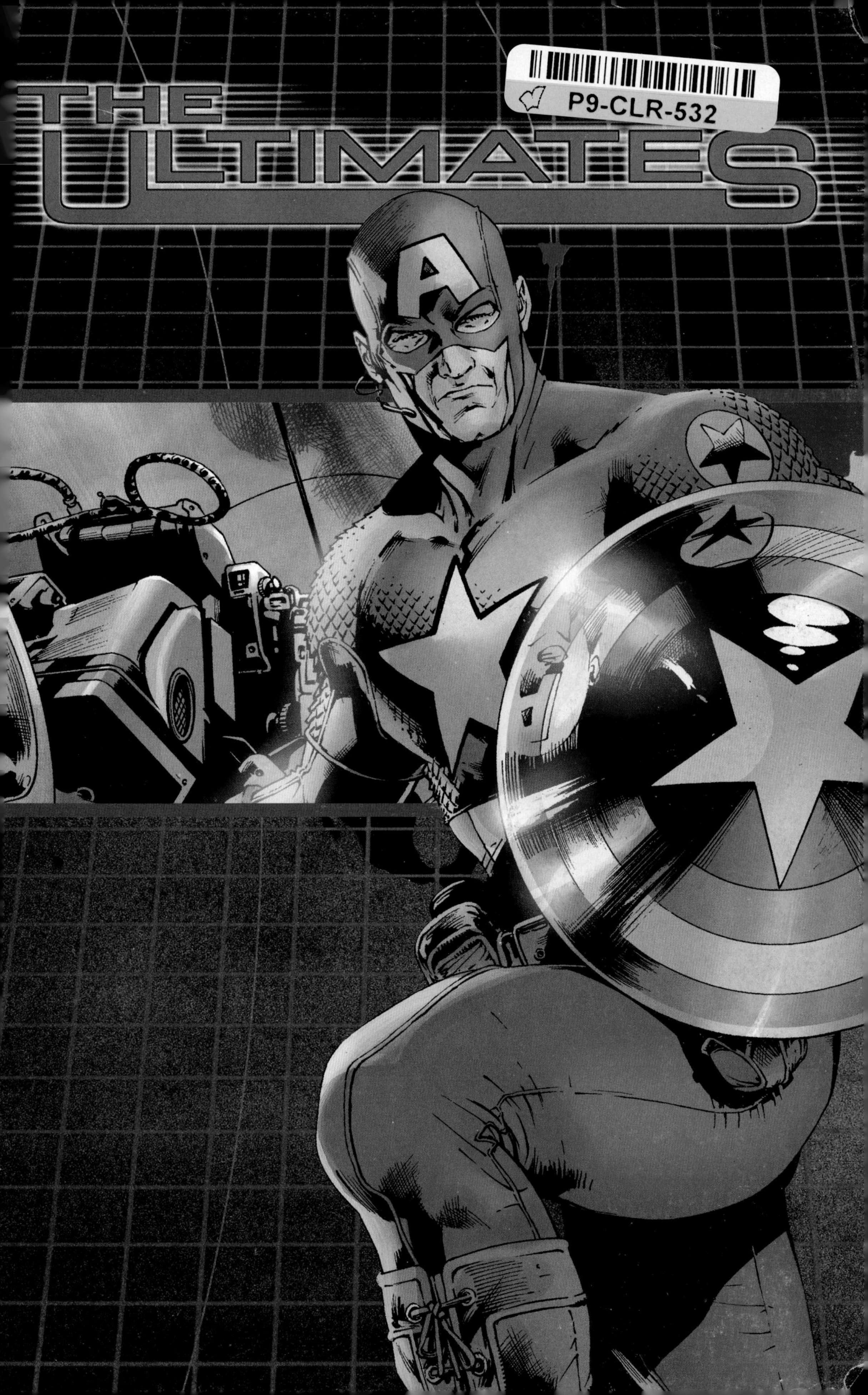
THE ULTIMATES

ULTIMATES

writer **Mark Millar**

pencils **Bryan Hitch**

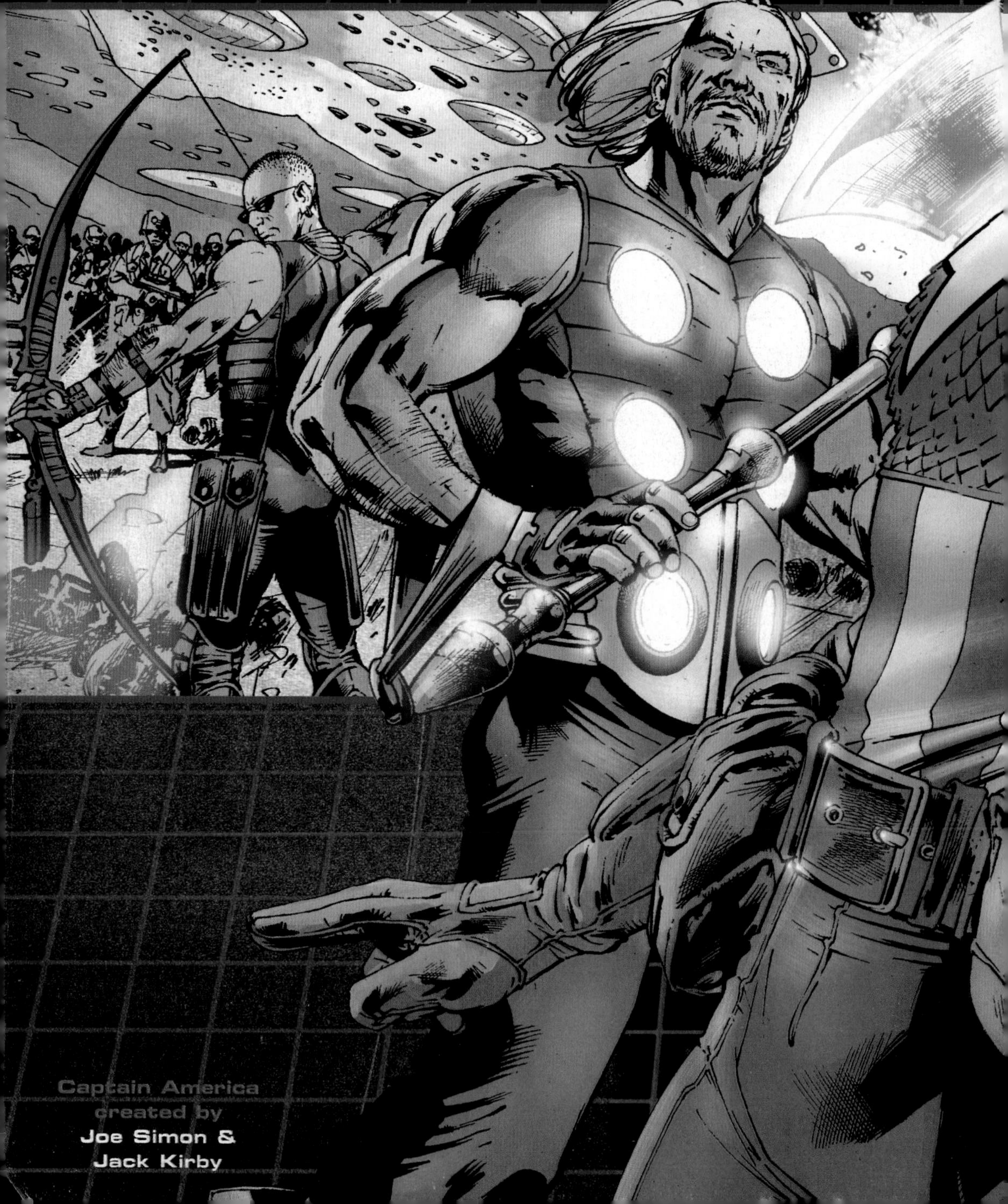

Captain America
created by
Joe Simon &
Jack Kirby

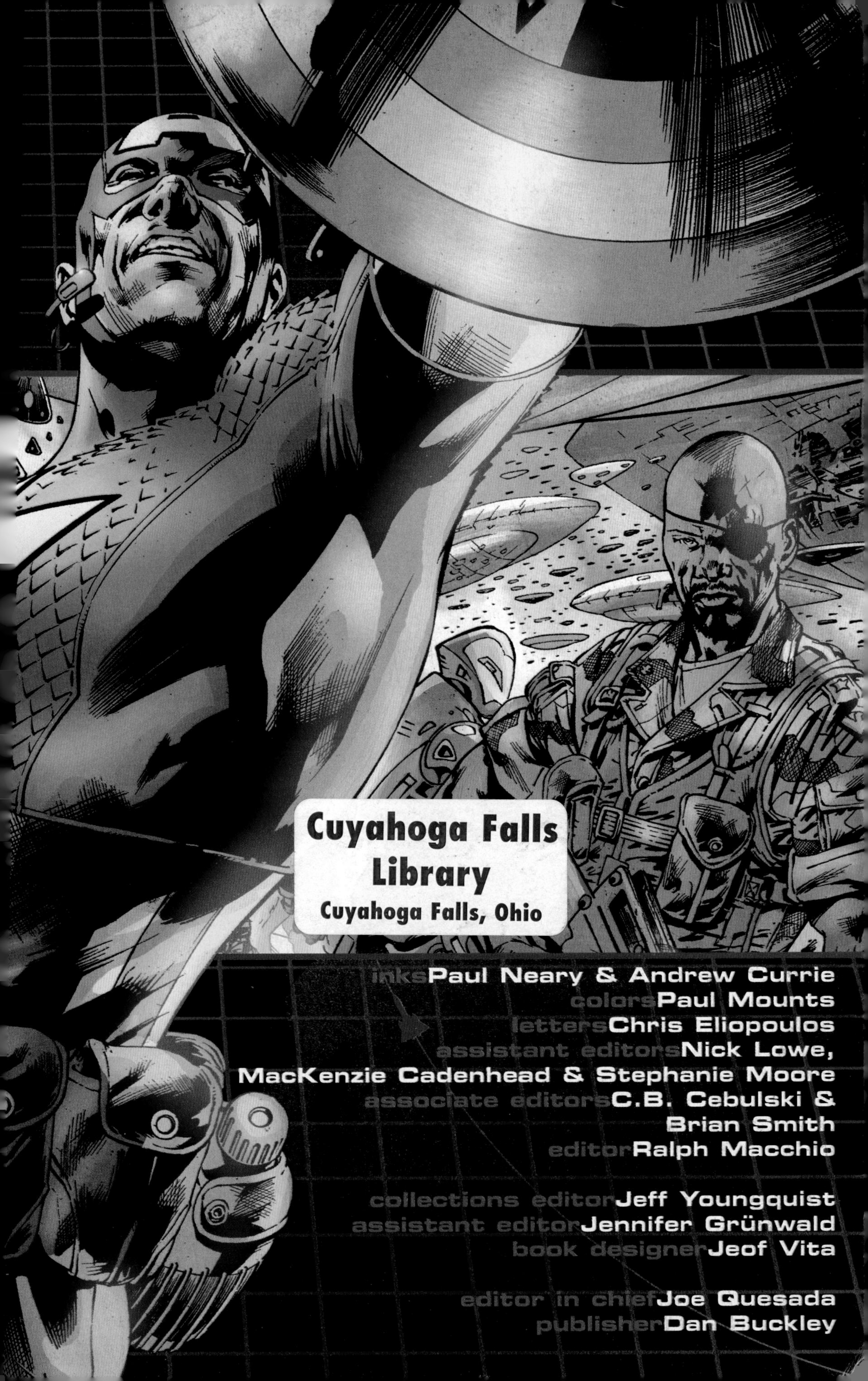

inks Paul Neary & Andrew Currie
colors Paul Mounts
letters Chris Eliopoulos
assistant editors Nick Lowe,
MacKenzie Cadenhead & Stephanie Moore
associate editors C.B. Cebulski &
Brian Smith
editor Ralph Macchio

collections editor Jeff Youngquist
assistant editor Jennifer Grünwald
book designer Jeof Vita

editor in chief Joe Quesada
publisher Dan Buckley

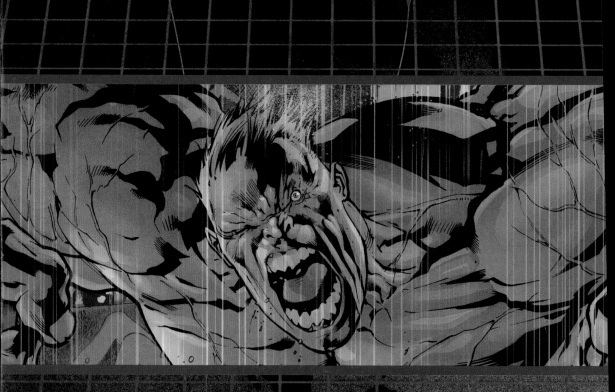

PREVIOUSLY

The Ultimates have successfully defeated their first real threat.

In the event now known as "The Hulk Incident," the team was forced to battle one of their own, causing the destruction of midtown Manhattan and the deaths of hundreds of innocents. However, their victory solidified their status as the world's premiere defense system, and catapulted them to super stardom in the public eye — but all is not as it seems.

Dr. Bruce Banner, the genius who turned himself into the monstrosity known as the Hulk, is now in custody. His future status as part of the team, as well as his health both mentally and physically, is unknown.

An argument between Giant Man and the Wasp, AKA Dr. and Mrs. Henry Pym, takes a brutally violent turn. After shrinking down to Wasp size, Janet is overrun and possibly killed by a horde of ants — controlled by none other than her husband.

CHAPTER SEVEN

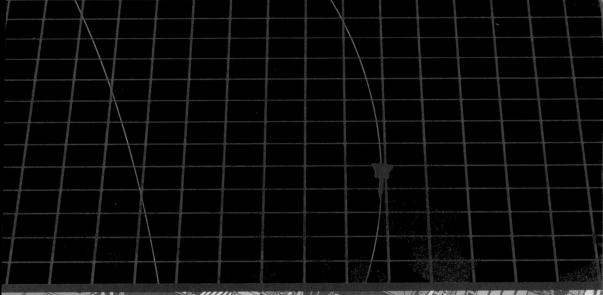

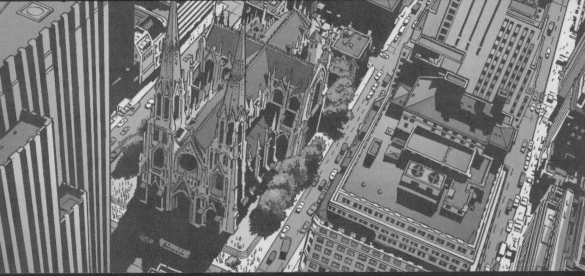

HOMELAND SECURITY

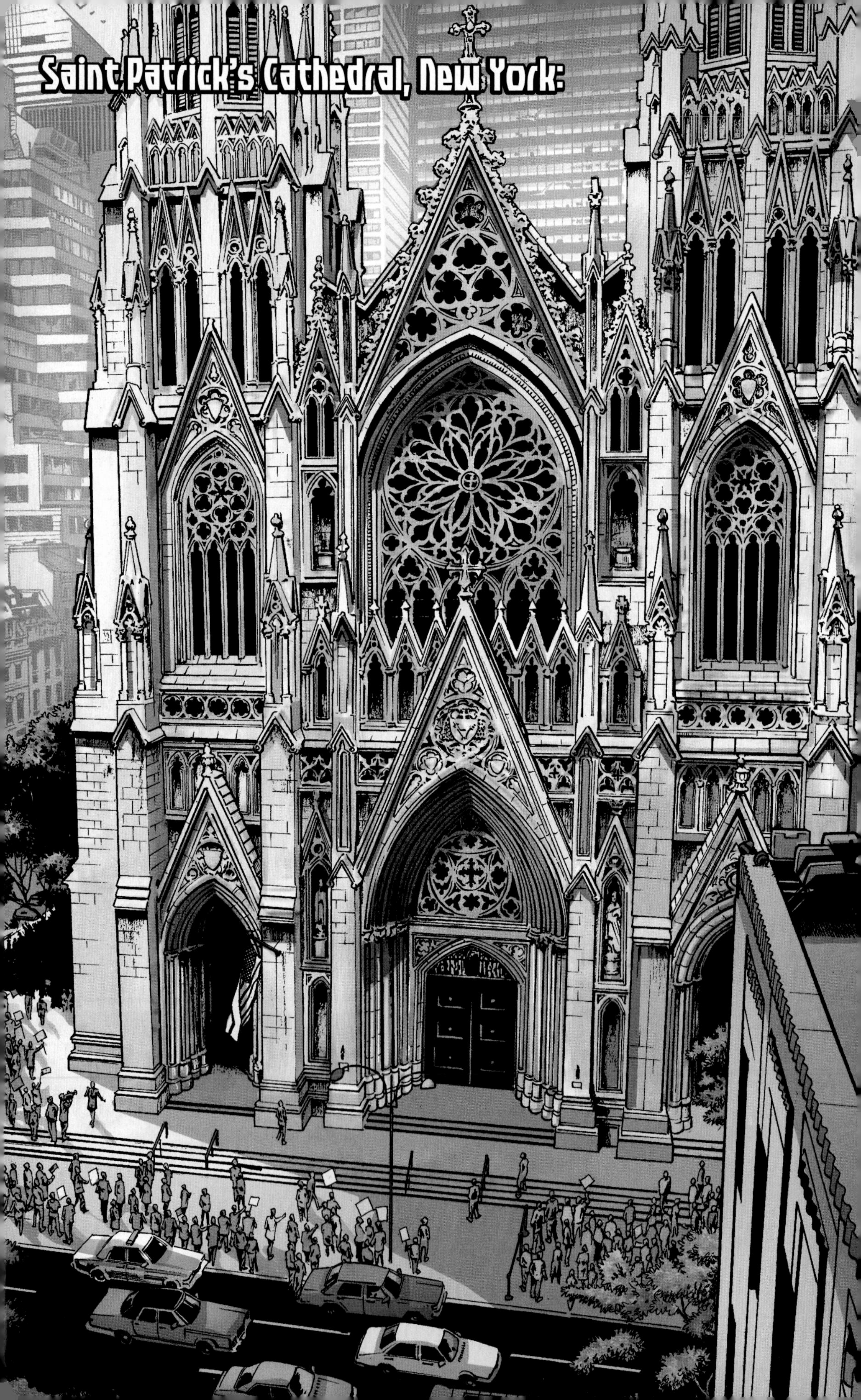
Saint Patrick's Cathedral, New York:

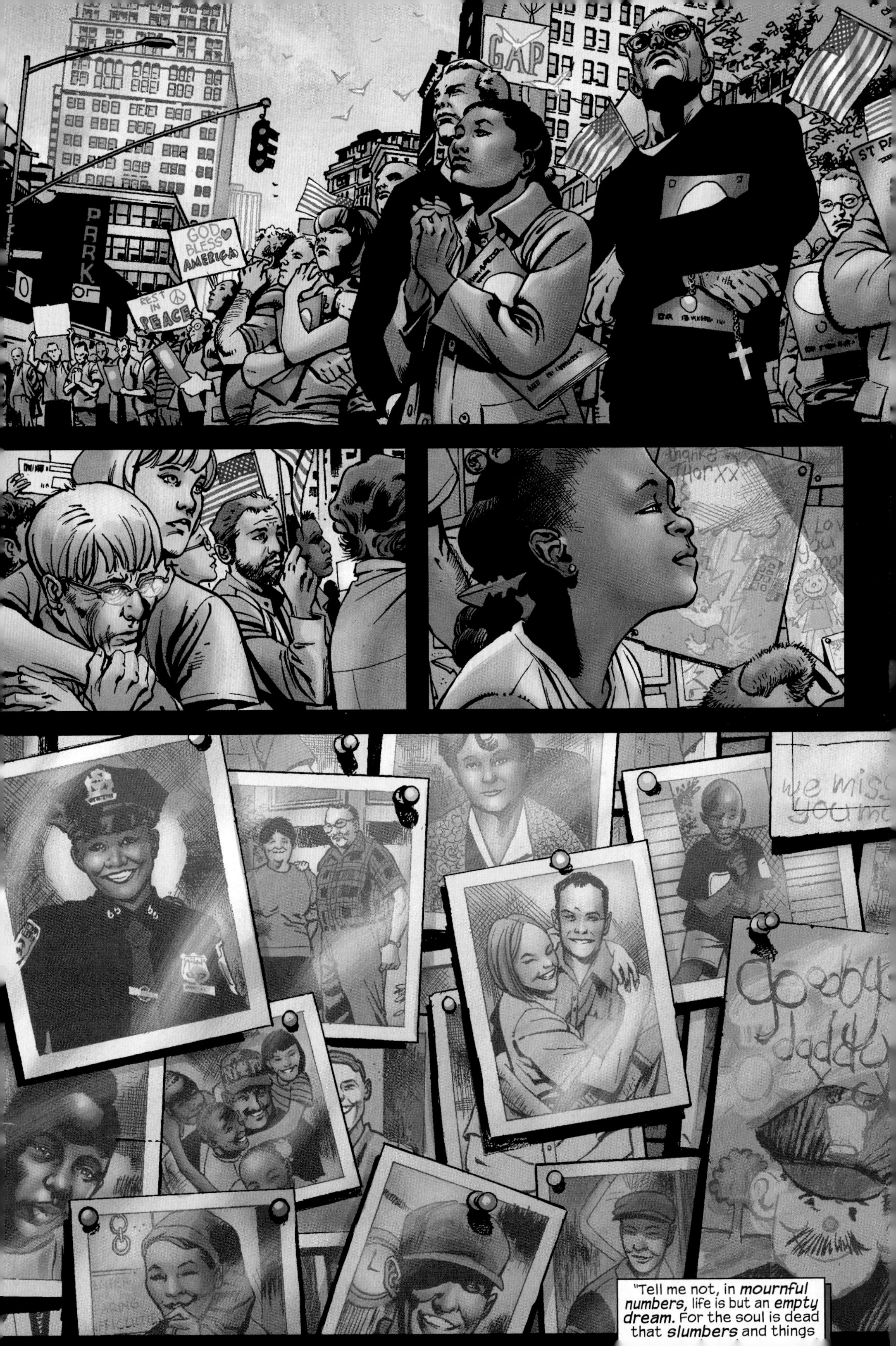
GAP
GOD BLESS AMERICA
REST IN PEACE
"Tell me not, in *mournful numbers,* life is but an *empty dream.* For the soul is dead that *slumbers* and things

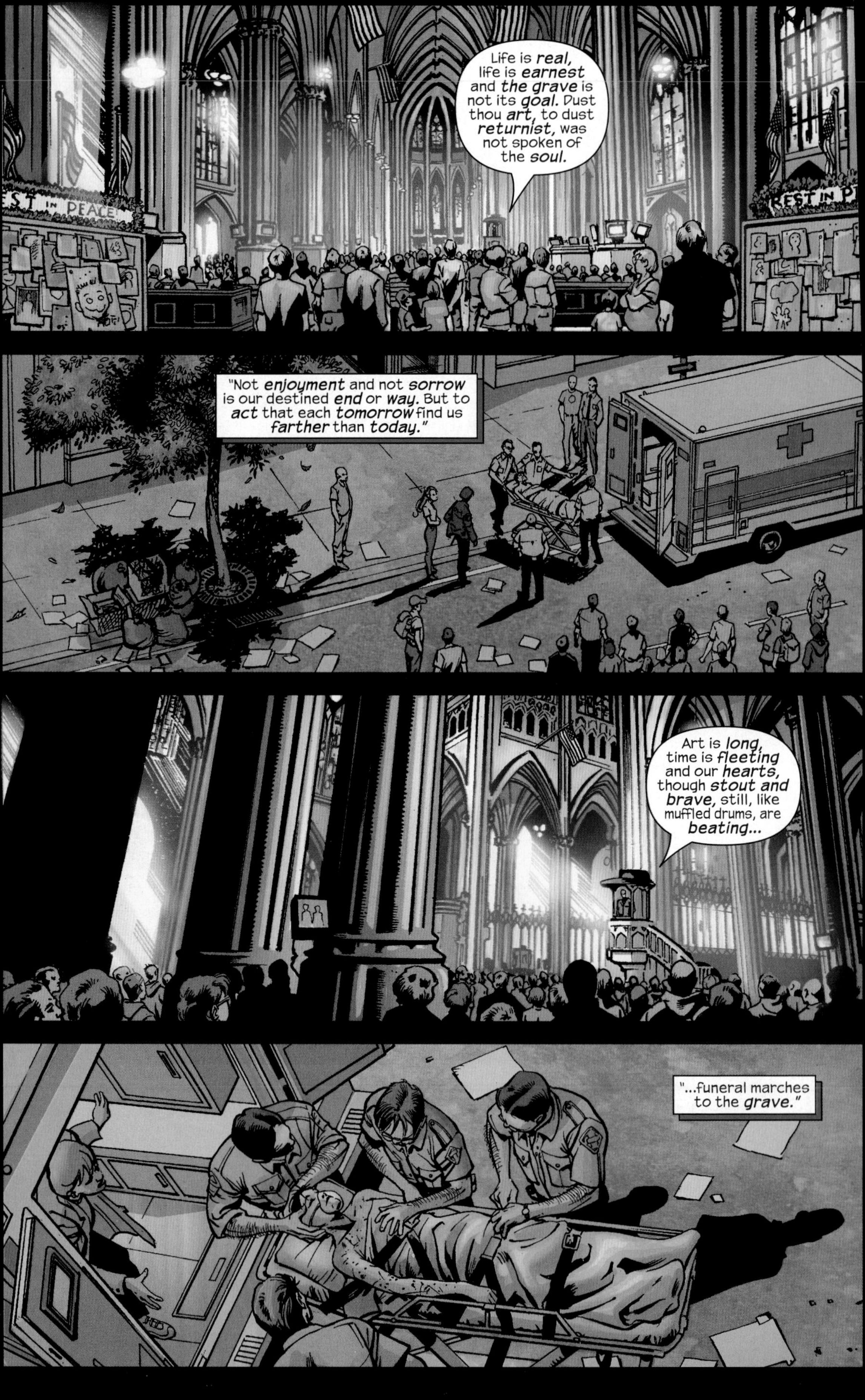
REST IN PEACE
Life is real, life is earnest and the grave is not its goal. Dust thou art, to dust returnist, was not spoken of the soul.
REST IN P
"Not enjoyment and not sorrow is our destined end or way. But to act that each tomorrow find us farther than today."
Art is long, time is fleeting and our hearts, though stout and brave, still, like muffled drums, are beating...
"...funeral marches to the grave."

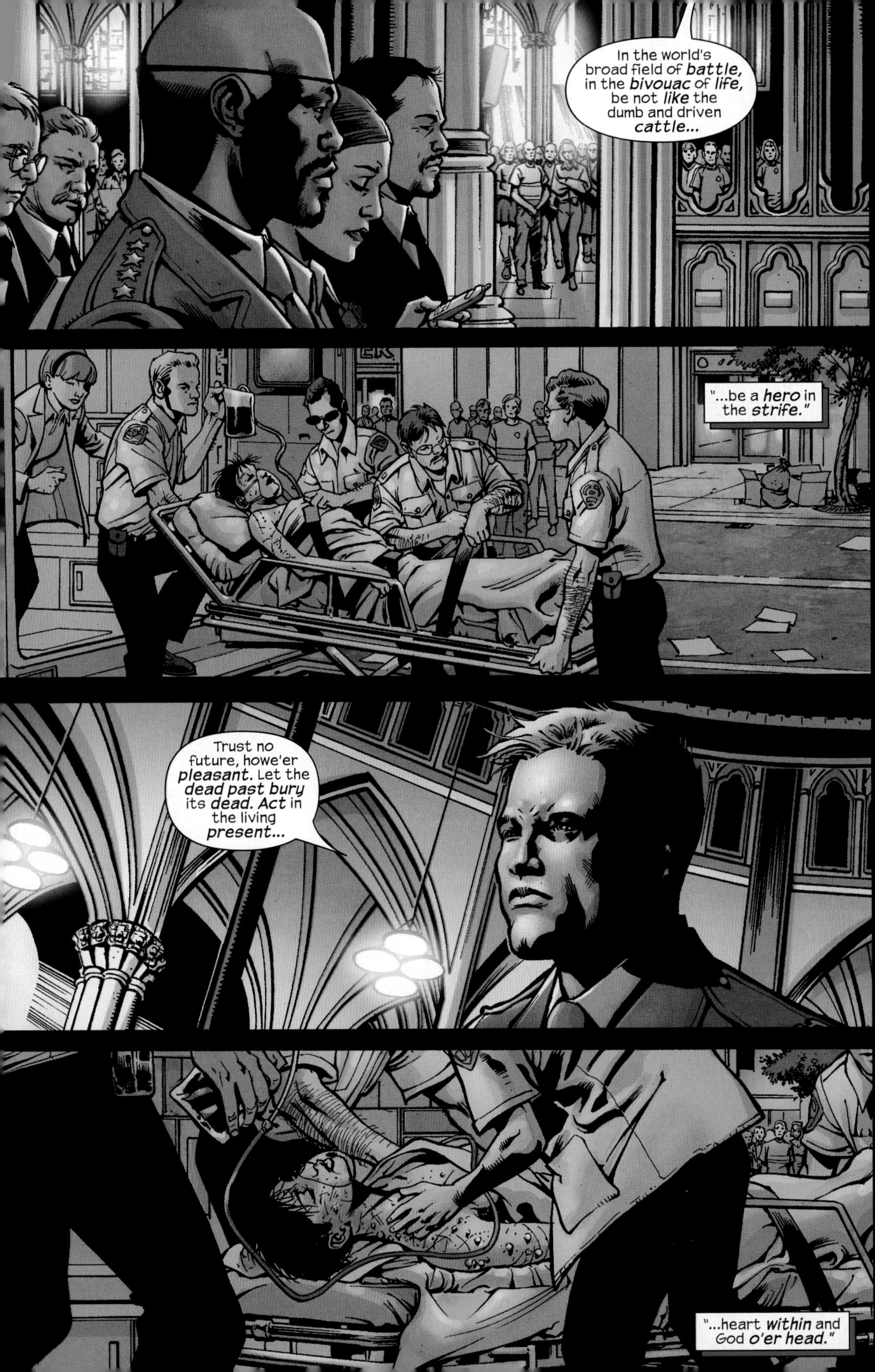

In the world's broad field of *battle,* in the *bivouac* of *life,* be not *like* the dumb and driven *cattle...*
"...be a *hero* in the *strife."*
Trust no future, howe'er *pleasant.* Let the *dead past bury* its *dead. Act* in the living *present...*
"...heart *within* and God *o'er head."*

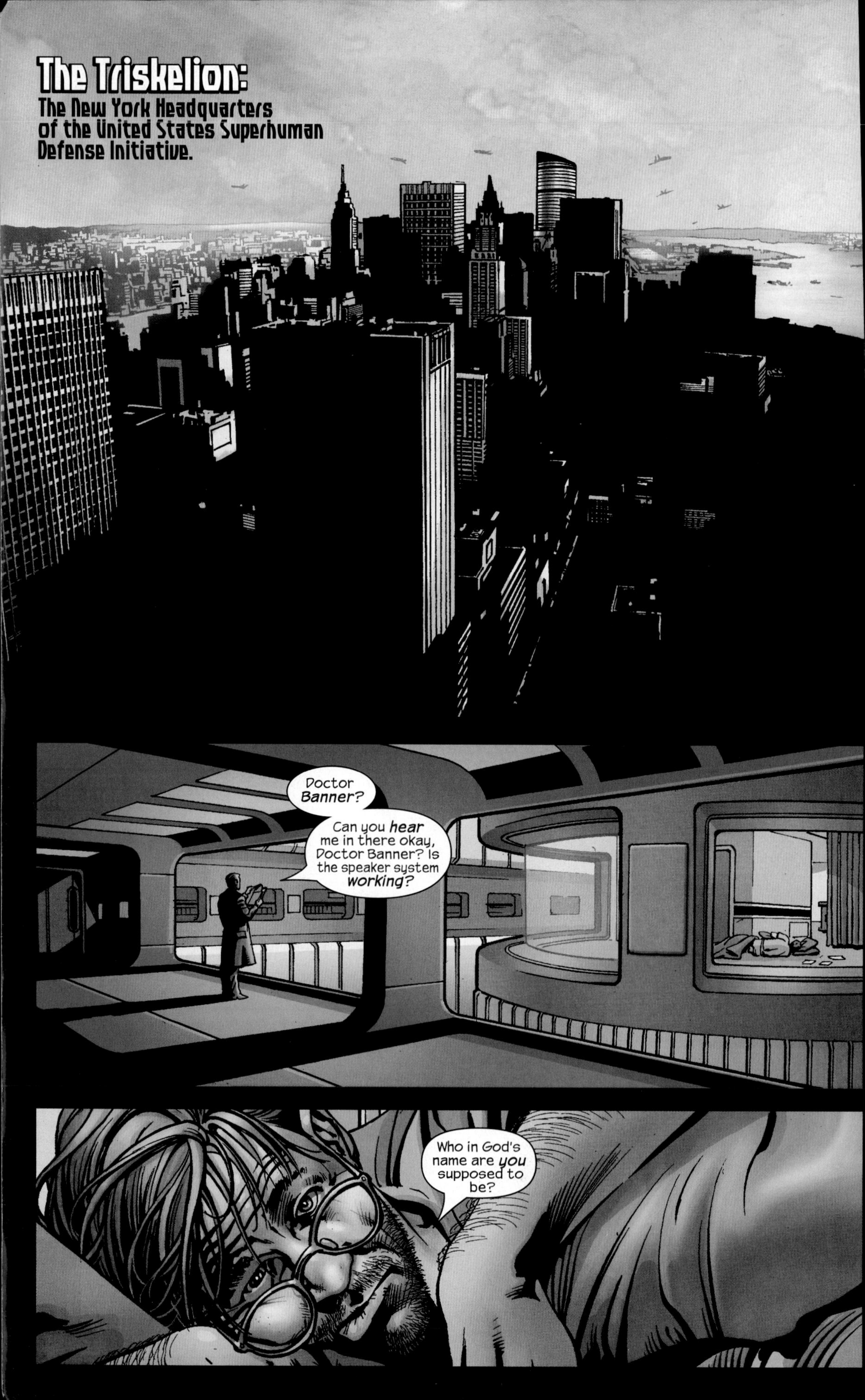
The Triskelion:
The New York Headquarters of the United States Superhuman Defense Initiative.
Doctor Banner?
Can you hear me in there okay, Doctor Banner? Is the speaker system working?
Who in God's name are you supposed to be?

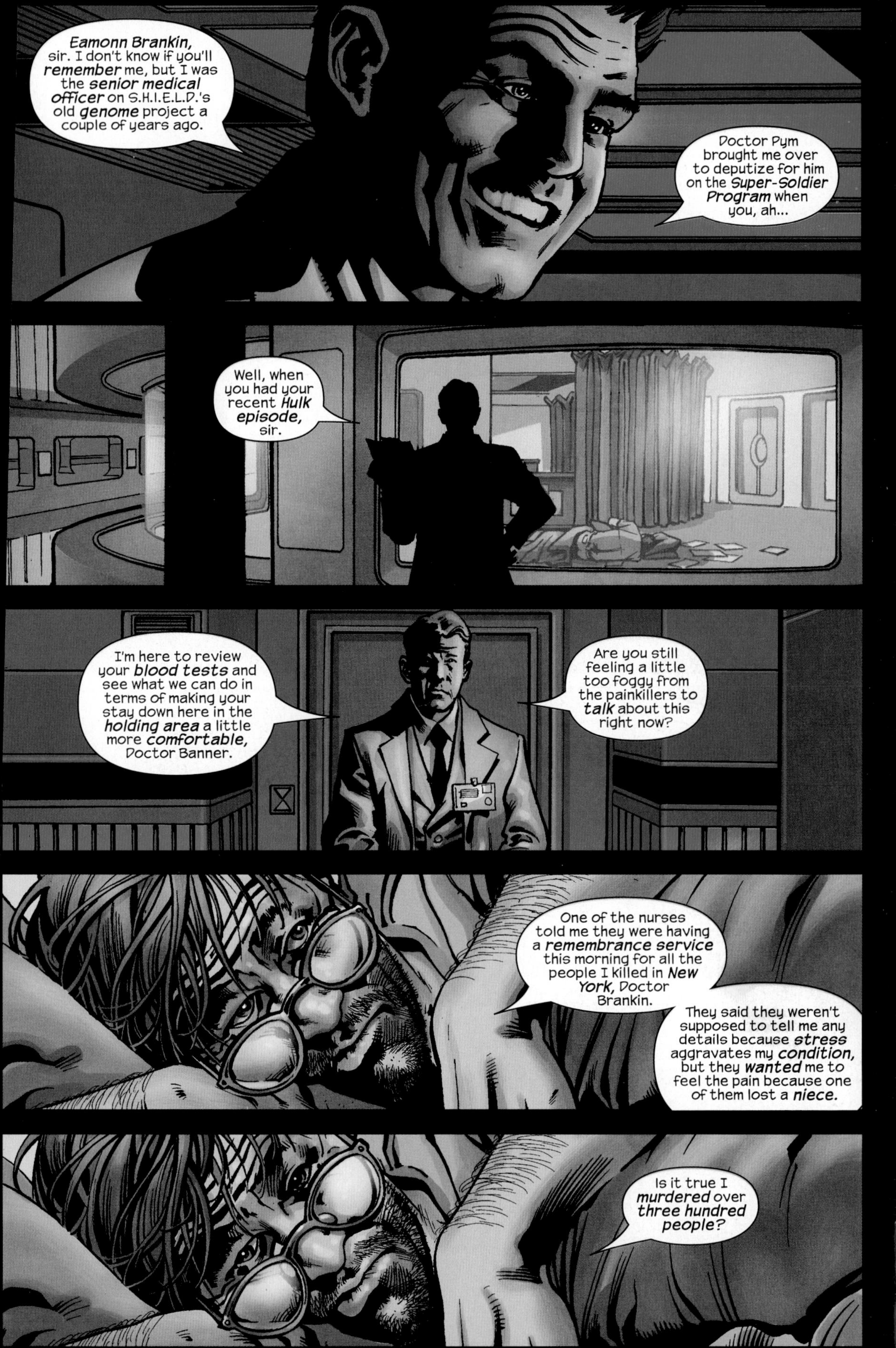
Eamonn Brankin, sir. I don't know if you'll remember me, but I was the senior medical officer on S.H.I.E.L.D.'s old genome project a couple of years ago.
Doctor Pym brought me over to deputize for him on the Super-Soldier Program when you, ah...
Well, when you had your recent Hulk episode, sir.
I'm here to review your blood tests and see what we can do in terms of making your stay down here in the holding area a little more comfortable, Doctor Banner.
Are you still feeling a little too foggy from the painkillers to talk about this right now?
One of the nurses told me they were having a remembrance service this morning for all the people I killed in New York, Doctor Brankin.
They said they weren't supposed to tell me any details because stress aggravates my condition, but they wanted me to feel the pain because one of them lost a niece.
Is it true I murdered over three hundred people?

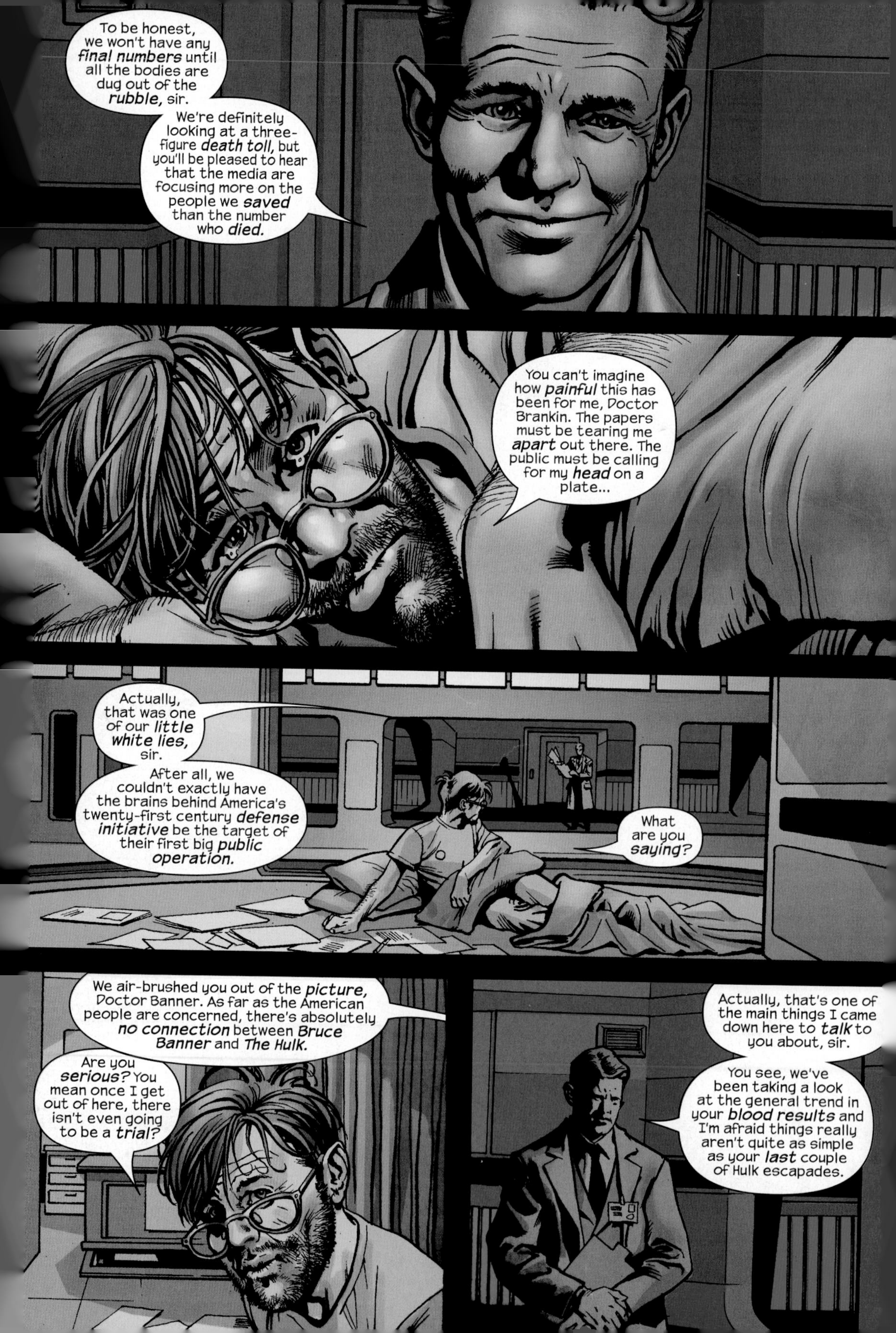

To be honest, we won't have any final numbers until all the bodies are dug out of the rubble, sir.
We're definitely looking at a three-figure death toll, but you'll be pleased to hear that the media are focusing more on the people we saved than the number who died.
You can't imagine how painful this has been for me, Doctor Brankin. The papers must be tearing me apart out there. The public must be calling for my head on a plate...
Actually, that was one of our little white lies, sir.
After all, we couldn't exactly have the brains behind America's twenty-first century defense initiative be the target of their first big public operation.
What are you saying?
We air-brushed you out of the picture, Doctor Banner. As far as the American people are concerned, there's absolutely no connection between Bruce Banner and The Hulk.
Are you serious? You mean once I get out of here, there isn't even going to be a trial?
Actually, that's one of the main things I came down here to talk to you about, sir.
You see, we've been taking a look at the general trend in your blood results and I'm afraid things really aren't quite as simple as your last couple of Hulk escapades.

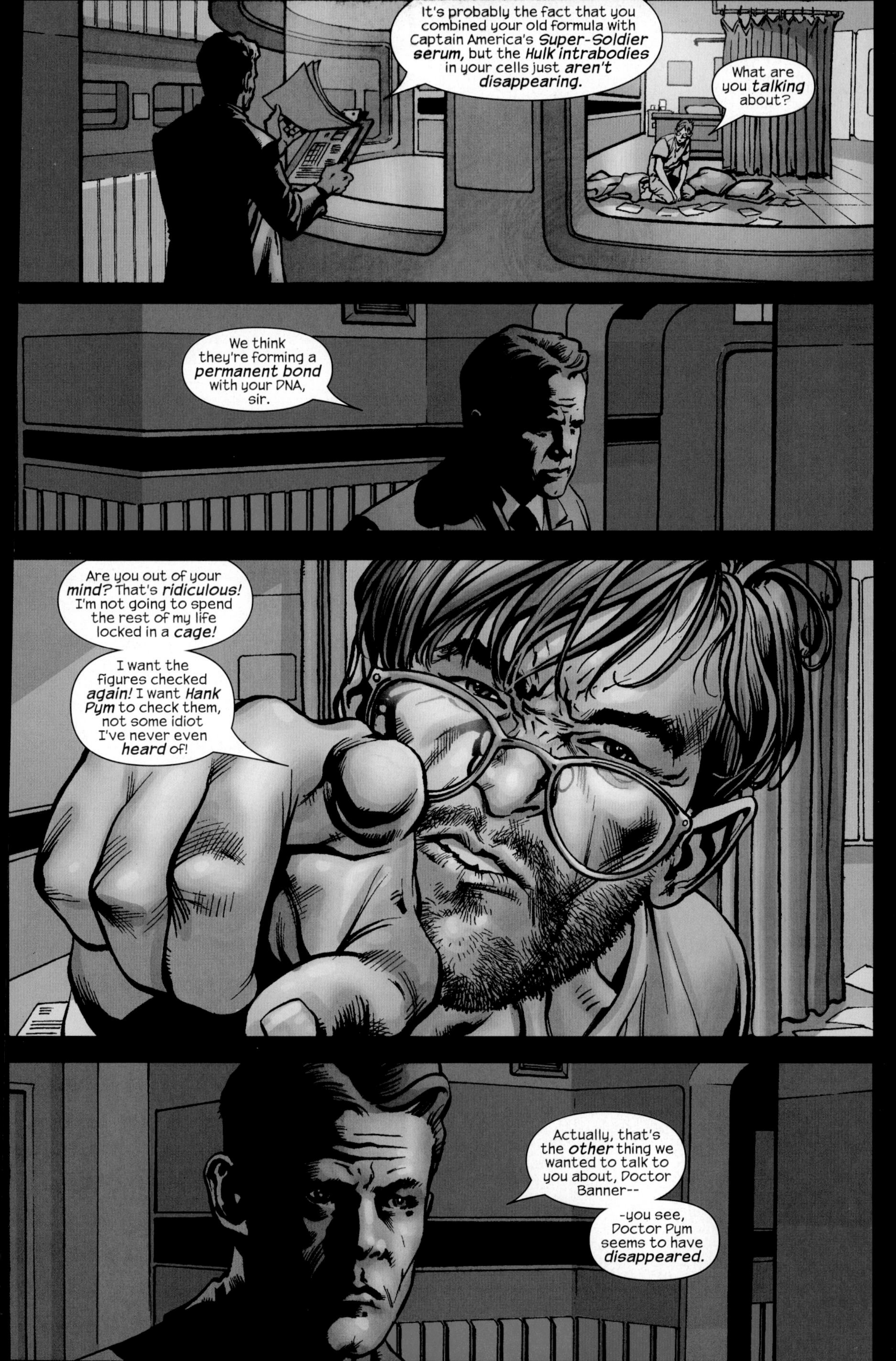
It's probably the fact that you combined your old formula with Captain America's Super-Soldier serum, but the Hulk intrabodies in your cells just aren't disappearing.
What are you talking about?
We think they're forming a permanent bond with your DNA, sir.
Are you out of your mind? That's ridiculous! I'm not going to spend the rest of my life locked in a cage!
I want the figures checked again! I want Hank Pym to check them, not some idiot I've never even heard of!
Actually, that's the other thing we wanted to talk to you about, Doctor Banner--
-you see, Doctor Pym seems to have disappeared.

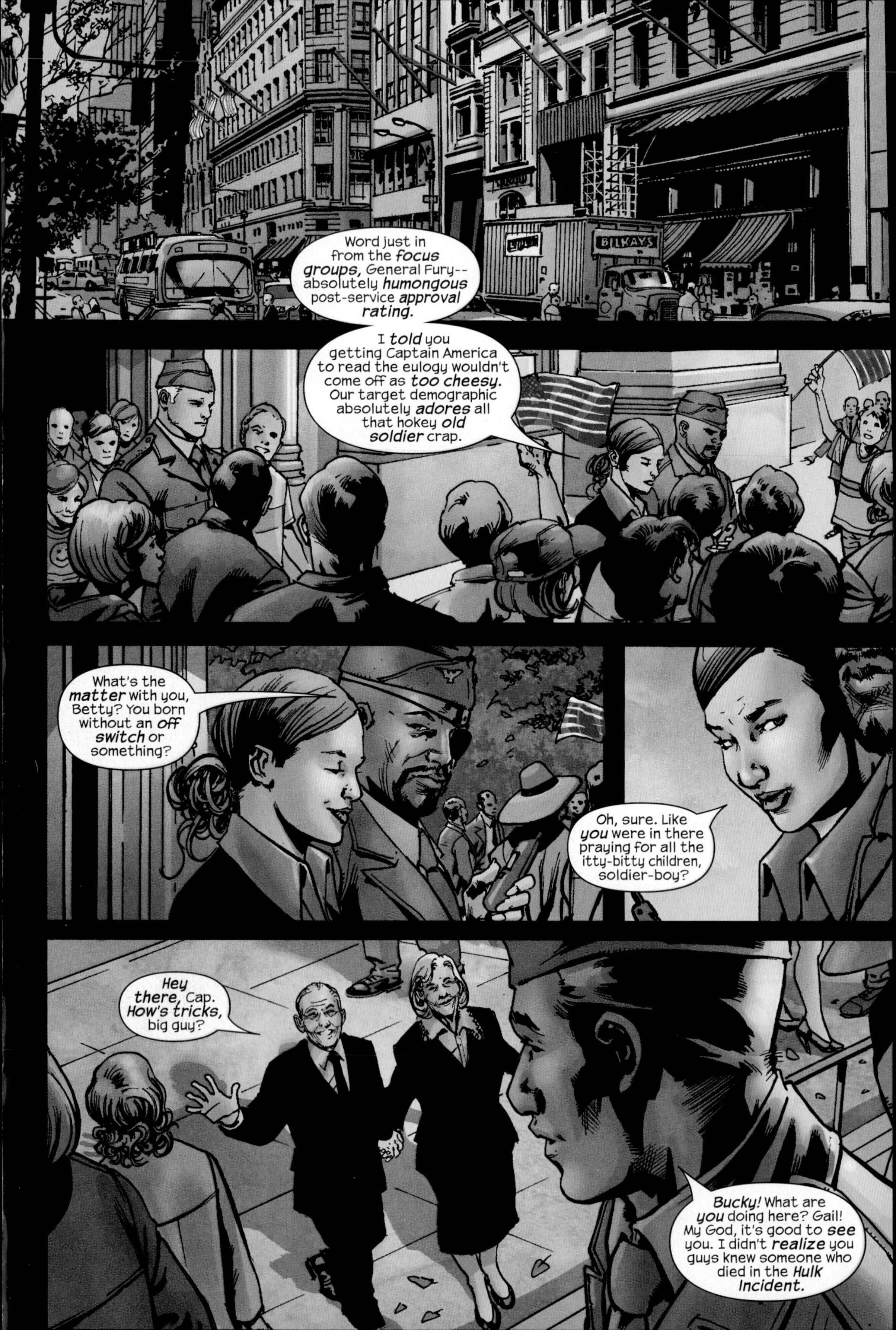

BILKAYS
Word just in from the focus groups, General Fury-- absolutely humongous post-service approval rating.
I told you getting Captain America to read the eulogy wouldn't come off as too cheesy. Our target demographic absolutely adores all that hokey old soldier crap.
What's the matter with you, Betty? You born without an off switch or something?
Oh, sure. Like you were in there praying for all the itty-bitty children, soldier-boy?
Hey there, Cap. How's tricks, big guy?
Bucky! What are you doing here? Gail! My God, it's good to see you. I didn't realize you guys knew someone who died in the Hulk Incident.

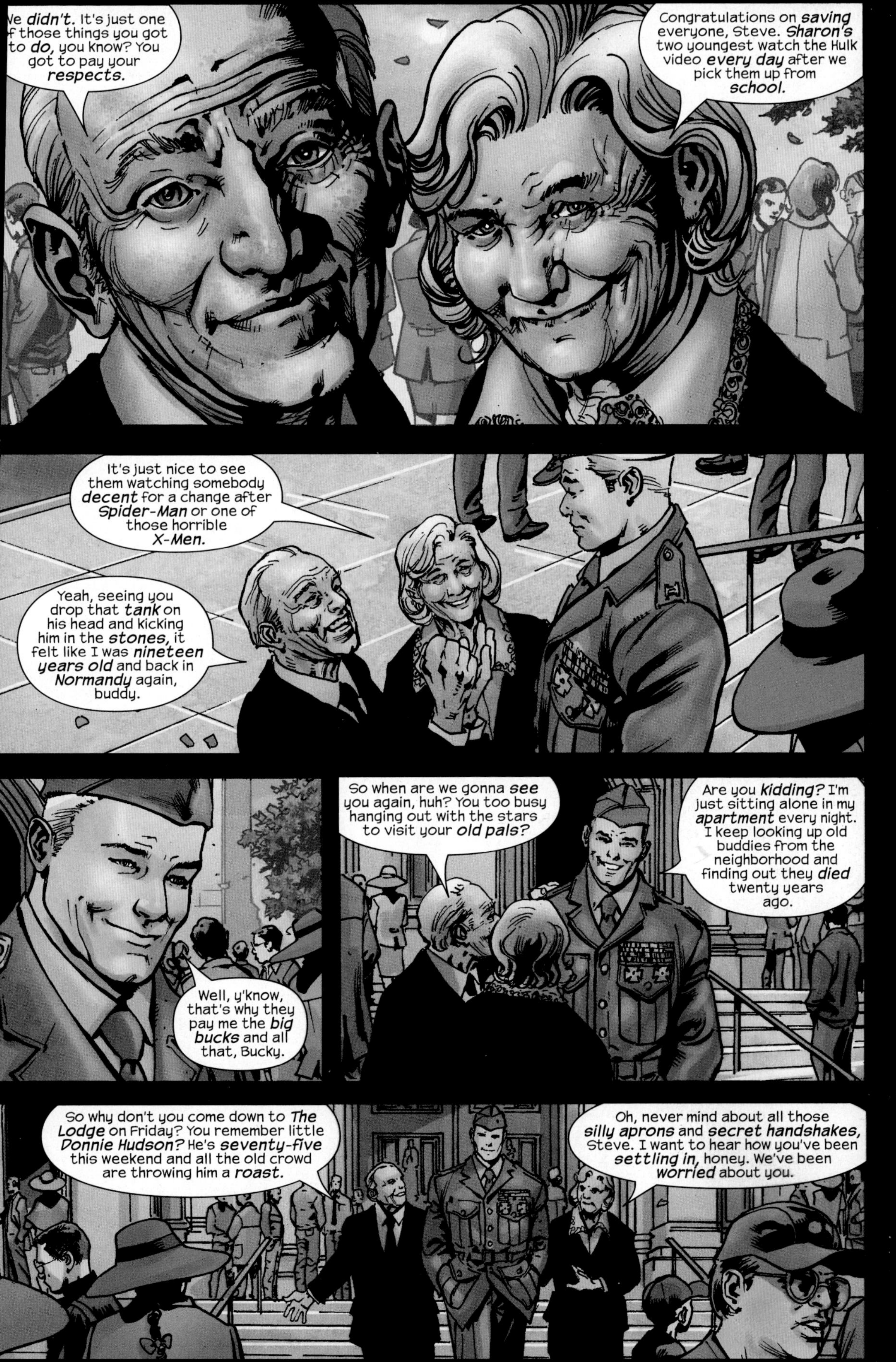

We didn't. It's just one of those things you got to do, you know? You got to pay your respects.
Congratulations on saving everyone, Steve. Sharon's two youngest watch the Hulk video every day after we pick them up from school.
It's just nice to see them watching somebody decent for a change after Spider-Man or one of those horrible X-Men.
Yeah, seeing you drop that tank on his head and kicking him in the stones, it felt like I was nineteen years old and back in Normandy again, buddy.
Well, y'know, that's why they pay me the big bucks and all that, Bucky.
So when are we gonna see you again, huh? You too busy hanging out with the stars to visit your old pals?
Are you kidding? I'm just sitting alone in my apartment every night. I keep looking up old buddies from the neighborhood and finding out they died twenty years ago.
So why don't you come down to The Lodge on Friday? You remember little Donnie Hudson? He's seventy-five this weekend and all the old crowd are throwing him a roast.
Oh, never mind about all those silly aprons and secret handshakes, Steve. I want to hear how you've been settling in, honey. We've been worried about you.

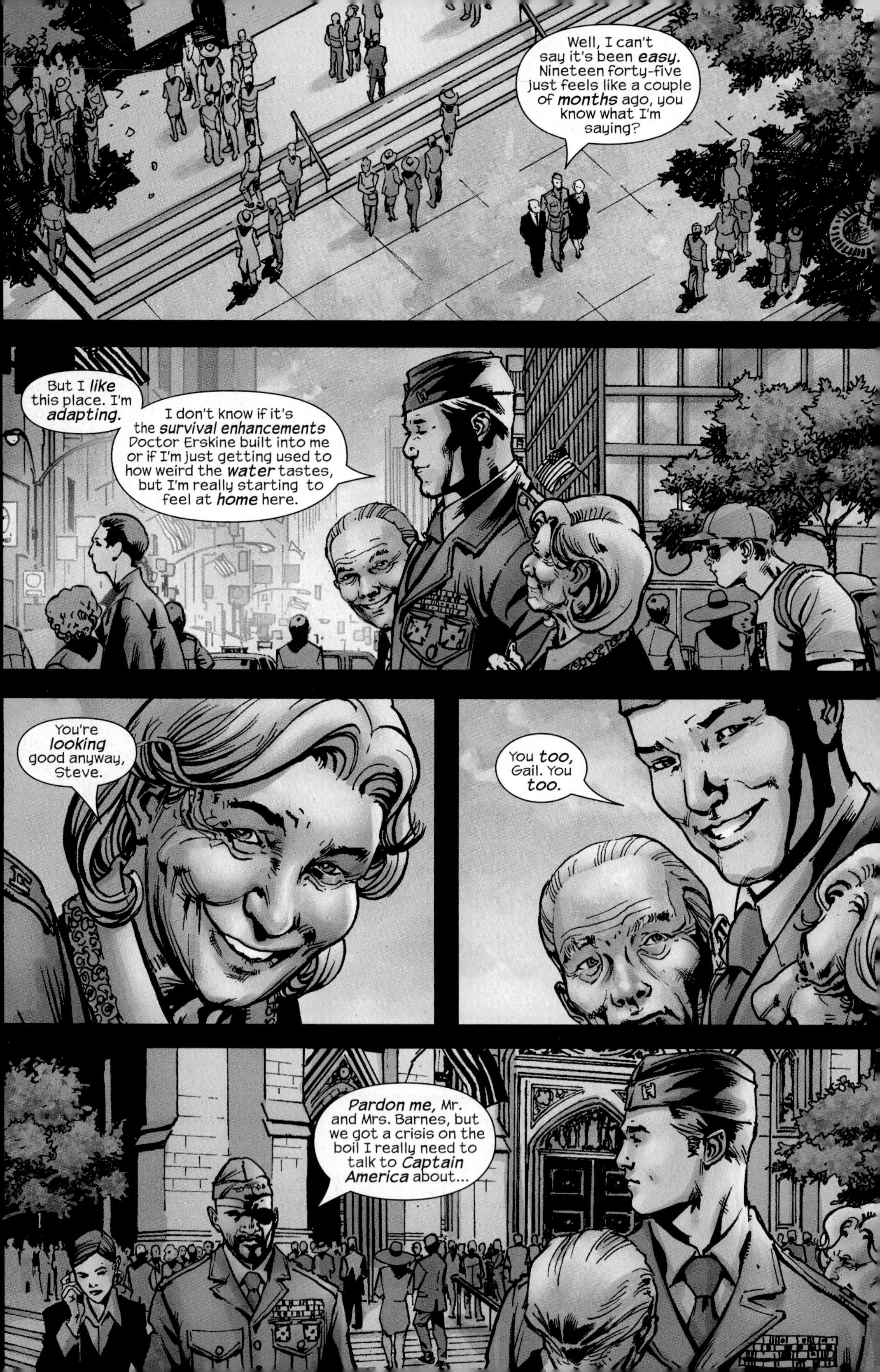
Well, I can't say it's been easy. Nineteen forty-five just feels like a couple of months ago, you know what I'm saying?
But I like this place. I'm adapting.
I don't know if it's the survival enhancements Doctor Erskine built into me or if I'm just getting used to how weird the water tastes, but I'm really starting to feel at home here.
You're looking good anyway, Steve.
You too, Gail. You too.
Pardon me, Mr. and Mrs. Barnes, but we got a crisis on the boil I really need to talk to Captain America about...

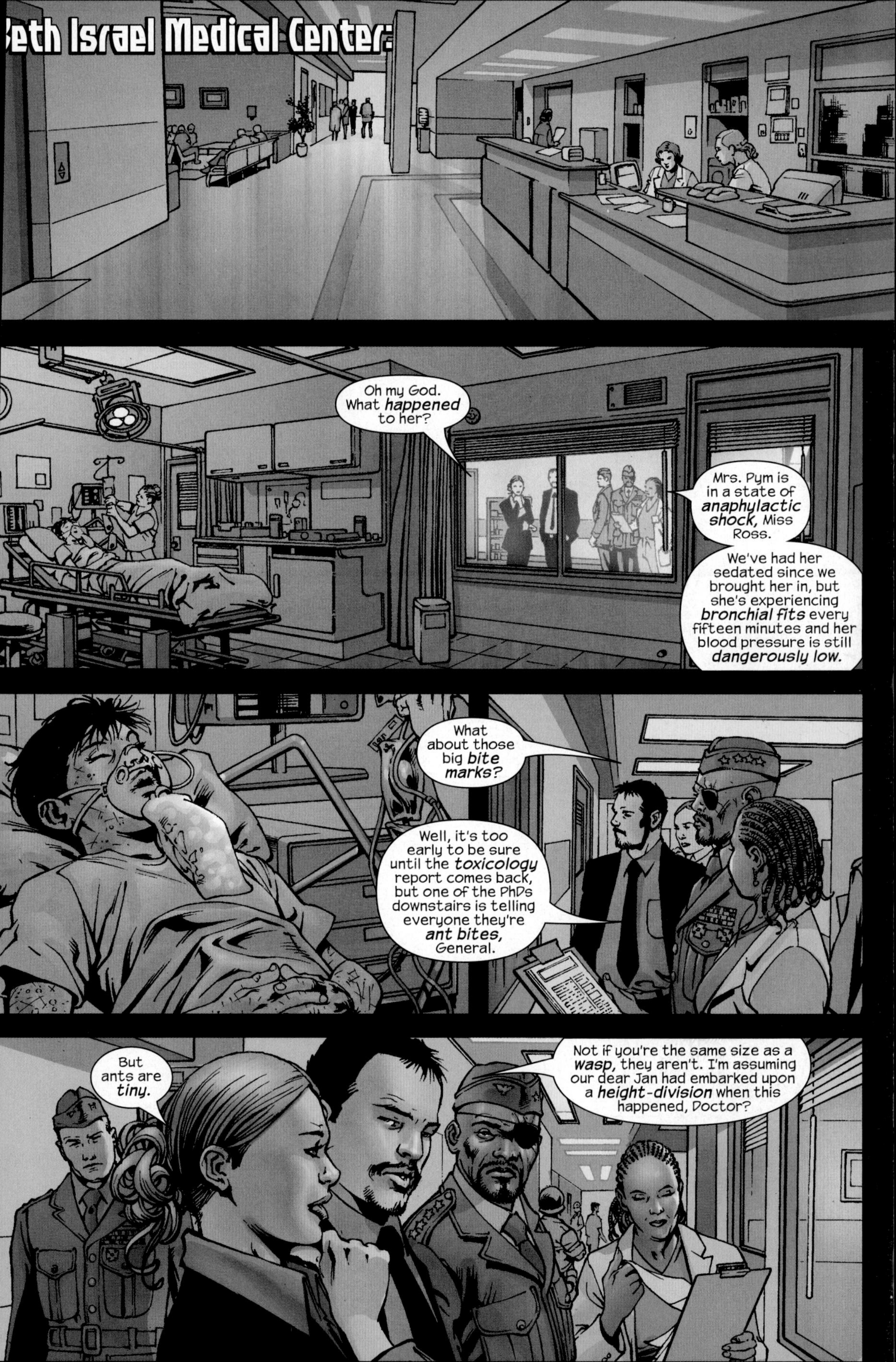
Beth Israel Medical Center:
Oh my God. What *happened* to her?
Mrs. Pym is in a state of *anaphylactic shock,* Miss Ross.
We've had her sedated since we brought her in, but she's experiencing *bronchial fits* every fifteen minutes and her blood pressure is still *dangerously low.*
What about those big *bite marks?*
Well, it's too early to be sure until the *toxicology* report comes back, but one of the PhDs downstairs is telling everyone they're *ant bites,* General.
But ants are *tiny.*
Not if you're the same size as a *wasp,* they aren't. I'm assuming our dear Jan had embarked upon a *height-division* when this happened, Doctor?

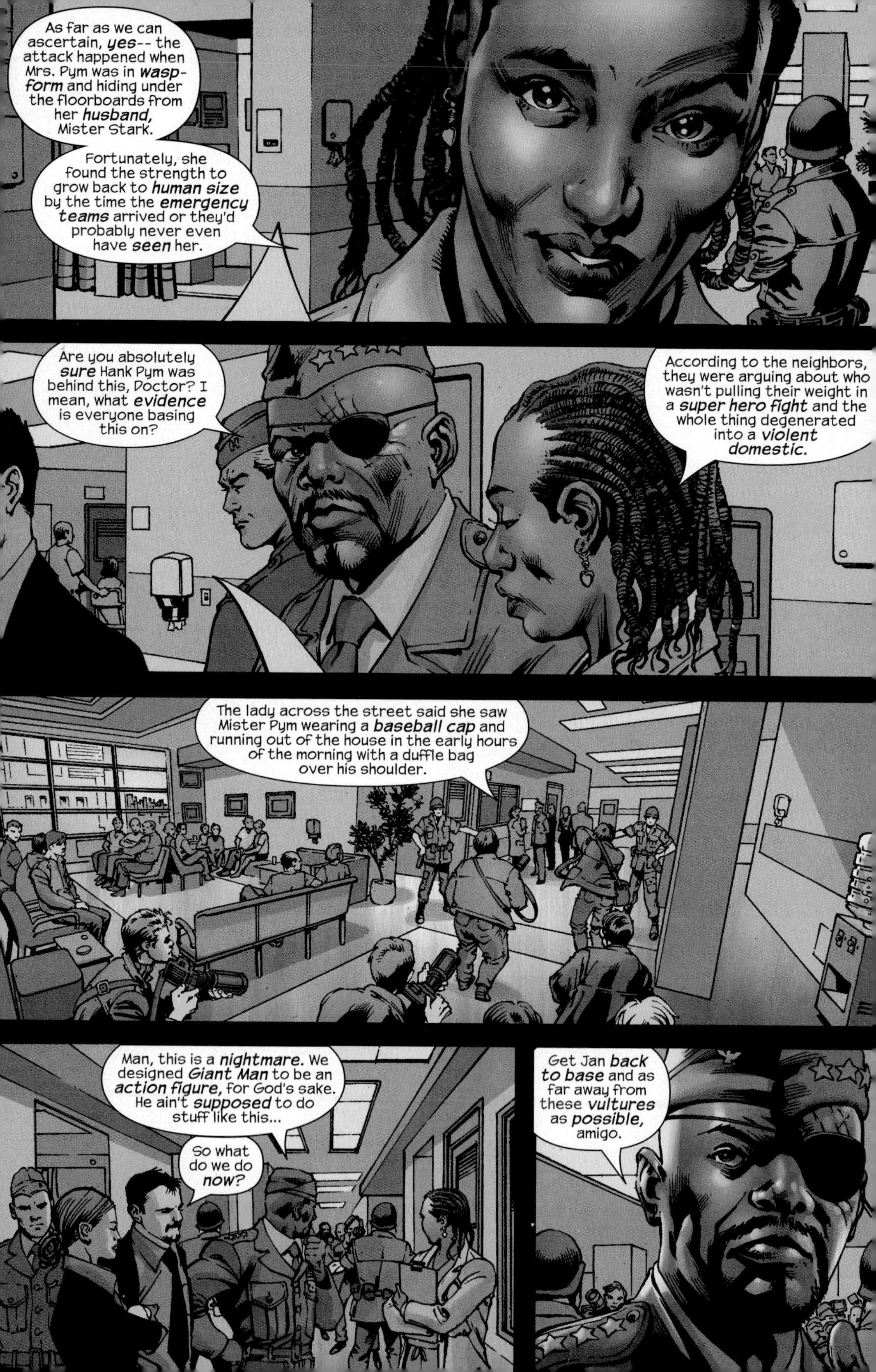
As far as we can ascertain, yes-- the attack happened when Mrs. Pym was in wasp-form and hiding under the floorboards from her husband, Mister Stark.
Fortunately, she found the strength to grow back to human size by the time the emergency teams arrived or they'd probably never even have seen her.
Are you absolutely sure Hank Pym was behind this, Doctor? I mean, what evidence is everyone basing this on?
According to the neighbors, they were arguing about who wasn't pulling their weight in a super hero fight and the whole thing degenerated into a violent domestic.
The lady across the street said she saw Mister Pym wearing a baseball cap and running out of the house in the early hours of the morning with a duffle bag over his shoulder.
Man, this is a nightmare. We designed Giant Man to be an action figure, for God's sake. He ain't supposed to do stuff like this...
So what do we do now?
Get Jan back to base and as far away from these vultures as possible, amigo.

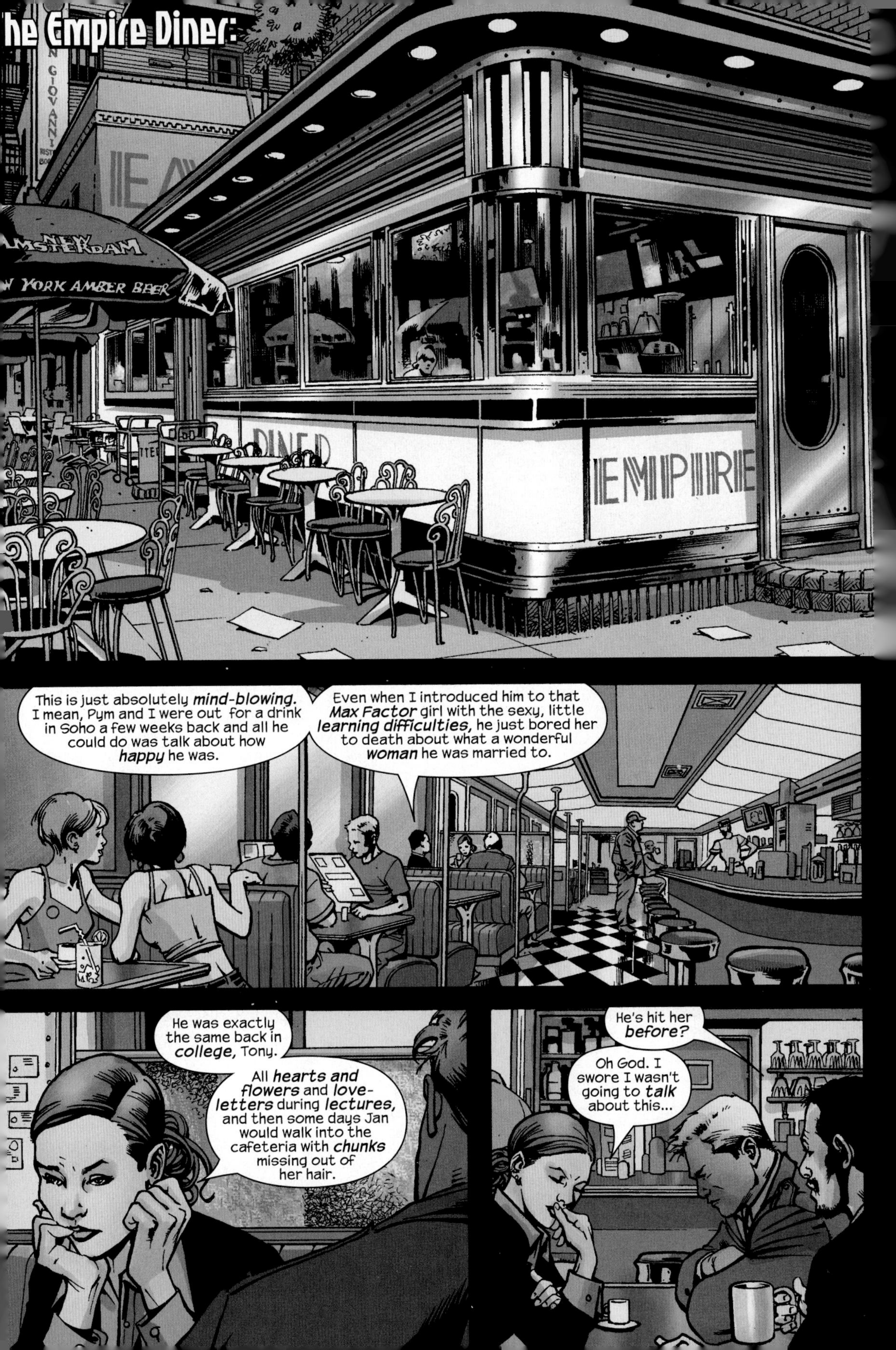
he Empire Diner:
NEW AMSTERDAM
N YORK AMBER BEER
EMPIRE
DINER
This is just absolutely mind-blowing. I mean, Pym and I were out for a drink in Soho a few weeks back and all he could do was talk about how happy he was.
Even when I introduced him to that Max Factor girl with the sexy, little learning difficulties, he just bored her to death about what a wonderful woman he was married to.
He was exactly the same back in college, Tony.
All hearts and flowers and love-letters during lectures, and then some days Jan would walk into the cafeteria with chunks missing out of her hair.
He's hit her before?
Oh God. I swore I wasn't going to talk about this...

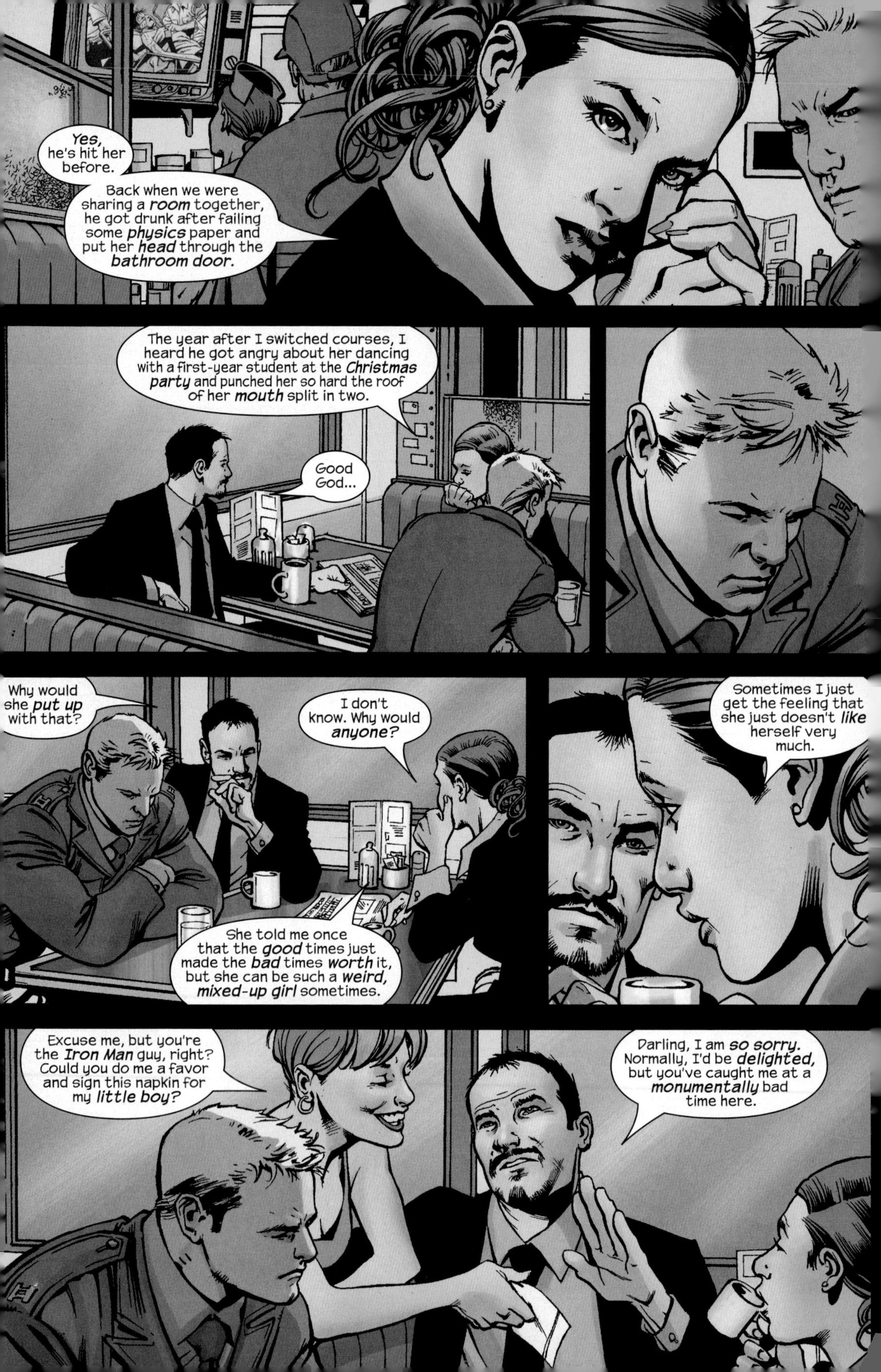
Yes, he's hit her before.
Back when we were sharing a room together, he got drunk after failing some physics paper and put her head through the bathroom door.
The year after I switched courses, I heard he got angry about her dancing with a first-year student at the Christmas party and punched her so hard the roof of her mouth split in two.
Good God...
Why would she put up with that?
I don't know. Why would anyone?
She told me once that the good times just made the bad times worth it, but she can be such a weird, mixed-up girl sometimes.
Sometimes I just get the feeling that she just doesn't like herself very much.
Excuse me, but you're the Iron Man guy, right? Could you do me a favor and sign this napkin for my little boy?
Darling, I am so sorry. Normally, I'd be delighted, but you've caught me at a monumentally bad time here.

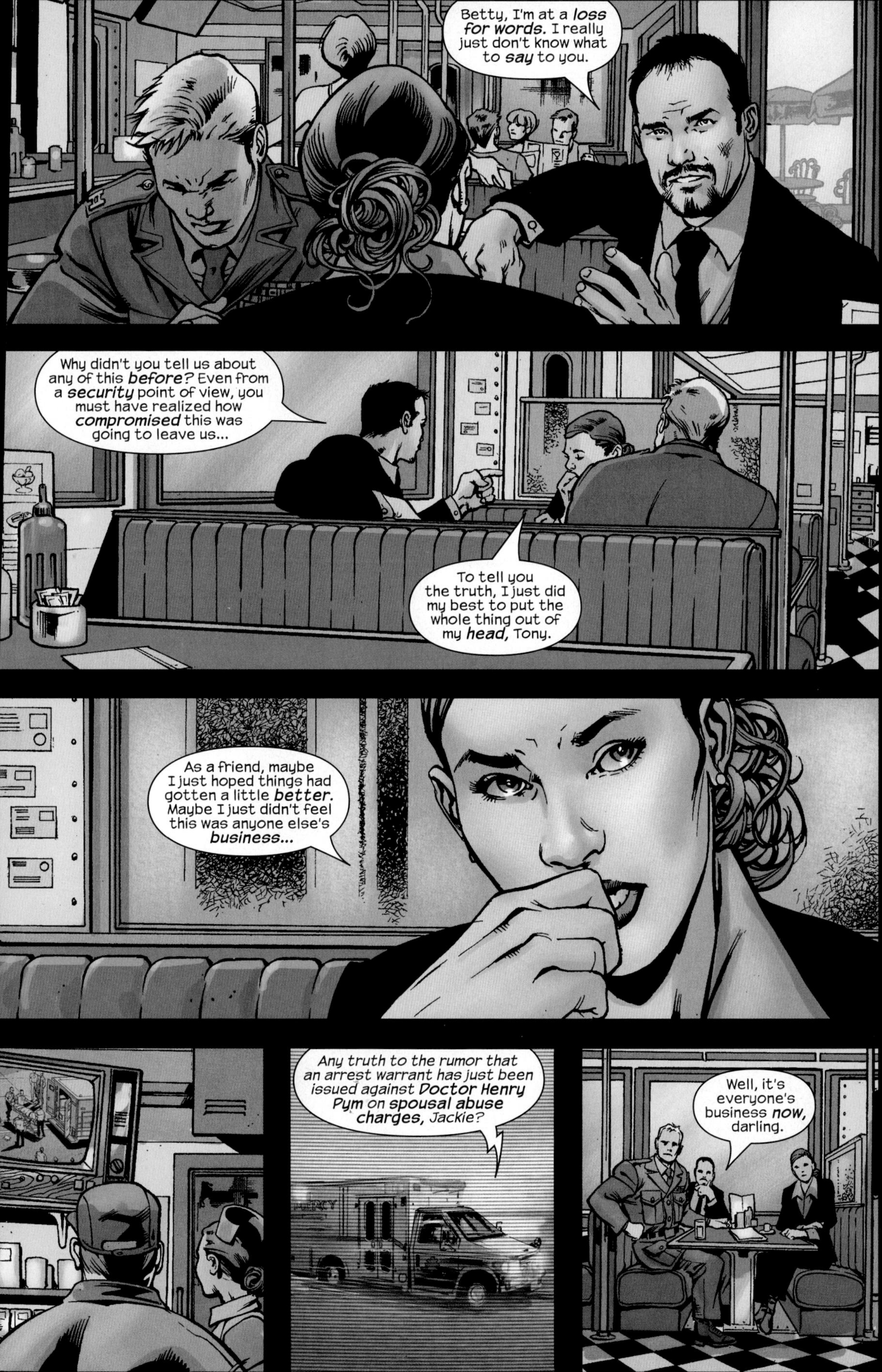
Betty, I'm at a loss for words. I really just don't know what to say to you.
Why didn't you tell us about any of this before? Even from a security point of view, you must have realized how compromised this was going to leave us...
To tell you the truth, I just did my best to put the whole thing out of my head, Tony.
As a friend, maybe I just hoped things had gotten a little better. Maybe I just didn't feel this was anyone else's business...
Any truth to the rumor that an arrest warrant has just been issued against Doctor Henry Pym on spousal abuse charges, Jackie?
Well, it's everyone's business now, darling.

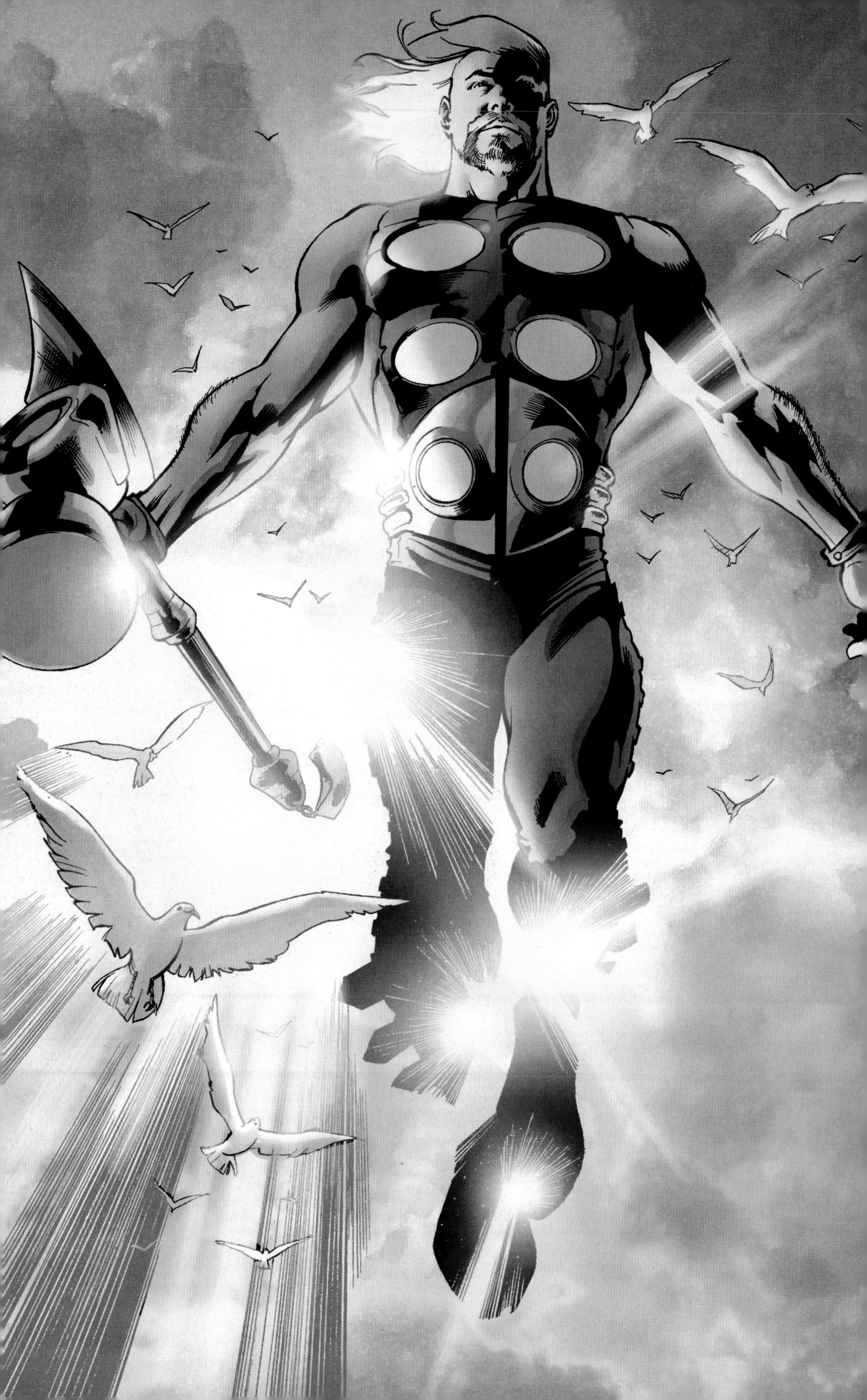

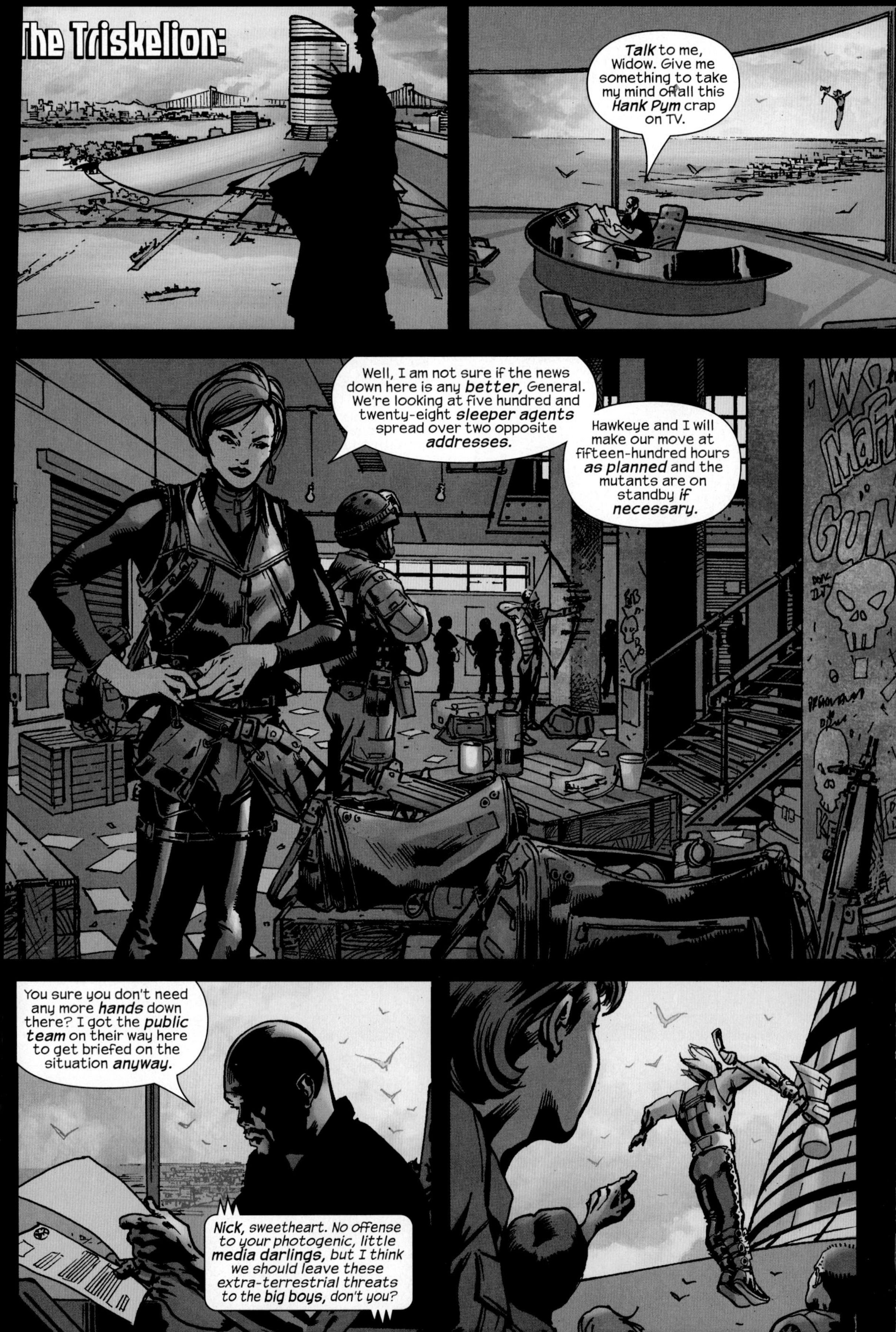
The Triskelion:
Talk to me, Widow. Give me something to take my mind off all this Hank Pym crap on TV.
Well, I am not sure if the news down here is any better, General. We're looking at five hundred and twenty-eight sleeper agents spread over two opposite addresses.
Hawkeye and I will make our move at fifteen-hundred hours as planned and the mutants are on standby if necessary.
You sure you don't need any more hands down there? I got the public team on their way here to get briefed on the situation anyway.
Nick, sweetheart. No offense to your photogenic, little media darlings, but I think we should leave these extra-terrestrial threats to the big boys, don't you?

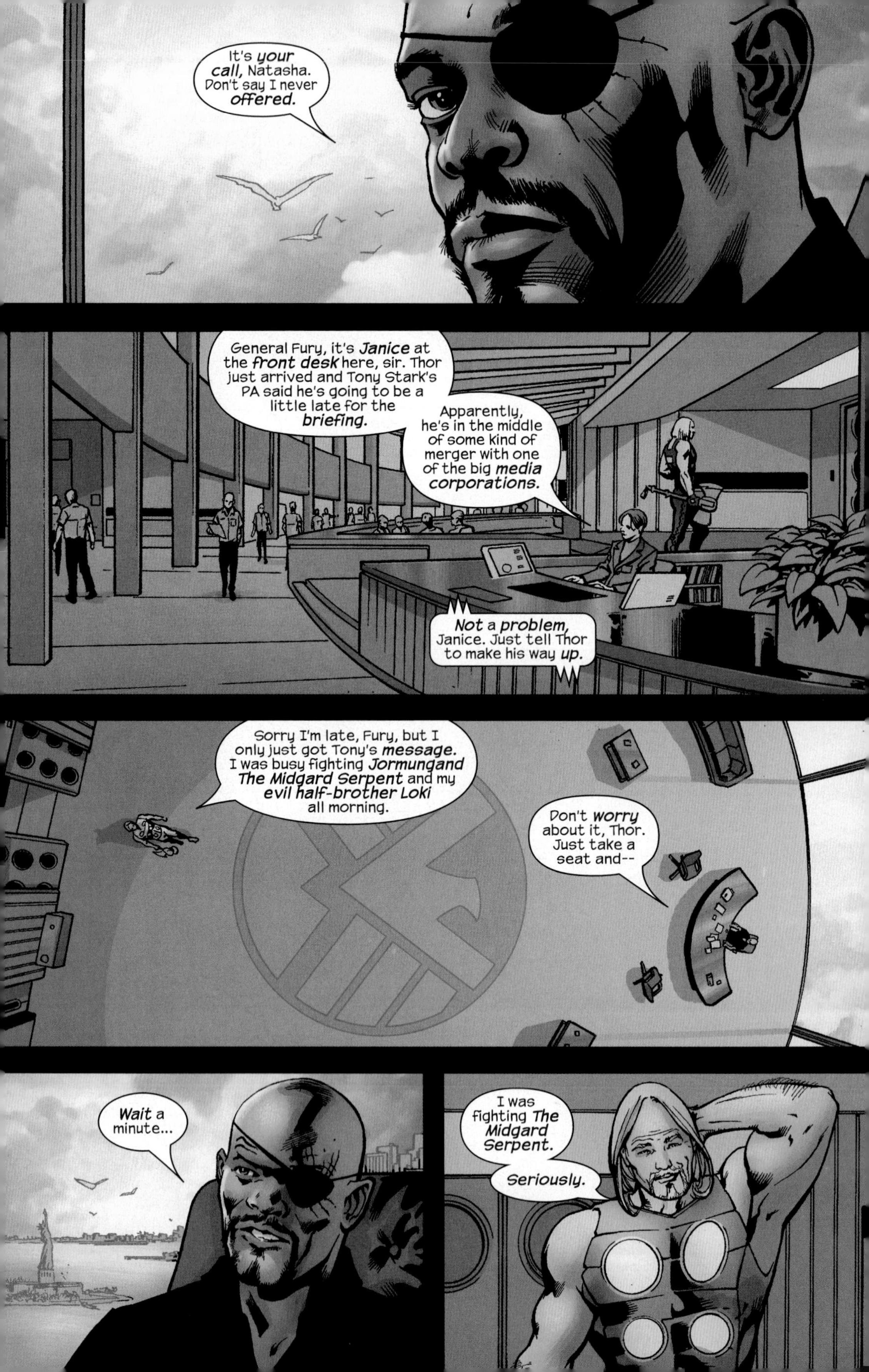
It's your call, Natasha. Don't say I never offered.
General Fury, it's Janice at the front desk here, sir. Thor just arrived and Tony Stark's PA said he's going to be a little late for the briefing.
Apparently, he's in the middle of some kind of merger with one of the big media corporations.
Not a problem, Janice. Just tell Thor to make his way up.
Sorry I'm late, Fury, but I only just got Tony's message. I was busy fighting Jormungand The Midgard Serpent and my evil half-brother Loki all morning.
Don't worry about it, Thor. Just take a seat and--
Wait a minute...
I was fighting The Midgard Serpent.
Seriously.

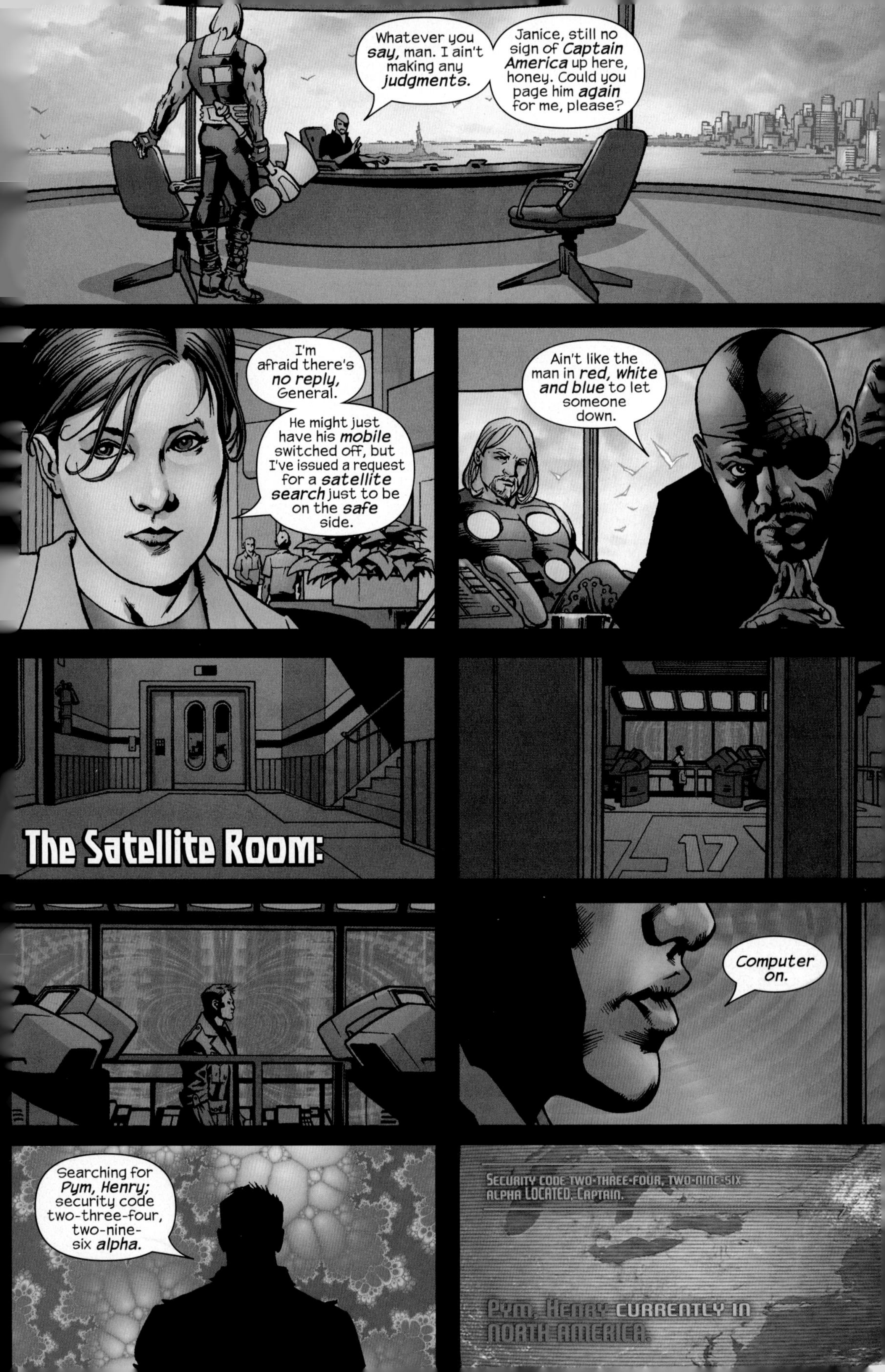

Whatever you say, man. I ain't making any judgments.
Janice, still no sign of Captain America up here, honey. Could you page him again for me, please?
I'm afraid there's no reply, General.
He might just have his mobile switched off, but I've issued a request for a satellite search just to be on the safe side.
Ain't like the man in red, white and blue to let someone down.
The Satellite Room:
17
Computer on.
Searching for Pym, Henry; security code two-three-four, two-nine-six alpha.
Security code two-three-four, two-nine-six alpha LOCATED, Captain.
Pym, Henry currently in North America.

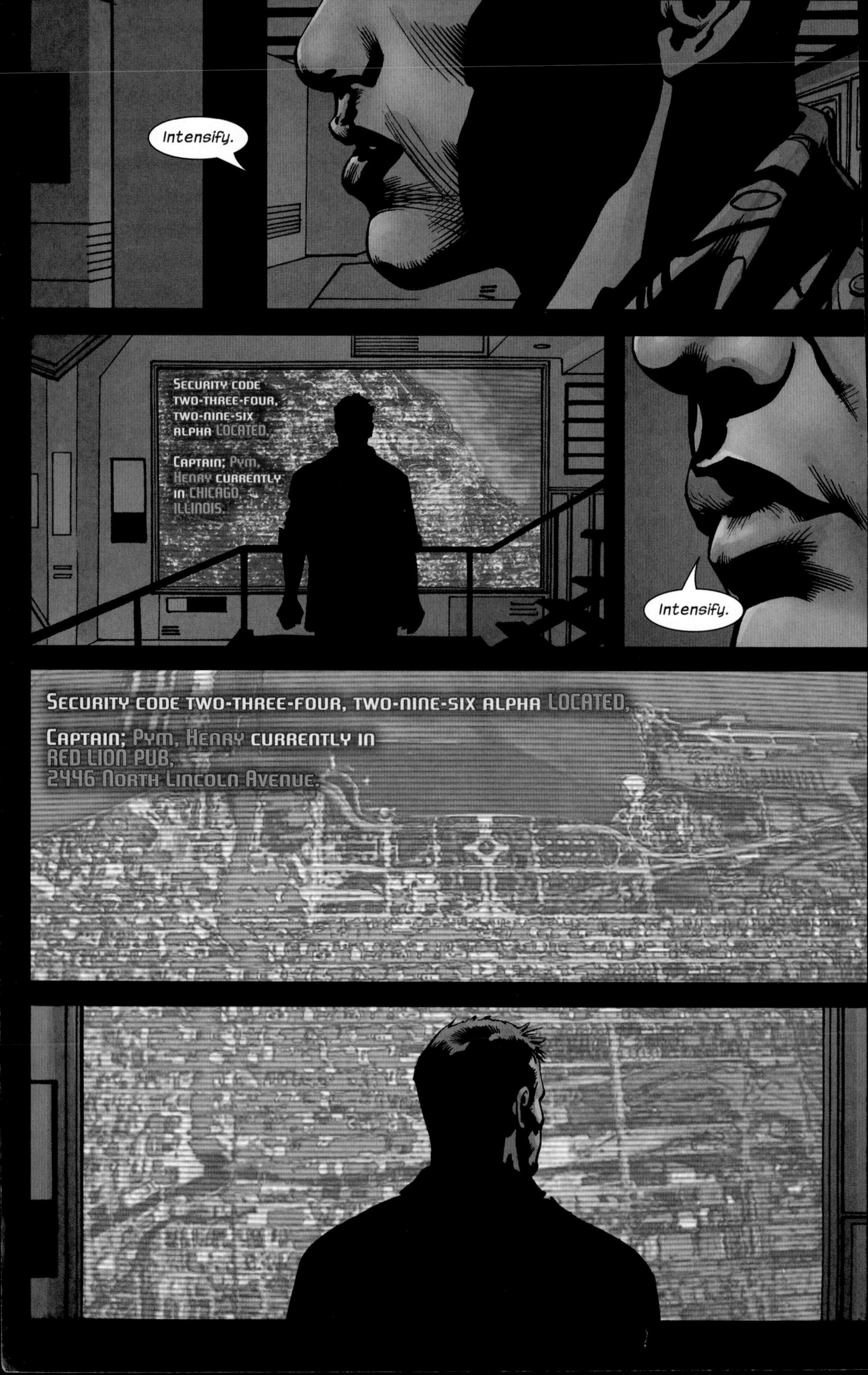
Intensify.
Security code two-three-four, two-nine-six alpha LOCATED.
Captain; Pym, Henry currently in CHICAGO, ILLINOIS.
Intensify.
Security code two-three-four, two-nine-six alpha LOCATED.
Captain; Pym, Henry currently in RED LION PUB, 2446 North Lincoln Avenue.

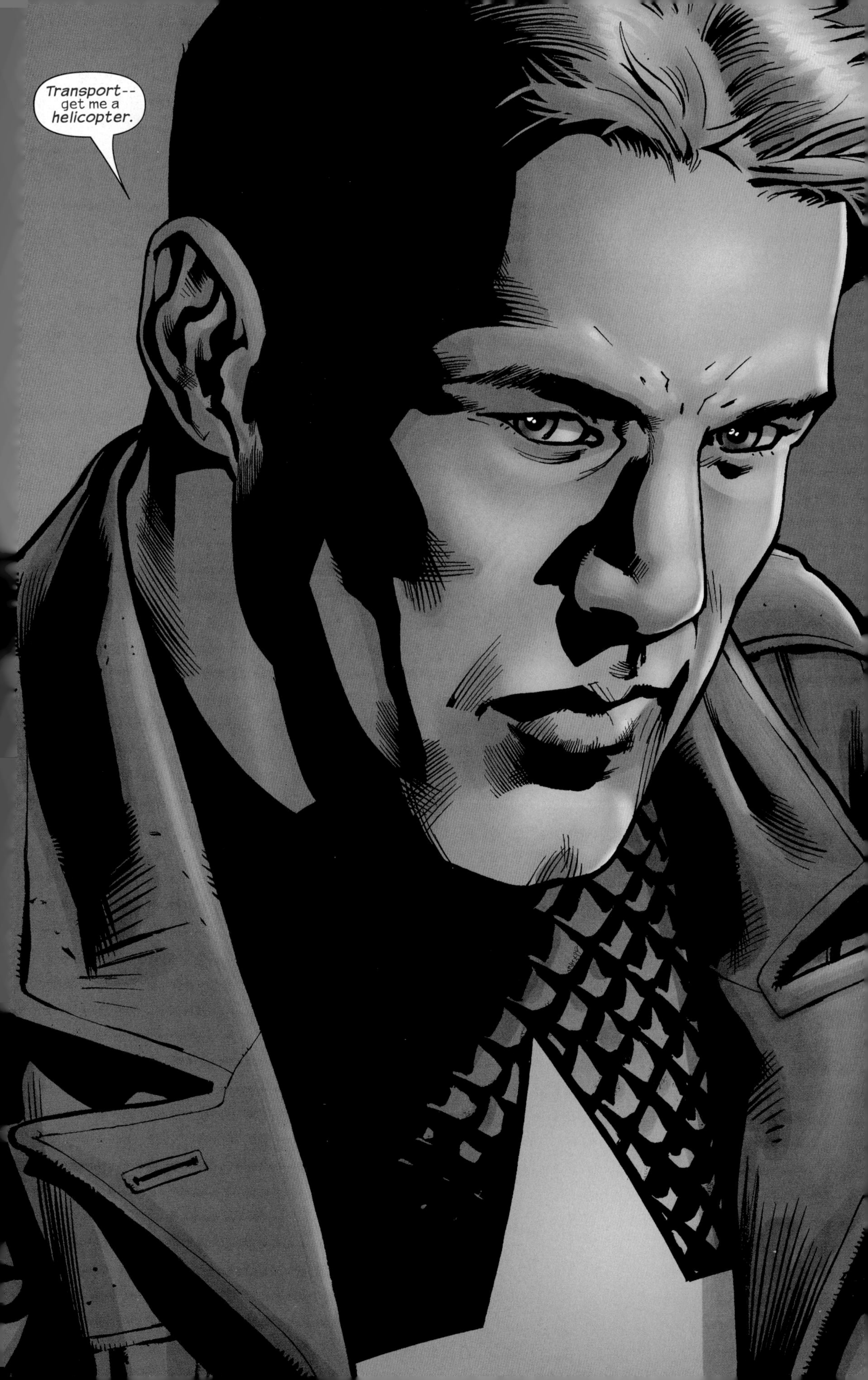
Transport-- get me a helicopter.

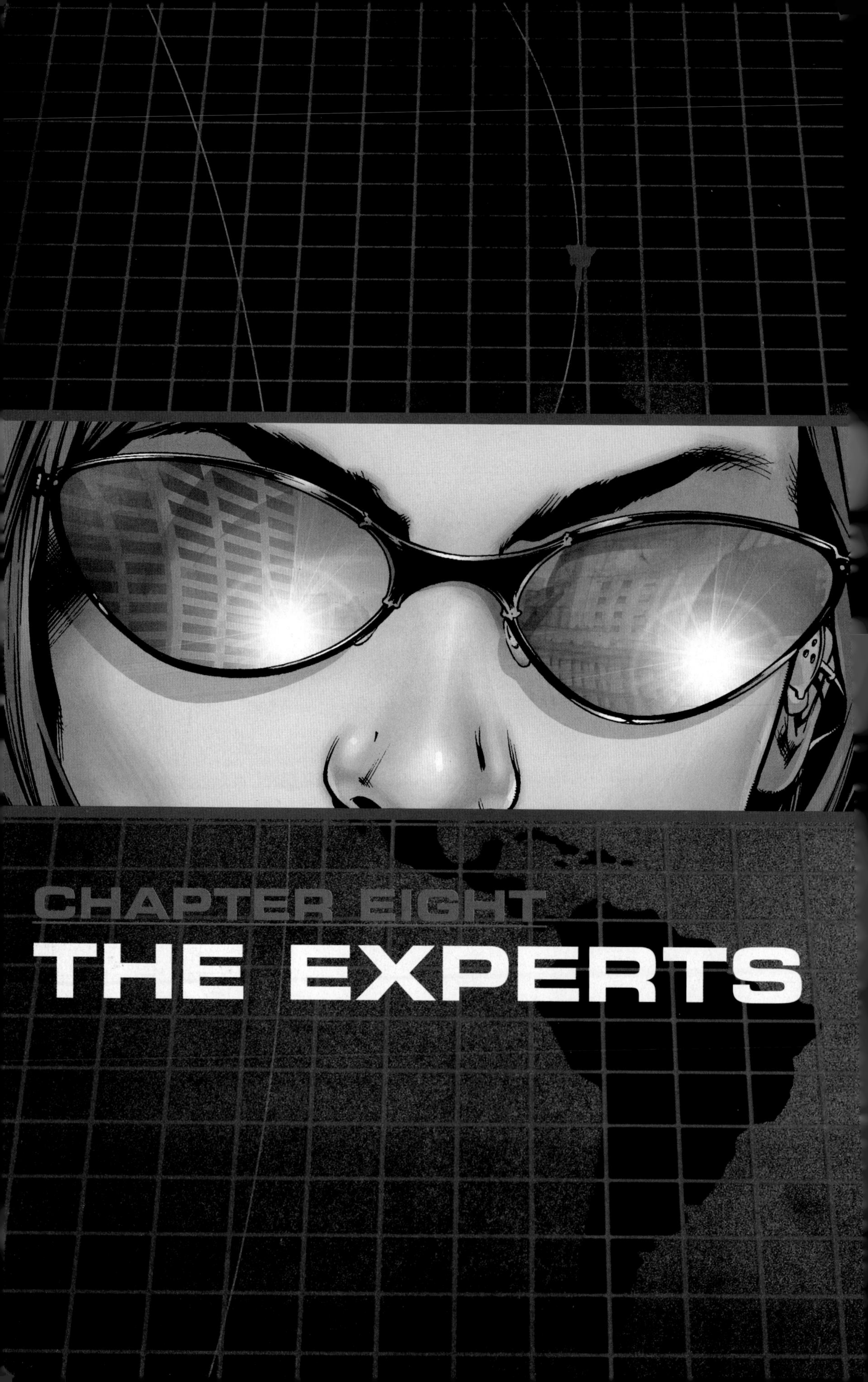
CHAPTER EIGHT
THE EXPERTS

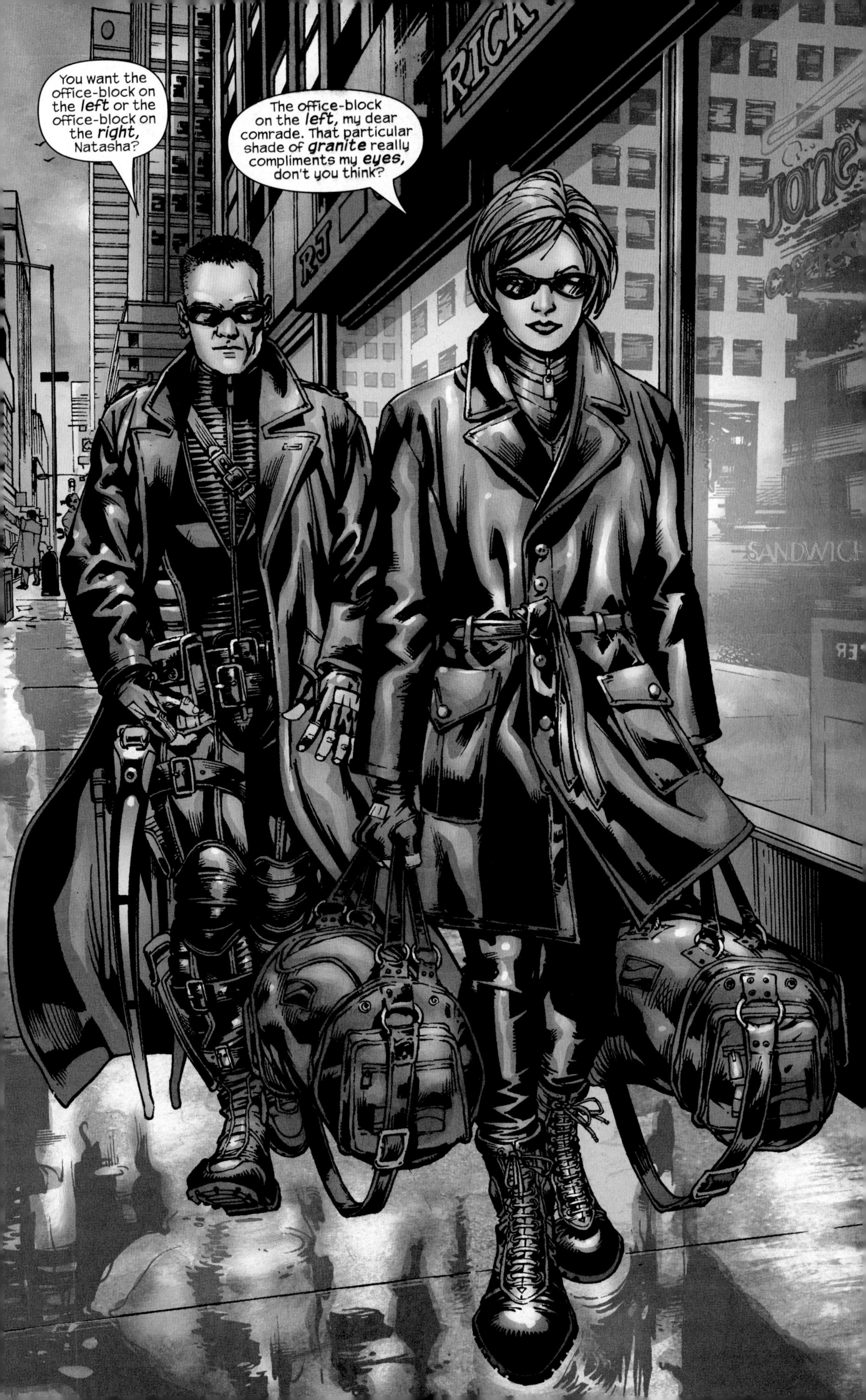
You want the office-block on the left or the office-block on the right, Natasha?
The office-block on the left, my dear comrade. That particular shade of granite really compliments my eyes, don't you think?
RICK
RJ
SANDWIC

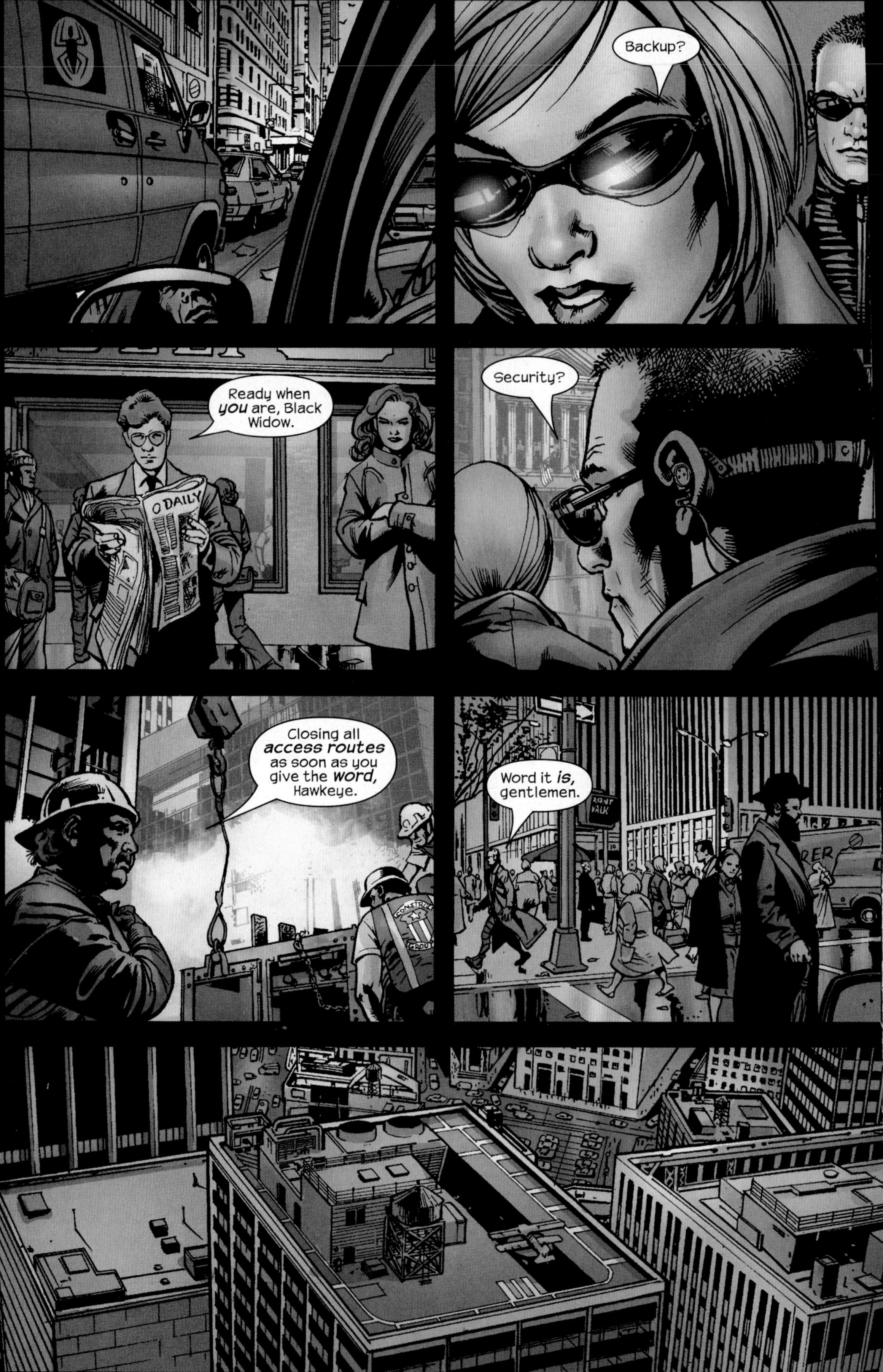
Backup?
Ready when *you* are, Black Widow.
Security?
Closing all ***access routes*** as soon as you give the ***word,*** Hawkeye.
Word it ***is,*** gentlemen.

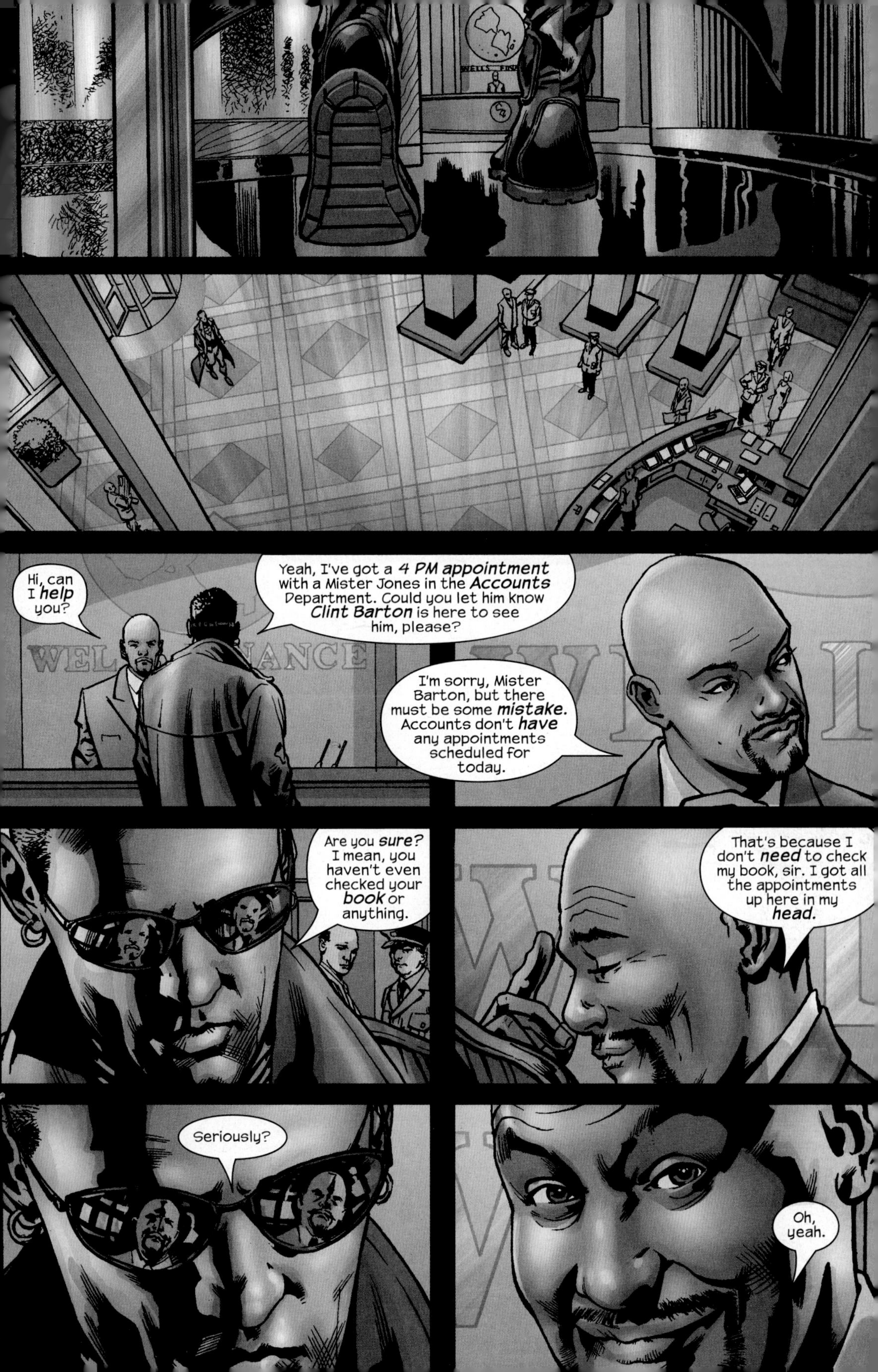
WELLS FINANCE
Hi, can I help you?
Yeah, I've got a 4 PM appointment with a Mister Jones in the Accounts Department. Could you let him know Clint Barton is here to see him, please?
I'm sorry, Mister Barton, but there must be some mistake. Accounts don't have any appointments scheduled for today.
Are you sure? I mean, you haven't even checked your book or anything.
That's because I don't need to check my book, sir. I got all the appointments up here in my head.
Seriously?
Oh, yeah.

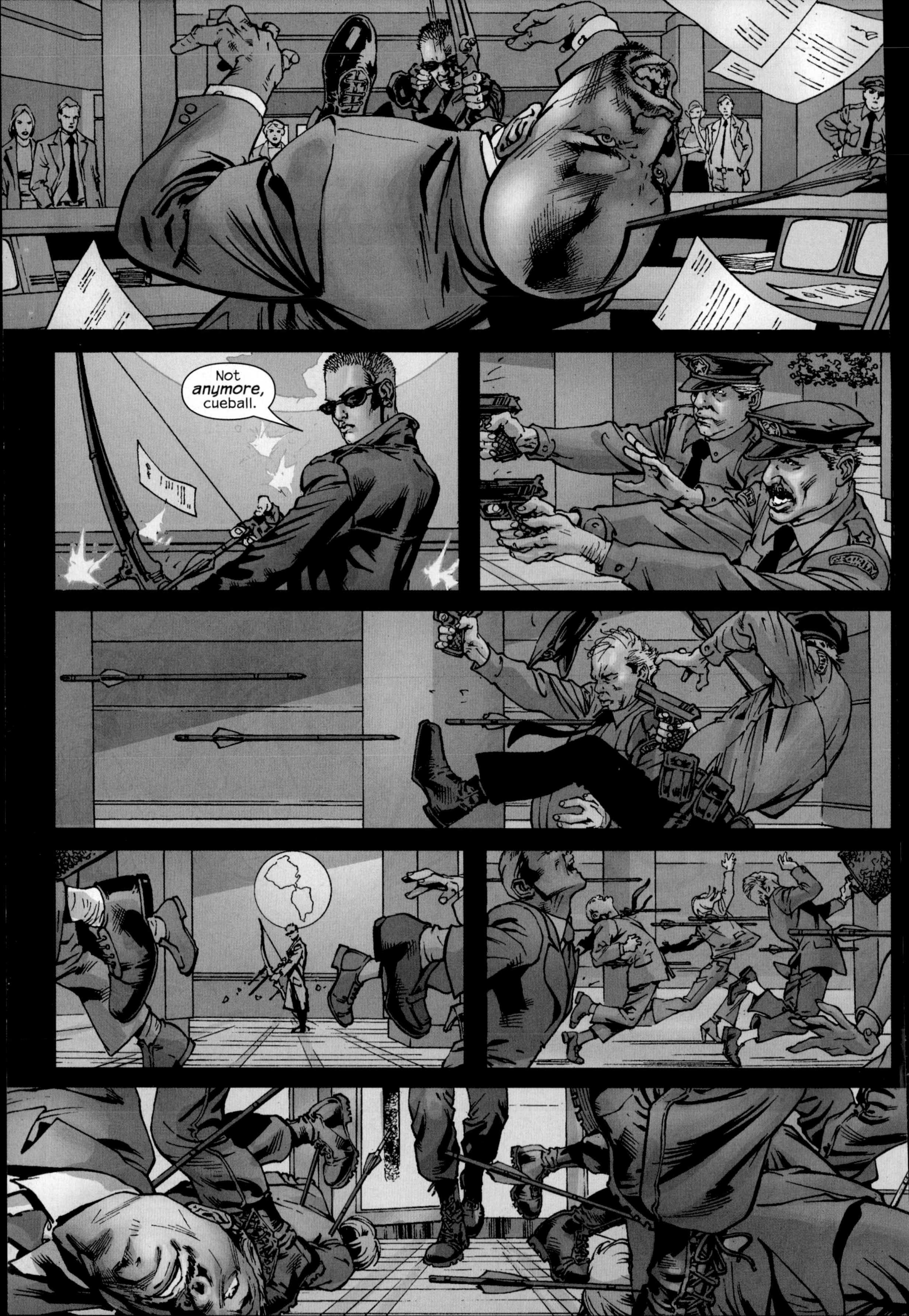
Not *anymore,* cueball.

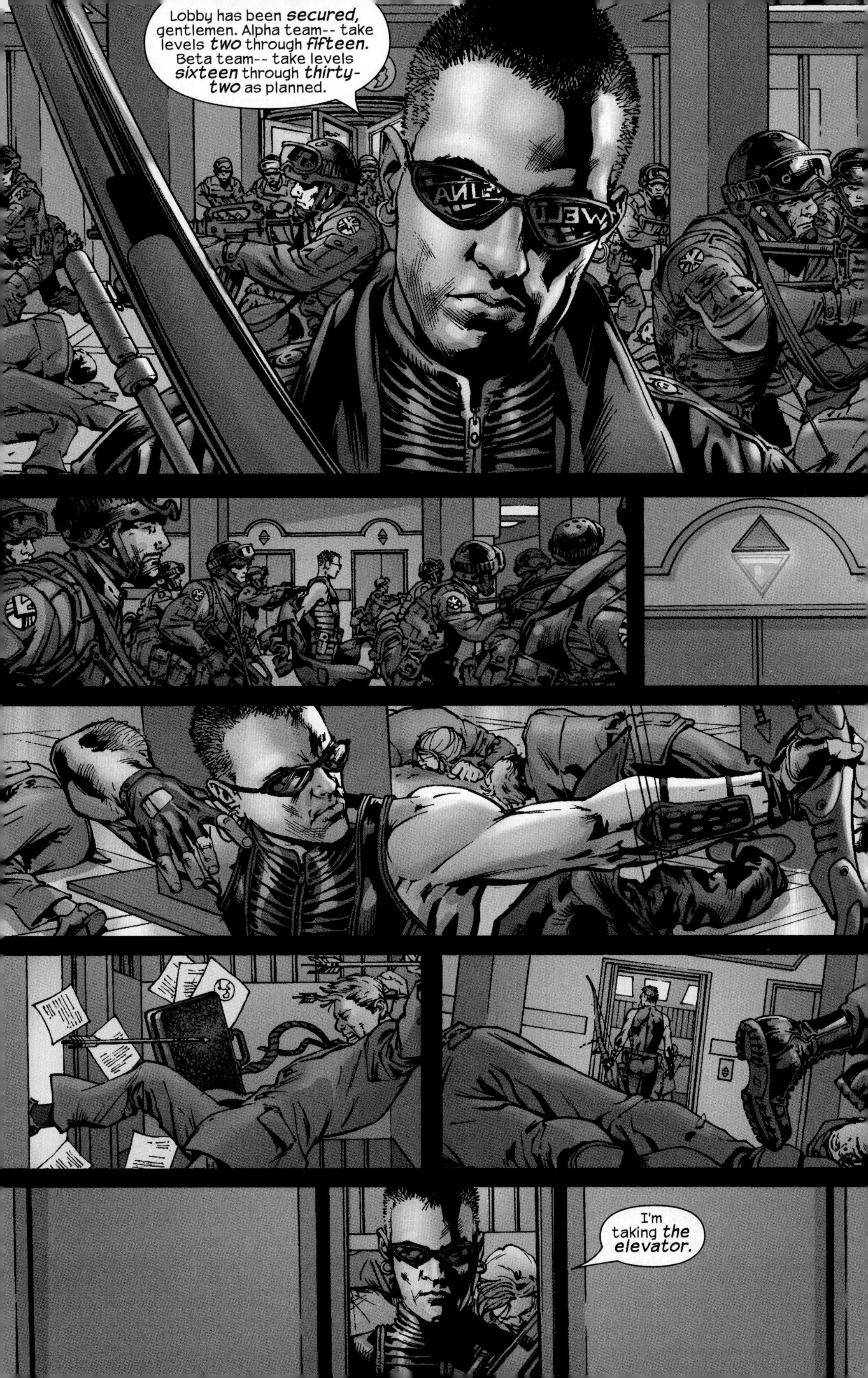
Lobby has been secured, gentlemen. Alpha team-- take levels two through fifteen. Beta team-- take levels sixteen through thirty-two as planned.
I'm taking the elevator.

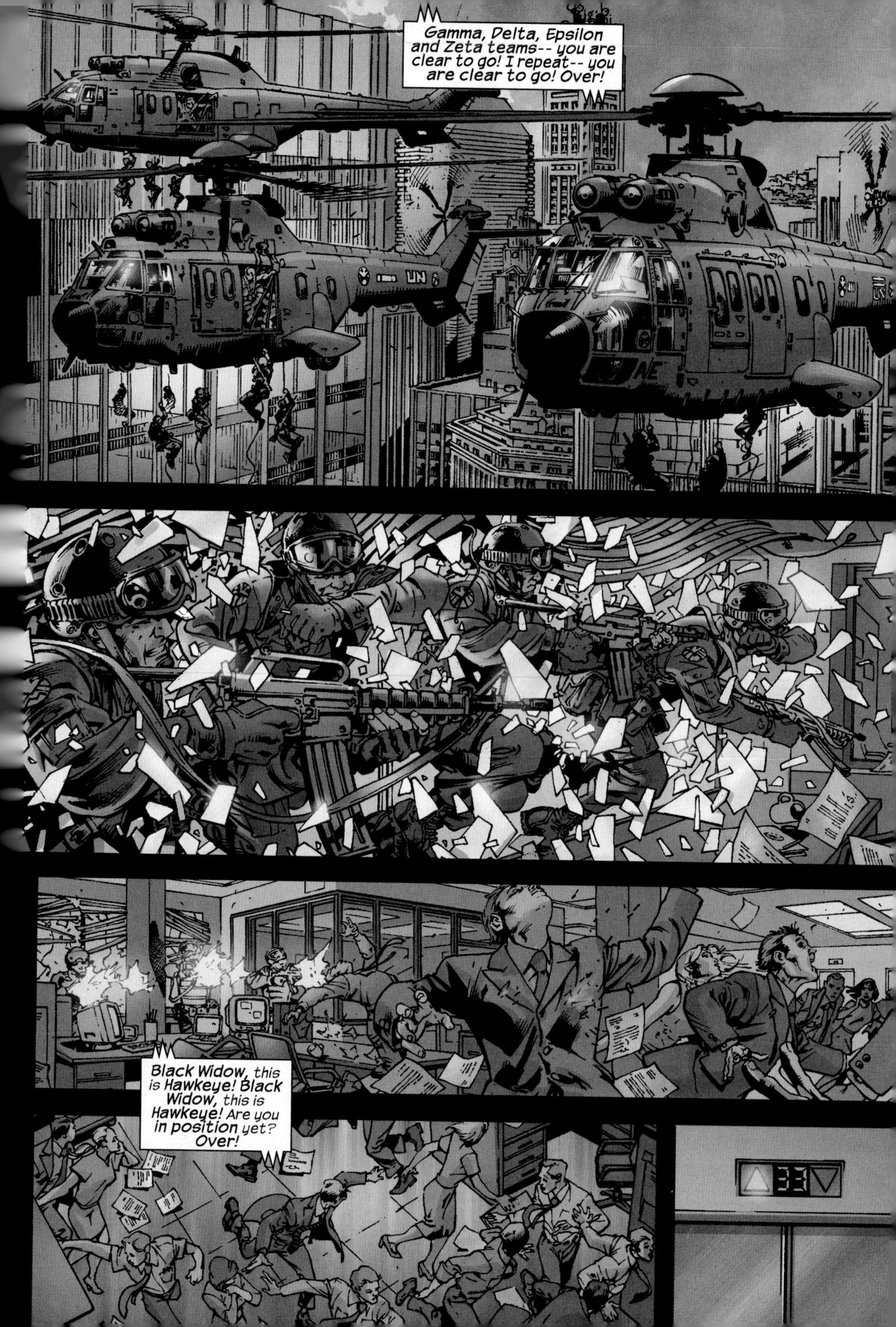
Gamma, Delta, Epsilon and Zeta teams-- you are clear to go! I repeat-- you are clear to go! Over!
Black Widow, this is Hawkeye! Black Widow, this is Hawkeye! Are you in position yet? Over!

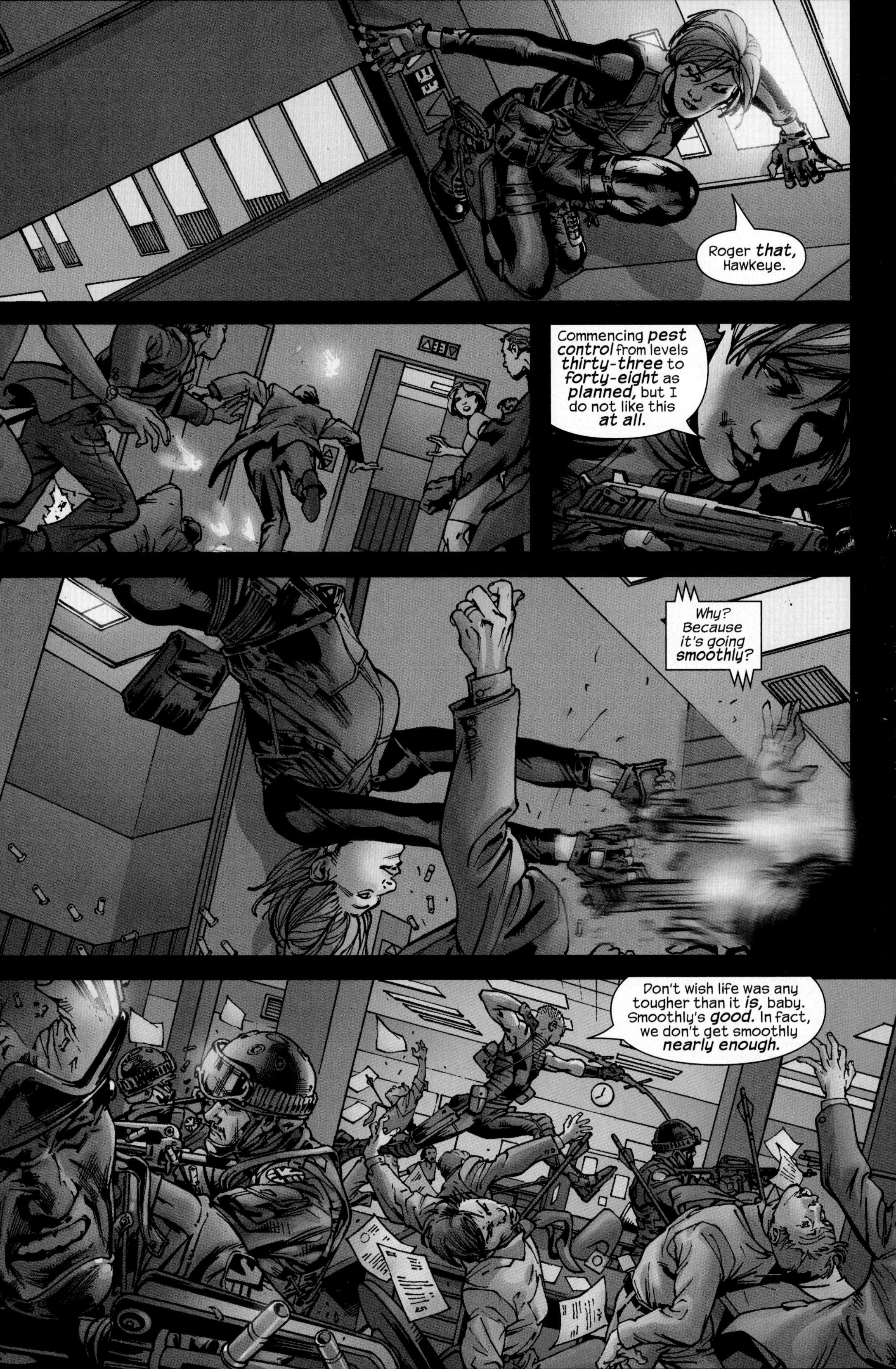

Roger that, Hawkeye.
Commencing pest control from levels thirty-three to forty-eight as planned, but I do not like this at all.
Why? Because it's going smoothly?
Don't wish life was any tougher than it is, baby. Smoothly's good. In fact, we don't get smoothly nearly enough.

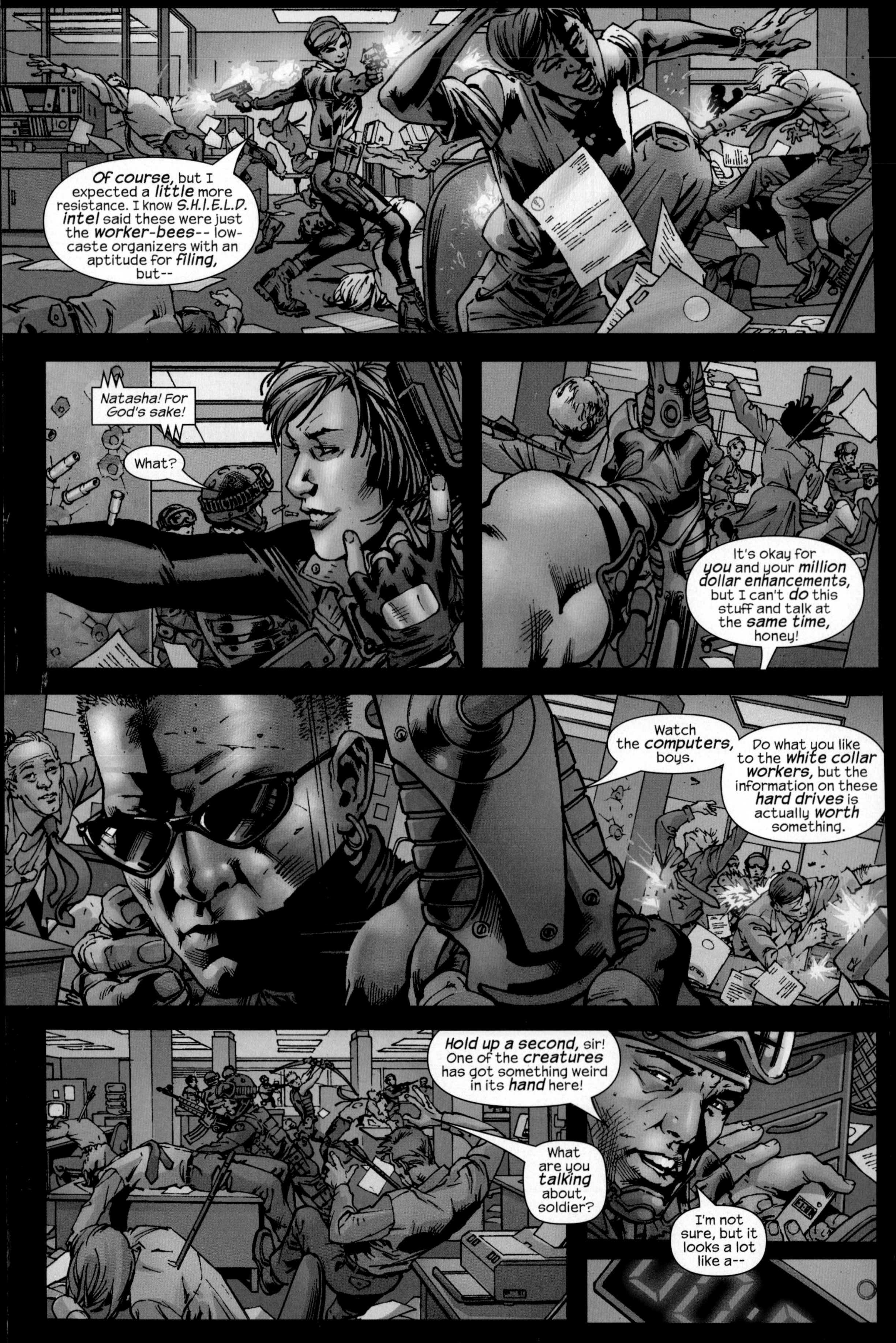

Of course, but I expected a little more resistance. I know S.H.I.E.L.D. intel said these were just the worker-bees-- low-caste organizers with an aptitude for filing, but--
Natasha! For God's sake!
What?
It's okay for you and your million dollar enhancements, but I can't do this stuff and talk at the same time, honey!
Watch the computers, boys.
Do what you like to the white collar workers, but the information on these hard drives is actually worth something.
Hold up a second, sir! One of the creatures has got something weird in its hand here!
What are you talking about, soldier?
I'm not sure, but it looks a lot like a--

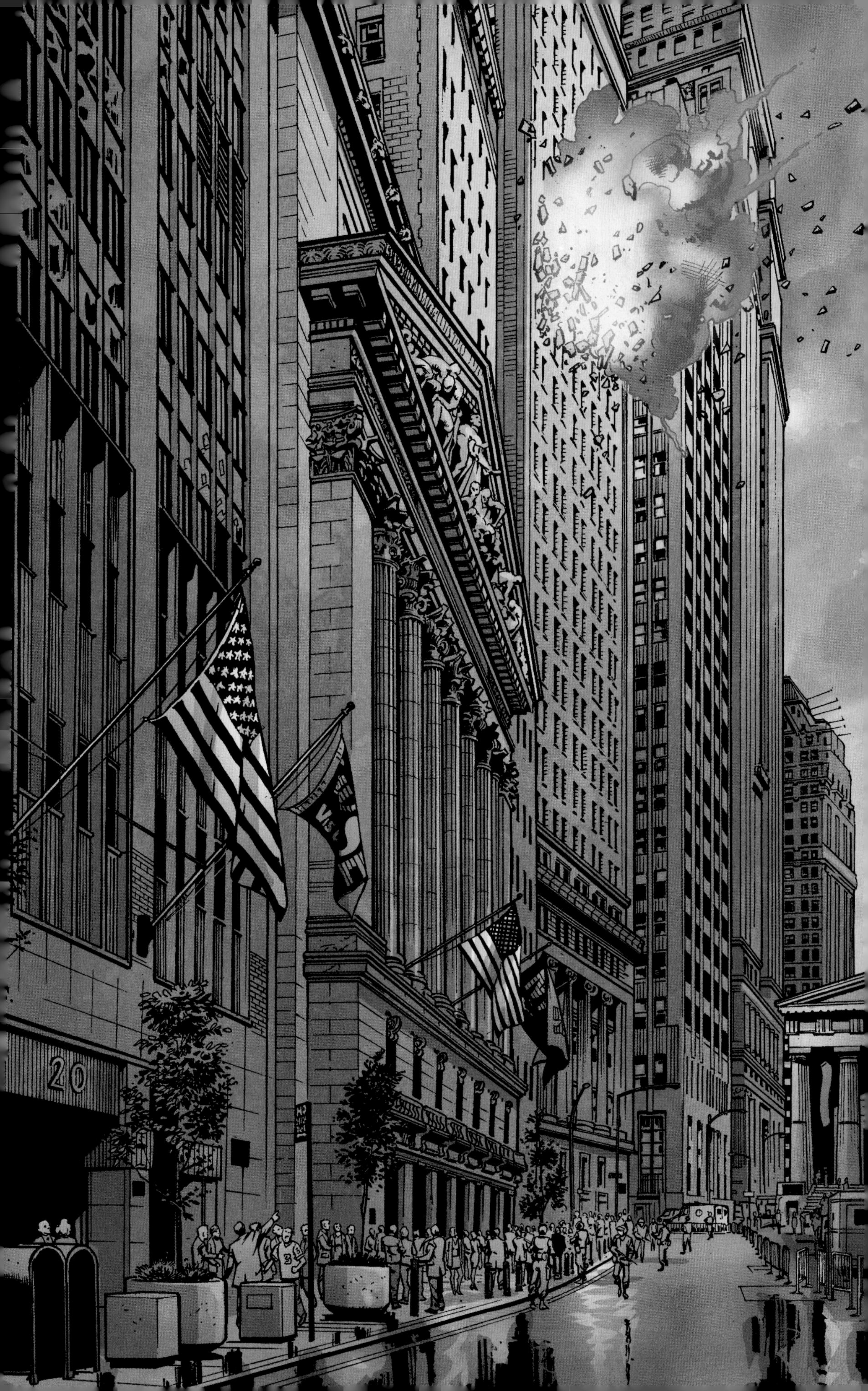
20

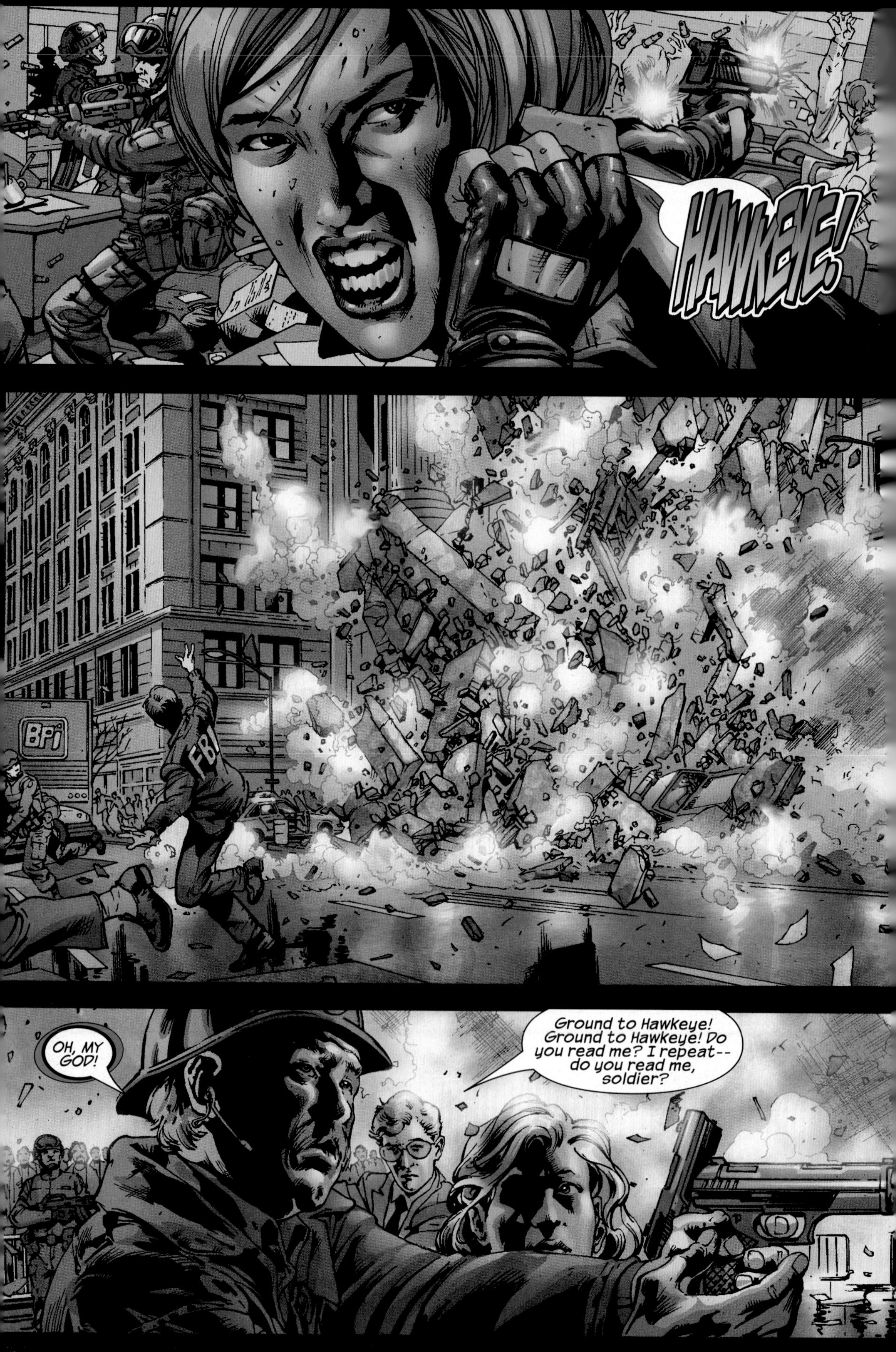
HAWKEYE!
FBI
BPI
OH, MY GOD!
Ground to Hawkeye! Ground to Hawkeye! Do you read me? I repeat-- do you read me, soldier?

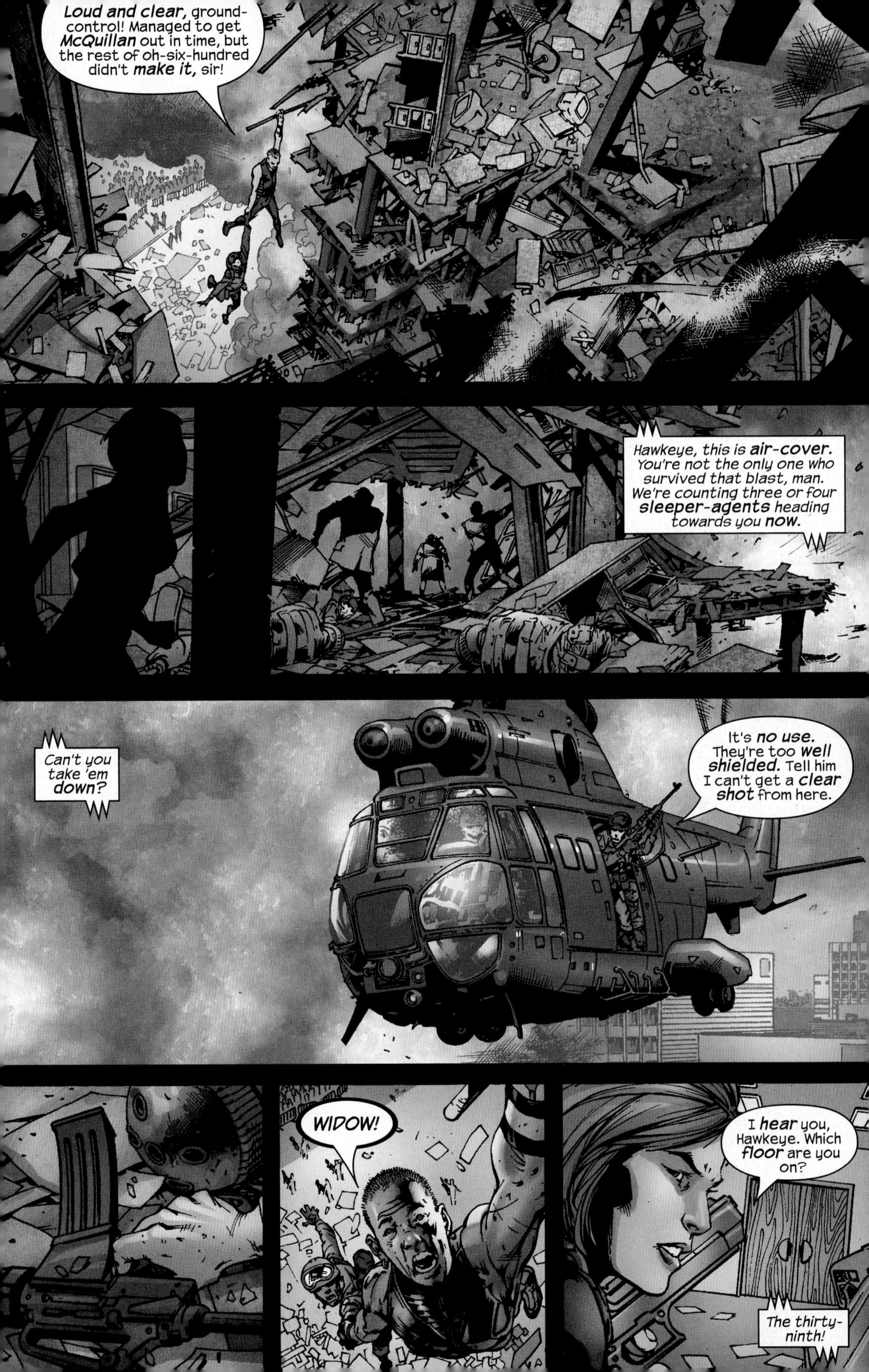
Loud and clear, ground-control! Managed to get McQuillan out in time, but the rest of oh-six-hundred didn't make it, sir!
Hawkeye, this is air-cover. You're not the only one who survived that blast, man. We're counting three or four sleeper-agents heading towards you now.
Can't you take 'em down?
It's no use. They're too well shielded. Tell him I can't get a clear shot from here.
WIDOW!
I hear you, Hawkeye. Which floor are you on?
The thirty-ninth!

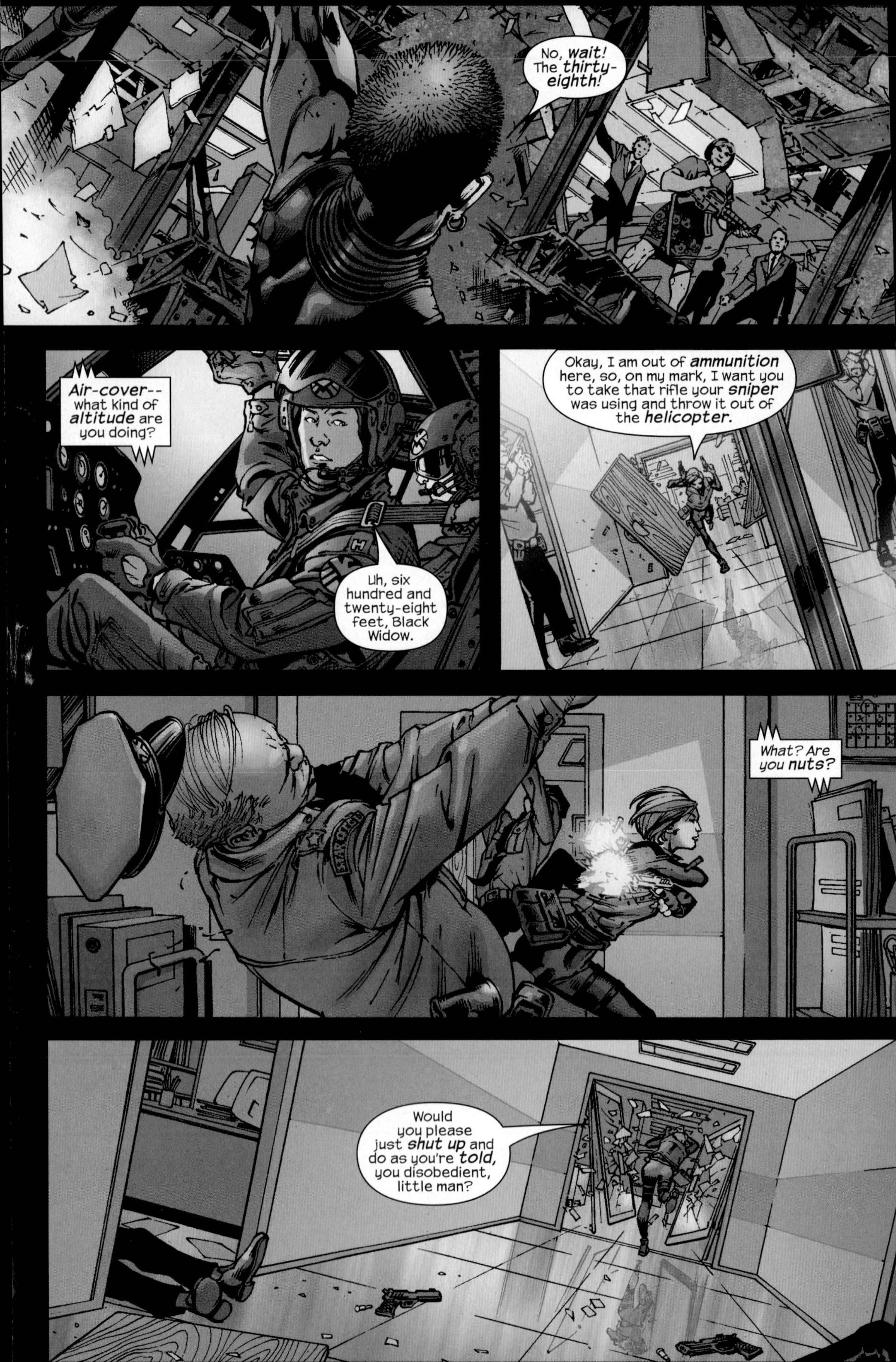

No, wait! The thirty-eighth!
Air-cover-- what kind of altitude are you doing?
Uh, six hundred and twenty-eight feet, Black Widow.
Okay, I am out of ammunition here, so, on my mark, I want you to take that rifle your sniper was using and throw it out of the helicopter.
What? Are you nuts?
Would you please just shut up and do as you're told, you disobedient, little man?

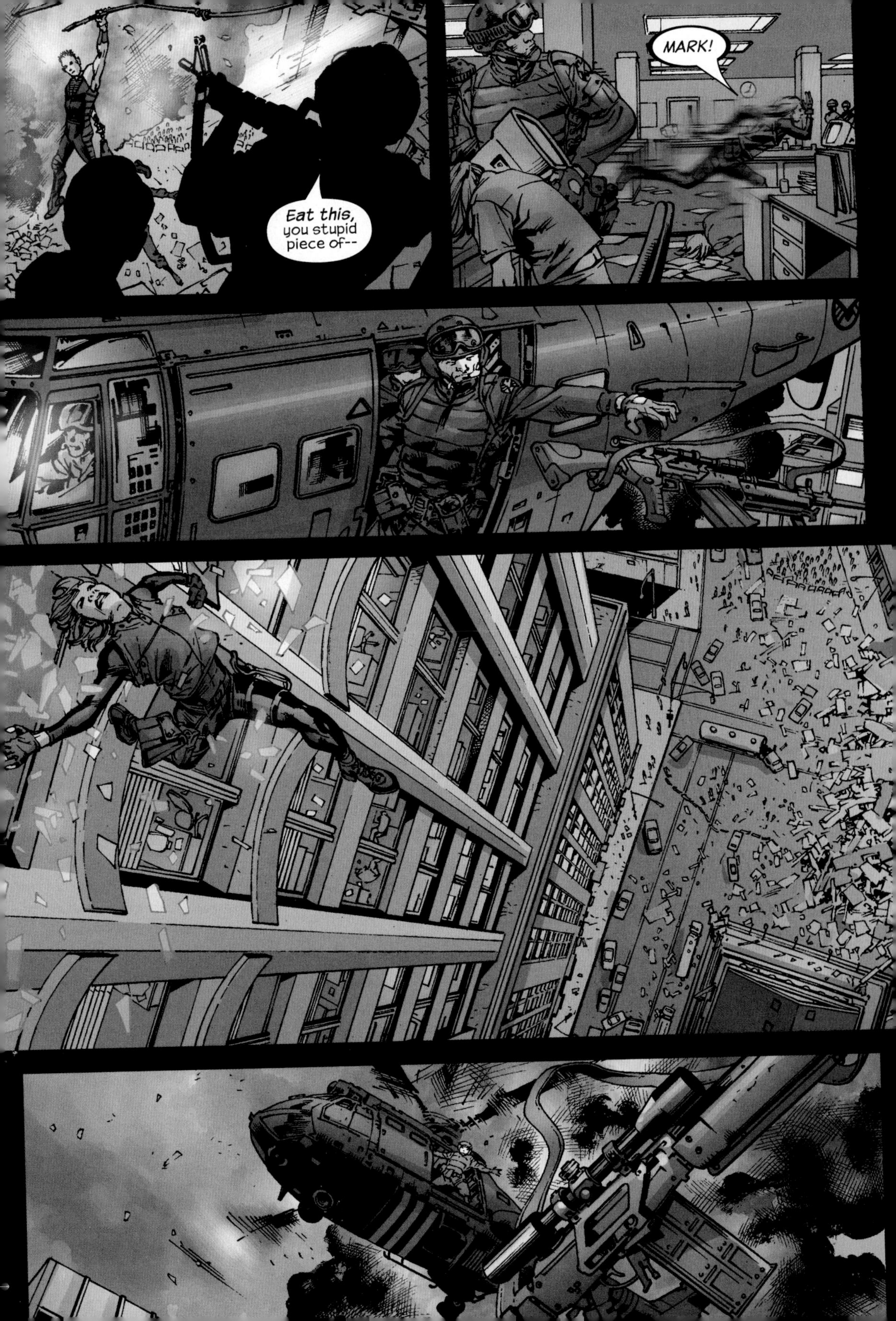
Eat this, you stupid piece of--
MARK!

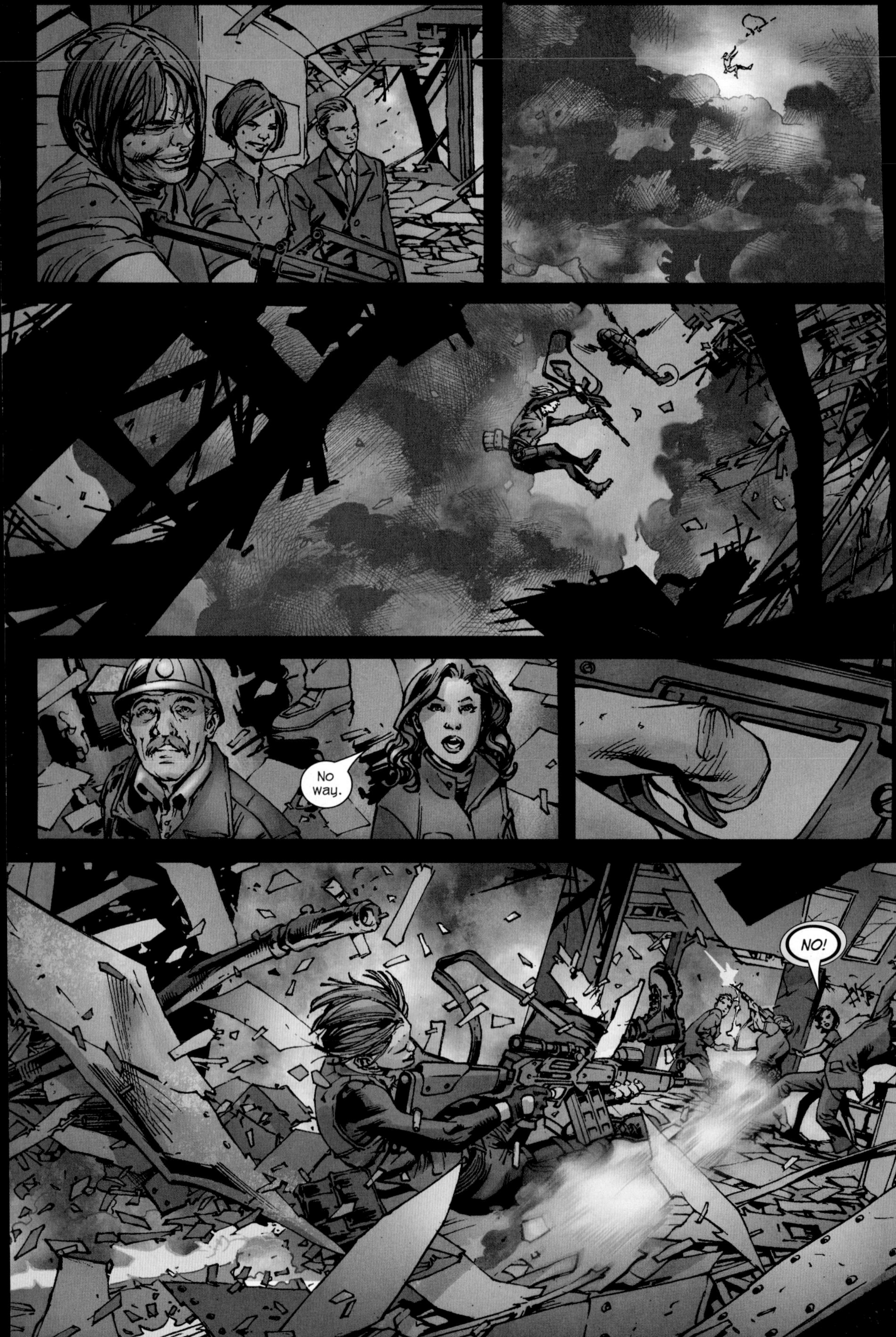
No way.
NO!

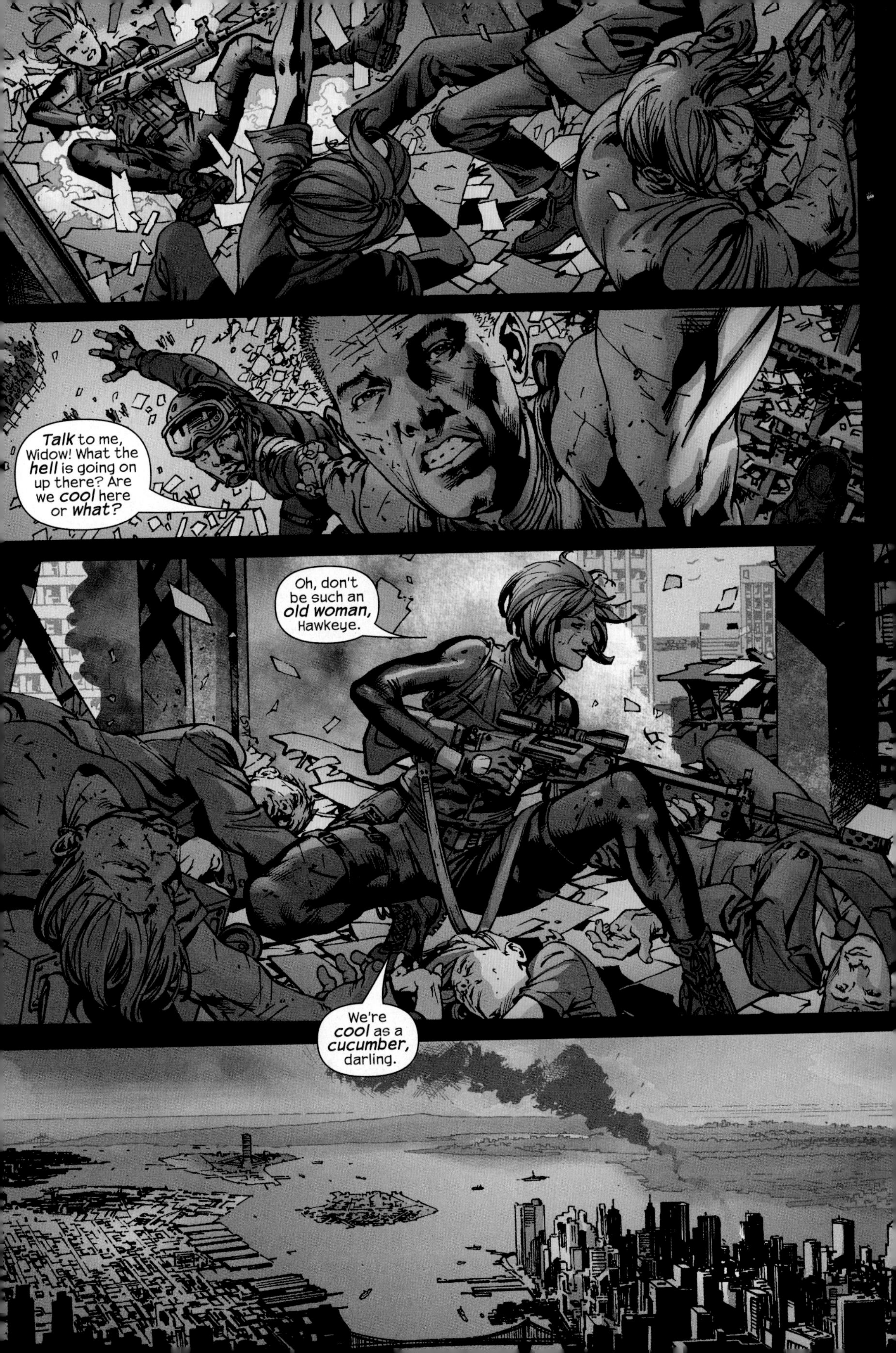
Talk to me, Widow! What the hell is going on up there? Are we cool here or what?
Oh, don't be such an old woman, Hawkeye.
We're cool as a cucumber, darling.

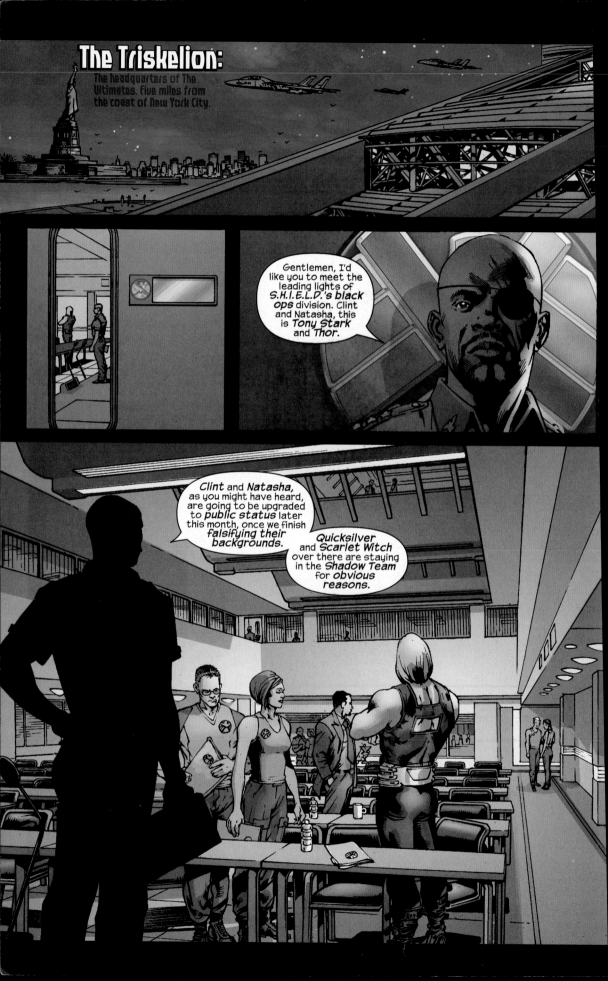

The Triskelion:

The headquarters of The Ultimates. Five miles from the coast of New York City.

Gentlemen, I'd like you to meet the leading lights of S.H.I.E.L.D.'s black ops division. Clint and Natasha, this is *Tony Stark* and *Thor*.

Clint and *Natasha*, as you might have heard, are going to be upgraded to *public status* later this month, once we finish *falsifying their backgrounds*.

Quicksilver and *Scarlet Witch* over there are staying in the *Shadow Team* for *obvious reasons*.

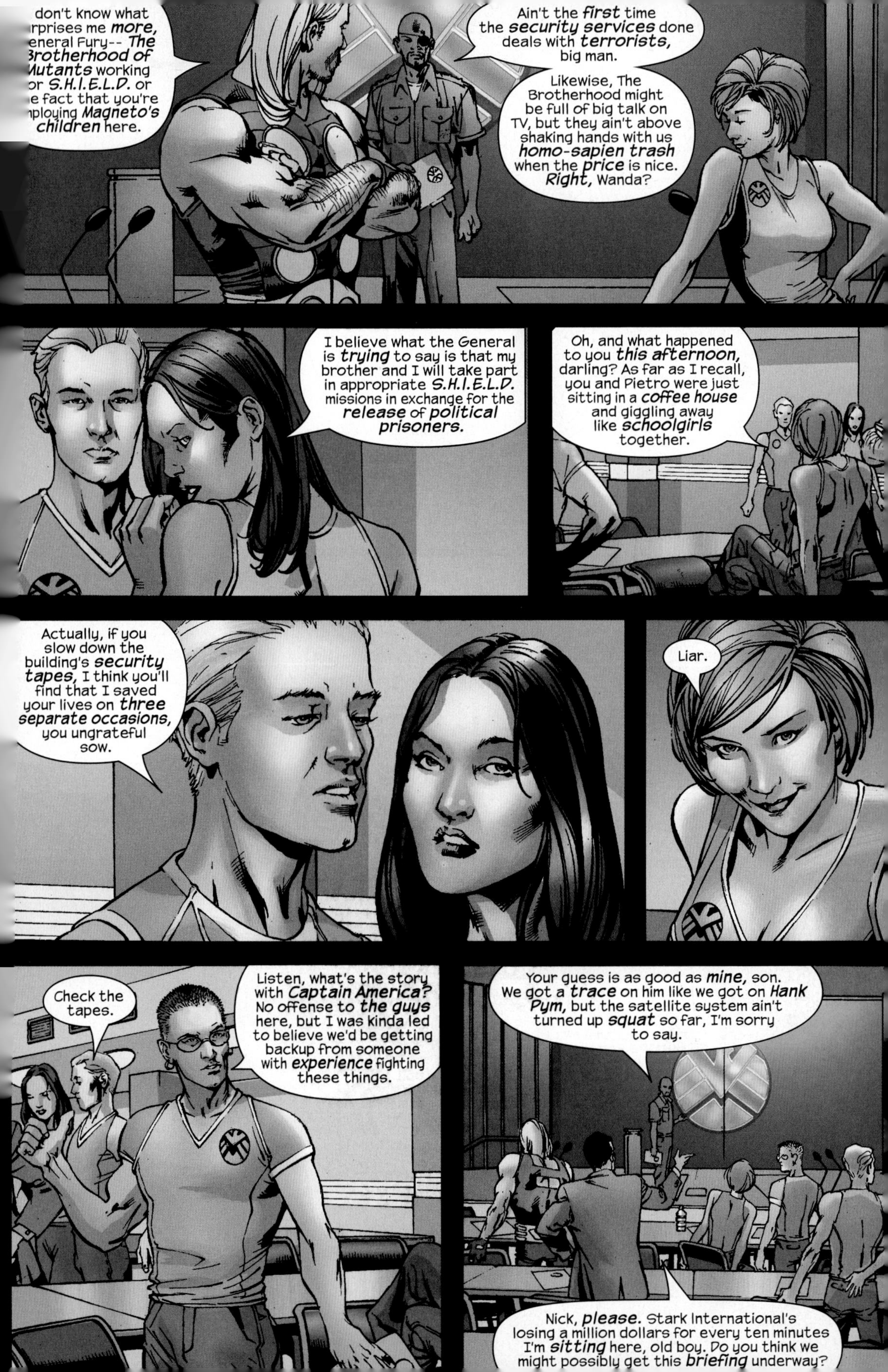
don't know what rprises me more, eneral Fury-- The Brotherhood of Mutants working or S.H.I.E.L.D. or e fact that you're nploying Magneto's children here.
Ain't the first time the security services done deals with terrorists, big man.
Likewise, The Brotherhood might be full of big talk on TV, but they ain't above shaking hands with us homo-sapien trash when the price is nice. Right, Wanda?
I believe what the General is trying to say is that my brother and I will take part in appropriate S.H.I.E.L.D. missions in exchange for the release of political prisoners.
Oh, and what happened to you this afternoon, darling? As far as I recall, you and Pietro were just sitting in a coffee house and giggling away like schoolgirls together.
Actually, if you slow down the building's security tapes, I think you'll find that I saved your lives on three separate occasions, you ungrateful sow.
Liar.
Check the tapes.
Listen, what's the story with Captain America? No offense to the guys here, but I was kinda led to believe we'd be getting backup from someone with experience fighting these things.
Your guess is as good as mine, son. We got a trace on him like we got on Hank Pym, but the satellite system ain't turned up squat so far, I'm sorry to say.
Nick, please. Stark International's losing a million dollars for every ten minutes I'm sitting here, old boy. Do you think we might possibly get this briefing underway?

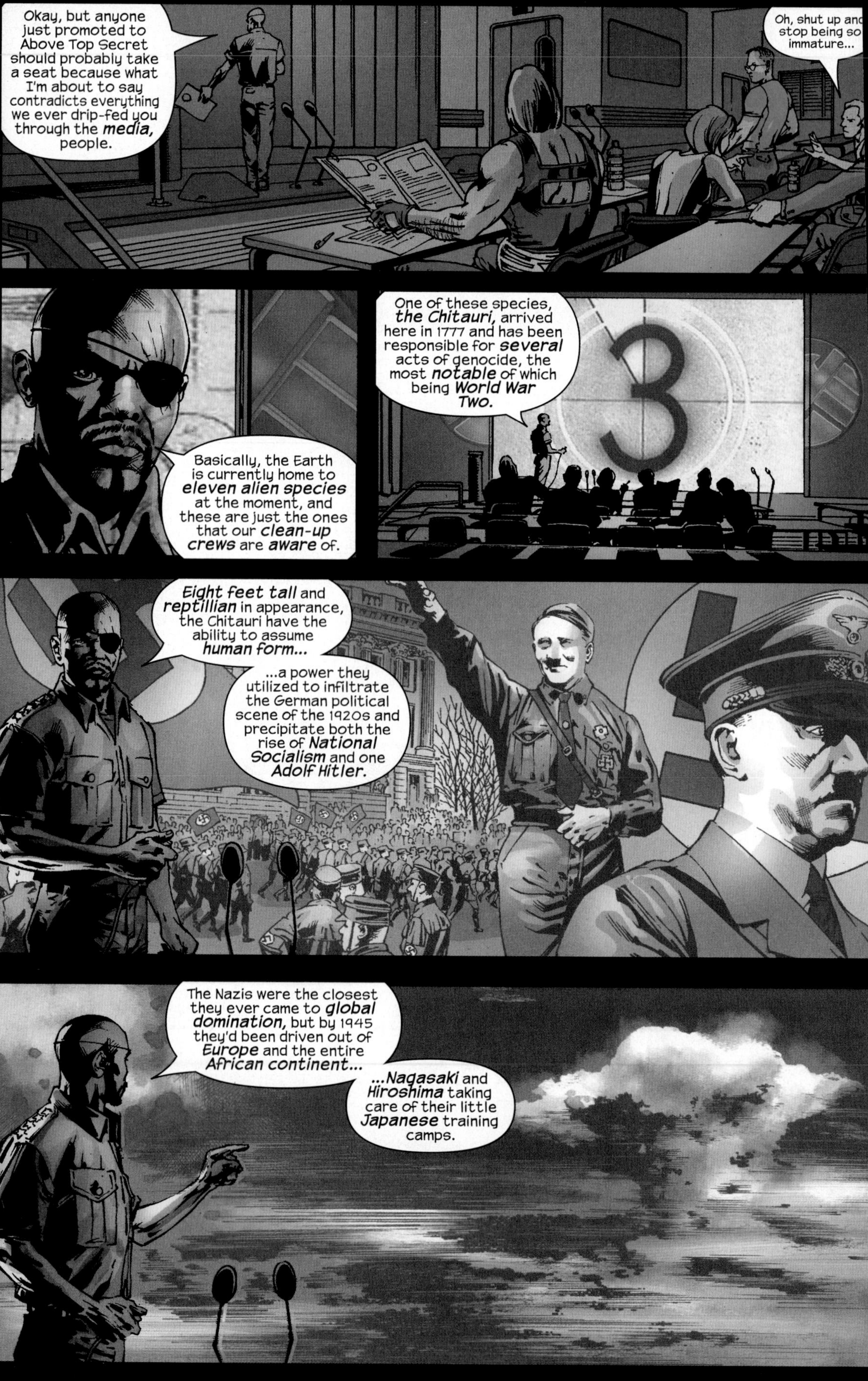
Okay, but anyone just promoted to Above Top Secret should probably take a seat because what I'm about to say contradicts everything we ever drip-fed you through the *media,* people.
Oh, shut up and stop being so immature...
Basically, the Earth is currently home to *eleven alien species* at the moment, and these are just the ones that our *clean-up crews* are *aware* of.
One of these species, *the Chitauri,* arrived here in 1777 and has been responsible for *several* acts of genocide, the most *notable* of which being *World War Two.*
Eight feet tall and *reptillian* in appearance, the Chitauri have the ability to assume *human form...*
...a power they utilized to infiltrate the German political scene of the 1920s and precipitate both the rise of *National Socialism* and one *Adolf Hitler.*
The Nazis were the closest they ever came to *global domination,* but by 1945 they'd been driven out of *Europe* and the entire *African continent...*
...Nagasaki and *Hiroshima* taking care of their little *Japanese* training camps.

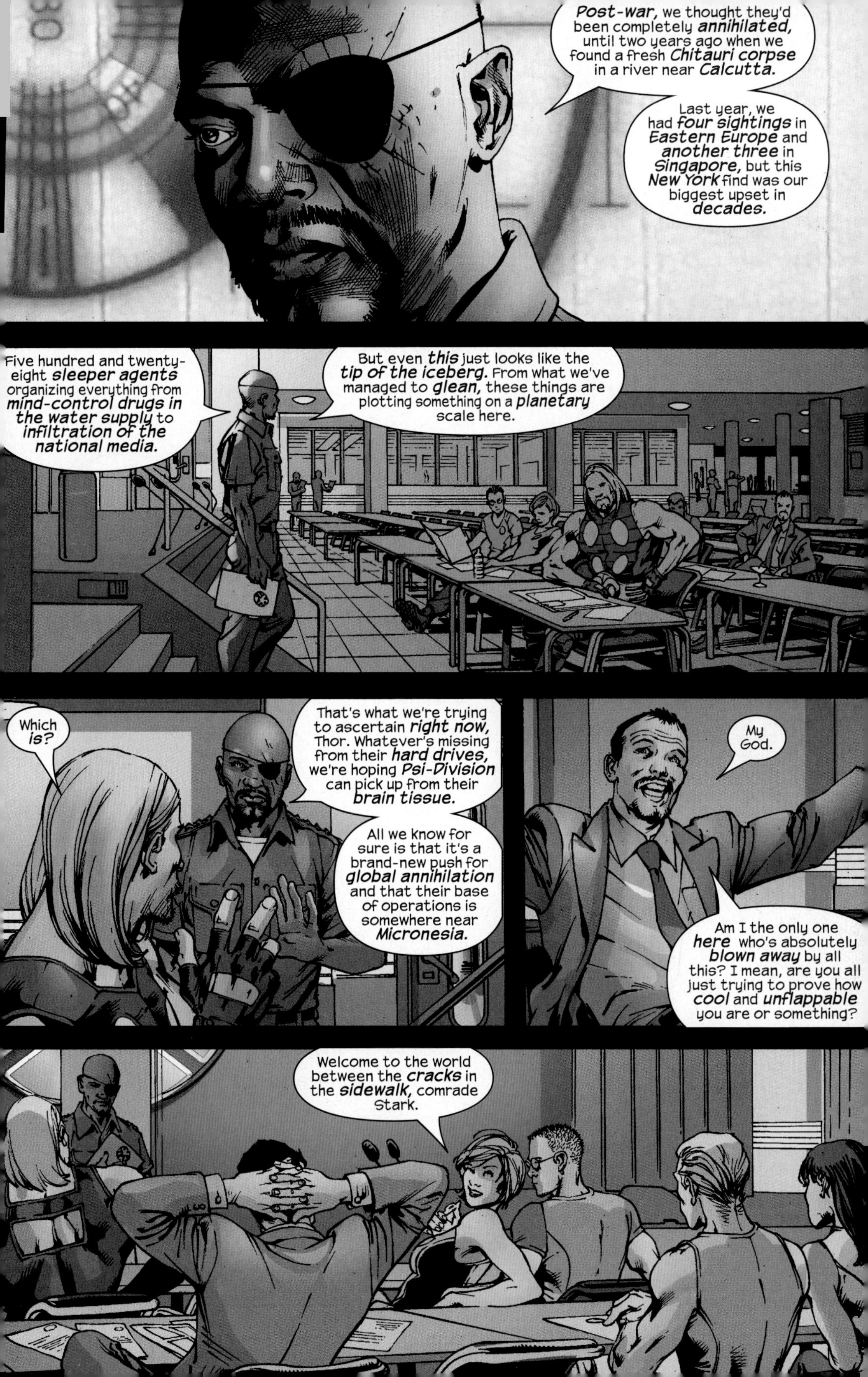
Post-war, we thought they'd been completely annihilated, until two years ago when we found a fresh Chitauri corpse in a river near Calcutta.
Last year, we had four sightings in Eastern Europe and another three in Singapore, but this New York find was our biggest upset in decades.
Five hundred and twenty-eight sleeper agents organizing everything from mind-control drugs in the water supply to infiltration of the national media.
But even this just looks like the tip of the iceberg. From what we've managed to glean, these things are plotting something on a planetary scale here.
Which is?
That's what we're trying to ascertain right now, Thor. Whatever's missing from their hard drives, we're hoping Psi-Division can pick up from their brain tissue.
All we know for sure is that it's a brand-new push for global annihilation and that their base of operations is somewhere near Micronesia.
My God.
Am I the only one here who's absolutely blown away by all this? I mean, are you all just trying to prove how cool and unflappable you are or something?
Welcome to the world between the cracks in the sidewalk, comrade Stark.

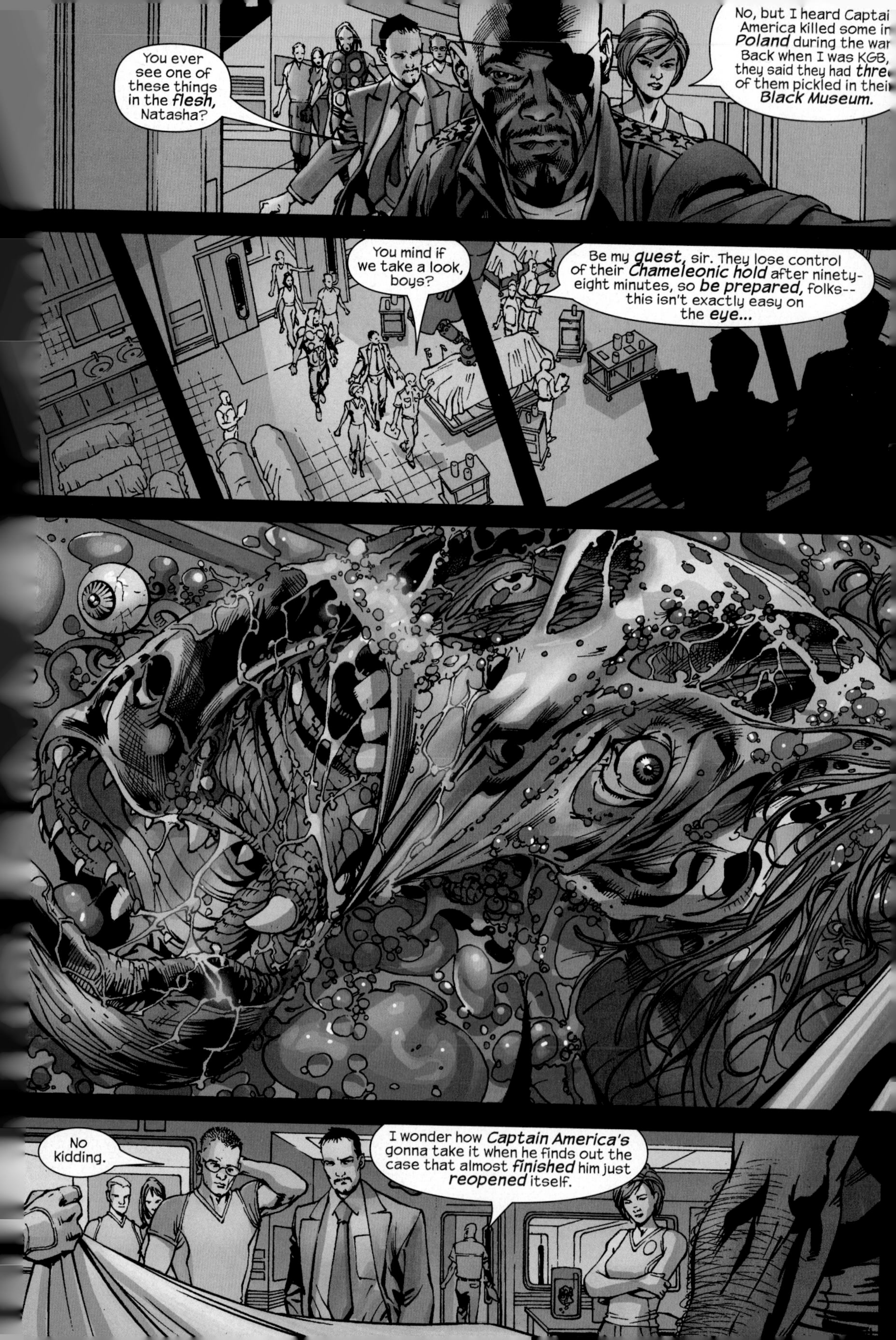
You ever see one of these things in the flesh, Natasha?
No, but I heard Captai America killed some in Poland during the war Back when I was KGB, they said they had thre of them pickled in thei Black Museum.
You mind if we take a look, boys?
Be my guest, sir. They lose control of their Chameleonic hold after ninety-eight minutes, so be prepared, folks-- this isn't exactly easy on the eye...
No kidding.
I wonder how Captain America's gonna take it when he finds out the case that almost finished him just reopened itself.

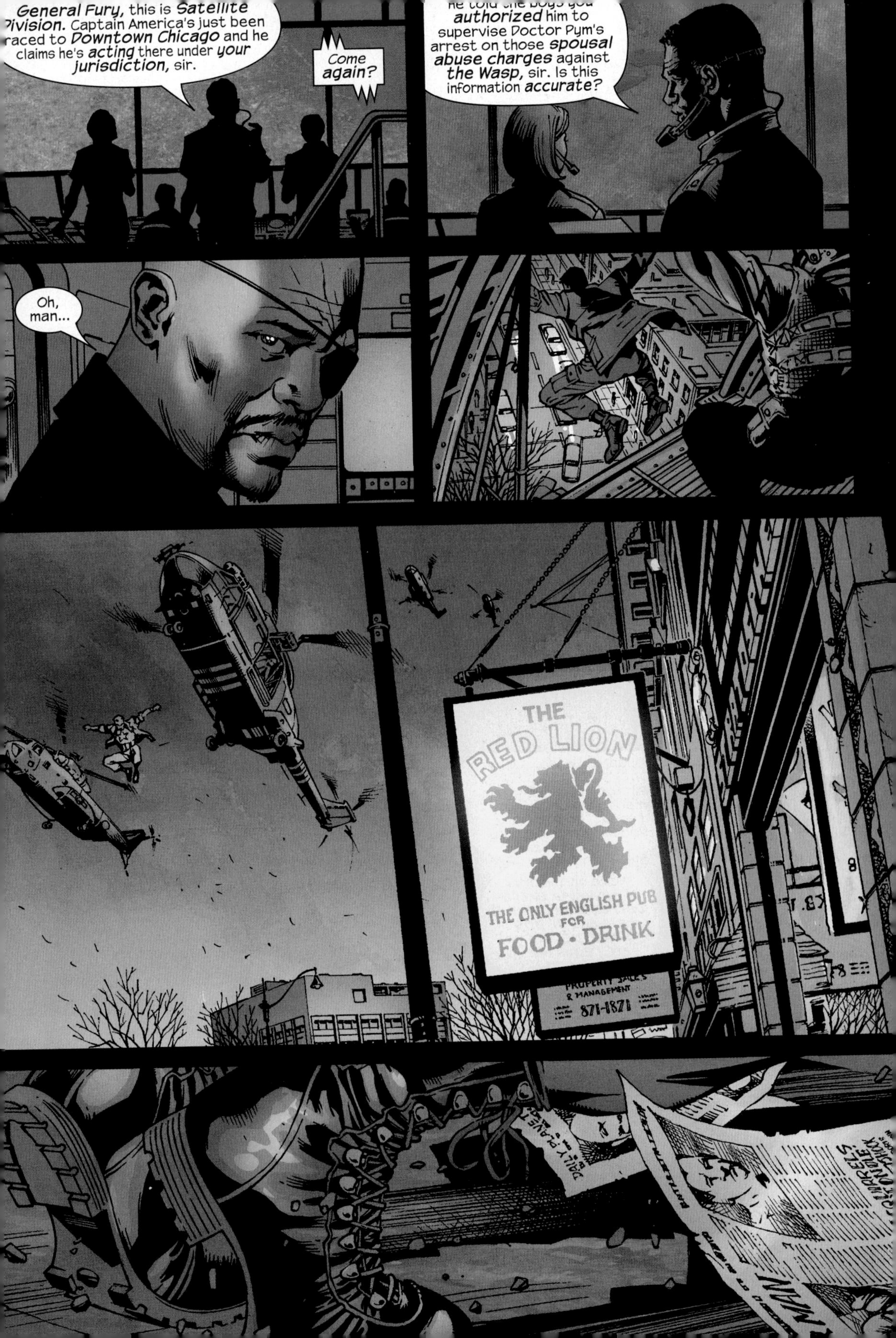
General Fury, this is Satellite Division. Captain America's just been traced to Downtown Chicago and he claims he's acting there under your jurisdiction, sir.
Come again?
He told the boys you authorized him to supervise Doctor Pym's arrest on those spousal abuse charges against the Wasp, sir. Is this information accurate?
Oh, man...
THE RED LION
THE ONLY ENGLISH PUB FOR FOOD • DRINK
PROPERTY SALES & MANAGEMENT
871-1871

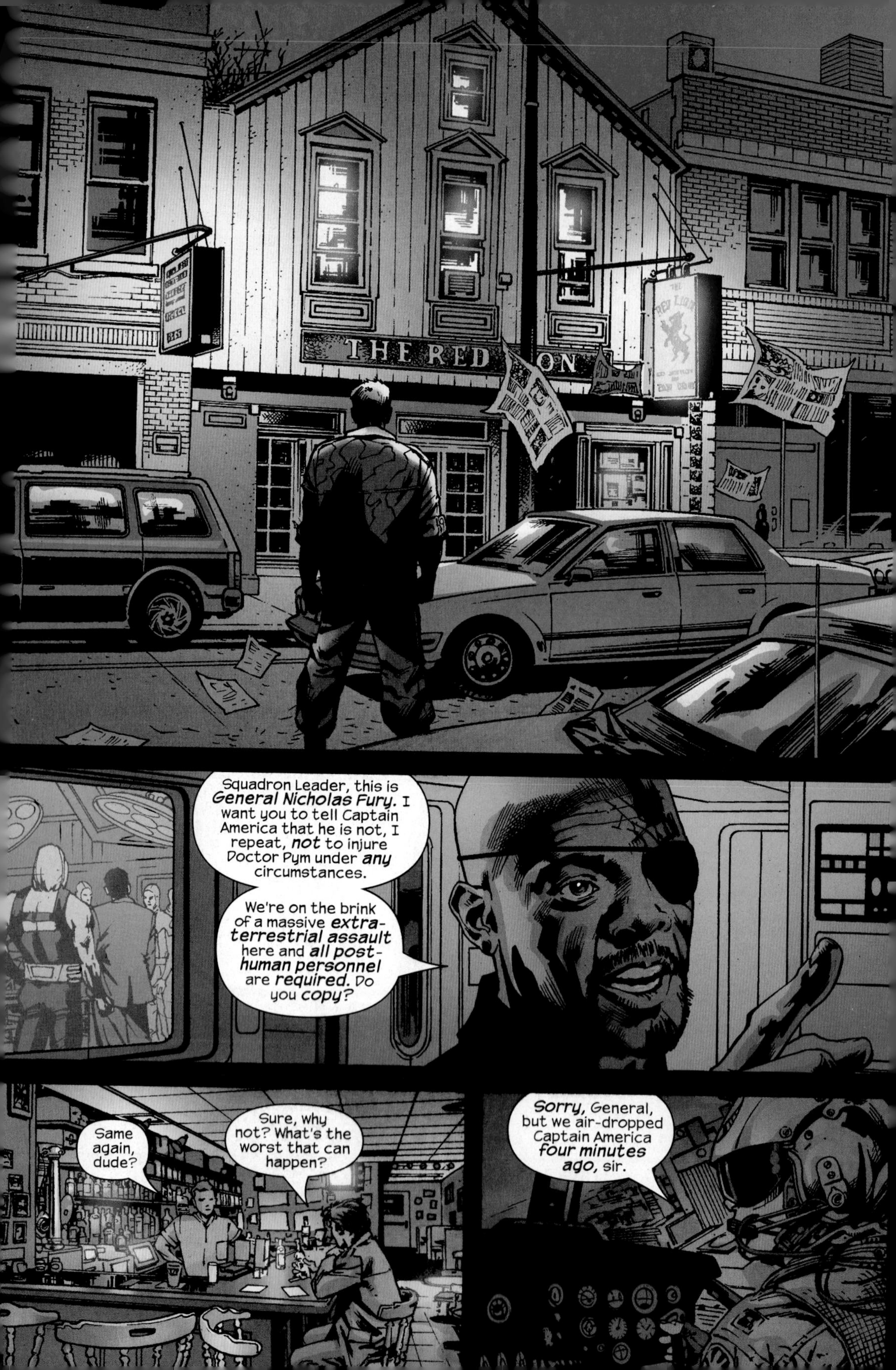

THE RED L ON
Squadron Leader, this is General Nicholas Fury. I want you to tell Captain America that he is not, I repeat, not to injure Doctor Pym under any circumstances.
We're on the brink of a massive extra-terrestrial assault here and all post-human personnel are required. Do you copy?
Same again, dude?
Sure, why not? What's the worst that can happen?
Sorry, General, but we air-dropped Captain America four minutes ago, sir.

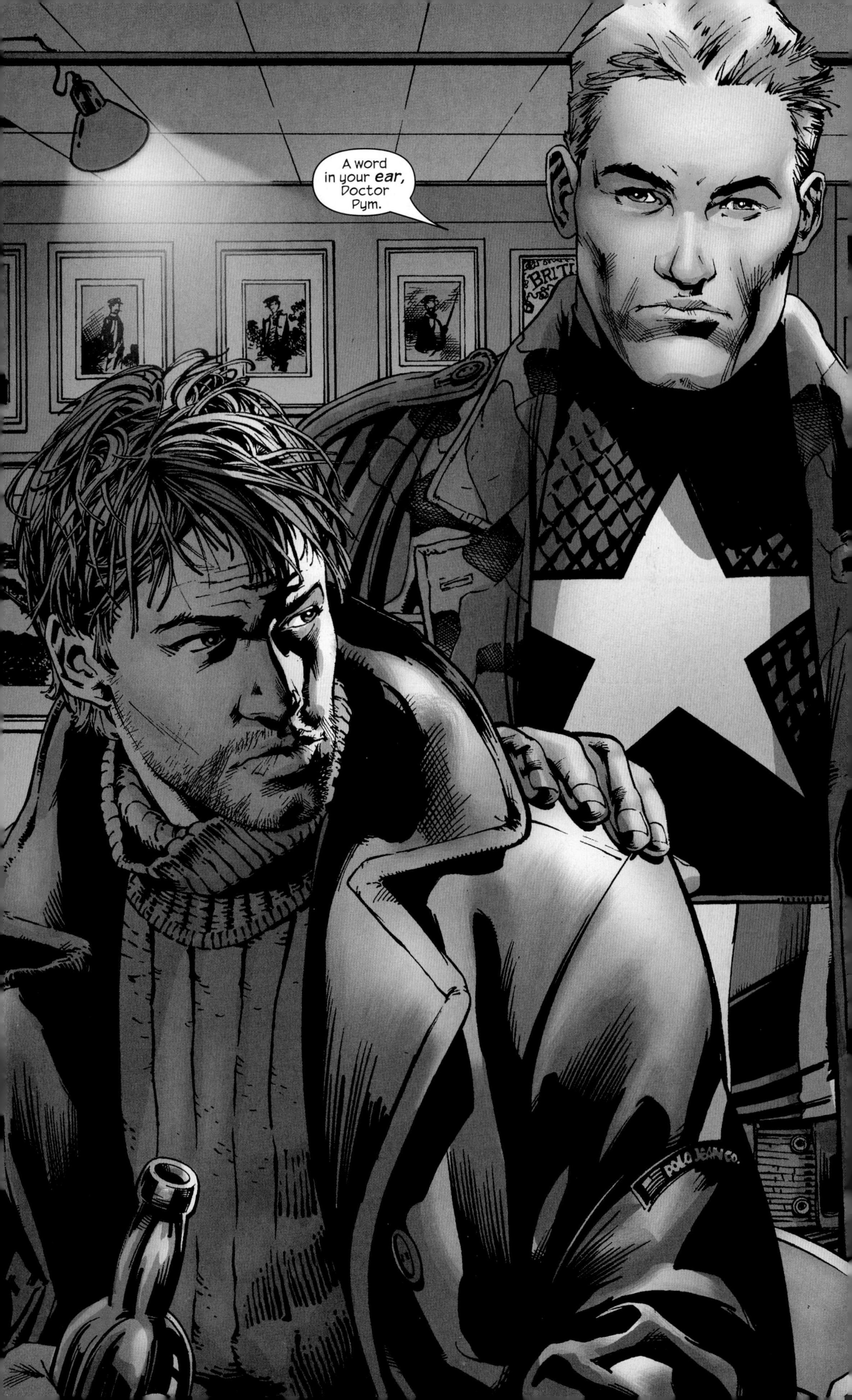
A word in your ear, Doctor Pym.
BRITI
POLO JEAN CO.

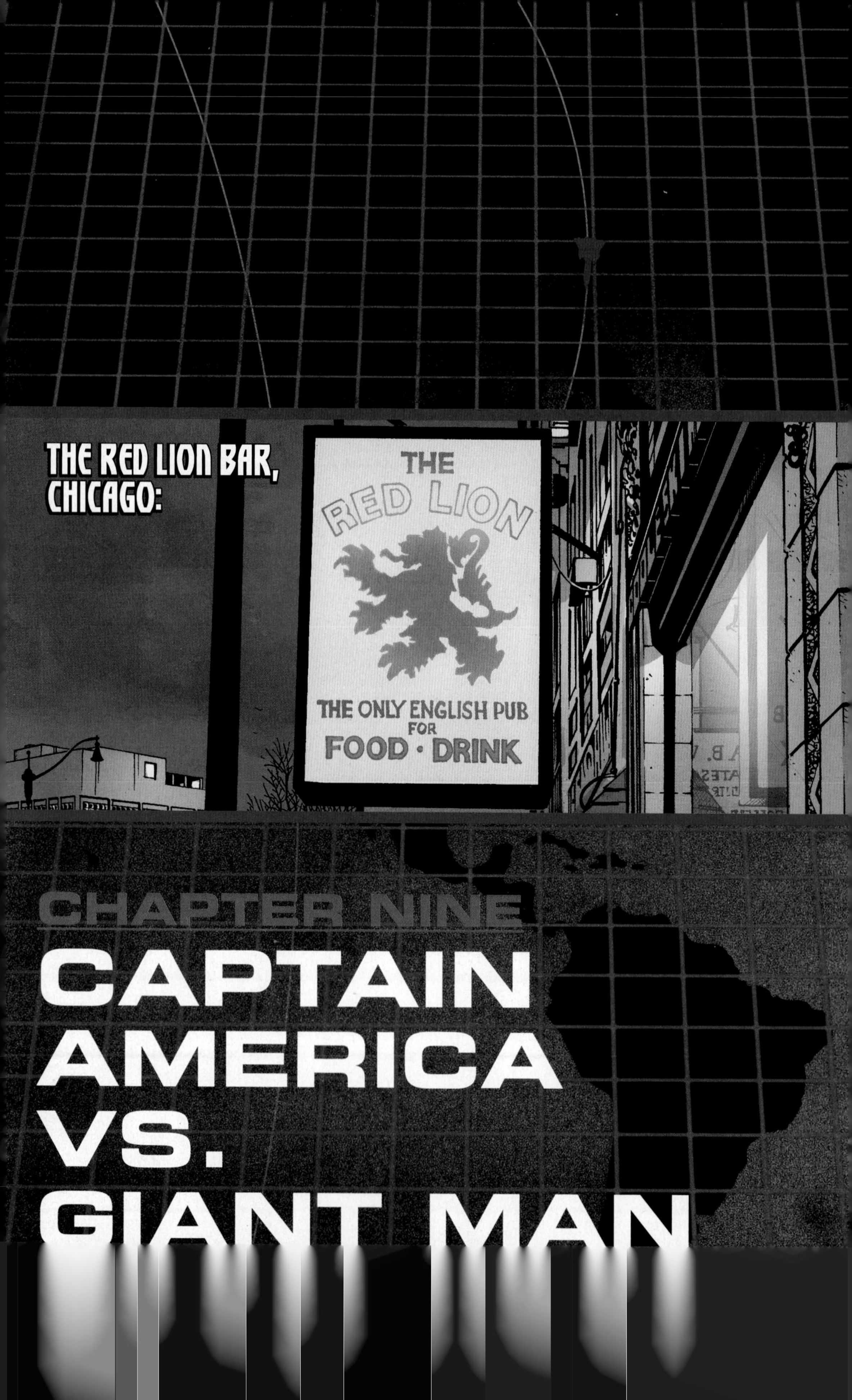
THE RED LION BAR, CHICAGO:
THE RED LION
THE ONLY ENGLISH PUB FOR FOOD · DRINK
CHAPTER NINE
CAPTAIN AMERICA VS. GIANT MAN

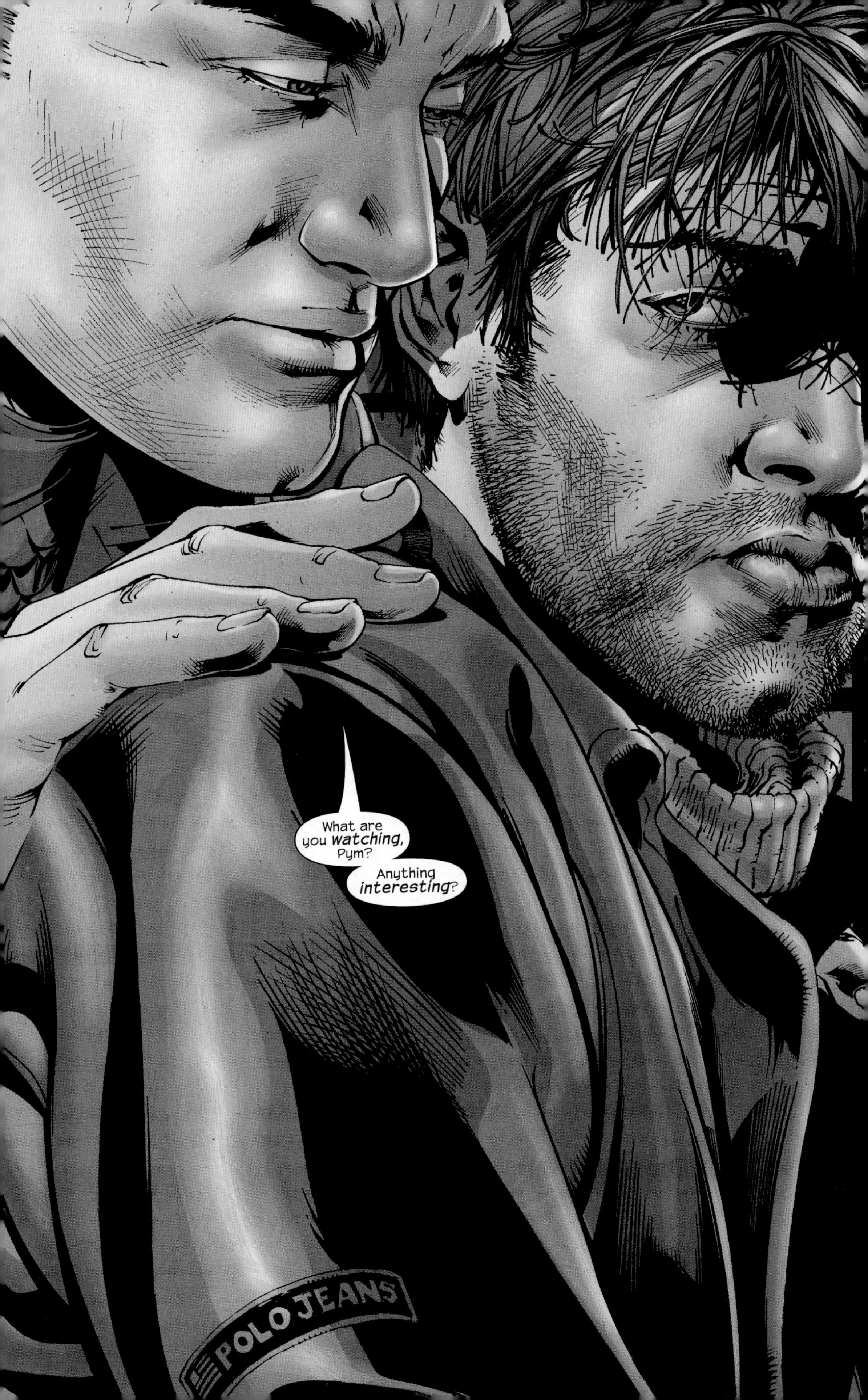
What are you watching, Pym?
Anything interesting?
POLO JEANS

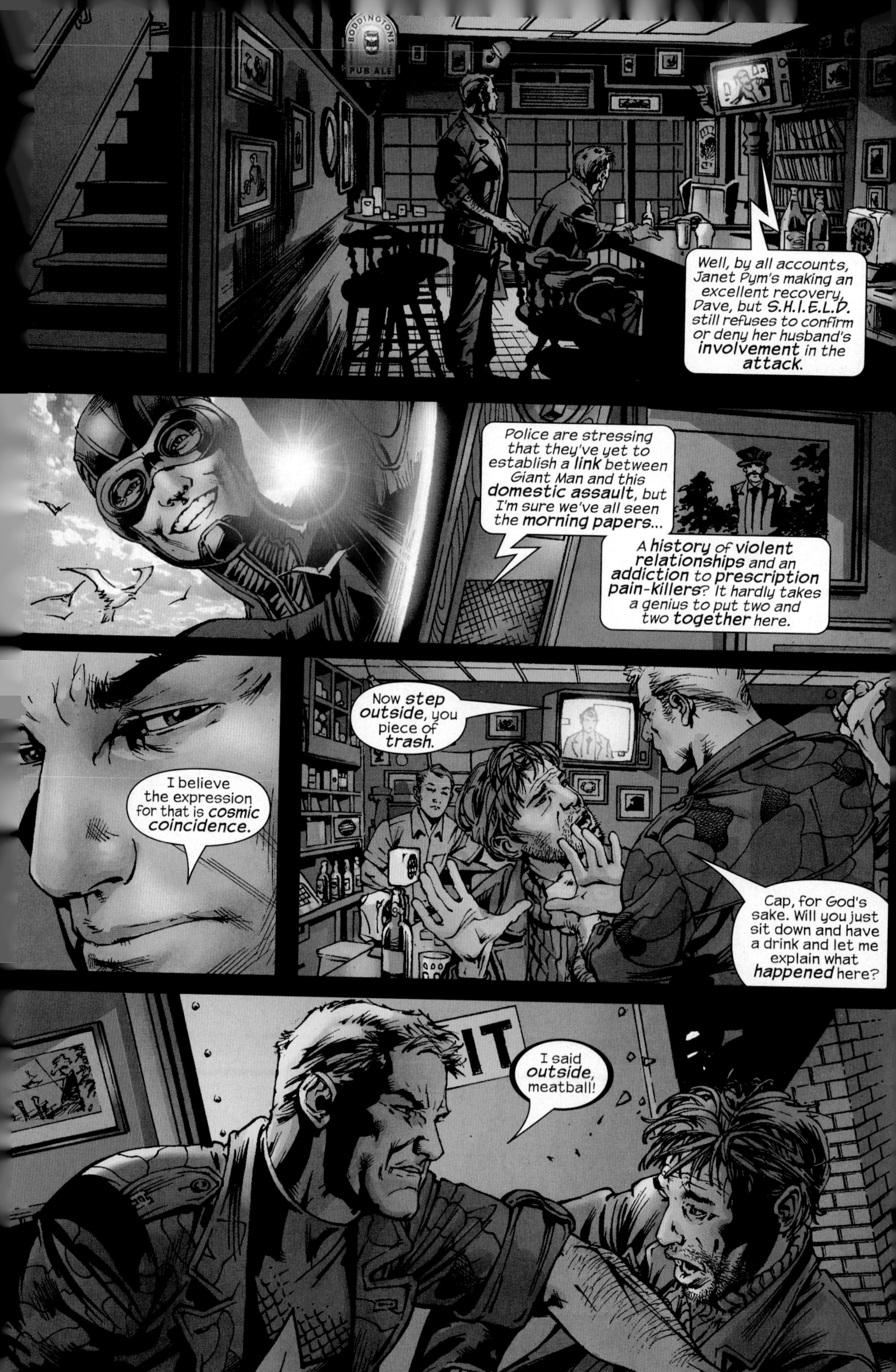
BODDINGTONS
PUB ALE
Well, by all accounts, Janet Pym's making an excellent recovery, Dave, but S.H.I.E.L.D. still refuses to confirm or deny her husband's involvement in the attack.
Police are stressing that they've yet to establish a link between Giant Man and this domestic assault, but I'm sure we've all seen the morning papers...
A history of violent relationships and an addiction to prescription pain-killers? It hardly takes a genius to put two and two together here.
I believe the expression for that is cosmic coincidence.
Now step outside, you piece of trash.
Cap, for God's sake. Will you just sit down and have a drink and let me explain what happened here?
IT
I said outside, meatball!

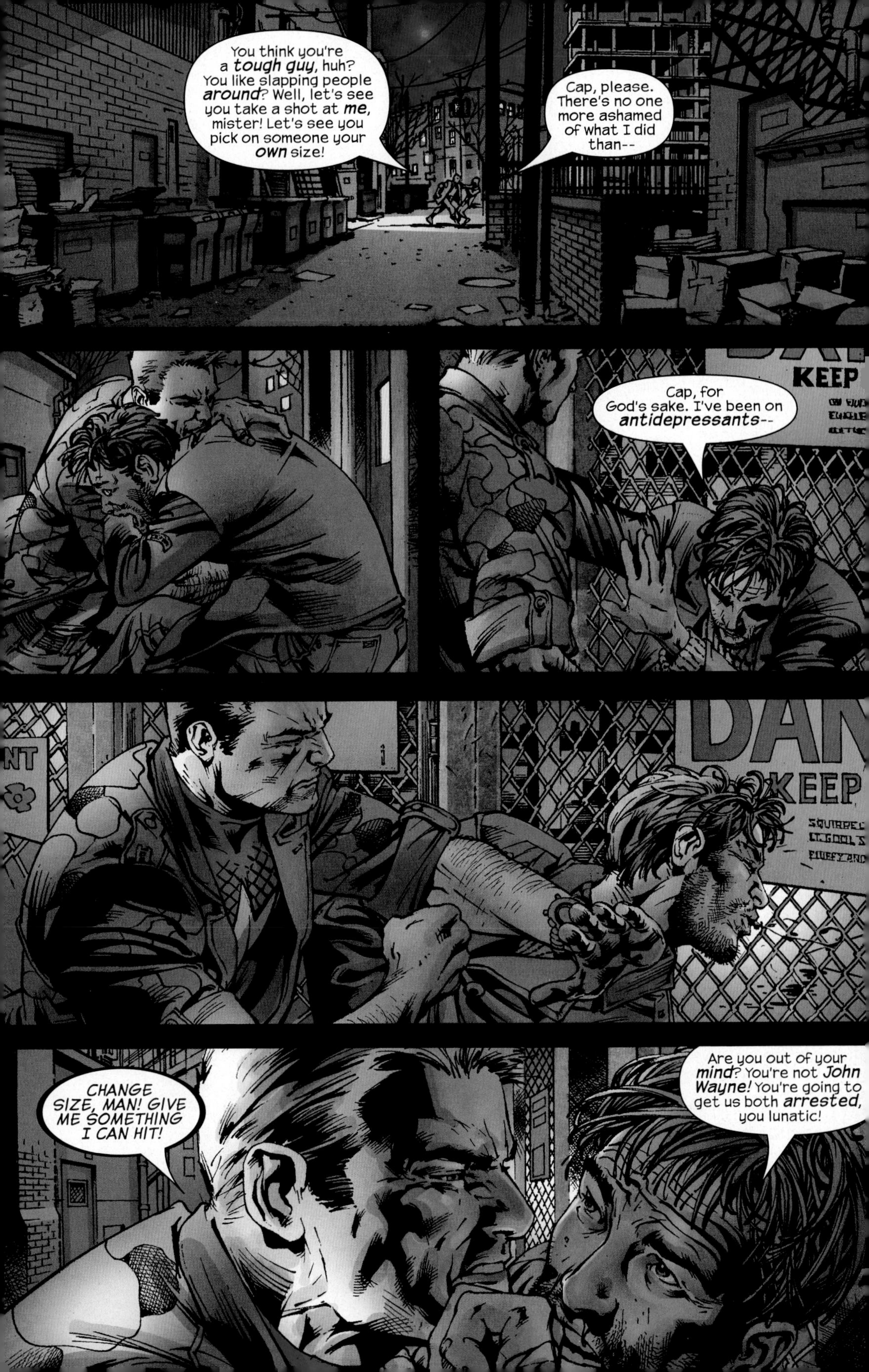
You think you're a tough guy, huh? You like slapping people around? Well, let's see you take a shot at me, mister! Let's see you pick on someone your own size!
Cap, please. There's no one more ashamed of what I did than--
KEEP
Cap, for God's sake. I've been on antidepressants--
KEEP
CHANGE SIZE, MAN! GIVE ME SOMETHING I CAN HIT!
Are you out of your mind? You're not John Wayne! You're going to get us both arrested, you lunatic!

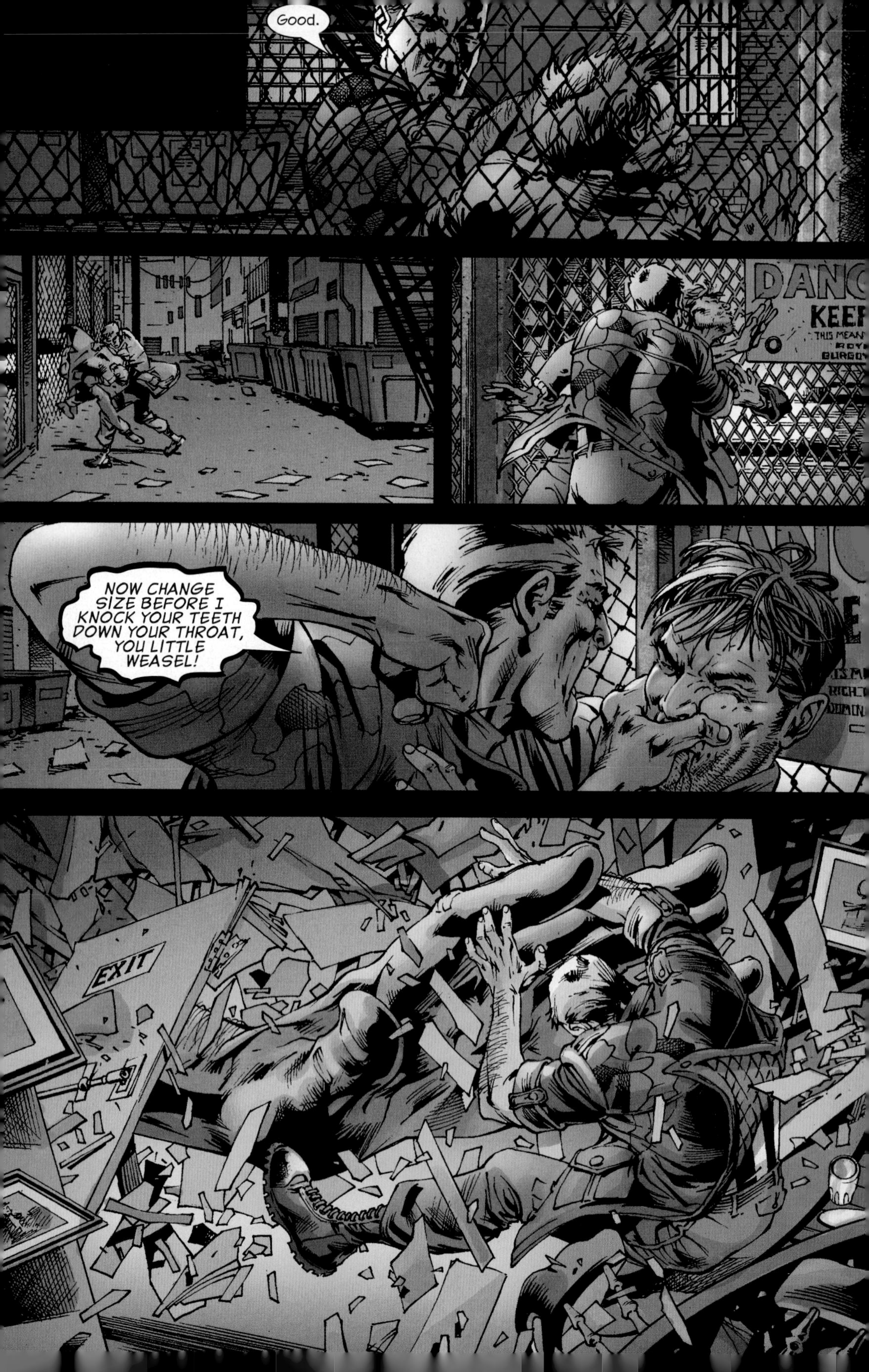
Good.
NOW CHANGE SIZE BEFORE I KNOCK YOUR TEETH DOWN YOUR THROAT, YOU LITTLE WEASEL!
EXIT

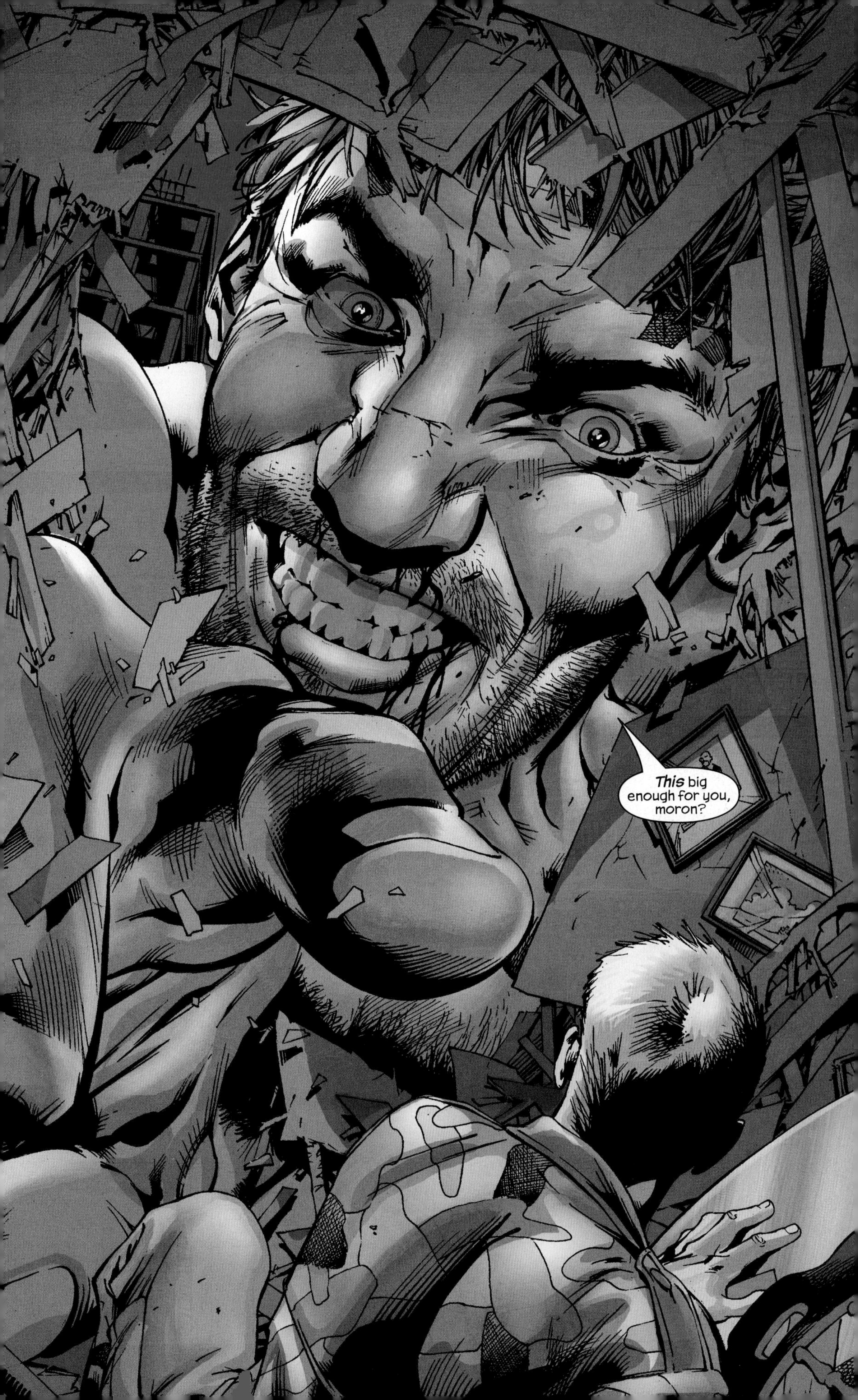
This big enough for you, moron?

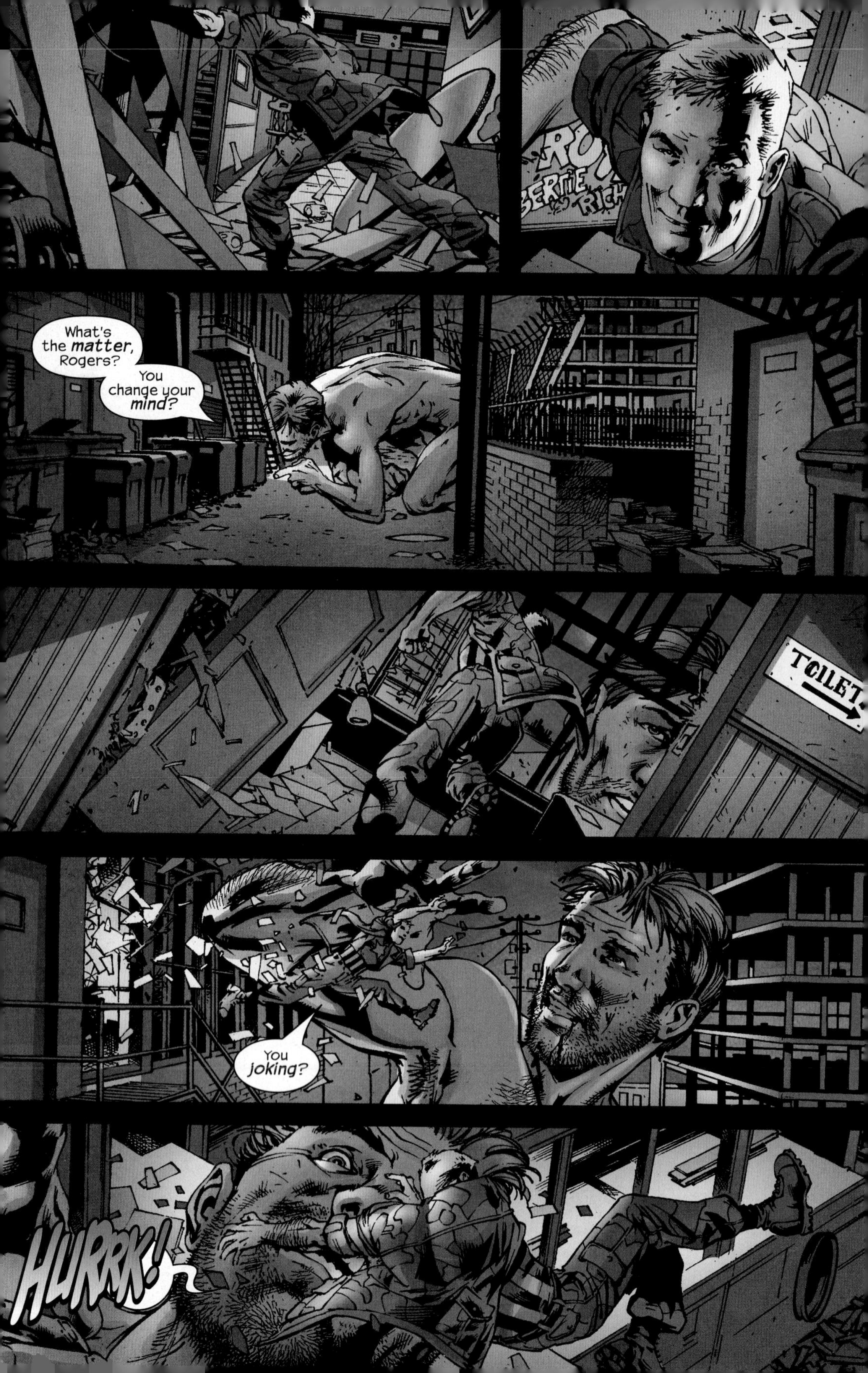
ROU
BERTIE
RICH
What's the matter, Rogers?
You change your mind?
TOILET
You joking?
HURRK!

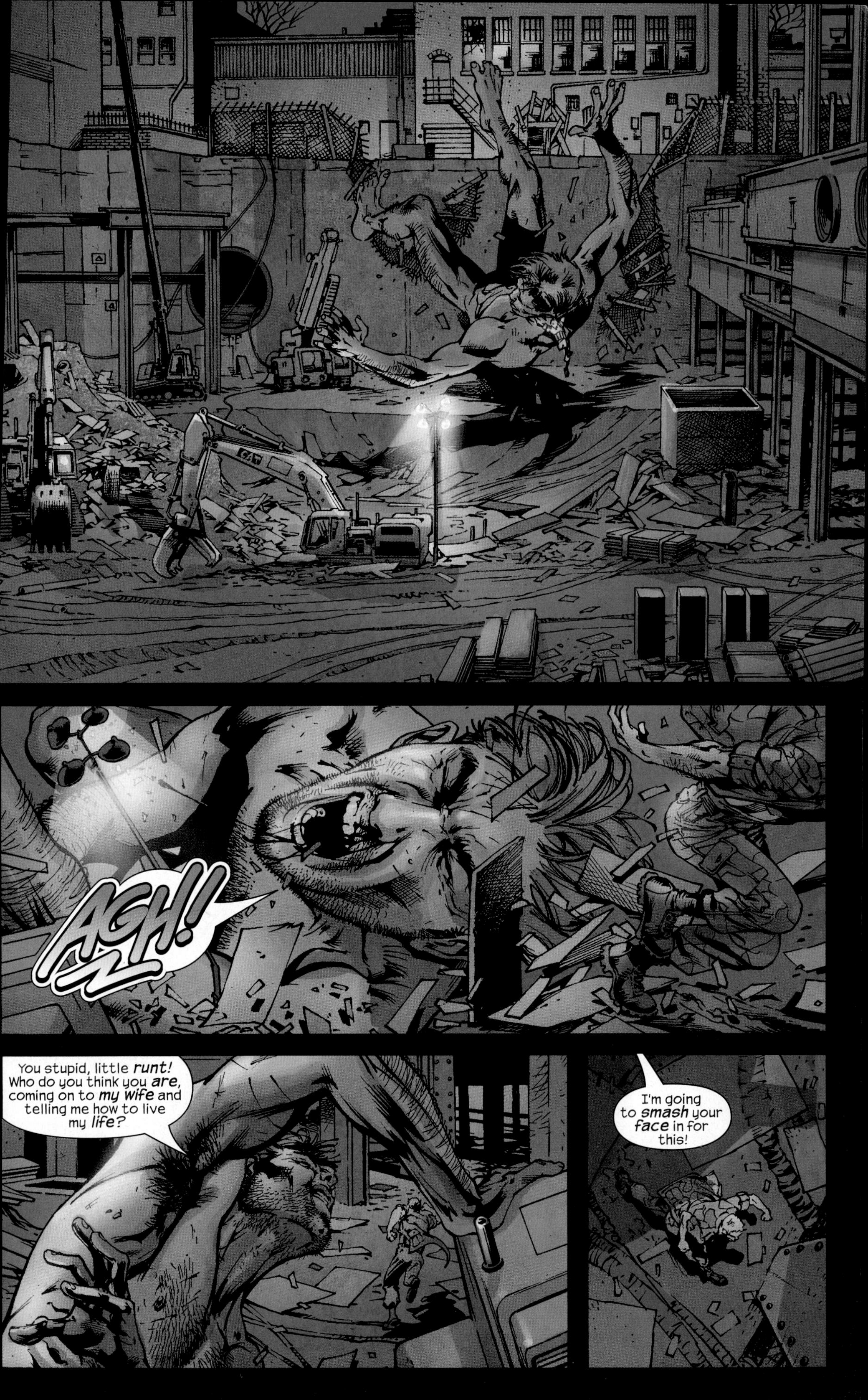
AGH!
You stupid, little runt! Who do you think you are, coming on to my wife and telling me how to live my life?
I'm going to smash your face in for this!

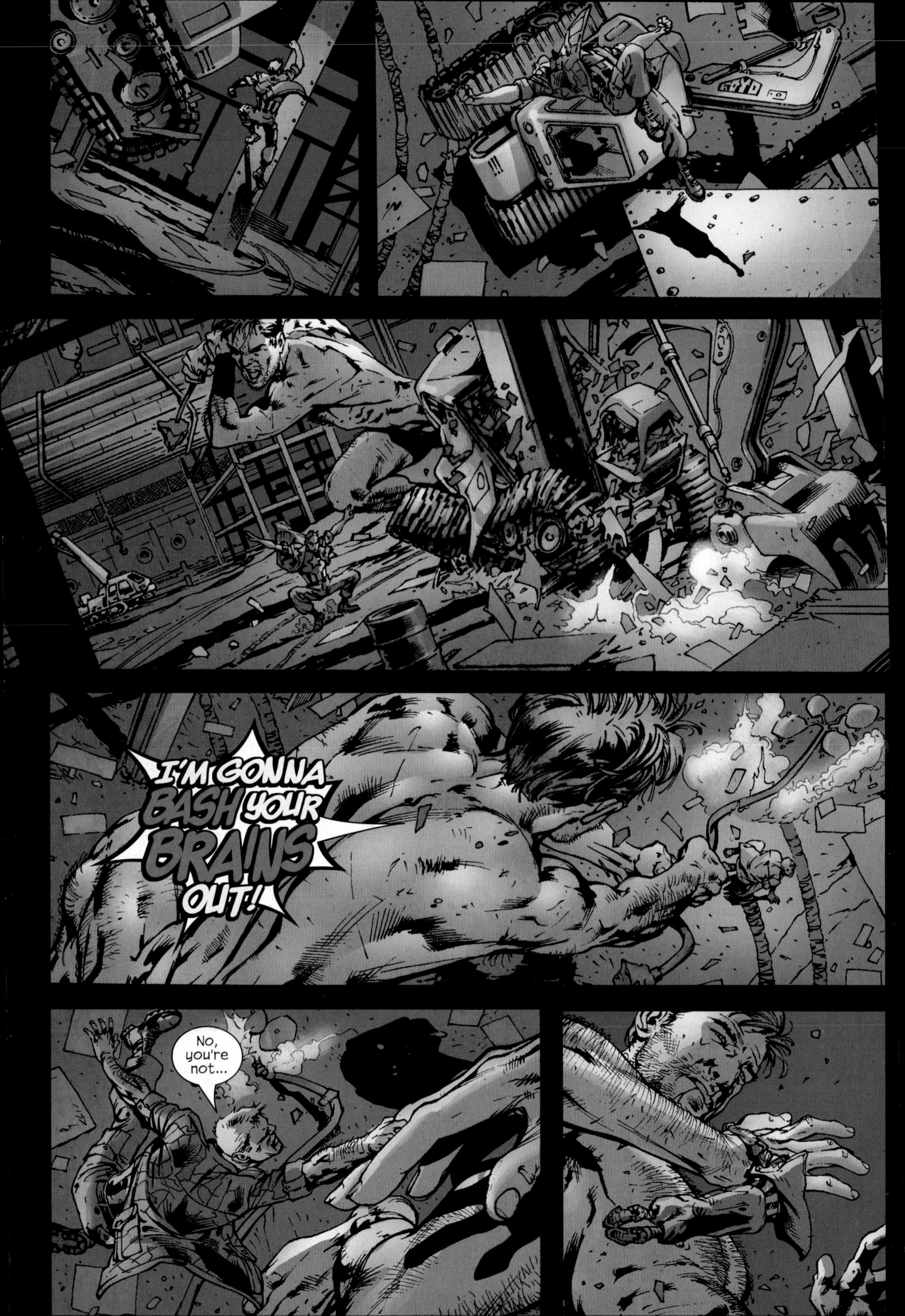
I'M GONNA BASH YOUR BRAINS OUT!
No, you're not...

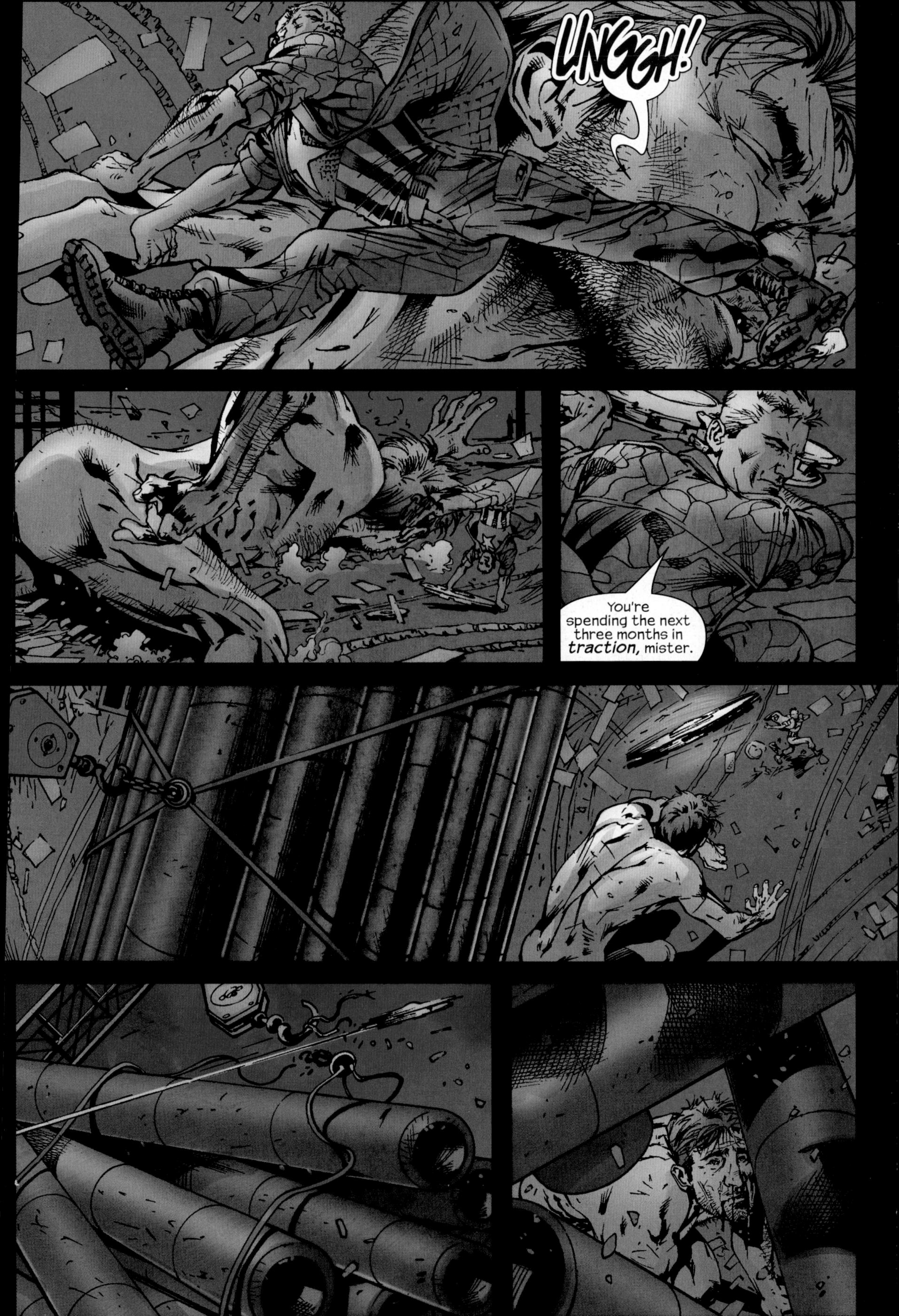
UNGGH!
You're spending the next three months in traction, mister.

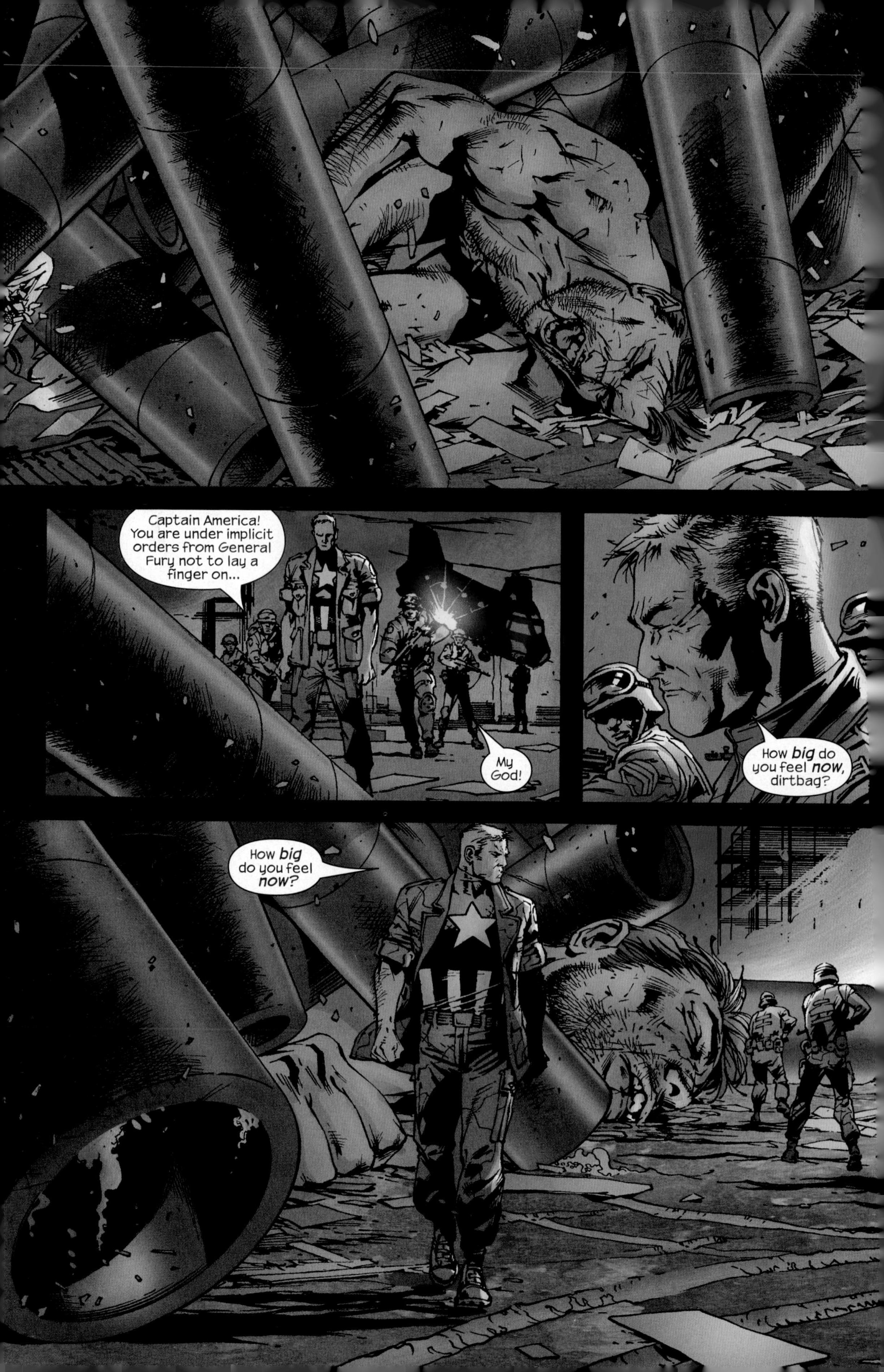
Captain America! You are under implicit orders from General Fury not to lay a finger on...
My God!
How **big** do you feel **now**, dirtbag?
How **big** do you feel **now**?

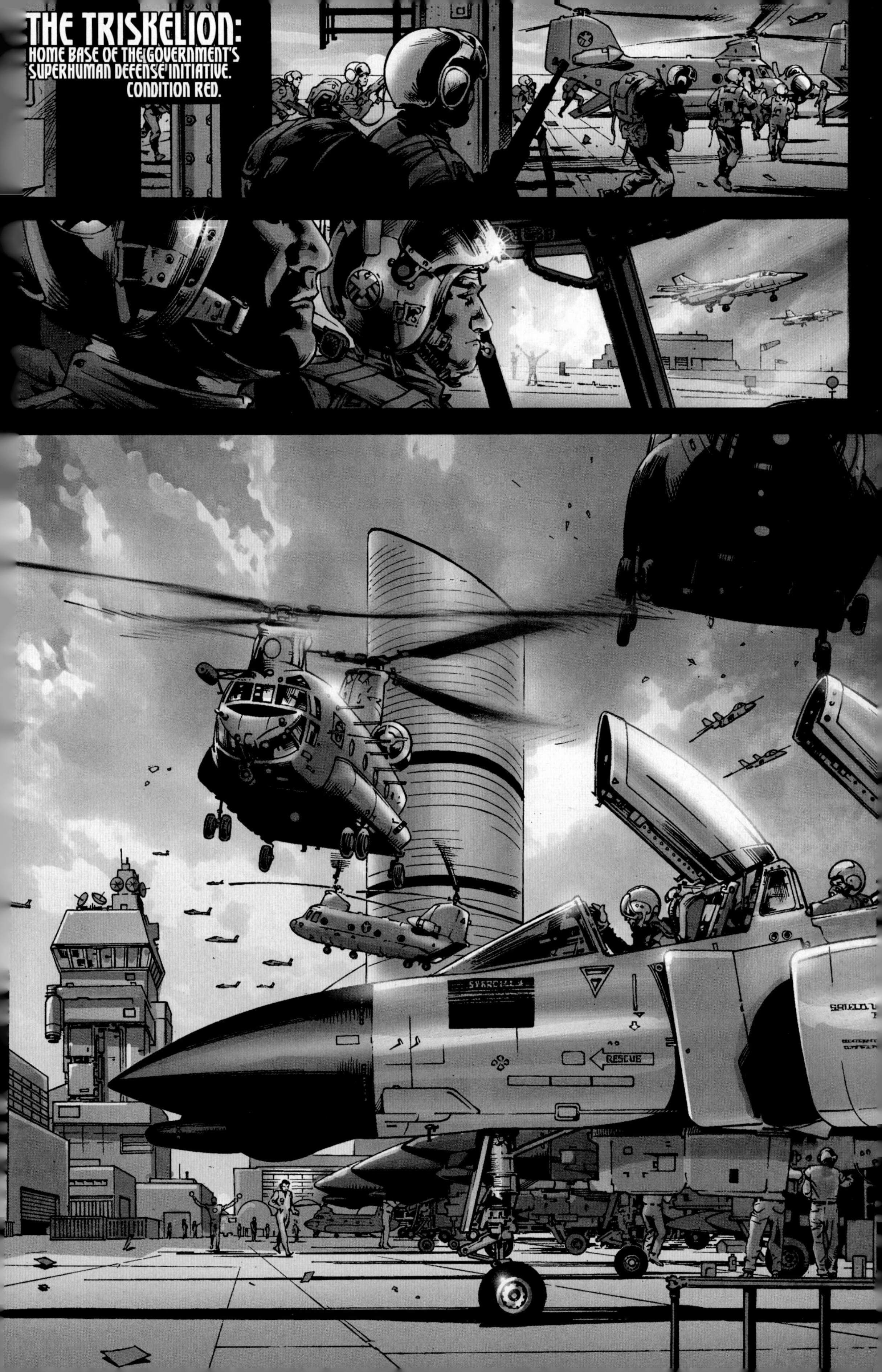

THE TRISKELION:
HOME BASE OF THE GOVERNMENT'S SUPERHUMAN DEFENSE INITIATIVE.
CONDITION RED.
RESCUE

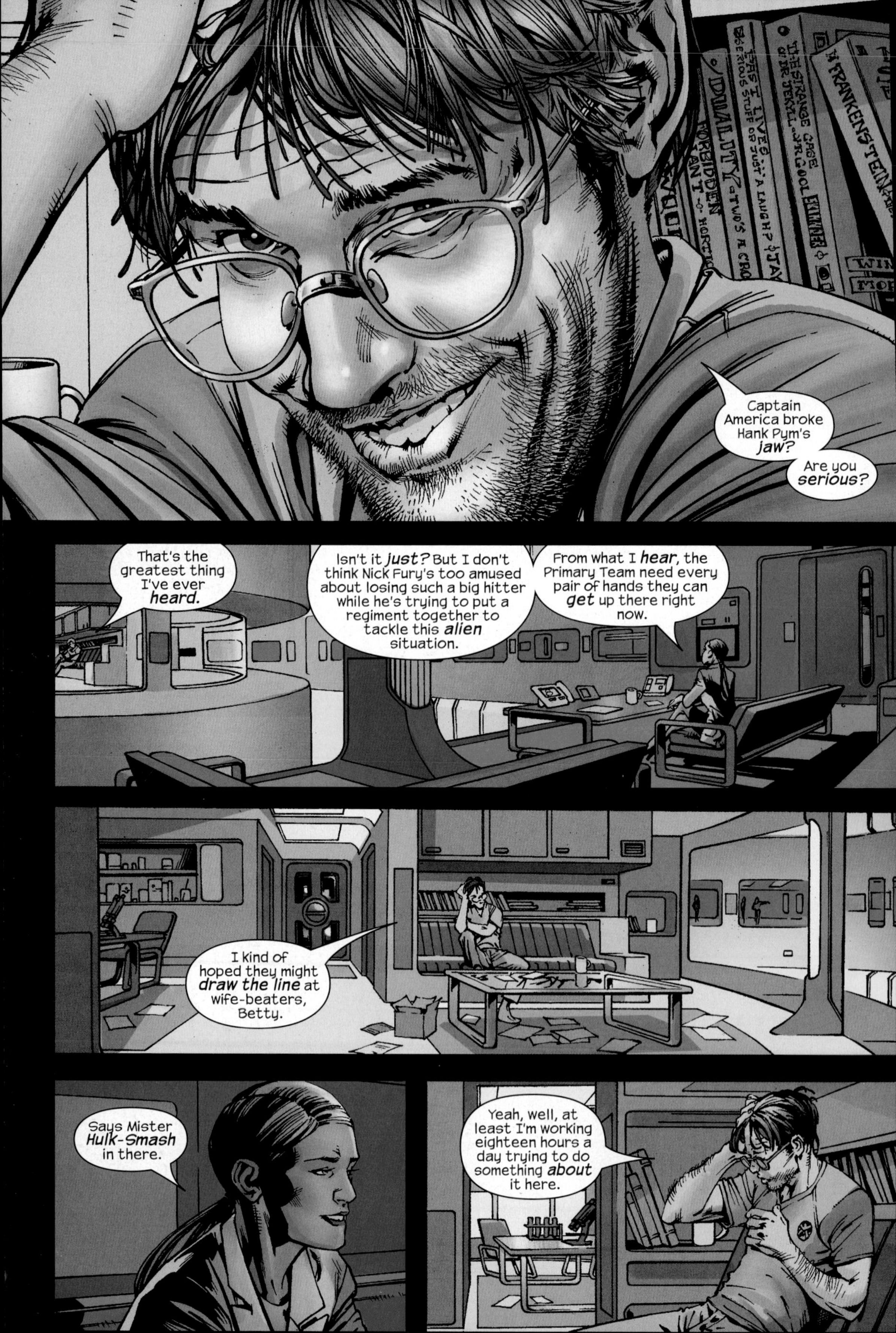

Captain America broke Hank Pym's *jaw?*
Are you *serious?*
That's the greatest thing I've ever *heard.*
Isn't it *just?* But I don't think Nick Fury's too amused about losing such a big hitter while he's trying to put a regiment together to tackle this *alien* situation.
From what I *hear,* the Primary Team need every pair of hands they can *get* up there right now.
I kind of hoped they might *draw the line* at wife-beaters, Betty.
Says Mister *Hulk-Smash* in there.
Yeah, well, at least I'm working eighteen hours a day trying to do something *about* it here.

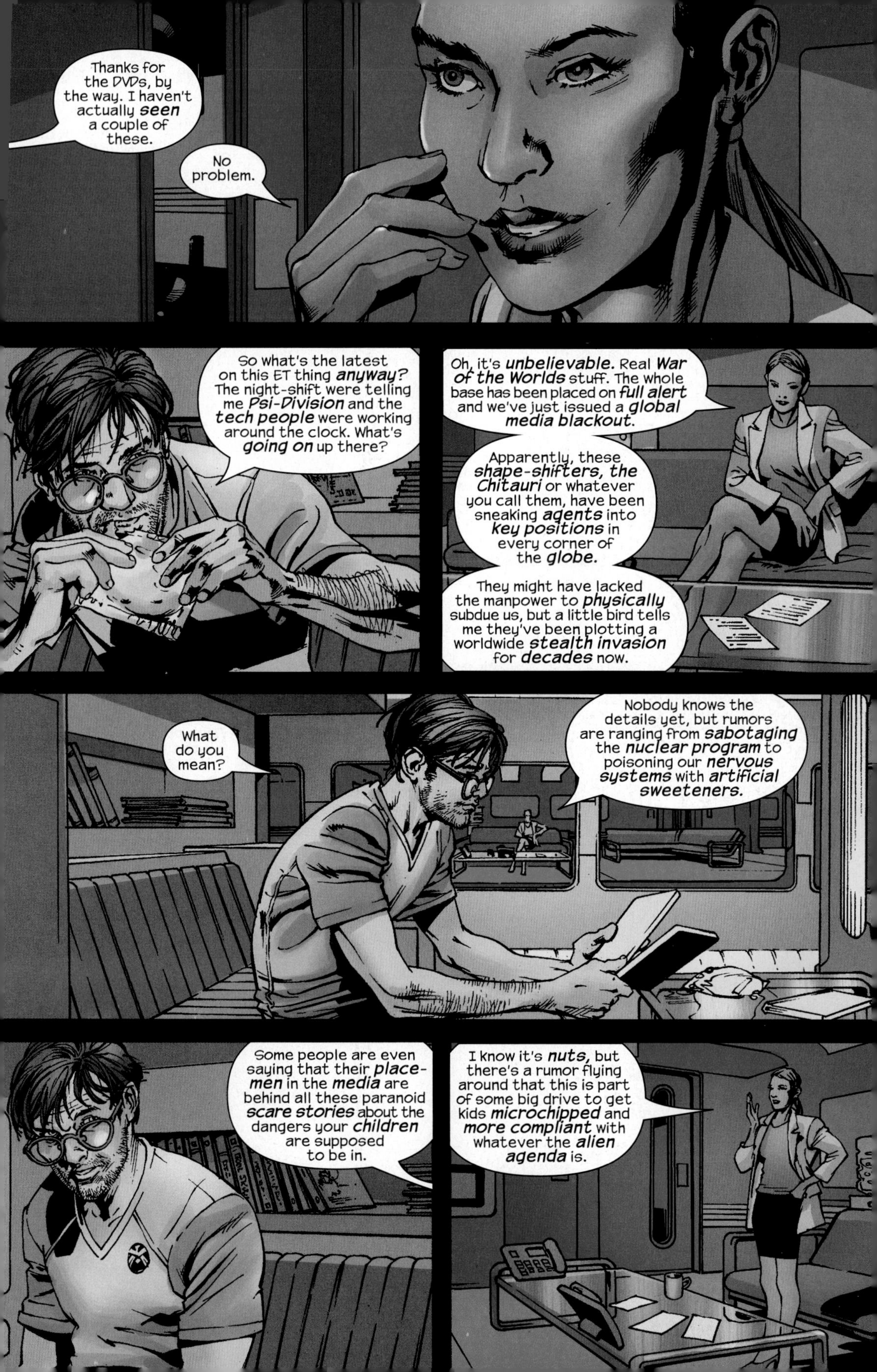

Thanks for the DVDs, by the way. I haven't actually seen a couple of these.
No problem.
So what's the latest on this ET thing anyway? The night-shift were telling me Psi-Division and the tech people were working around the clock. What's going on up there?
Oh, it's unbelievable. Real War of the Worlds stuff. The whole base has been placed on full alert and we've just issued a global media blackout.
Apparently, these shape-shifters, the Chitauri or whatever you call them, have been sneaking agents into key positions in every corner of the globe.
They might have lacked the manpower to physically subdue us, but a little bird tells me they've been plotting a worldwide stealth invasion for decades now.
What do you mean?
Nobody knows the details yet, but rumors are ranging from sabotaging the nuclear program to poisoning our nervous systems with artificial sweeteners.
Some people are even saying that their place-men in the media are behind all these paranoid scare stories about the dangers your children are supposed to be in.
I know it's nuts, but there's a rumor flying around that this is part of some big drive to get kids microchipped and more compliant with whatever the alien agenda is.

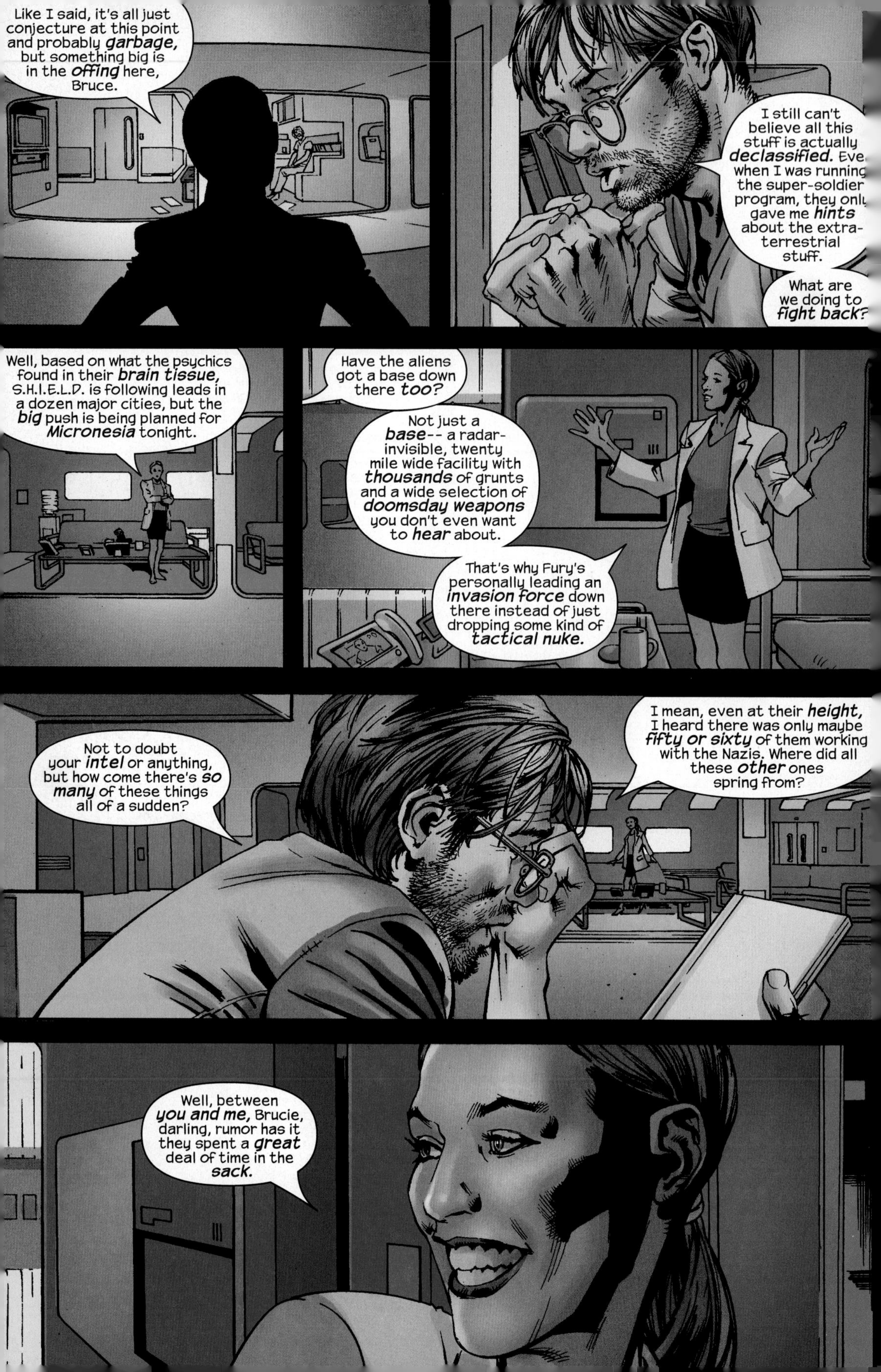
Like I said, it's all just conjecture at this point and probably *garbage*, but something big is in the *offing* here, Bruce.
I still can't believe all this stuff is actually *declassified*. Eve when I was running the super-soldier program, they onl gave me *hints* about the extra-terrestrial stuff.
What are we doing to *fight back?*
Well, based on what the psychics found in their *brain tissue*, S.H.I.E.L.D. is following leads in a dozen major cities, but the *big* push is being planned for *Micronesia* tonight.
Have the aliens got a base down there *too?*
Not just a *base*-- a radar-invisible, twenty mile wide facility with *thousands* of grunts and a wide selection of *doomsday weapons* you don't even want to *hear* about.
That's why Fury's personally leading an *invasion force* down there instead of just dropping some kind of *tactical nuke.*
Not to doubt your *intel* or anything, but how come there's *so many* of these things all of a sudden?
I mean, even at their *height*, I heard there was only maybe *fifty or sixty* of them working with the Nazis. Where did all these *other* ones spring from?
Well, between *you and me*, Brucie, darling, rumor has it they spent a *great* deal of time in the *sack.*

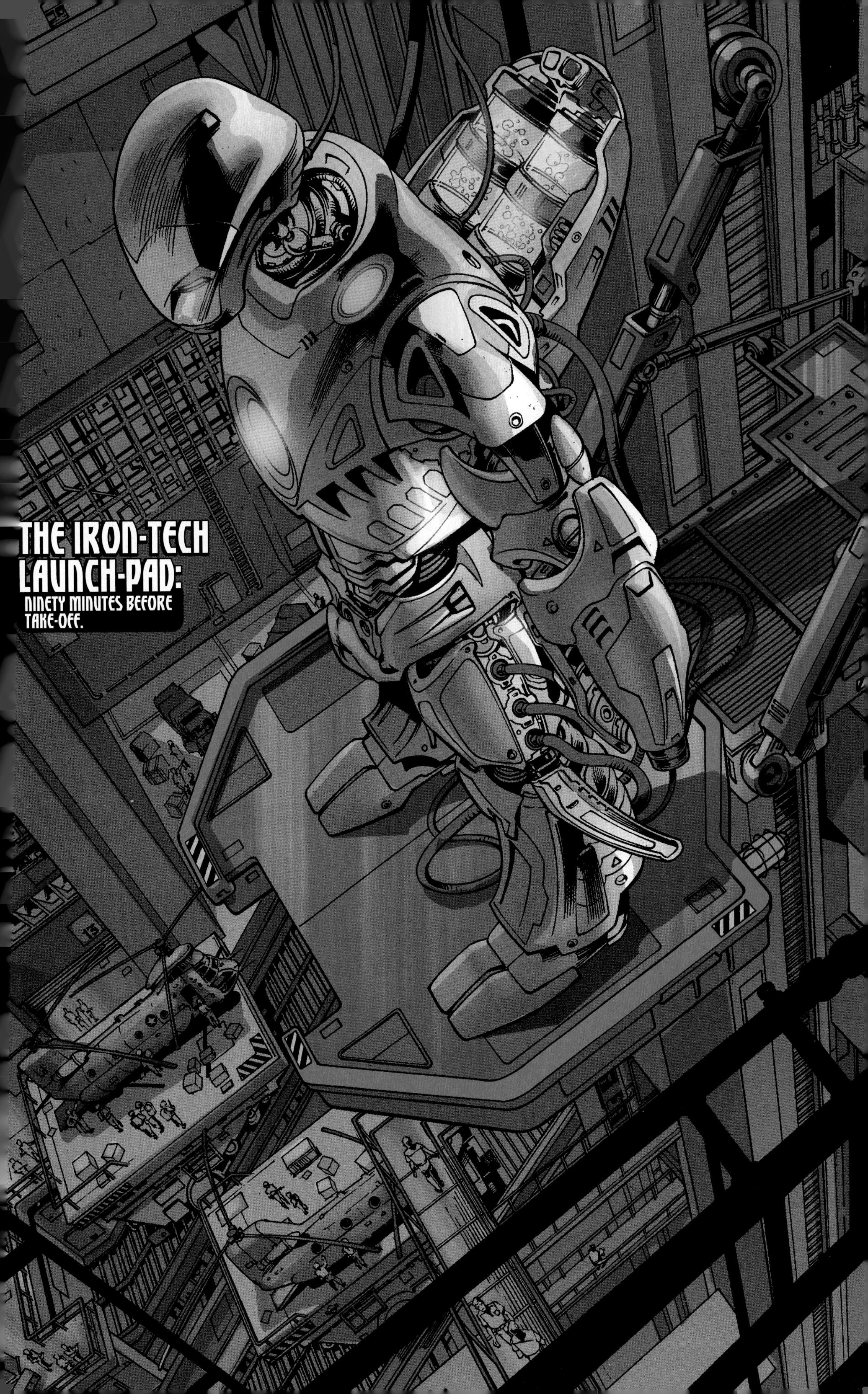
THE IRON-TECH LAUNCH-PAD:
NINETY MINUTES BEFORE TAKE-OFF.
13

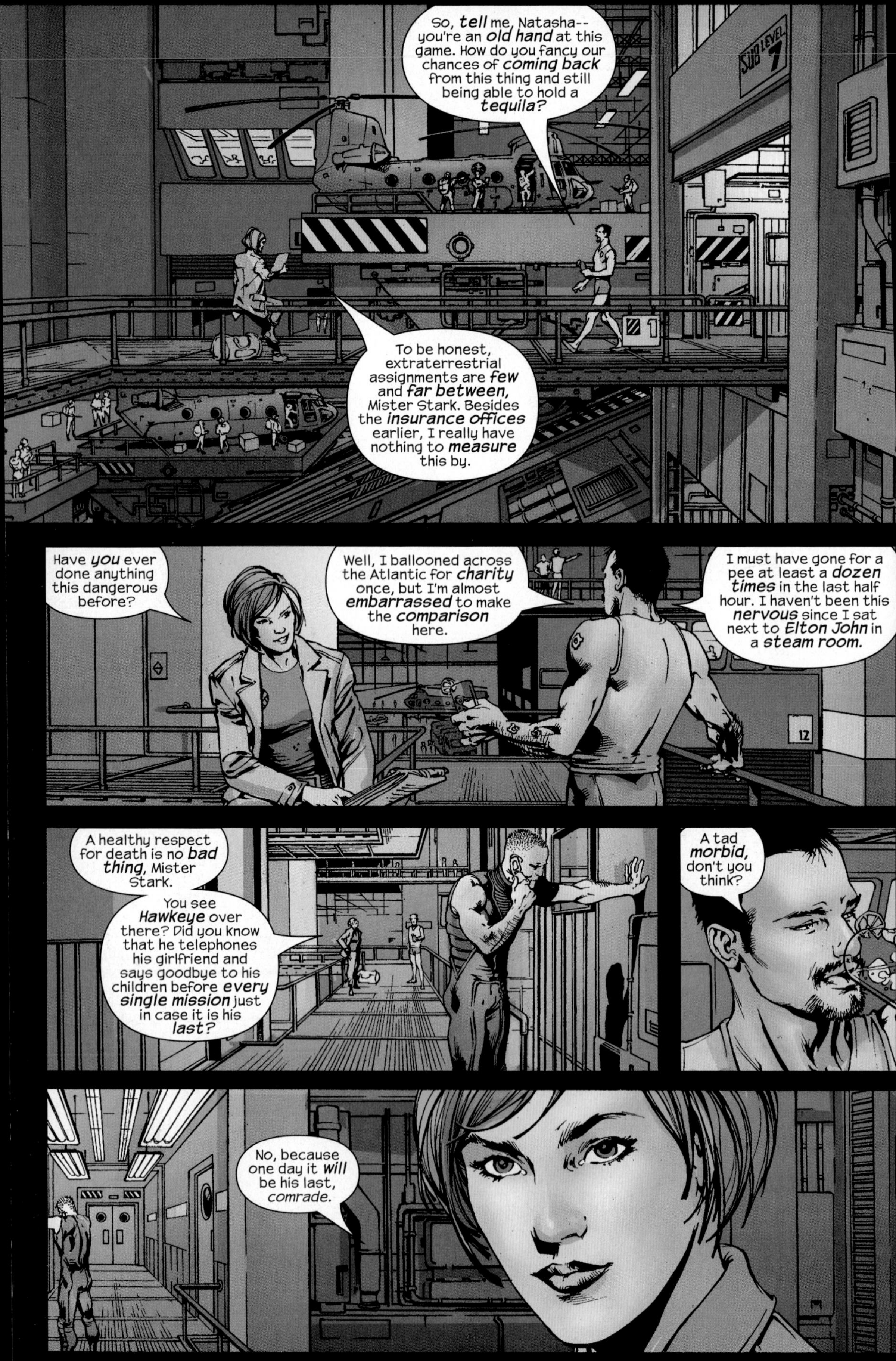

So, tell me, Natasha-- you're an old hand at this game. How do you fancy our chances of coming back from this thing and still being able to hold a tequila?
SUB LEVEL 7
To be honest, extraterrestrial assignments are few and far between, Mister Stark. Besides the insurance offices earlier, I really have nothing to measure this by.
Have you ever done anything this dangerous before?
Well, I ballooned across the Atlantic for charity once, but I'm almost embarrassed to make the comparison here.
I must have gone for a pee at least a dozen times in the last half hour. I haven't been this nervous since I sat next to Elton John in a steam room.
A healthy respect for death is no bad thing, Mister Stark.
You see Hawkeye over there? Did you know that he telephones his girlfriend and says goodbye to his children before every single mission just in case it is his last?
A tad morbid, don't you think?
No, because one day it will be his last, comrade.

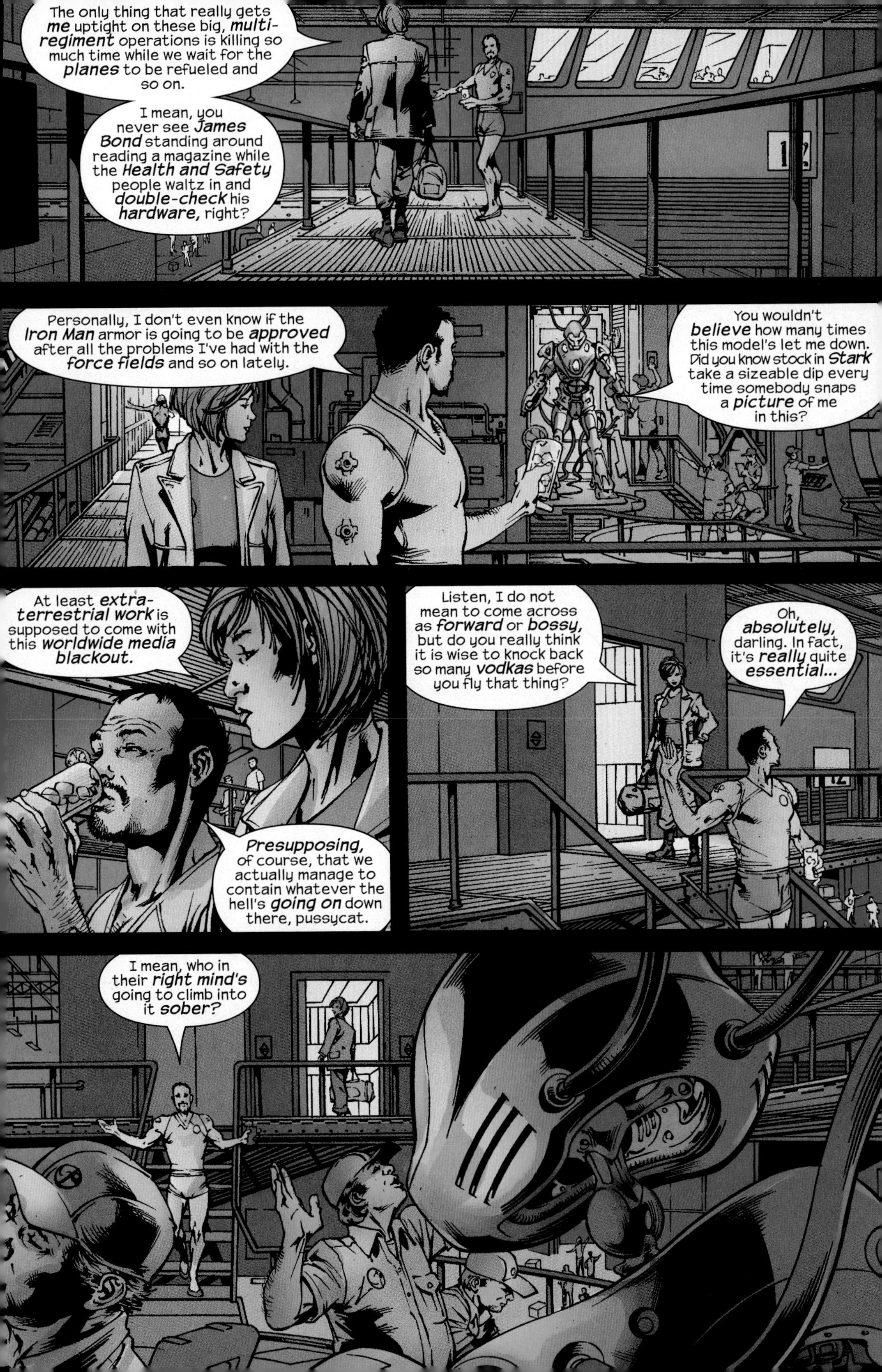
The only thing that really gets me uptight on these big, multi-regiment operations is killing so much time while we wait for the planes to be refueled and so on.
I mean, you never see James Bond standing around reading a magazine while the Health and Safety people waltz in and double-check his hardware, right?
Personally, I don't even know if the Iron Man armor is going to be approved after all the problems I've had with the force fields and so on lately.
You wouldn't believe how many times this model's let me down. Did you know stock in Stark take a sizeable dip every time somebody snaps a picture of me in this?
At least extra-terrestrial work is supposed to come with this worldwide media blackout.
Presupposing, of course, that we actually manage to contain whatever the hell's going on down there, pussycat.
Listen, I do not mean to come across as forward or bossy, but do you really think it is wise to knock back so many vodkas before you fly that thing?
Oh, absolutely, darling. In fact, it's really quite essential...
I mean, who in their right mind's going to climb into it sober?

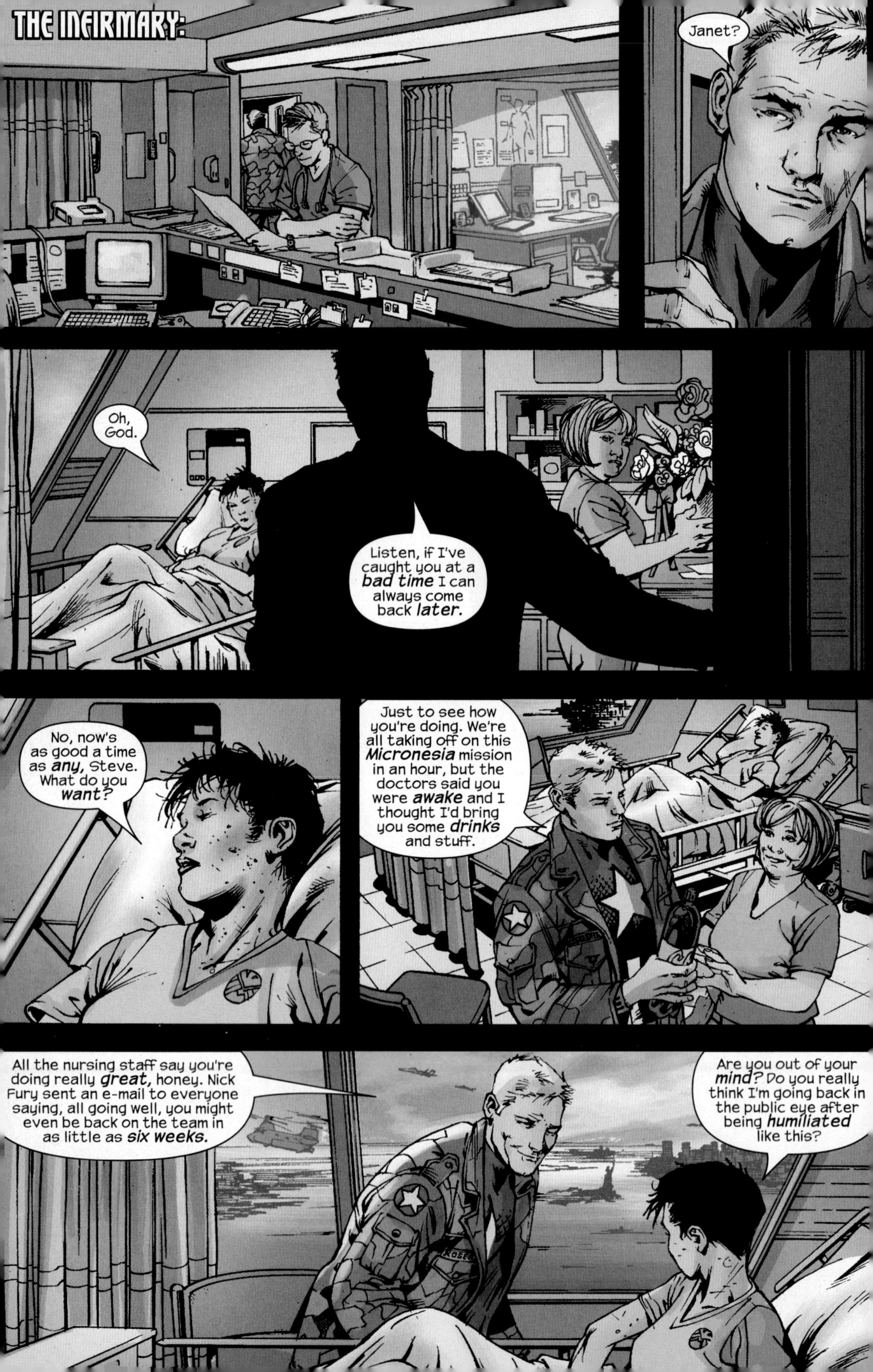
THE INFIRMARY:
Janet?
Oh, God.
Listen, if I've caught you at a bad time I can always come back later.
No, now's as good a time as any, Steve. What do you want?
Just to see how you're doing. We're all taking off on this Micronesia mission in an hour, but the doctors said you were awake and I thought I'd bring you some drinks and stuff.
All the nursing staff say you're doing really great, honey. Nick Fury sent an e-mail to everyone saying, all going well, you might even be back on the team in as little as six weeks.
Are you out of your mind? Do you really think I'm going back in the public eye after being humiliated like this?

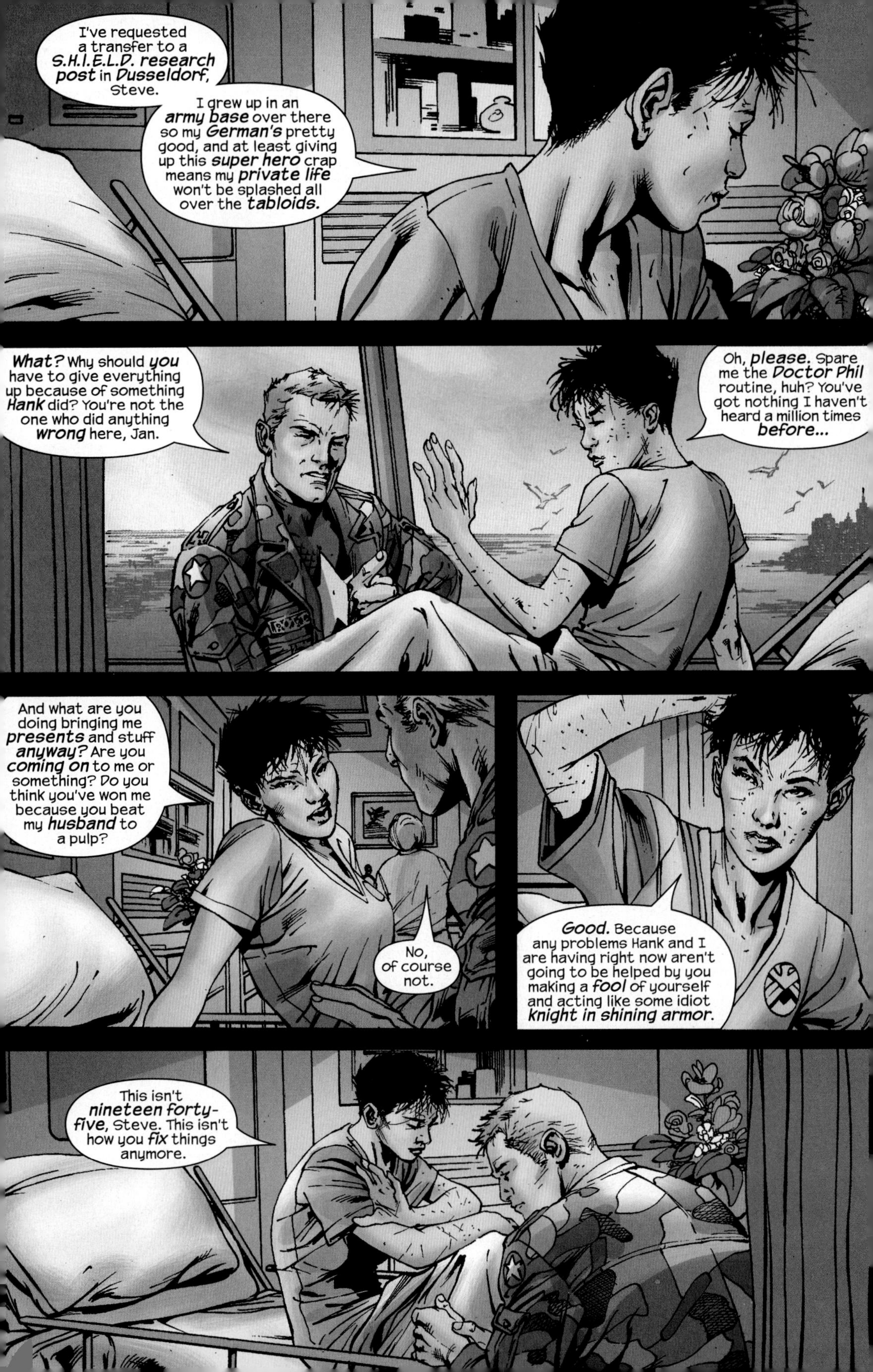
I've requested a transfer to a S.H.I.E.L.D. research post in Dusseldorf, Steve.
I grew up in an army base over there so my German's pretty good, and at least giving up this super hero crap means my private life won't be splashed all over the tabloids.
What? Why should you have to give everything up because of something Hank did? You're not the one who did anything wrong here, Jan.
Oh, please. Spare me the Doctor Phil routine, huh? You've got nothing I haven't heard a million times before...
And what are you doing bringing me presents and stuff anyway? Are you coming on to me or something? Do you think you've won me because you beat my husband to a pulp?
No, of course not.
Good. Because any problems Hank and I are having right now aren't going to be helped by you making a fool of yourself and acting like some idiot knight in shining armor.
This isn't nineteen forty-five, Steve. This isn't how you fix things anymore.

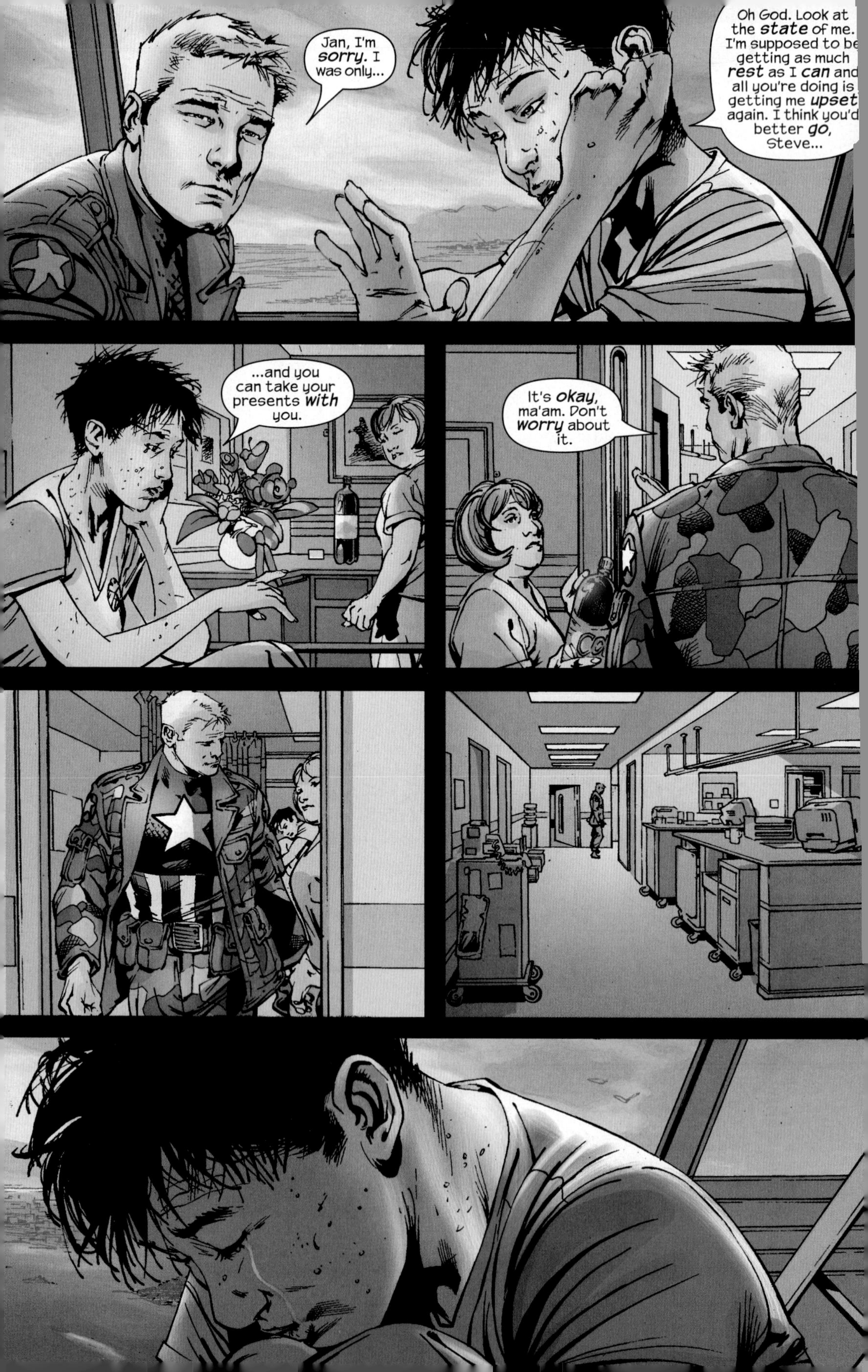
Jan, I'm sorry. I was only...
Oh God. Look at the state of me. I'm supposed to be getting as much rest as I can and all you're doing is getting me upset again. I think you'd better go, Steve...
...and you can take your presents with you.
It's okay, ma'am. Don't worry about it.

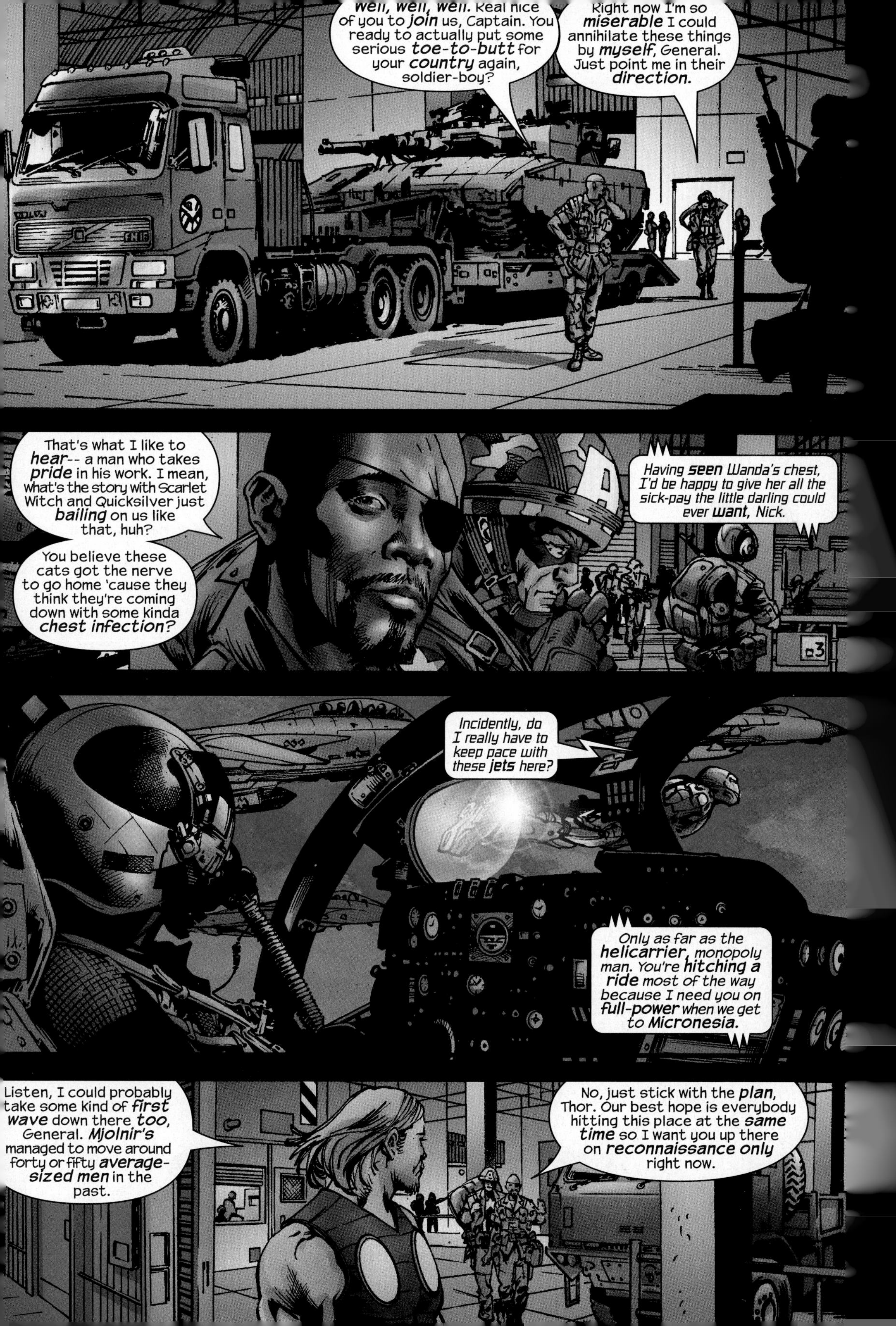
Well, well, well. Real nice of you to join us, Captain. You ready to actually put some serious toe-to-butt for your country again, soldier-boy?
Right now I'm so miserable I could annihilate these things by myself, General. Just point me in their direction.
That's what I like to hear-- a man who takes pride in his work. I mean, what's the story with Scarlet Witch and Quicksilver just bailing on us like that, huh?
You believe these cats got the nerve to go home 'cause they think they're coming down with some kinda chest infection?
Having seen Wanda's chest, I'd be happy to give her all the sick-pay the little darling could ever want, Nick.
Incidently, do I really have to keep pace with these jets here?
Only as far as the helicarrier, monopoly man. You're hitching a ride most of the way because I need you on full-power when we get to Micronesia.
Listen, I could probably take some kind of first wave down there too, General. Mjolnir's managed to move around forty or fifty average-sized men in the past.
No, just stick with the plan, Thor. Our best hope is everybody hitting this place at the same time so I want you up there on reconnaissance only right now.

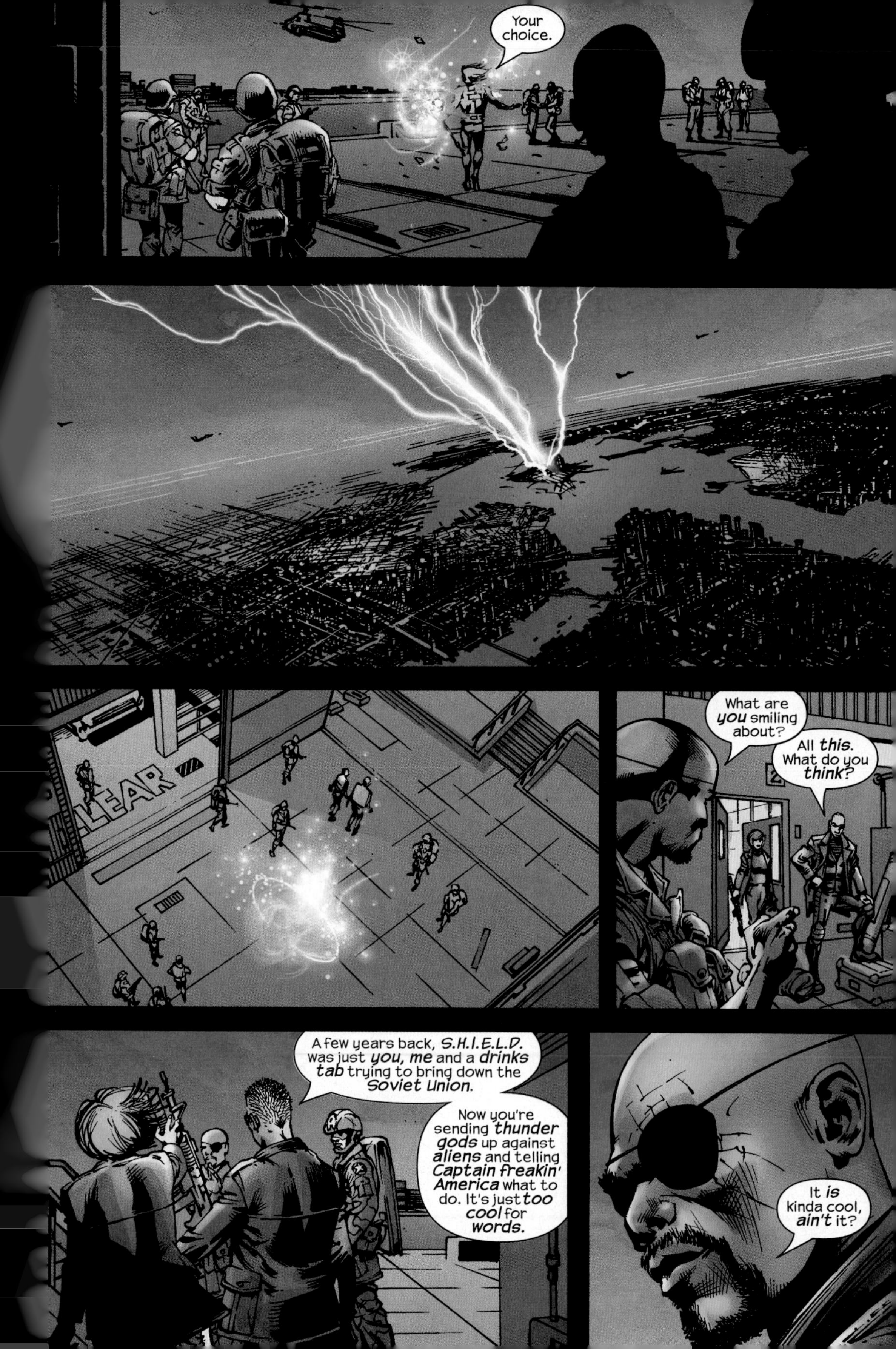
Your choice.
LEAR
What are you smiling about?
All this. What do you think?
A few years back, S.H.I.E.L.D. was just you, me and a drinks tab trying to bring down the Soviet Union.
Now you're sending thunder gods up against aliens and telling Captain freakin' America what to do. It's just too cool for words.
It is kinda cool, ain't it?

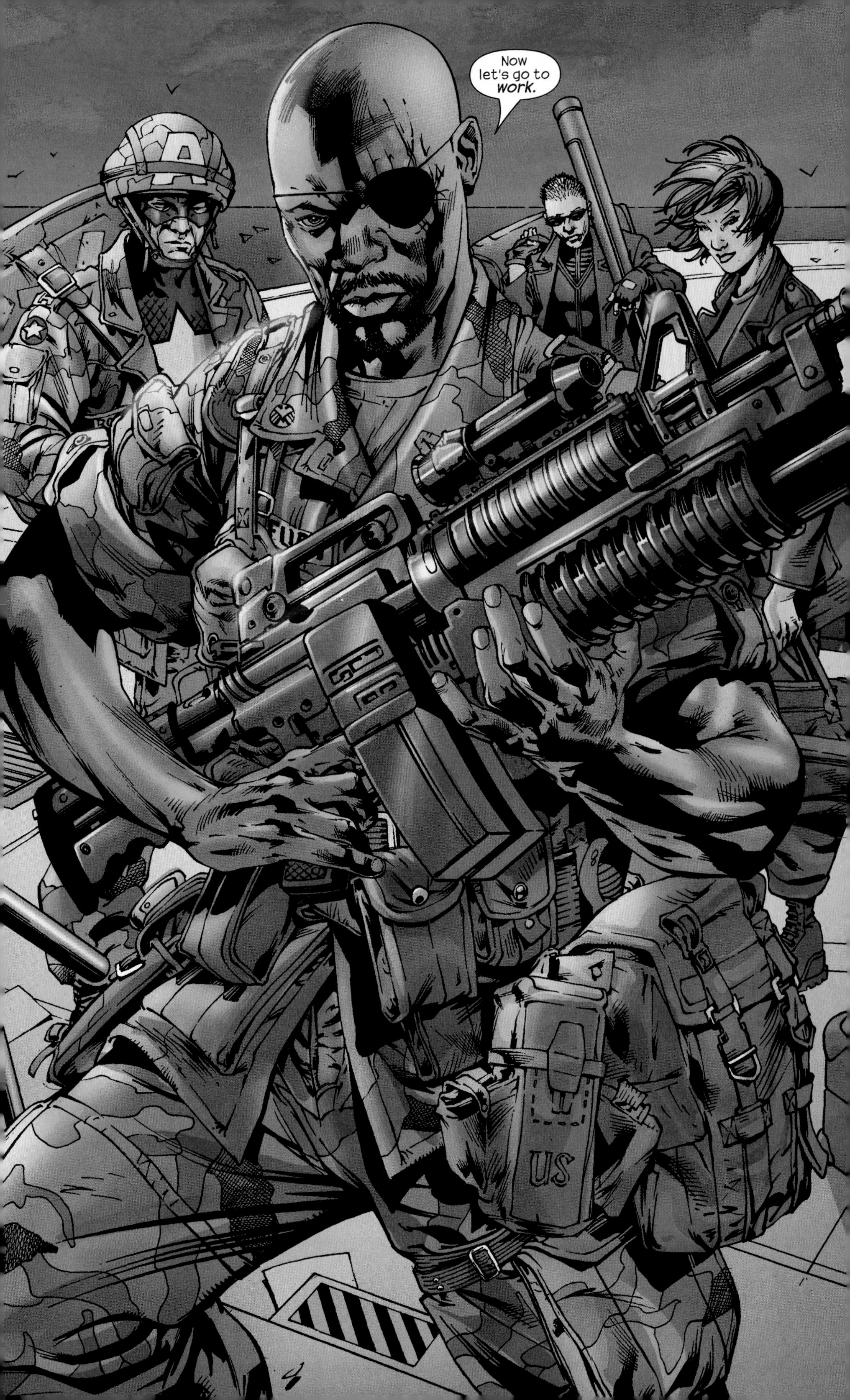
Now let's go to **work.**

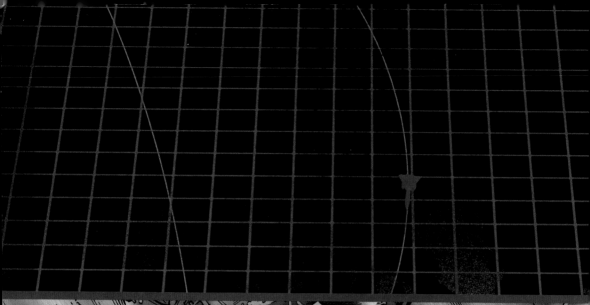

CHAPTER TEN
DEVILS IN DISGUISE

Poland, 1944:
I hope you were not feeling *optimistic* about this mission, Captain America.
424:075

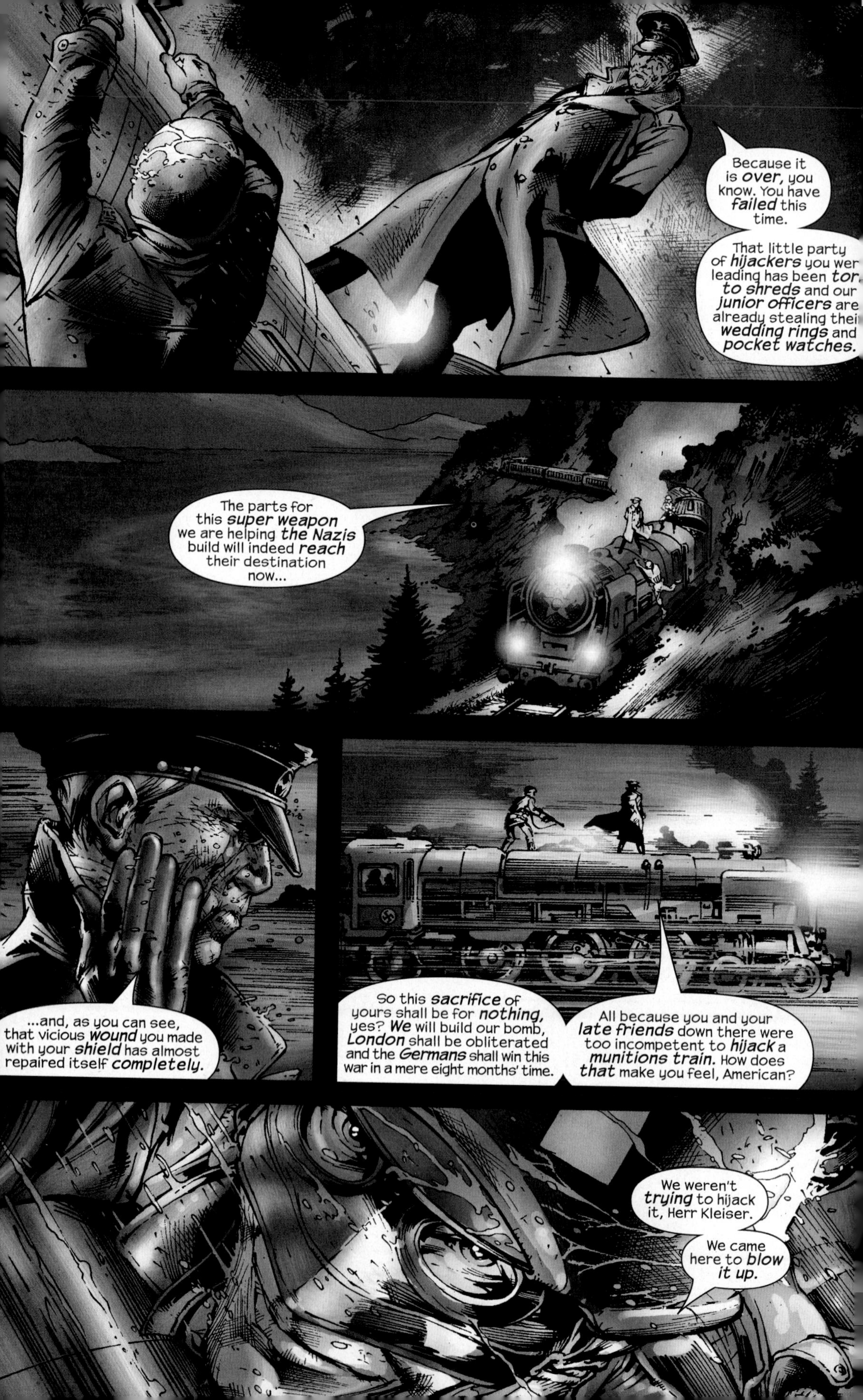
Because it is over, you know. You have failed this time.
That little party of hijackers you wer leading has been tor to shreds and our junior officers are already stealing thei wedding rings and pocket watches.
The parts for this super weapon we are helping the Nazis build will indeed reach their destination now...
...and, as you can see, that vicious wound you made with your shield has almost repaired itself completely.
So this sacrifice of yours shall be for nothing, yes? We will build our bomb, London shall be obliterated and the Germans shall win this war in a mere eight months' time.
All because you and your late friends down there were too incompetent to hijack a munitions train. How does that make you feel, American?
We weren't trying to hijack it, Herr Kleiser.
We came here to blow it up.

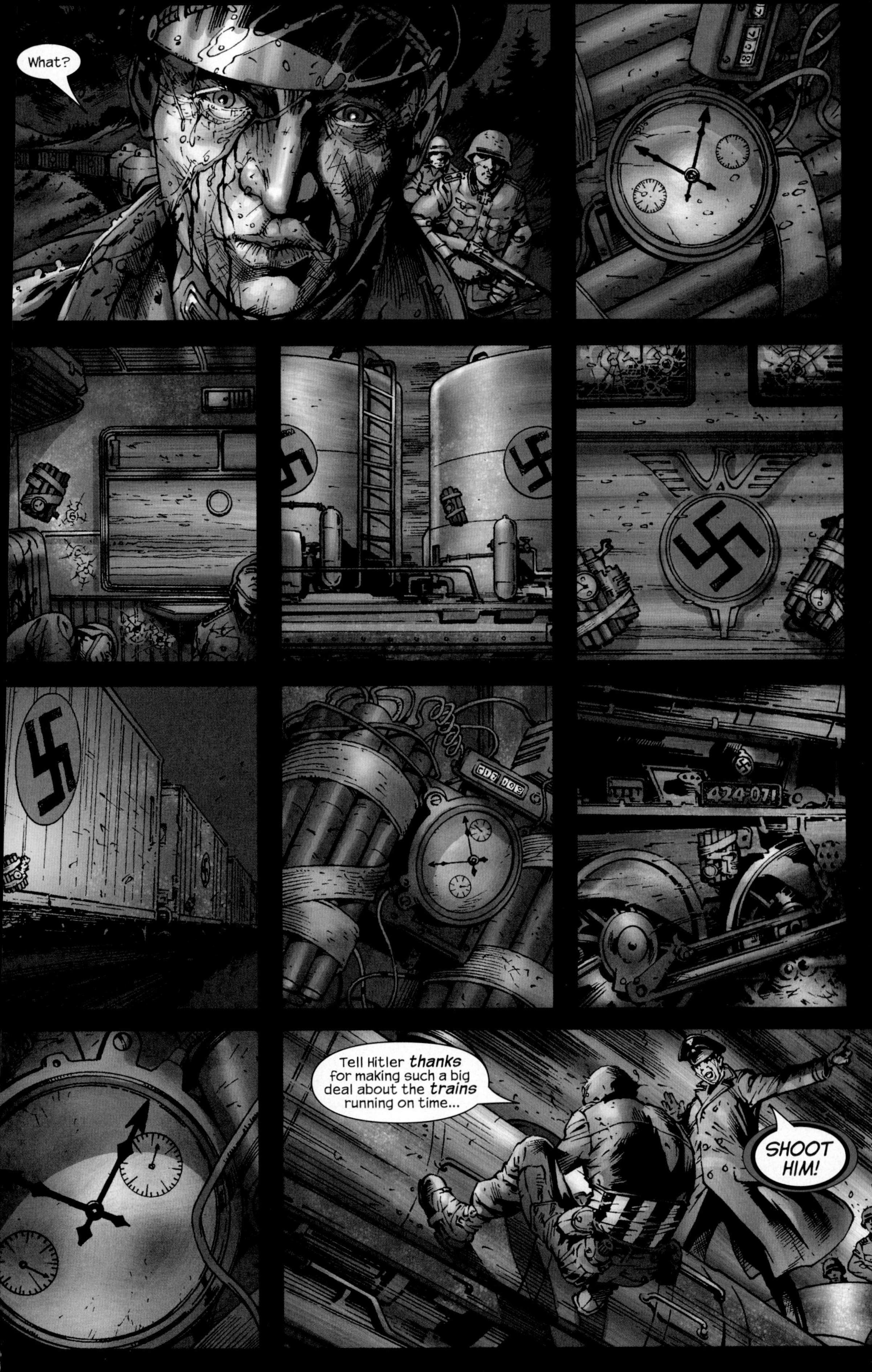
What?
Tell Hitler *thanks* for making such a big deal about the *trains* running on time...
SHOOT HIM!

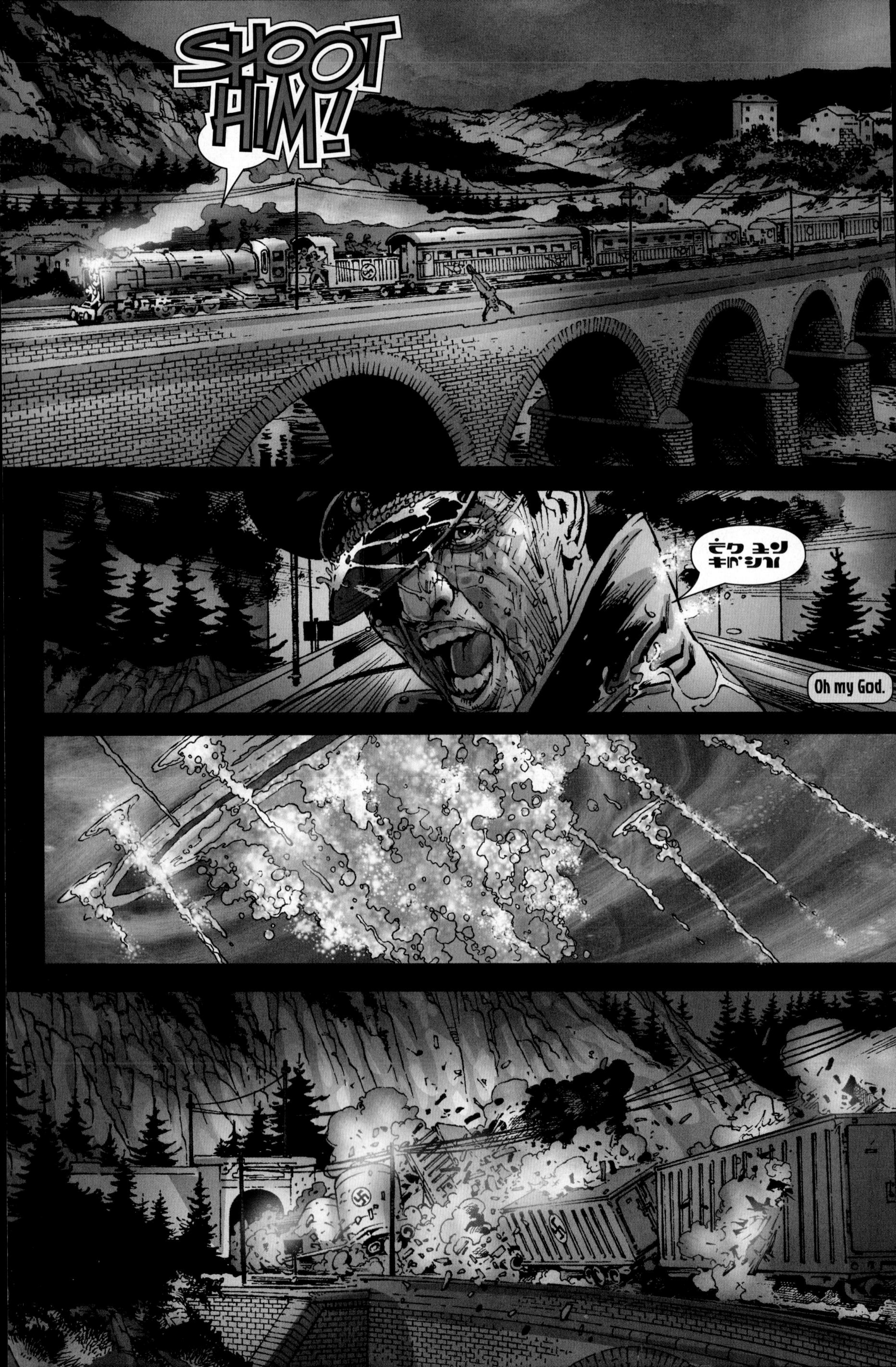
SHOOT HIM!
Oh my God.

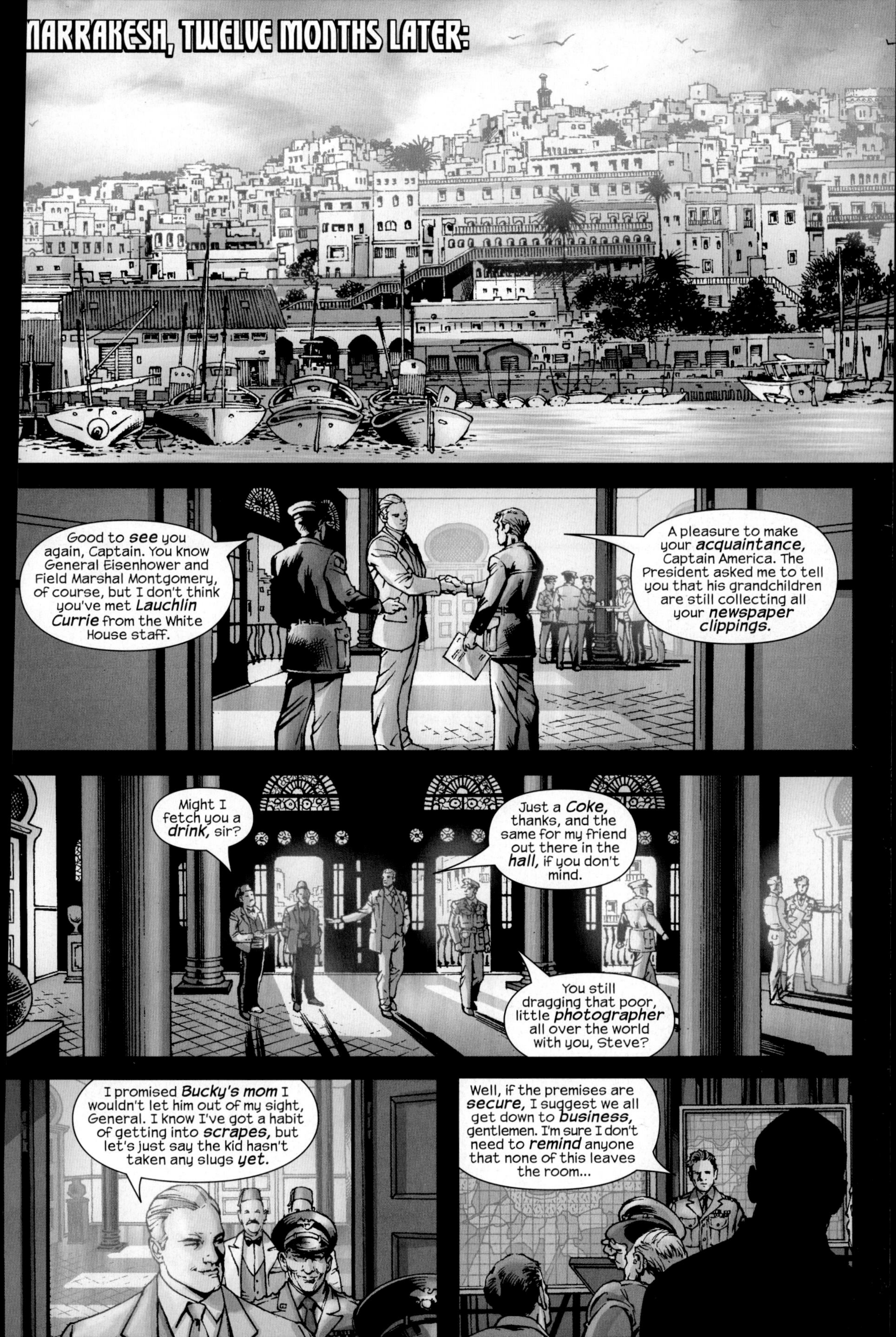
MARRAKESH, TWELVE MONTHS LATER:
Good to see you again, Captain. You know General Eisenhower and Field Marshal Montgomery, of course, but I don't think you've met Lauchlin Currie from the White House staff.
A pleasure to make your acquaintance, Captain America. The President asked me to tell you that his grandchildren are still collecting all your newspaper clippings.
Might I fetch you a drink, sir?
Just a Coke, thanks, and the same for my friend out there in the hall, if you don't mind.
You still dragging that poor, little photographer all over the world with you, Steve?
I promised Bucky's mom I wouldn't let him out of my sight, General. I know I've got a habit of getting into scrapes, but let's just say the kid hasn't taken any slugs yet.
Well, if the premises are secure, I suggest we all get down to business, gentlemen. I'm sure I don't need to remind anyone that none of this leaves the room...

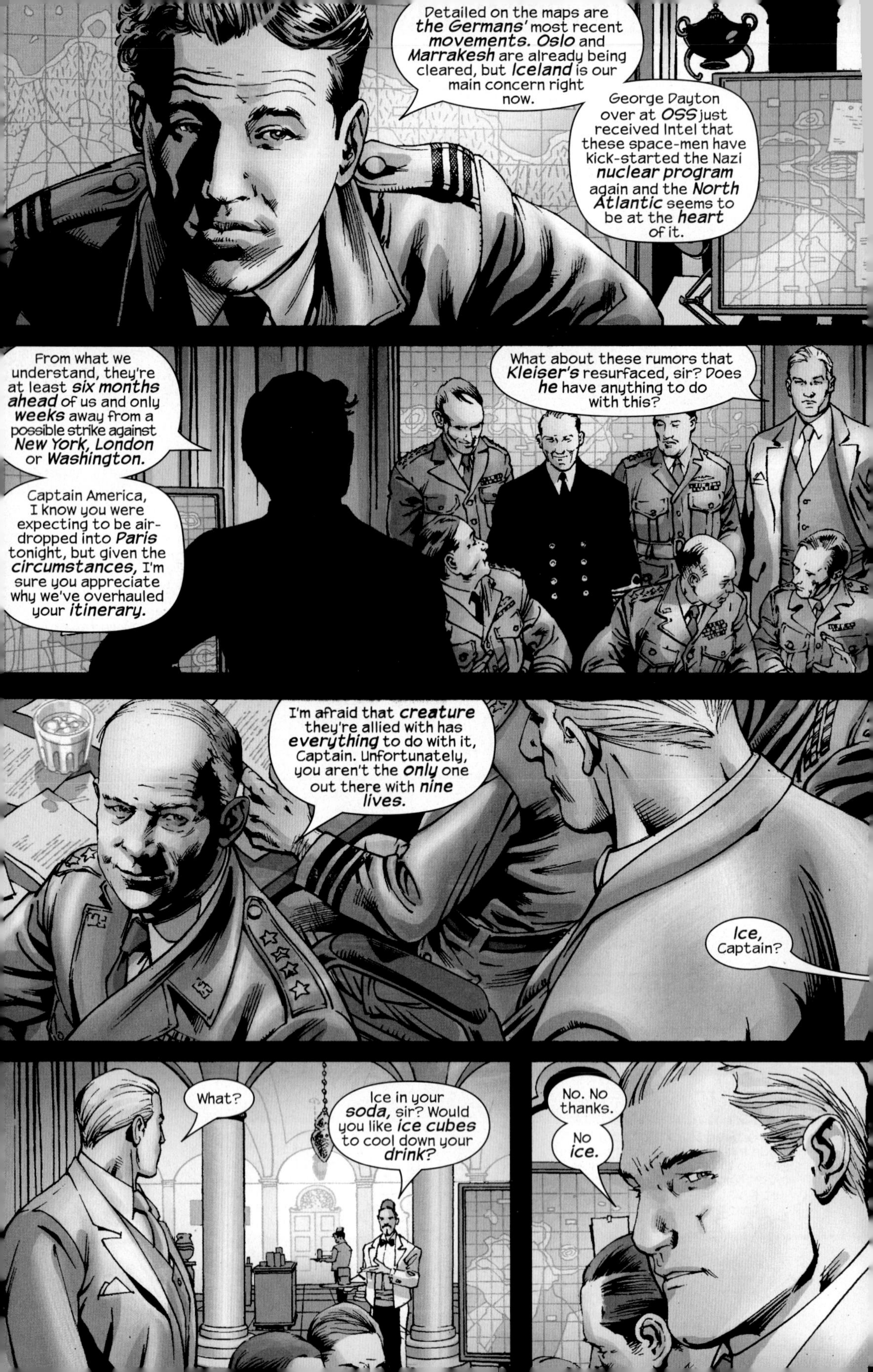

Detailed on the maps are the Germans' most recent movements. Oslo and Marrakesh are already being cleared, but Iceland is our main concern right now.
George Dayton over at OSS just received Intel that these space-men have kick-started the Nazi nuclear program again and the North Atlantic seems to be at the heart of it.
From what we understand, they're at least six months ahead of us and only weeks away from a possible strike against New York, London or Washington.
Captain America, I know you were expecting to be air-dropped into Paris tonight, but given the circumstances, I'm sure you appreciate why we've overhauled your itinerary.
What about these rumors that Kleiser's resurfaced, sir? Does he have anything to do with this?
I'm afraid that creature they're allied with has everything to do with it, Captain. Unfortunately, you aren't the only one out there with nine lives.
Ice, Captain?
What?
Ice in your soda, sir? Would you like ice cubes to cool down your drink?
No. No thanks.
No ice.

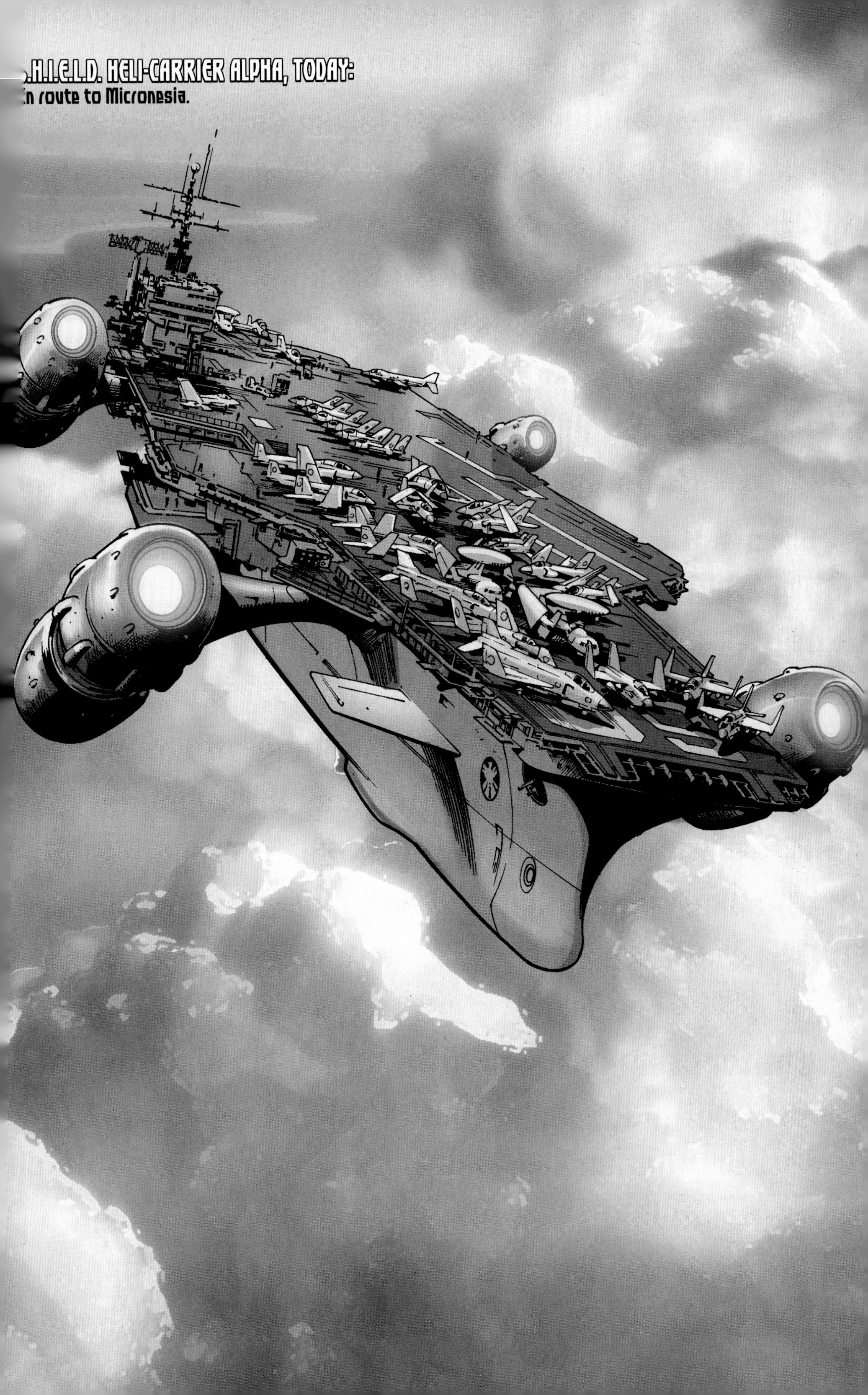
.H.I.E.L.D. HELI-CARRIER ALPHA, TODAY:
n route to Micronesia.

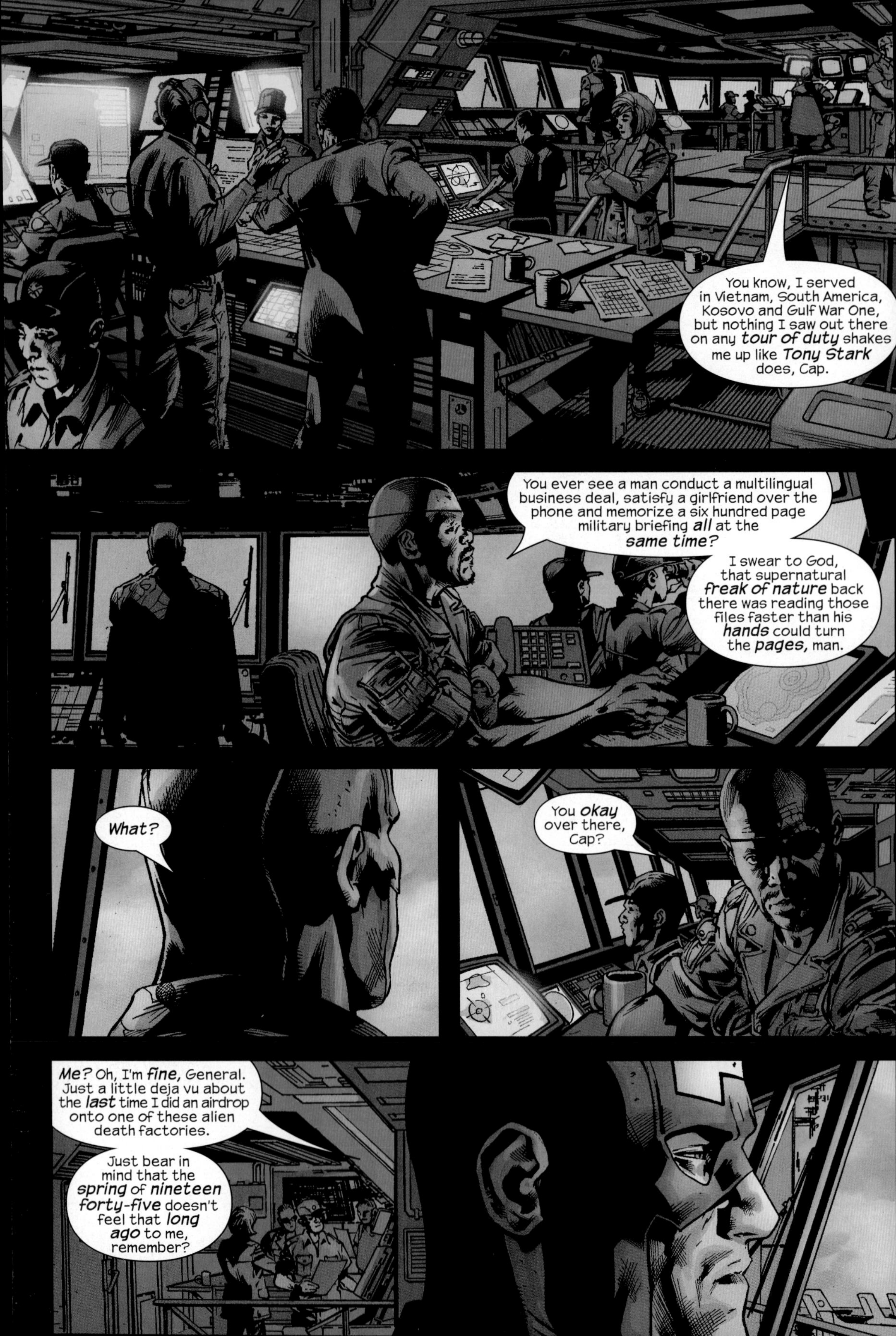
You know, I served in Vietnam, South America, Kosovo and Gulf War One, but nothing I saw out there on any tour of duty shakes me up like Tony Stark does, Cap.
You ever see a man conduct a multilingual business deal, satisfy a girlfriend over the phone and memorize a six hundred page military briefing all at the same time?
I swear to God, that supernatural freak of nature back there was reading those files faster than his hands could turn the pages, man.
What?
You okay over there, Cap?
Me? Oh, I'm fine, General. Just a little deja vu about the last time I did an airdrop onto one of these alien death factories.
Just bear in mind that the spring of nineteen forty-five doesn't feel that long ago to me, remember?

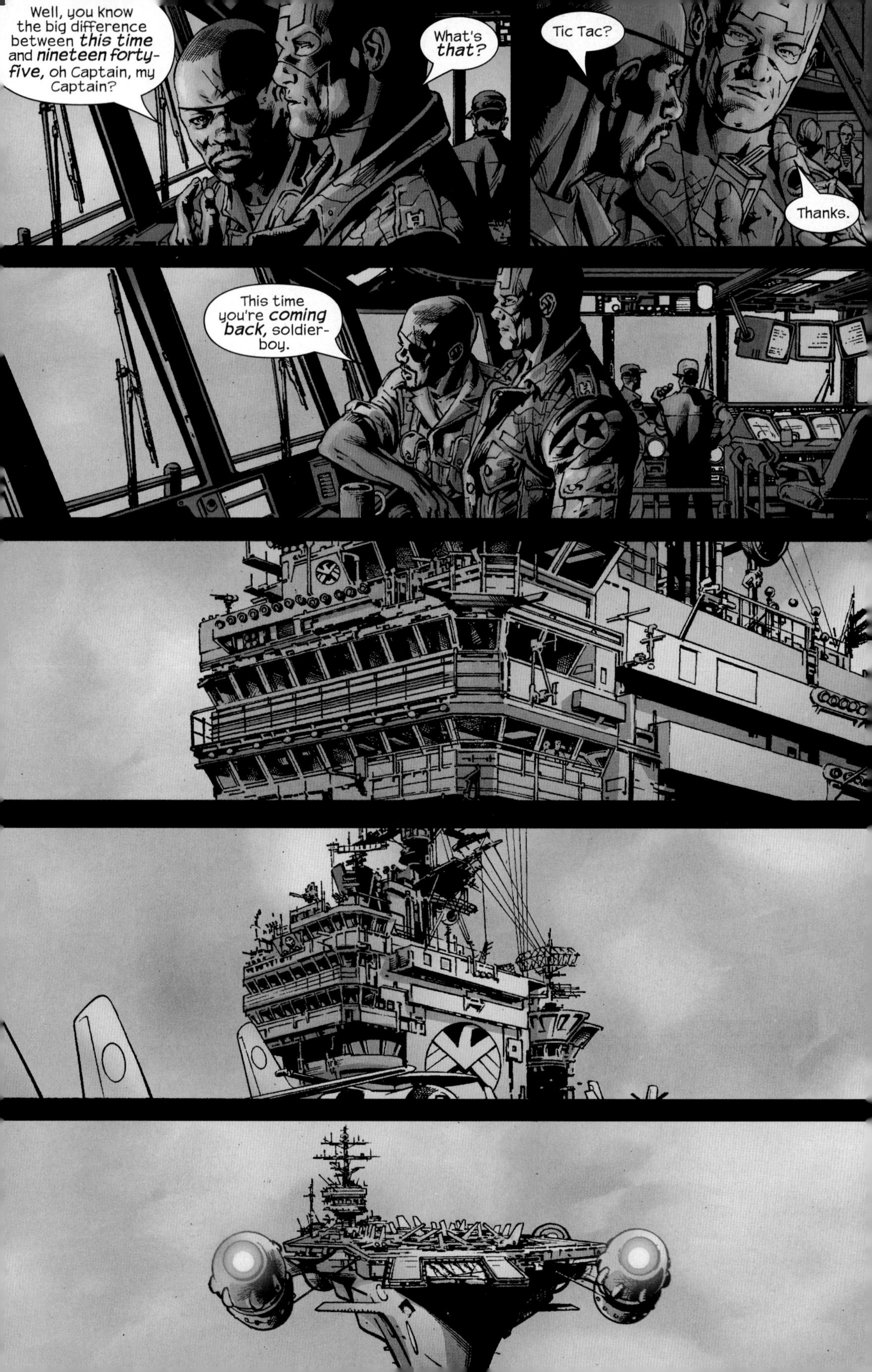
Well, you know the big difference between this time and nineteen forty-five, oh Captain, my Captain?
What's that?
Tic Tac?
Thanks.
This time you're coming back, soldier-boy.

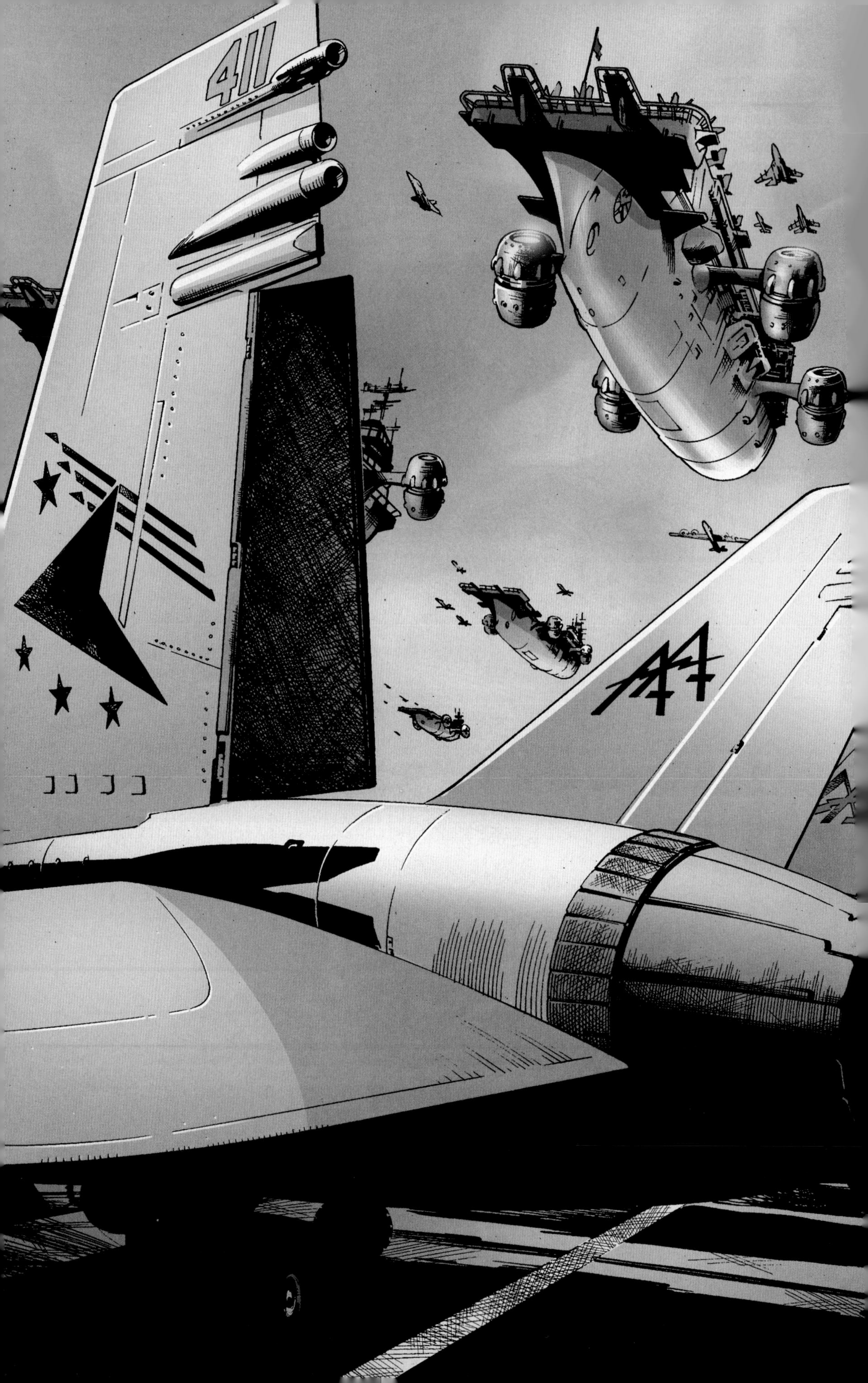

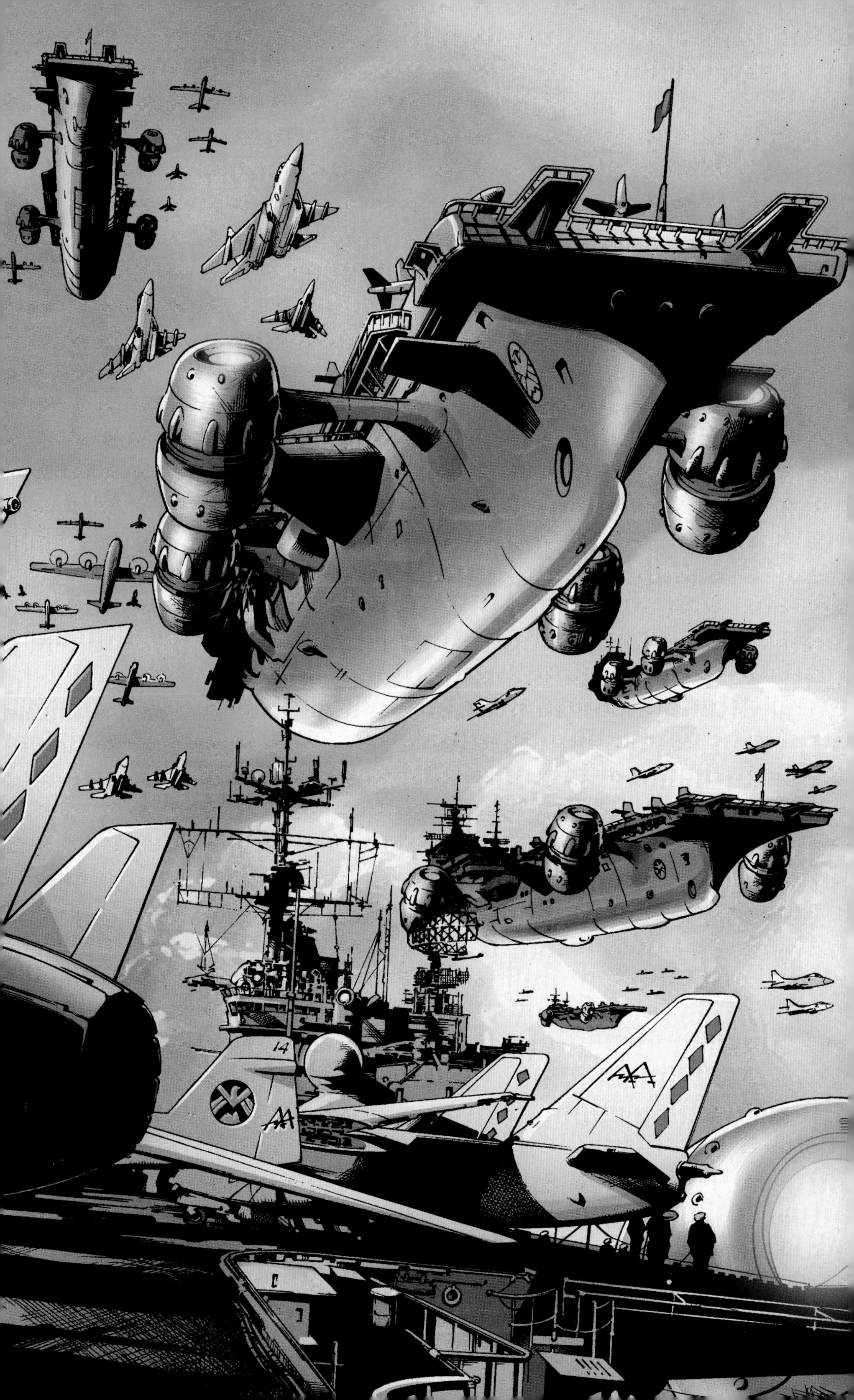

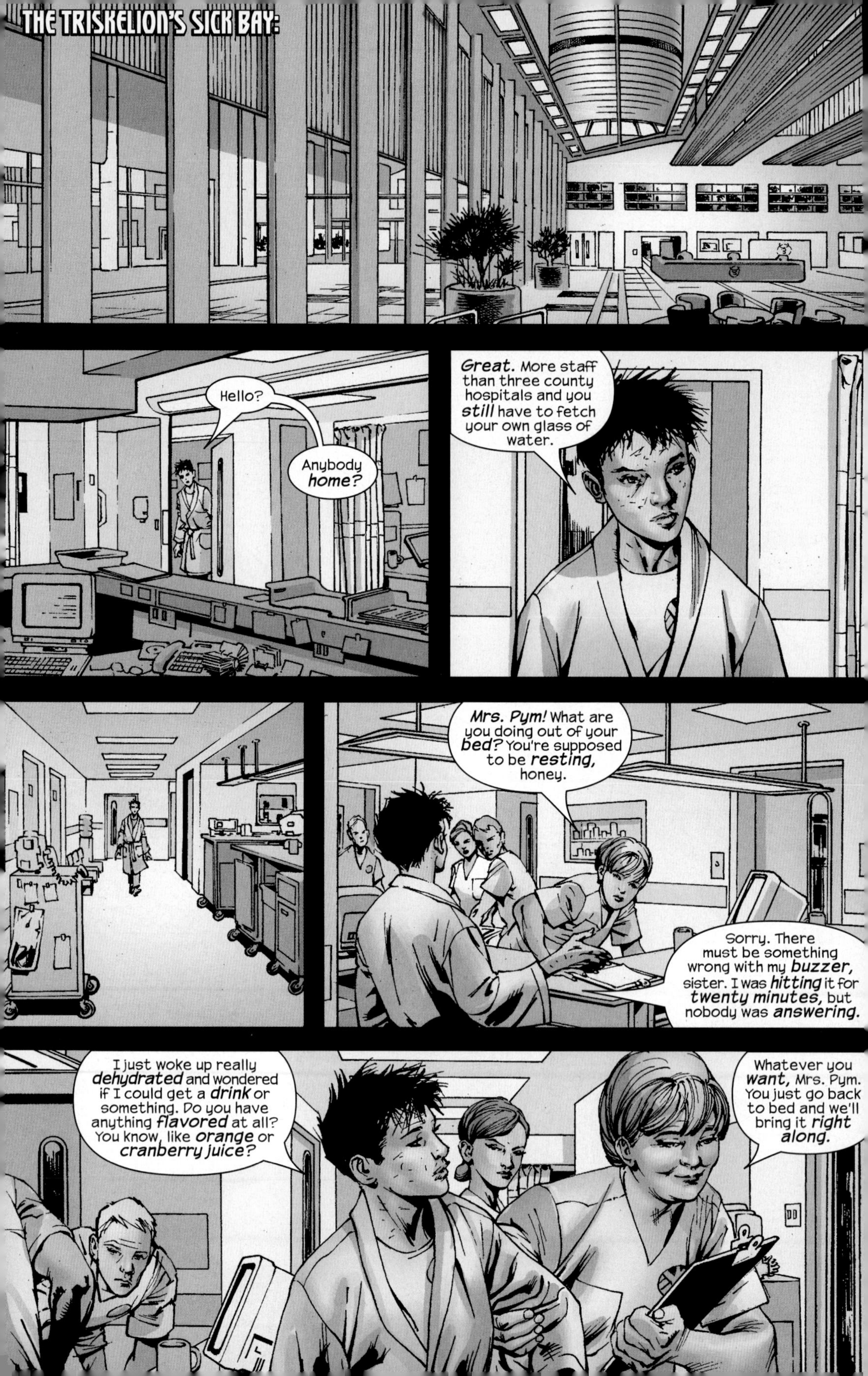
THE TRISKELION'S SICK BAY:
Hello?
Anybody home?
Great. More staff than three county hospitals and you still have to fetch your own glass of water.
Mrs. Pym! What are you doing out of your bed? You're supposed to be resting, honey.
Sorry. There must be something wrong with my buzzer, sister. I was hitting it for twenty minutes, but nobody was answering.
I just woke up really dehydrated and wondered if I could get a drink or something. Do you have anything flavored at all? You know, like orange or cranberry juice?
Whatever you want, Mrs. Pym. You just go back to bed and we'll bring it right along.

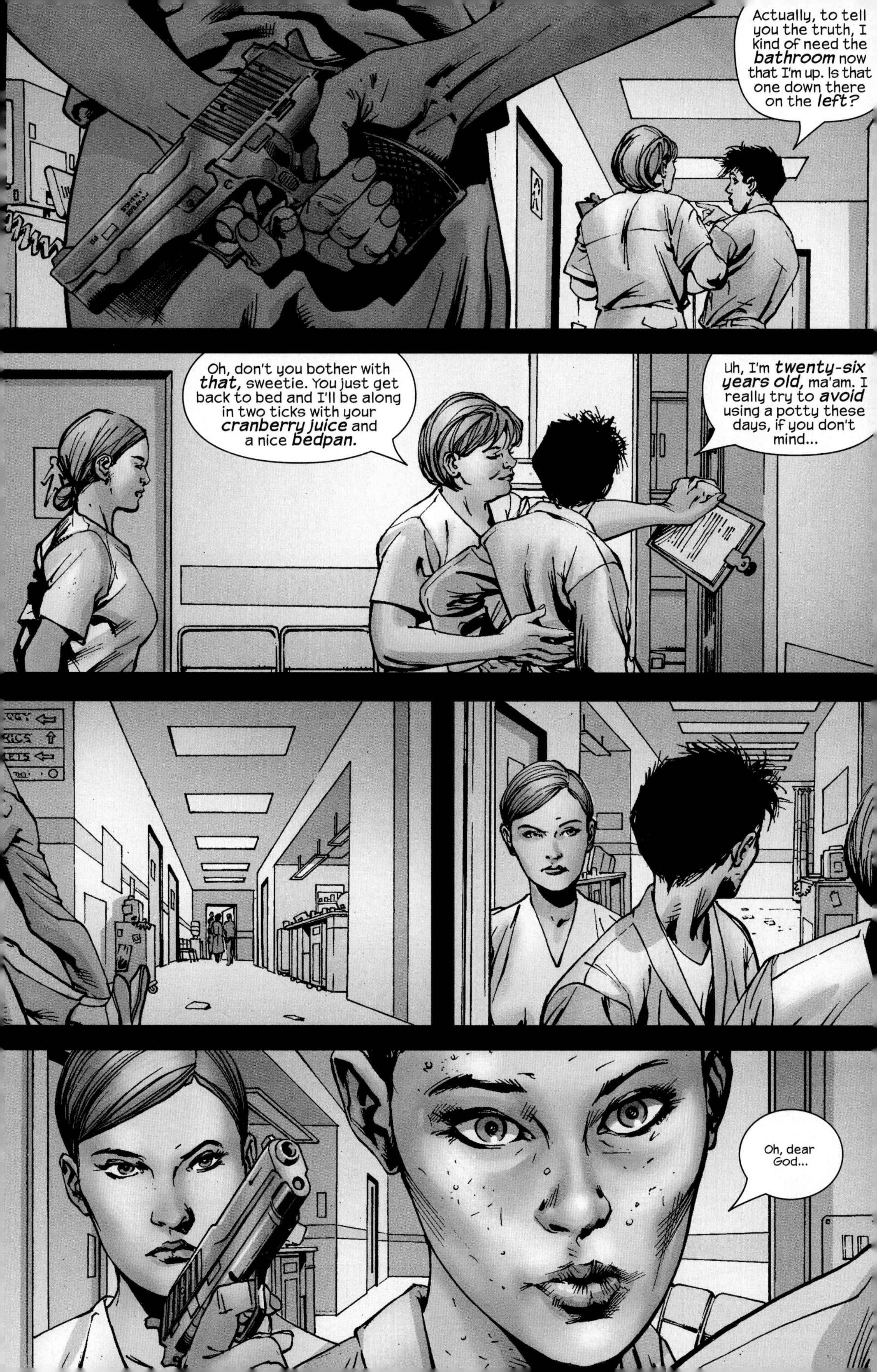
Actually, to tell you the truth, I kind of need the bathroom now that I'm up. Is that one down there on the left?
Oh, don't you bother with that, sweetie. You just get back to bed and I'll be along in two ticks with your cranberry juice and a nice bedpan.
Uh, I'm twenty-six years old, ma'am. I really try to avoid using a potty these days, if you don't mind...
Oh, dear God...

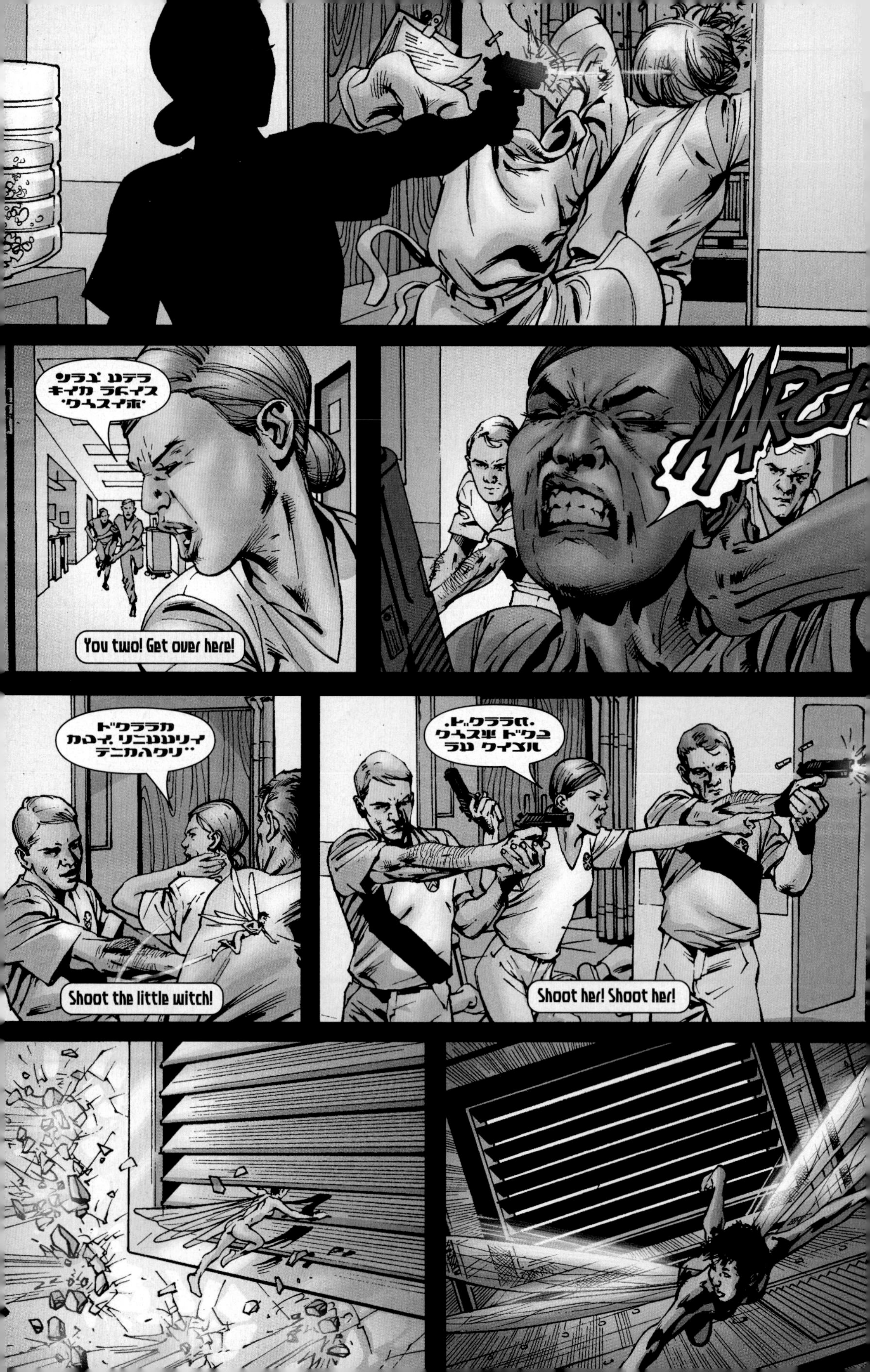
You two! Get over here!
AARGH
Shoot the little witch!
Shoot her! Shoot her!

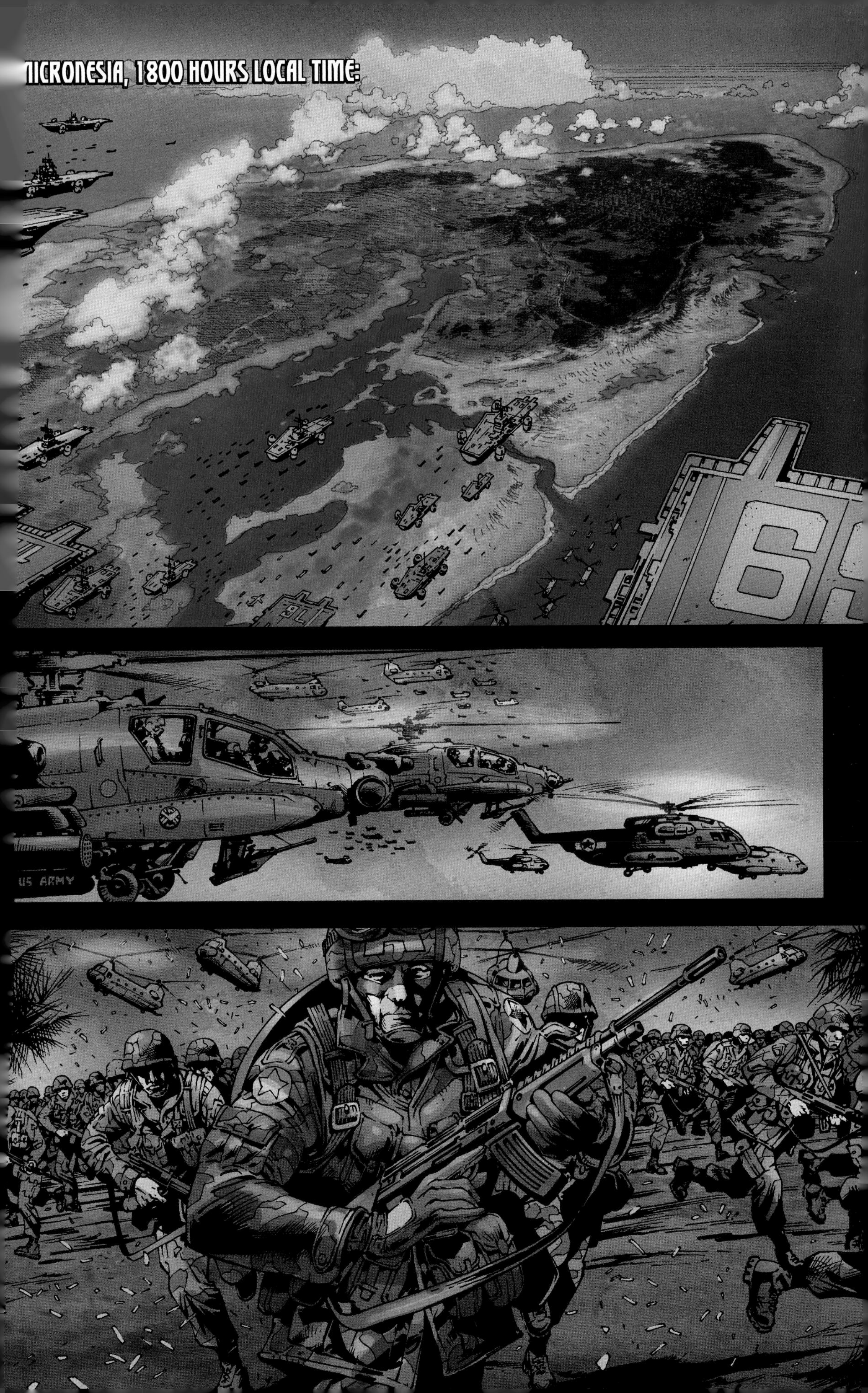
MICRONESIA, 1800 HOURS LOCAL TIME:
US ARMY

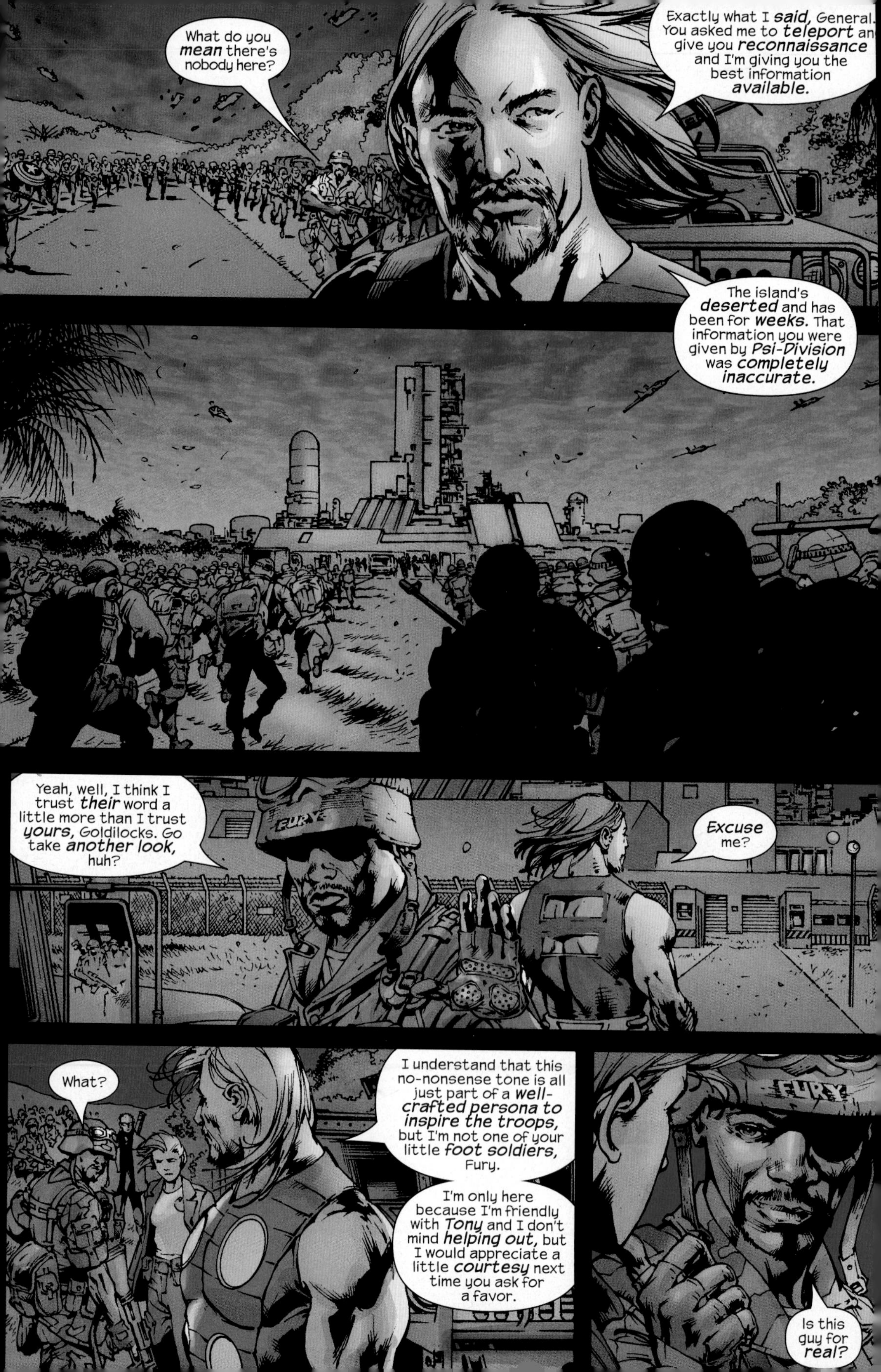
What do you mean there's nobody here?
Exactly what I said, General. You asked me to teleport and give you reconnaissance and I'm giving you the best information available.
The island's deserted and has been for weeks. That information you were given by Psi-Division was completely inaccurate.
Yeah, well, I think I trust their word a little more than I trust yours, Goldilocks. Go take another look, huh?
Excuse me?
What?
I understand that this no-nonsense tone is all just part of a well-crafted persona to inspire the troops, but I'm not one of your little foot soldiers, Fury.
I'm only here because I'm friendly with Tony and I don't mind helping out, but I would appreciate a little courtesy next time you ask for a favor.
Is this guy for real?

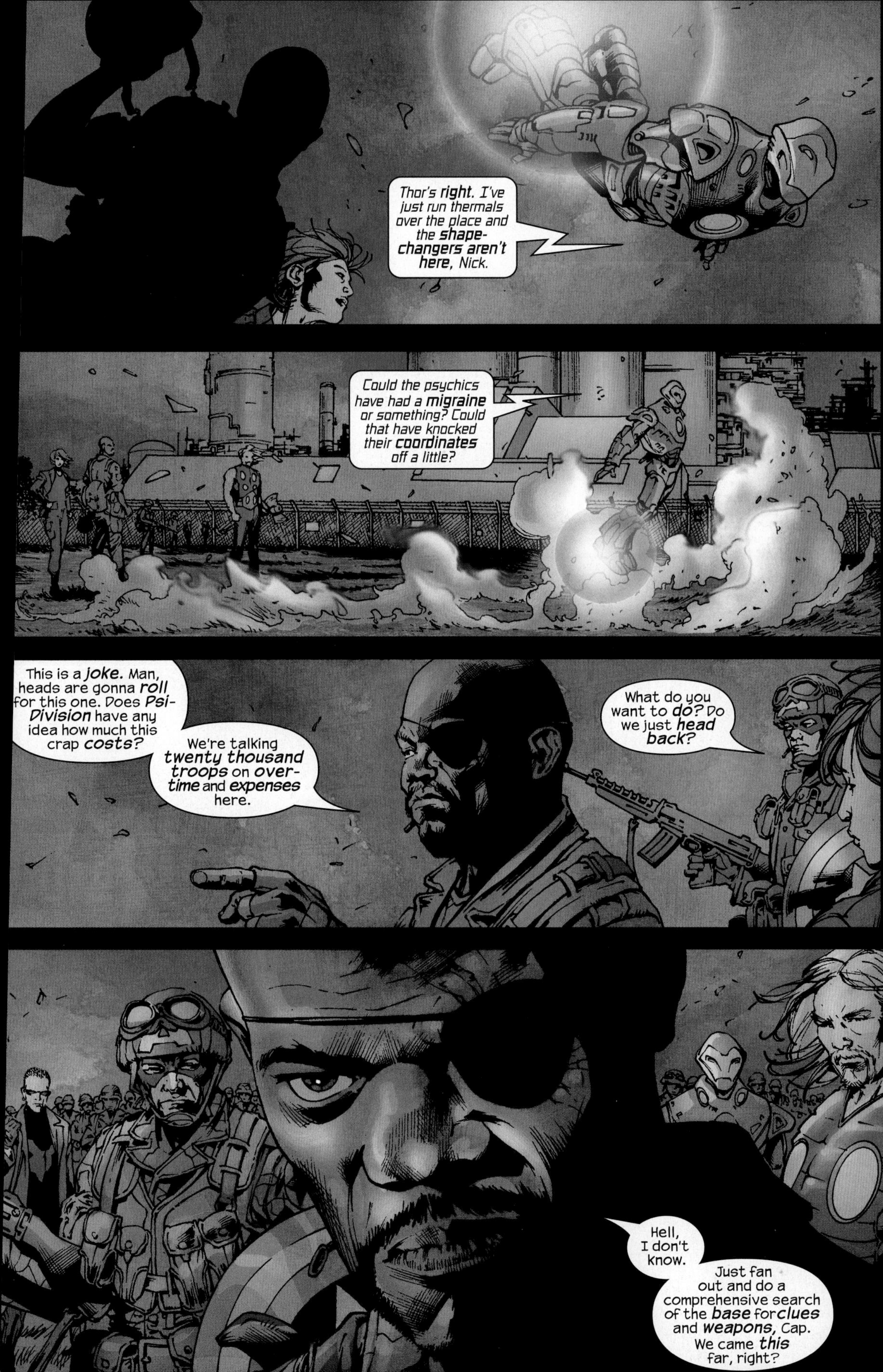

Thor's right. I've just run thermals over the place and the shape-changers aren't here, Nick.
Could the psychics have had a migraine or something? Could that have knocked their coordinates off a little?
This is a joke. Man, heads are gonna roll for this one. Does Psi-Division have any idea how much this crap costs?
We're talking twenty thousand troops on over-time and expenses here.
What do you want to do? Do we just head back?
Hell, I don't know.
Just fan out and do a comprehensive search of the base for clues and weapons, Cap. We came this far, right?

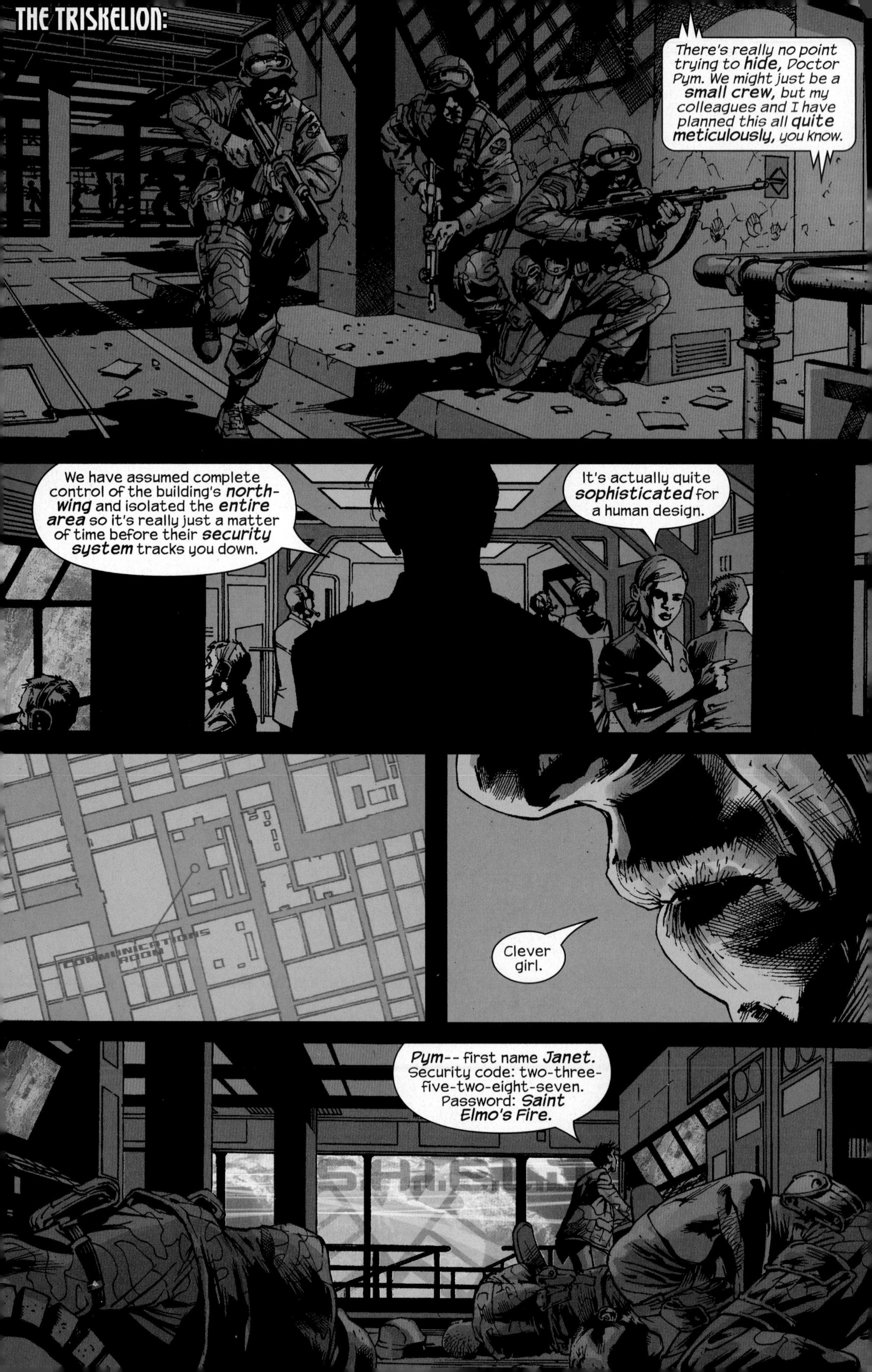
THE TRISKELION:
There's really no point trying to hide, Doctor Pym. We might just be a small crew, but my colleagues and I have planned this all quite meticulously, you know.
We have assumed complete control of the building's north-wing and isolated the entire area so it's really just a matter of time before their security system tracks you down.
It's actually quite sophisticated for a human design.
COMMUNICATIONS ROOM
Clever girl.
Pym-- first name Janet. Security code: two-three-five-two-eight-seven. Password: Saint Elmo's Fire.

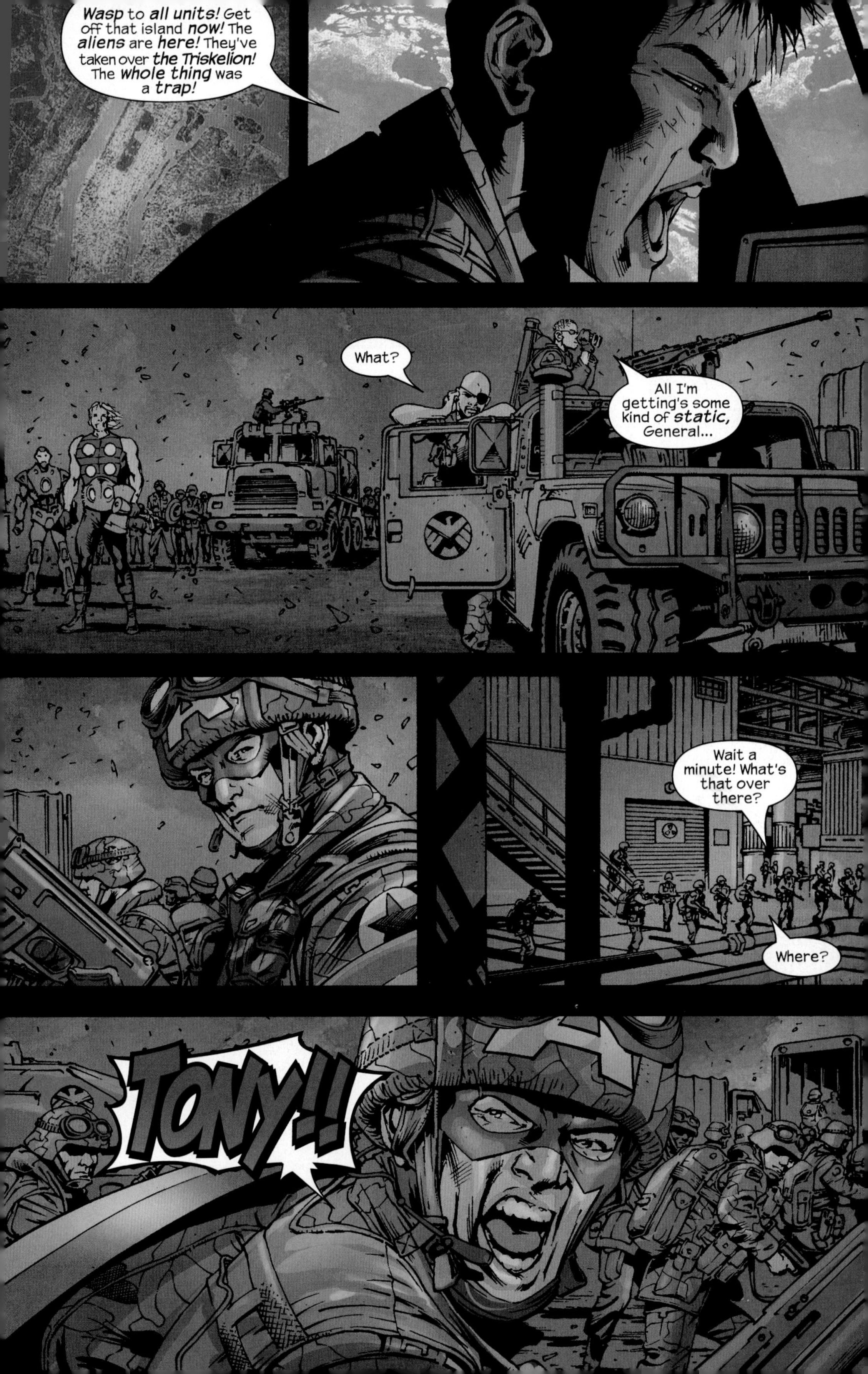
Wasp to all units! Get off that island now! The aliens are here! They've taken over the Triskelion! The whole thing was a trap!
What?
All I'm getting's some kind of static, General...
Wait a minute! What's that over there?
Where?
TONY!!

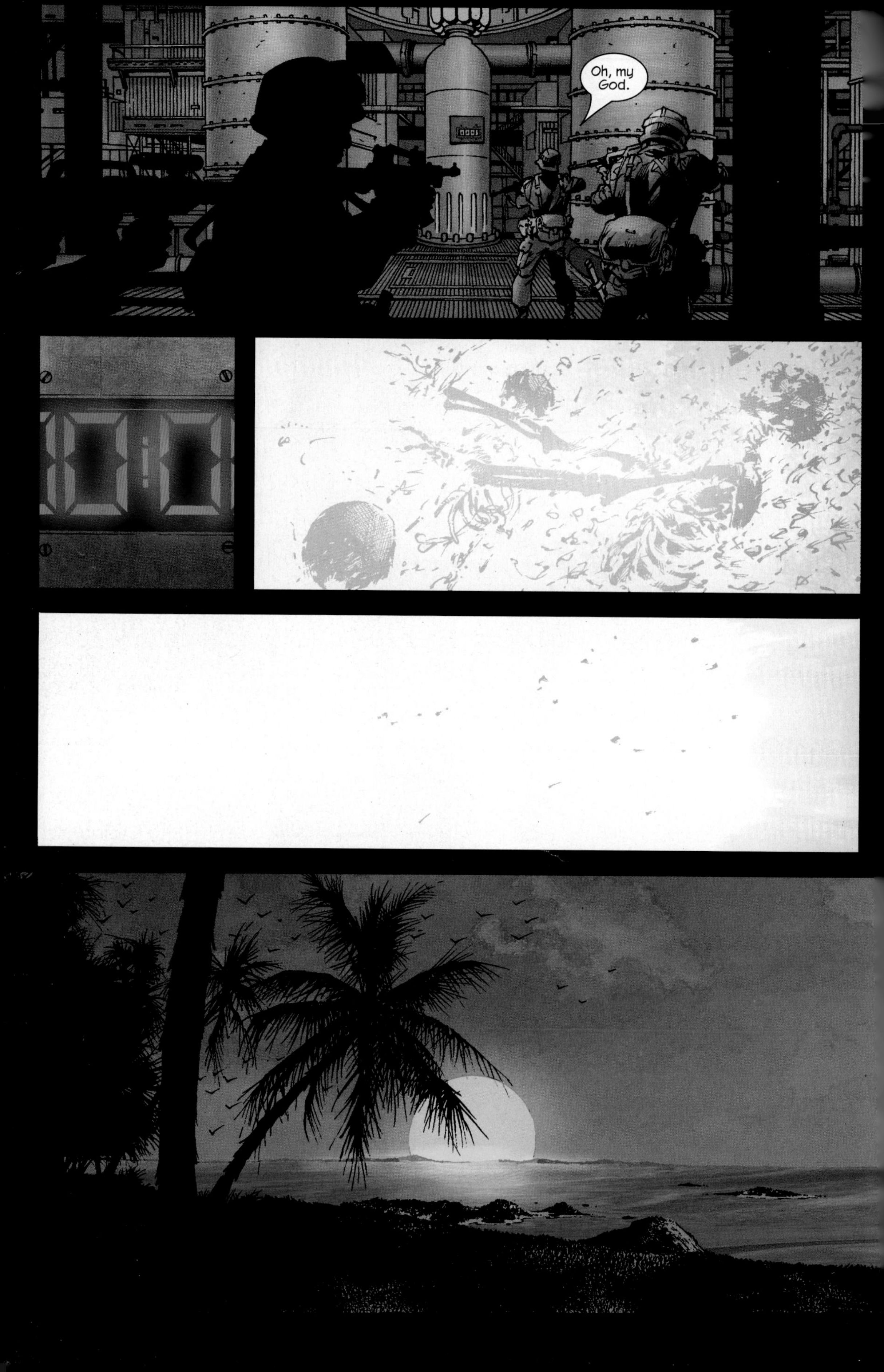
Oh, my God.

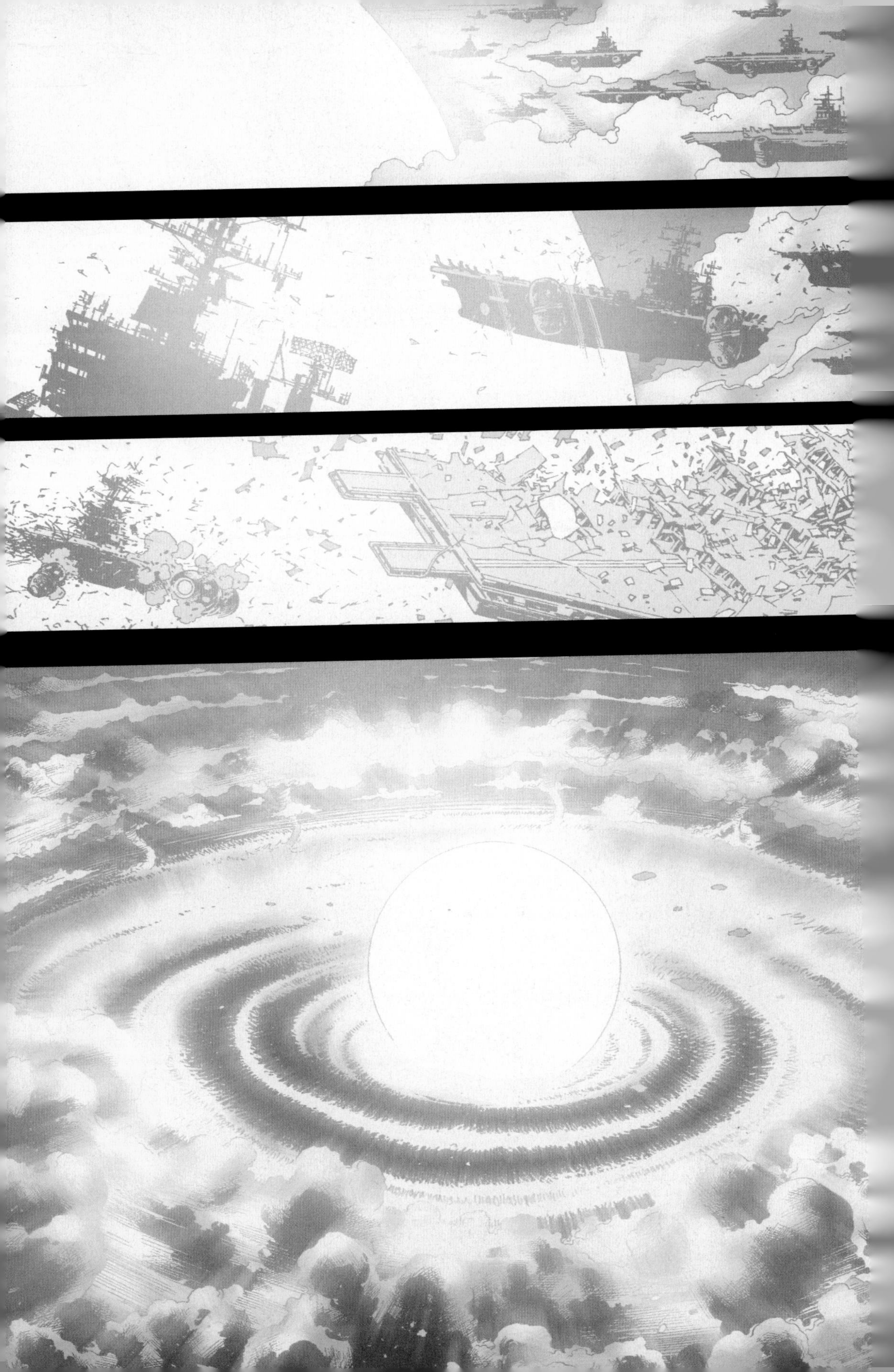

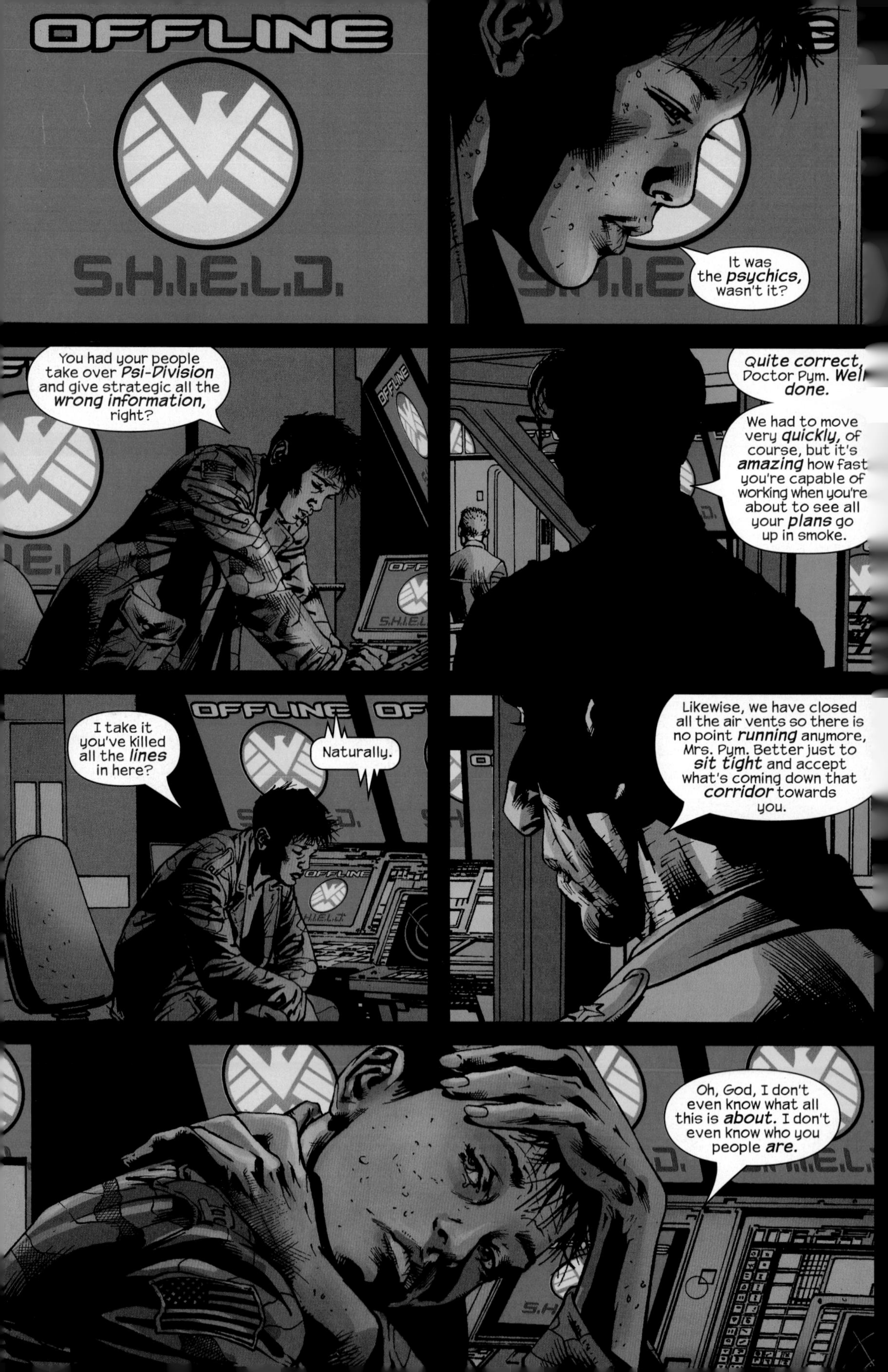
OFFLINE
S.H.I.E.L.D.
It was the psychics, wasn't it?
You had your people take over Psi-Division and give strategic all the wrong information, right?
Quite correct, Doctor Pym. Well done.
We had to move very quickly, of course, but it's amazing how fast you're capable of working when you're about to see all your plans go up in smoke.
I take it you've killed all the lines in here?
Naturally.
Likewise, we have closed all the air vents so there is no point running anymore, Mrs. Pym. Better just to sit tight and accept what's coming down that corridor towards you.
Oh, God, I don't even know what all this is about. I don't even know who you people are.

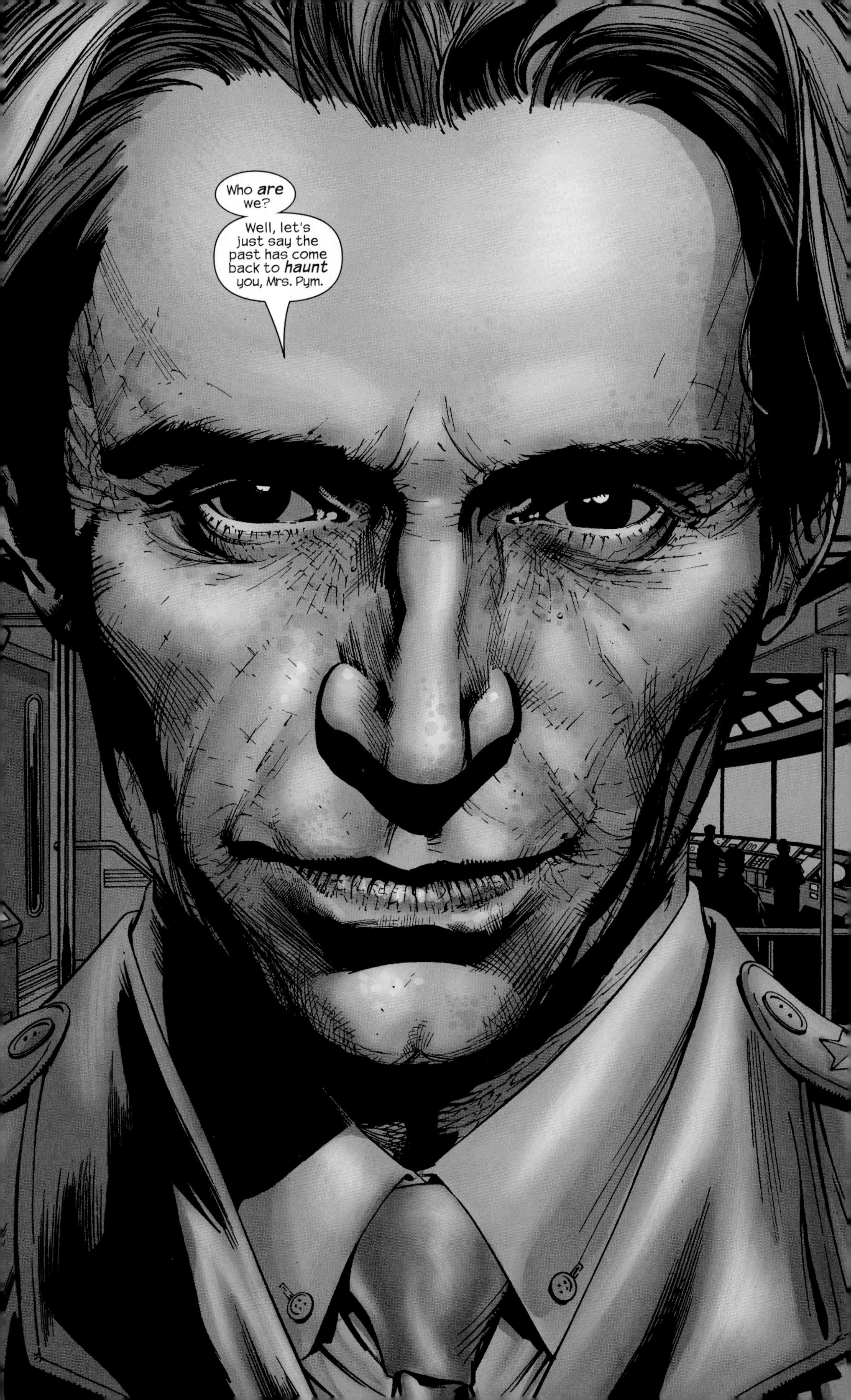
Who *are* we?
Well, let's just say the past has come back to *haunt* you, Mrs. Pym.

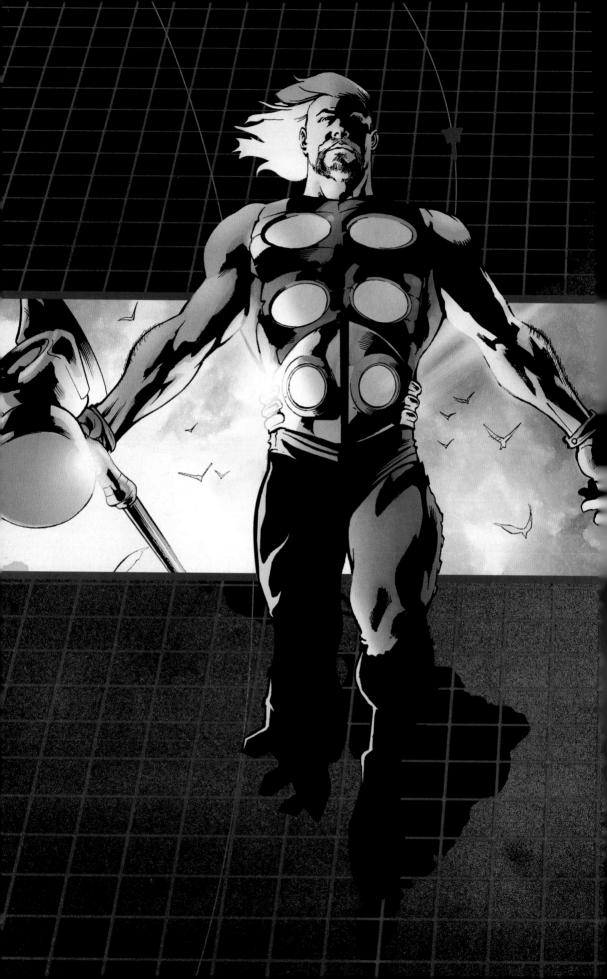

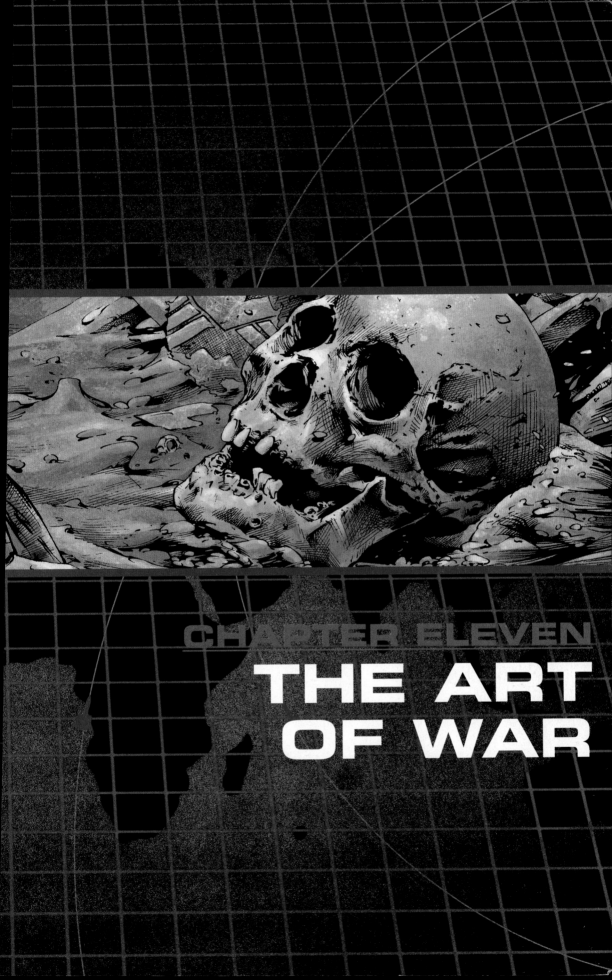

CHAPTER ELEVEN

THE ART OF WAR

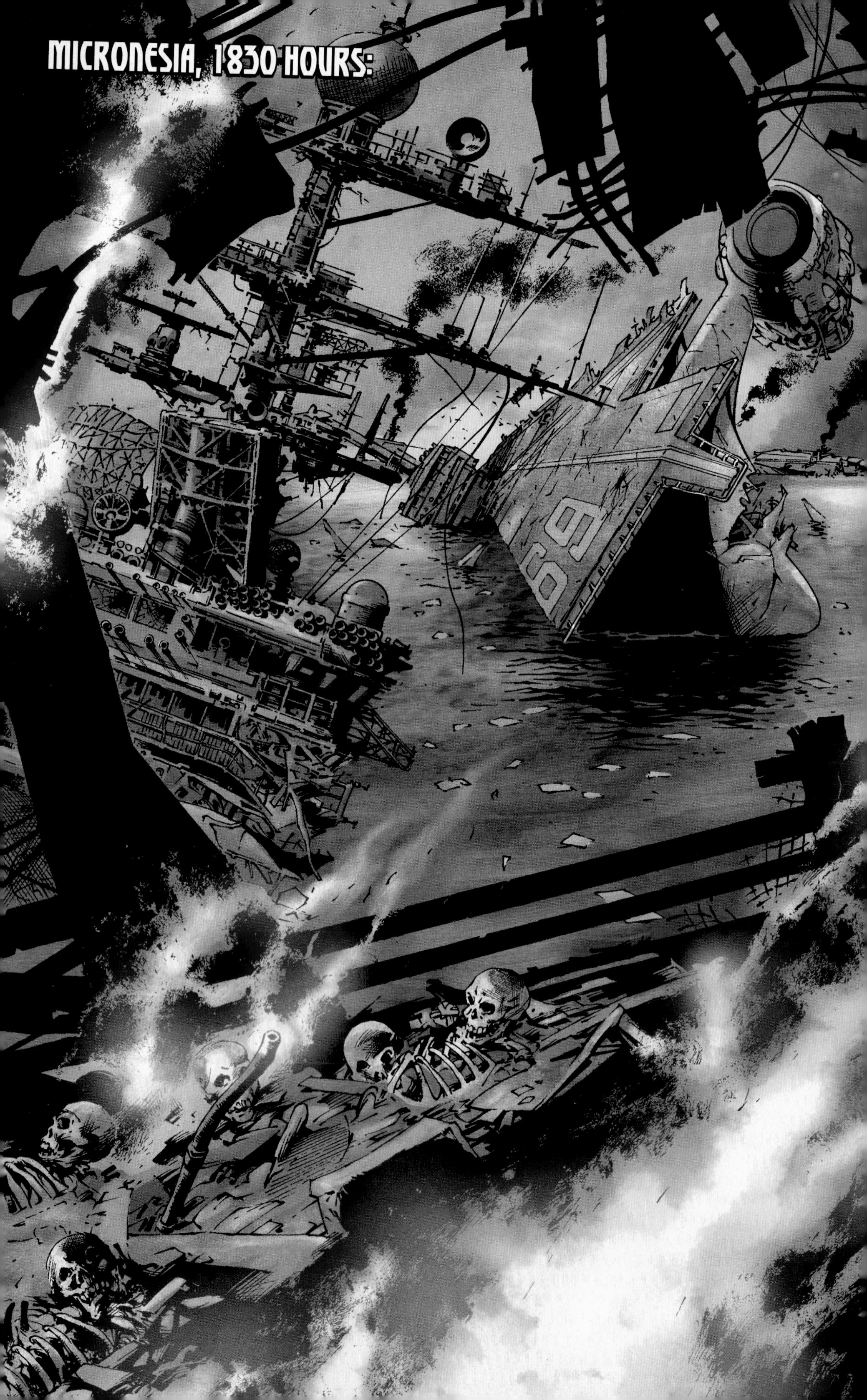
MICRONESIA, 1830 HOURS:

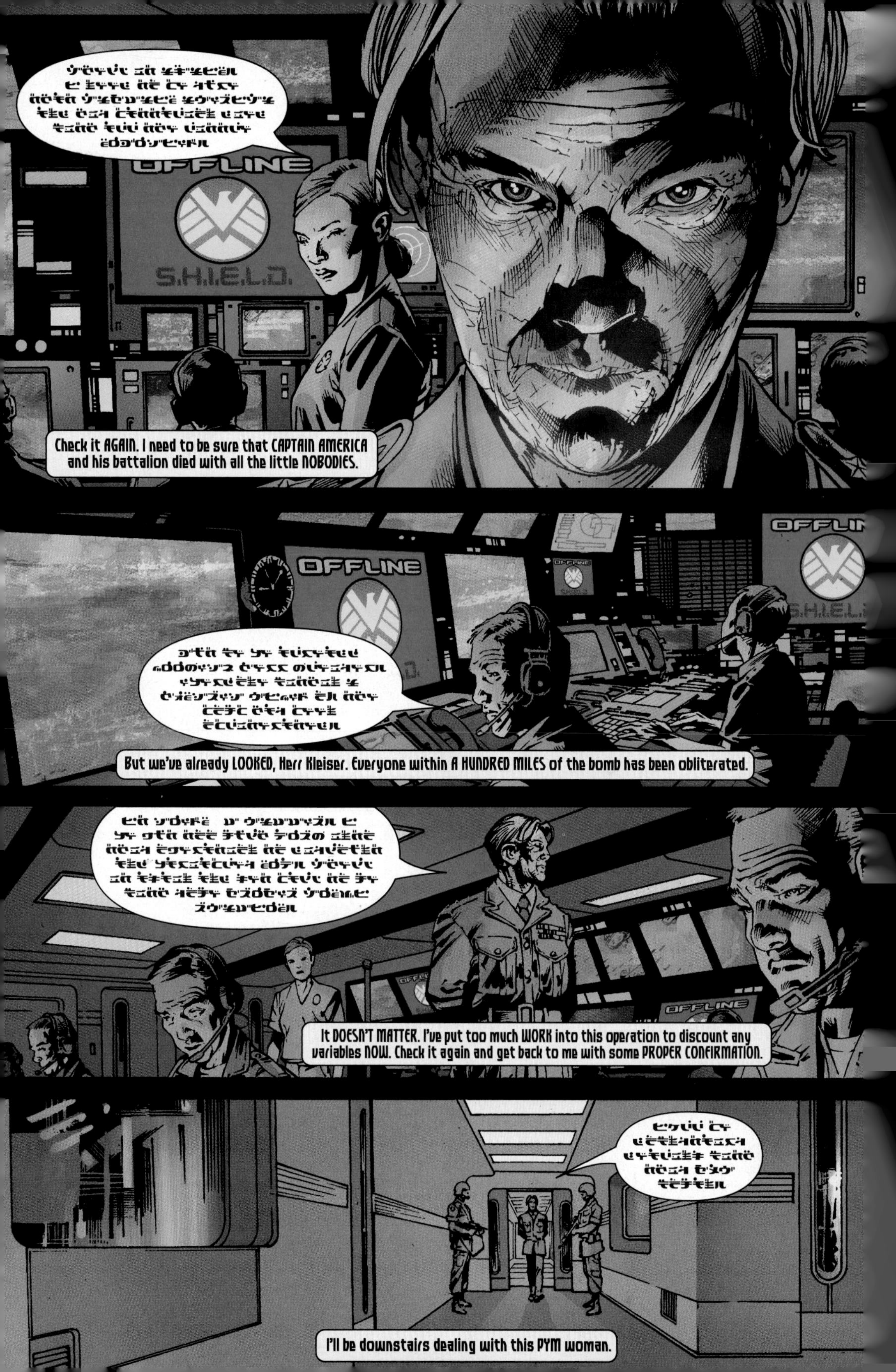
OFFLINE
S.H.I.E.L.D.
Check it AGAIN. I need to be sure that CAPTAIN AMERICA and his battalion died with all the little NOBODIES.
OFFLINE
OFFLINE
But we've already LOOKED, Herr Kleiser. Everyone within A HUNDRED MILES of the bomb has been obliterated.
It DOESN'T MATTER. I've put too much WORK into this operation to discount any variables NOW. Check it again and get back to me with some PROPER CONFIRMATION.
OFFLINE
I'll be downstairs dealing with this PYM woman.

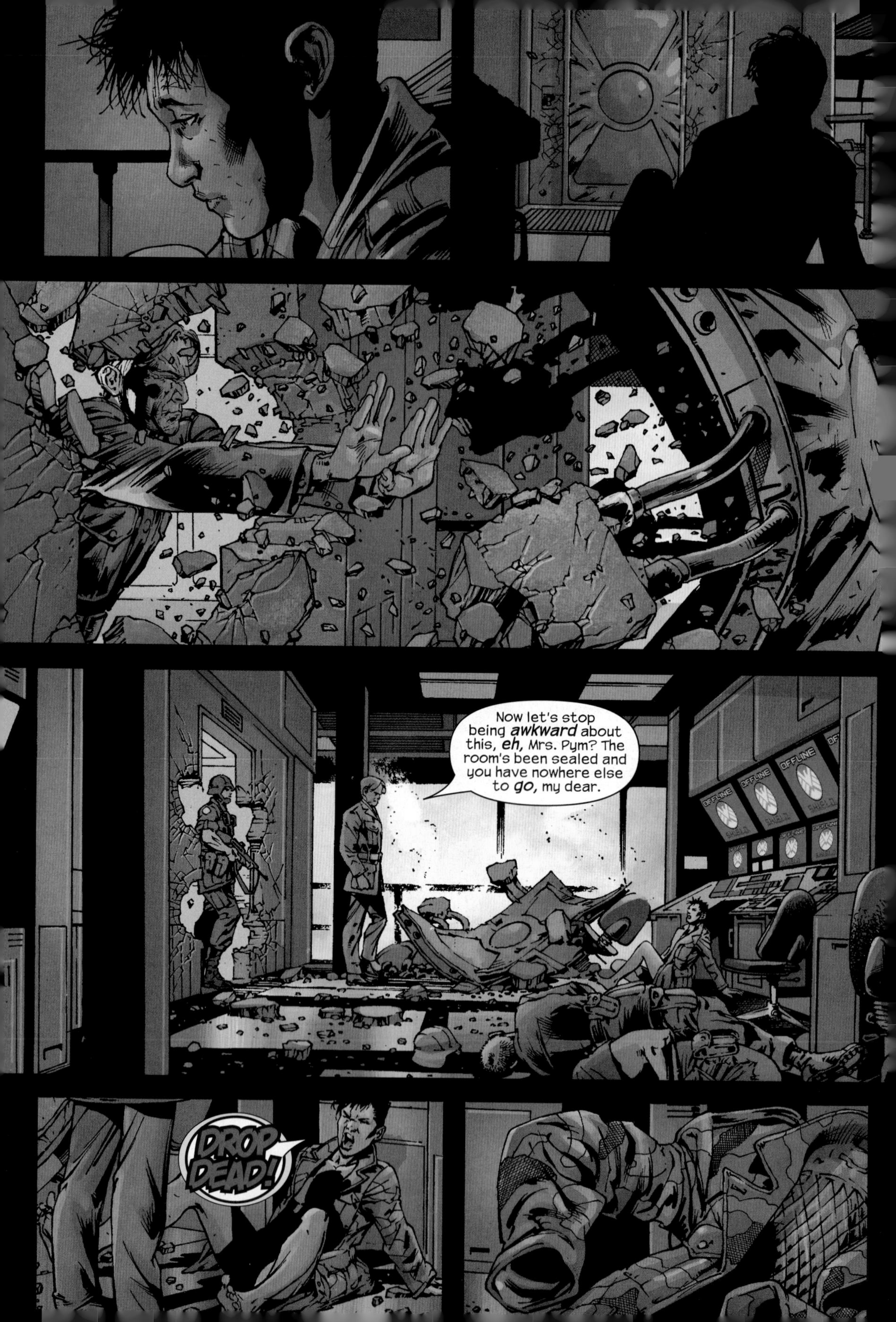
Now let's stop being awkward about this, eh, Mrs. Pym? The room's been sealed and you have nowhere else to go, my dear.
OFFLINE
SHIELD
DROP DEAD!

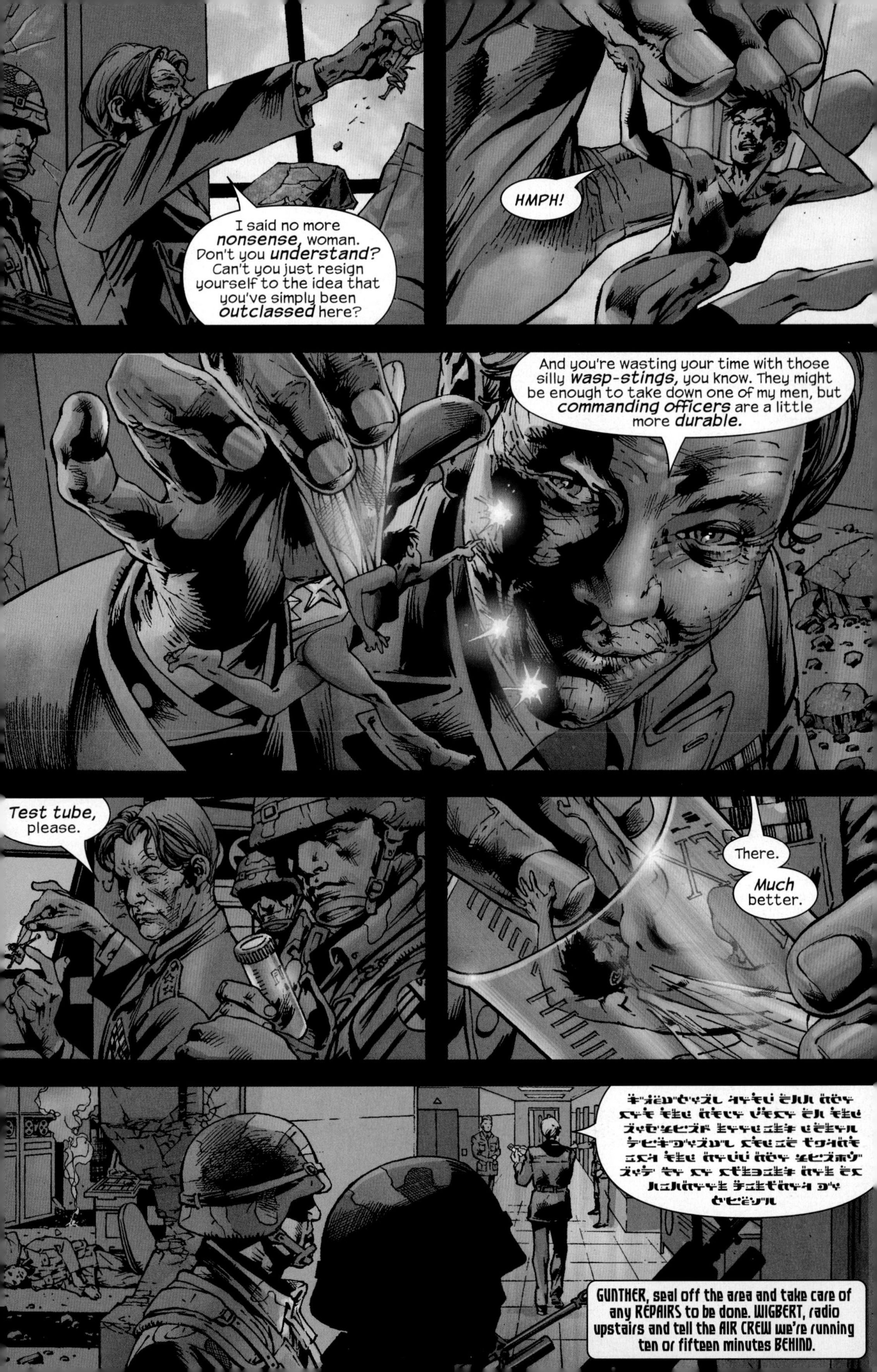
I said no more nonsense, woman. Don't you understand? Can't you just resign yourself to the idea that you've simply been outclassed here?
HMPH!
And you're wasting your time with those silly wasp-stings, you know. They might be enough to take down one of my men, but commanding officers are a little more durable.
Test tube, please.
There.
Much better.
GUNTHER, seal off the area and take care of any REPAIRS to be done. WIGBERT, radio upstairs and tell the AIR CREW we're running ten or fifteen minutes BEHIND.

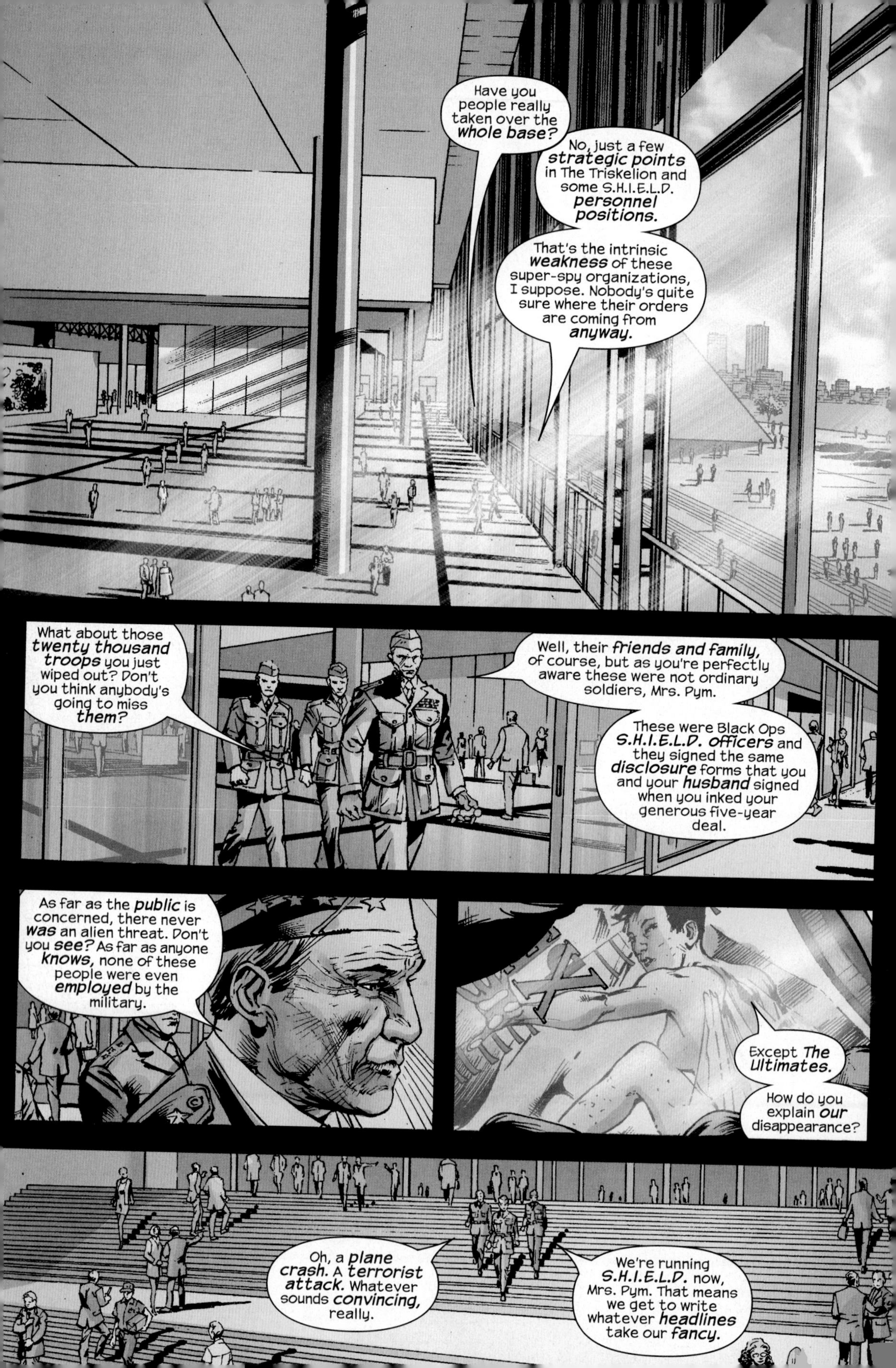
Have you people really taken over the whole base?
No, just a few strategic points in The Triskelion and some S.H.I.E.L.D. personnel positions.
That's the intrinsic weakness of these super-spy organizations, I suppose. Nobody's quite sure where their orders are coming from anyway.
What about those twenty thousand troops you just wiped out? Don't you think anybody's going to miss them?
Well, their friends and family, of course, but as you're perfectly aware these were not ordinary soldiers, Mrs. Pym.
These were Black Ops S.H.I.E.L.D. officers and they signed the same disclosure forms that you and your husband signed when you inked your generous five-year deal.
As far as the public is concerned, there never was an alien threat. Don't you see? As far as anyone knows, none of these people were even employed by the military.
Except The Ultimates.
How do you explain our disappearance?
Oh, a plane crash. A terrorist attack. Whatever sounds convincing, really.
We're running S.H.I.E.L.D. now, Mrs. Pym. That means we get to write whatever headlines take our fancy.

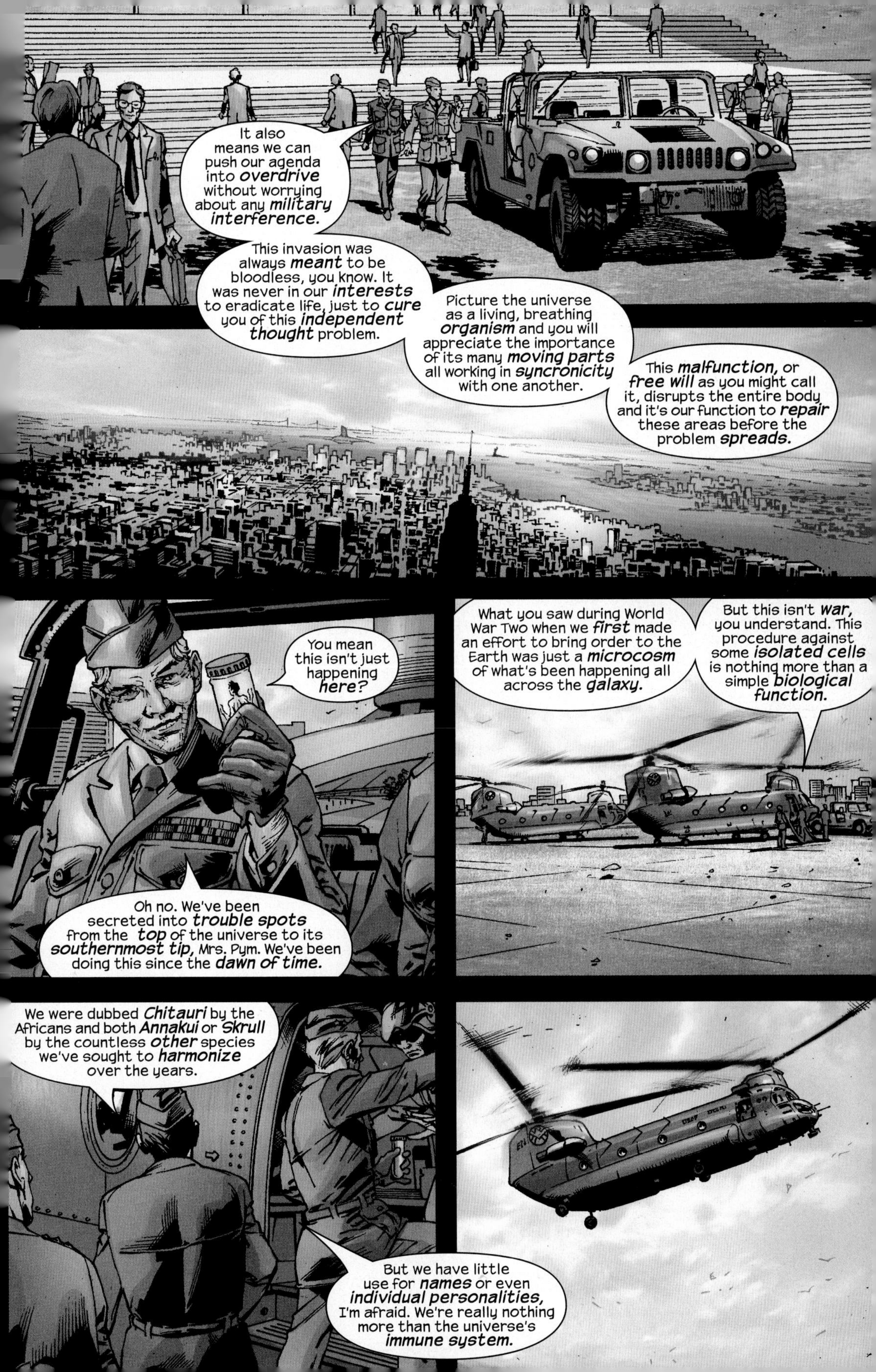
It also means we can push our agenda into overdrive without worrying about any military interference.
This invasion was always meant to be bloodless, you know. It was never in our interests to eradicate life, just to cure you of this independent thought problem.
Picture the universe as a living, breathing organism and you will appreciate the importance of its many moving parts all working in syncronicity with one another.
This malfunction, or free will as you might call it, disrupts the entire body and it's our function to repair these areas before the problem spreads.
You mean this isn't just happening here?
Oh no. We've been secreted into trouble spots from the top of the universe to its southernmost tip, Mrs. Pym. We've been doing this since the dawn of time.
What you saw during World War Two when we first made an effort to bring order to the Earth was just a microcosm of what's been happening all across the galaxy.
But this isn't war, you understand. This procedure against some isolated cells is nothing more than a simple biological function.
We were dubbed Chitauri by the Africans and both Annakui or Skrull by the countless other species we've sought to harmonize over the years.
But we have little use for names or even individual personalities, I'm afraid. We're really nothing more than the universe's immune system.

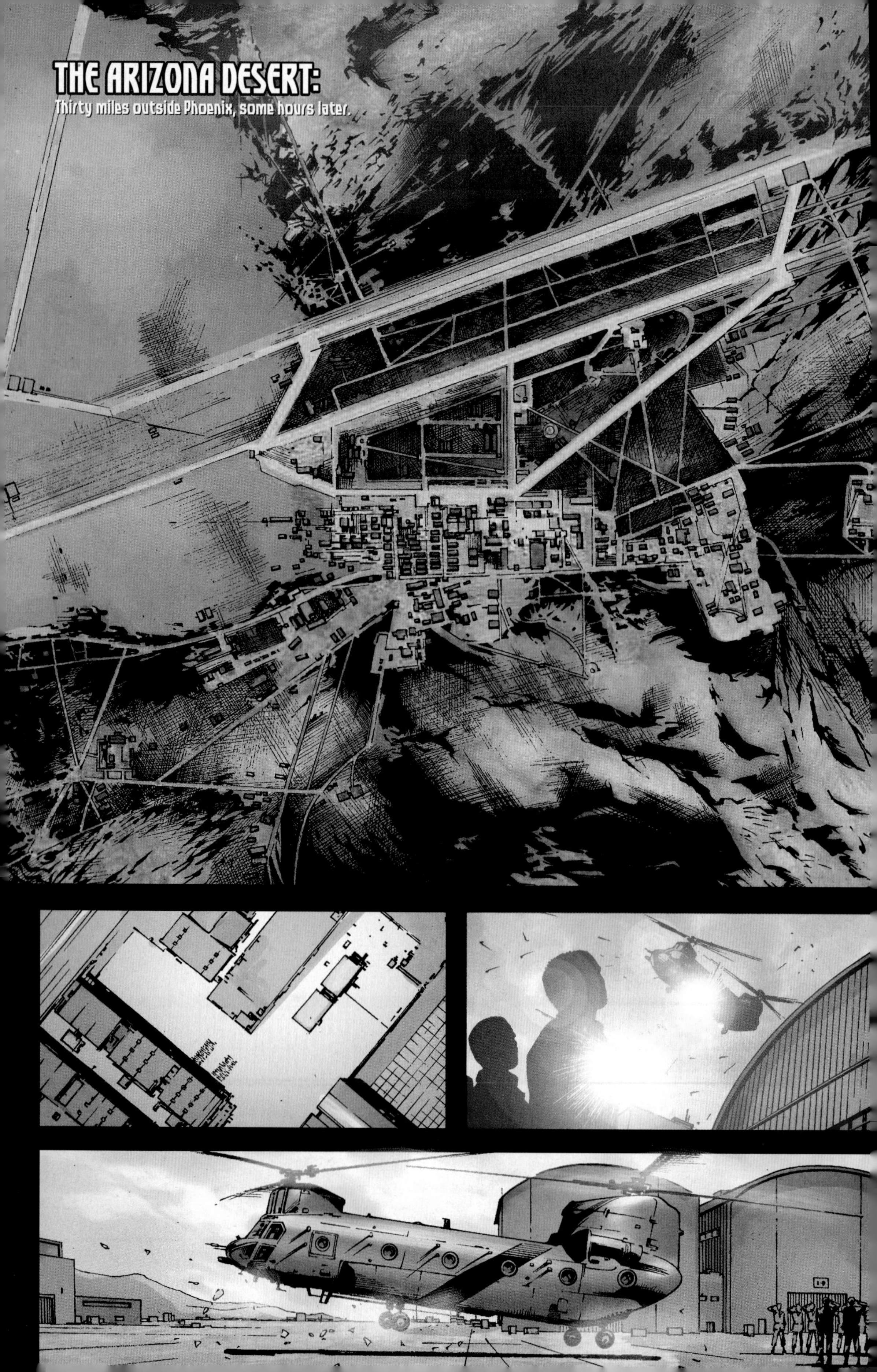
THE ARIZONA DESERT:
Thirty miles outside Phoenix, some hours later.

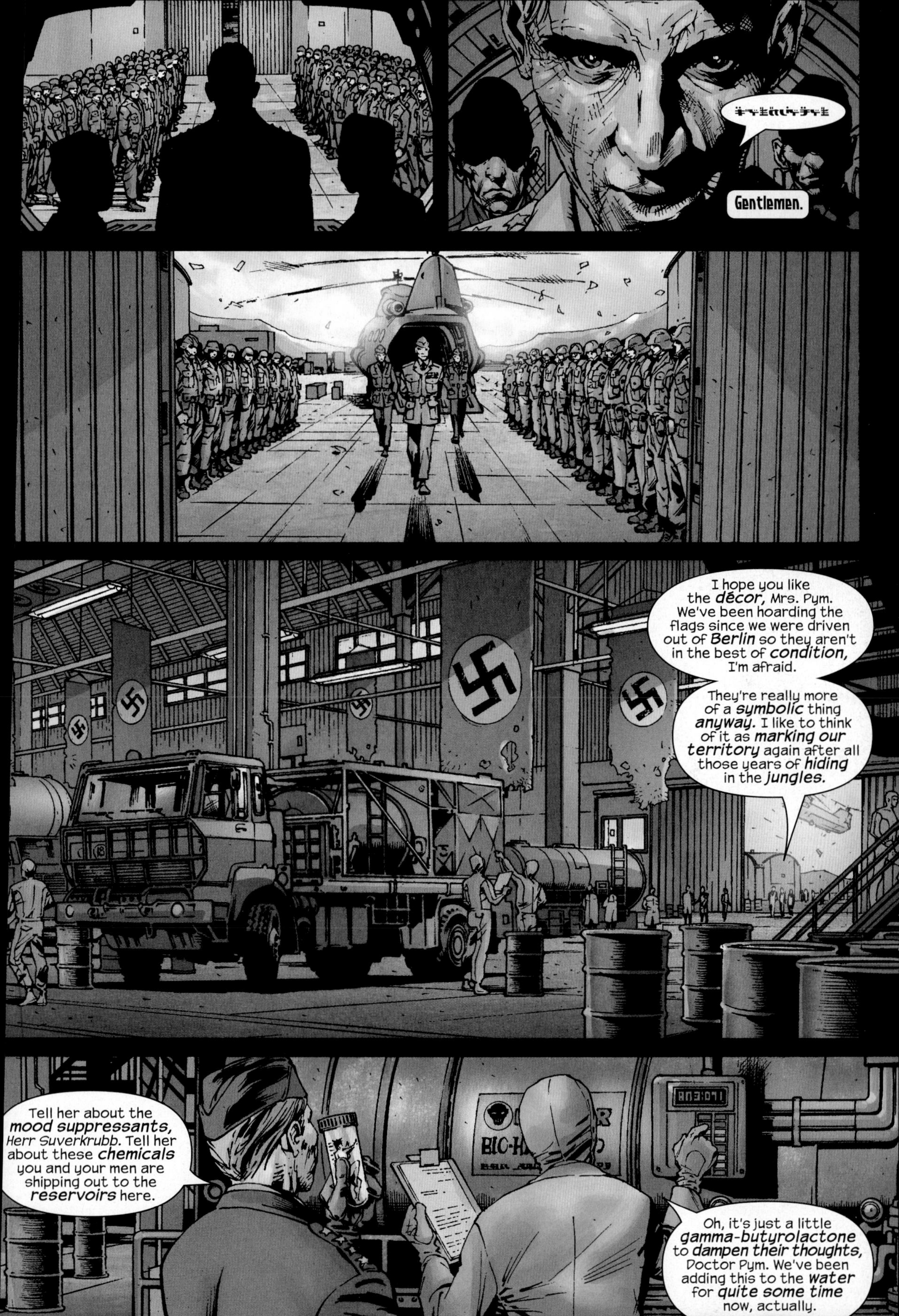
Gentlemen.
I hope you like the décor, Mrs. Pym. We've been hoarding the flags since we were driven out of Berlin so they aren't in the best of condition, I'm afraid.
They're really more of a symbolic thing anyway. I like to think of it as marking our territory again after all those years of hiding in the jungles.
Tell her about the mood suppressants, Herr Suverkrubb. Tell her about these chemicals you and your men are shipping out to the reservoirs here.
Oh, it's just a little gamma-butyrolactone to dampen their thoughts, Doctor Pym. We've been adding this to the water for quite some time now, actually.

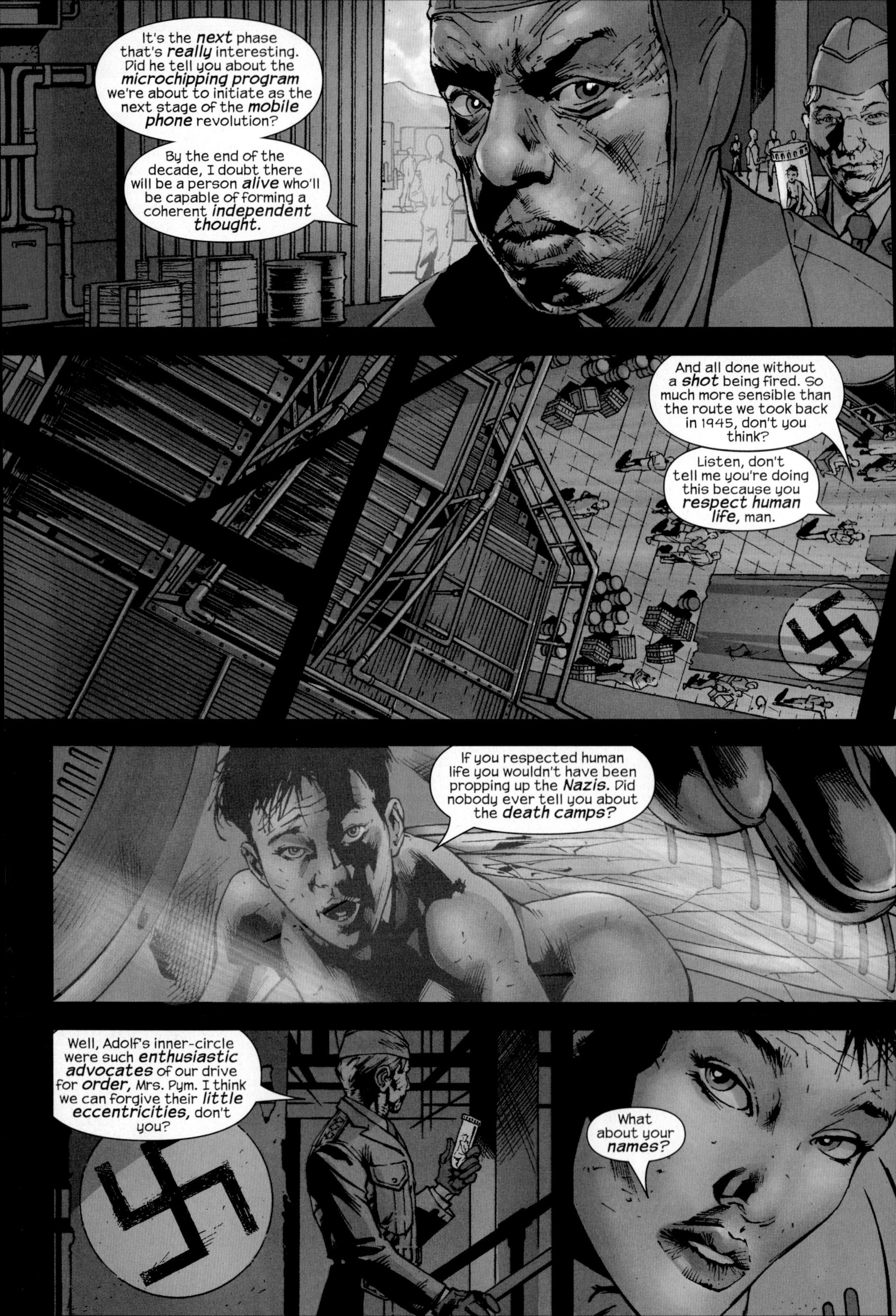

It's the next phase that's really interesting. Did he tell you about the microchipping program we're about to initiate as the next stage of the mobile phone revolution?
By the end of the decade, I doubt there will be a person alive who'll be capable of forming a coherent independent thought.
And all done without a shot being fired. So much more sensible than the route we took back in 1945, don't you think?
Listen, don't tell me you're doing this because you respect human life, man.
If you respected human life you wouldn't have been propping up the Nazis. Did nobody ever tell you about the death camps?
Well, Adolf's inner-circle were such enthusiastic advocates of our drive for order, Mrs. Pym. I think we can forgive their little eccentricities, don't you?
What about your names?

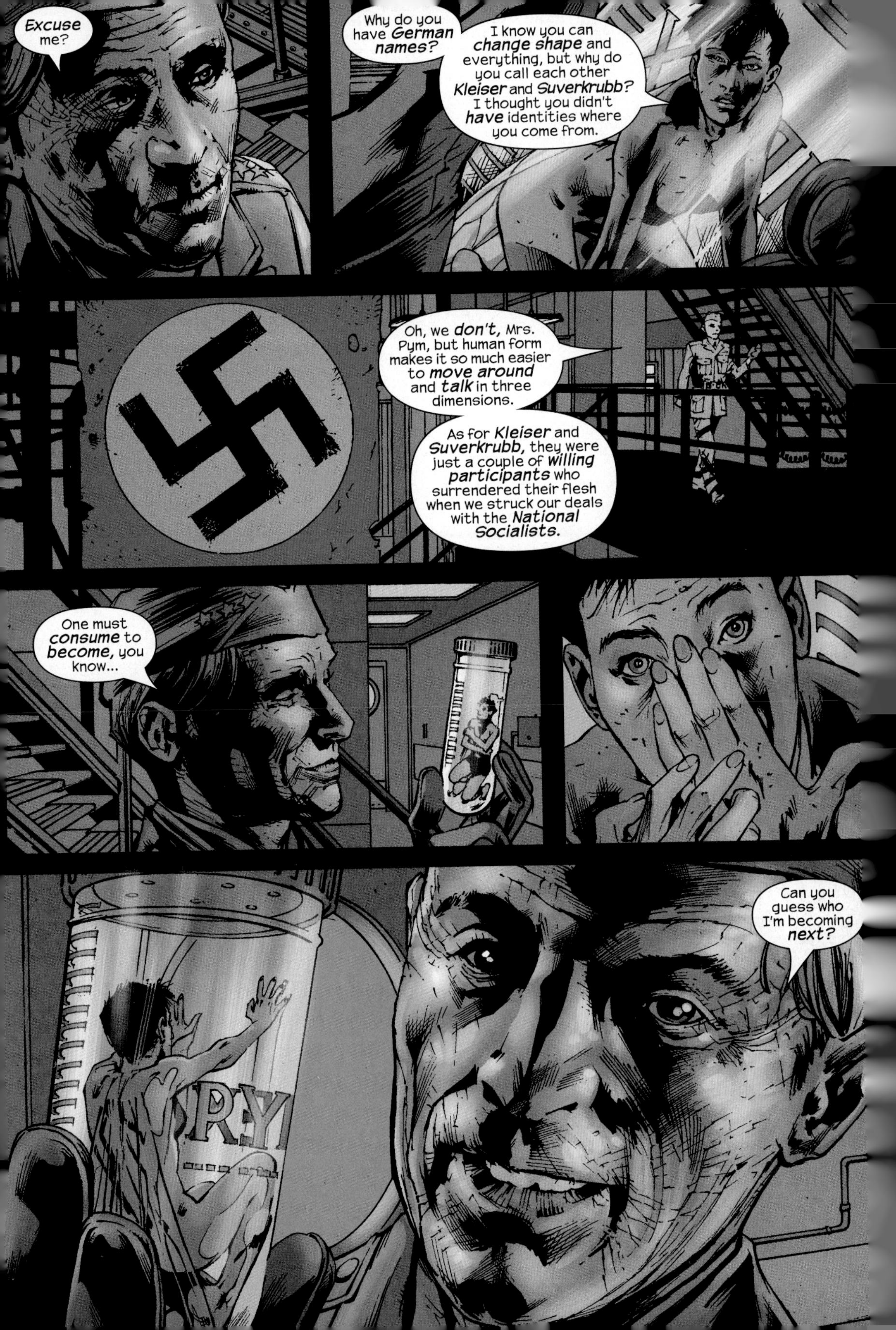
Excuse me?
Why do you have German names?
I know you can change shape and everything, but why do you call each other Kleiser and Suverkrubb? I thought you didn't have identities where you come from.
Oh, we don't, Mrs. Pym, but human form makes it so much easier to move around and talk in three dimensions.
As for Kleiser and Suverkrubb, they were just a couple of willing participants who surrendered their flesh when we struck our deals with the National Socialists.
One must consume to become, you know...
Can you guess who I'm becoming next?

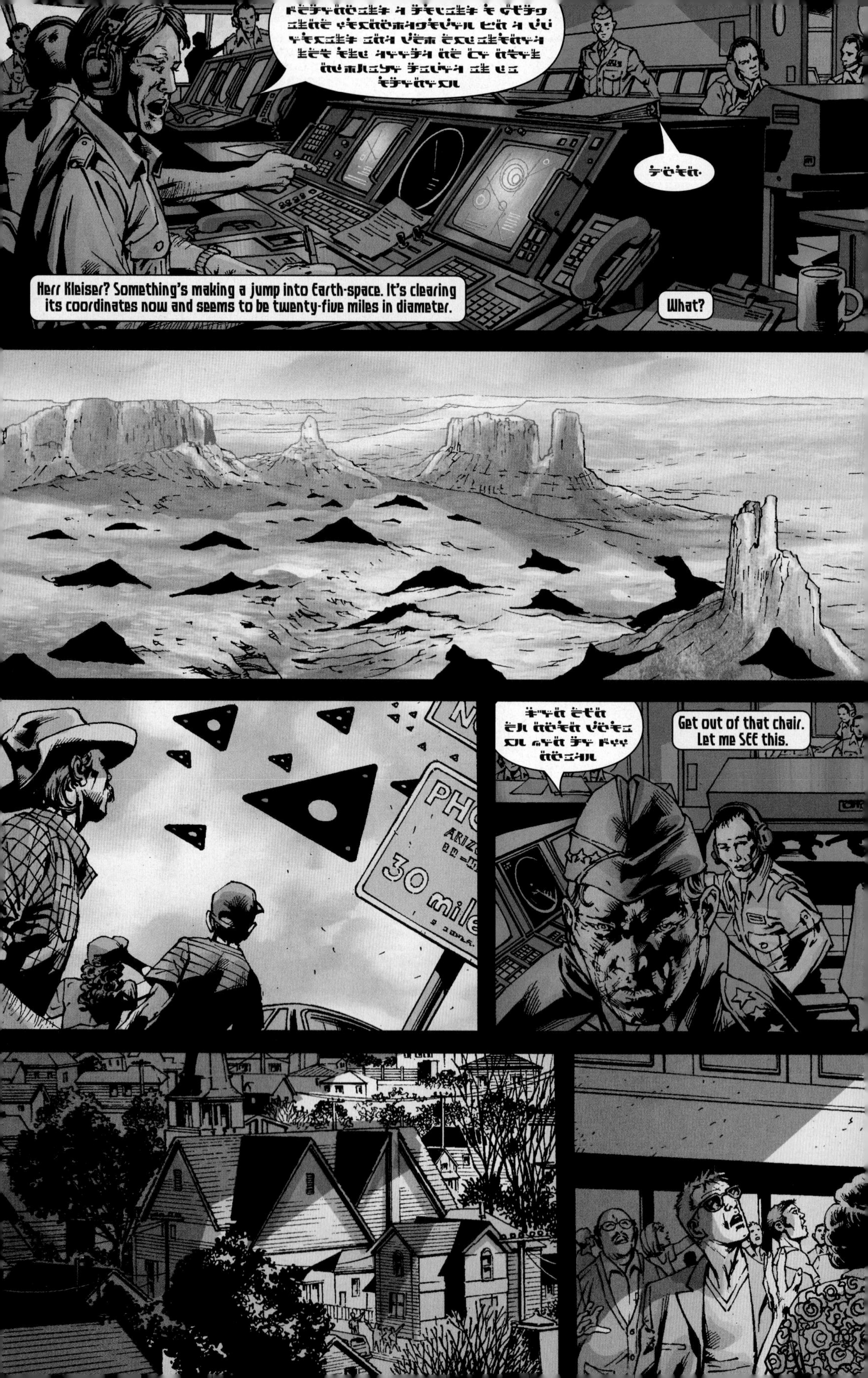
Herr Kleiser? Something's making a jump into Earth-space. It's clearing its coordinates now and seems to be twenty-five miles in diameter.
What?
Get out of that chair. Let me SEE this.

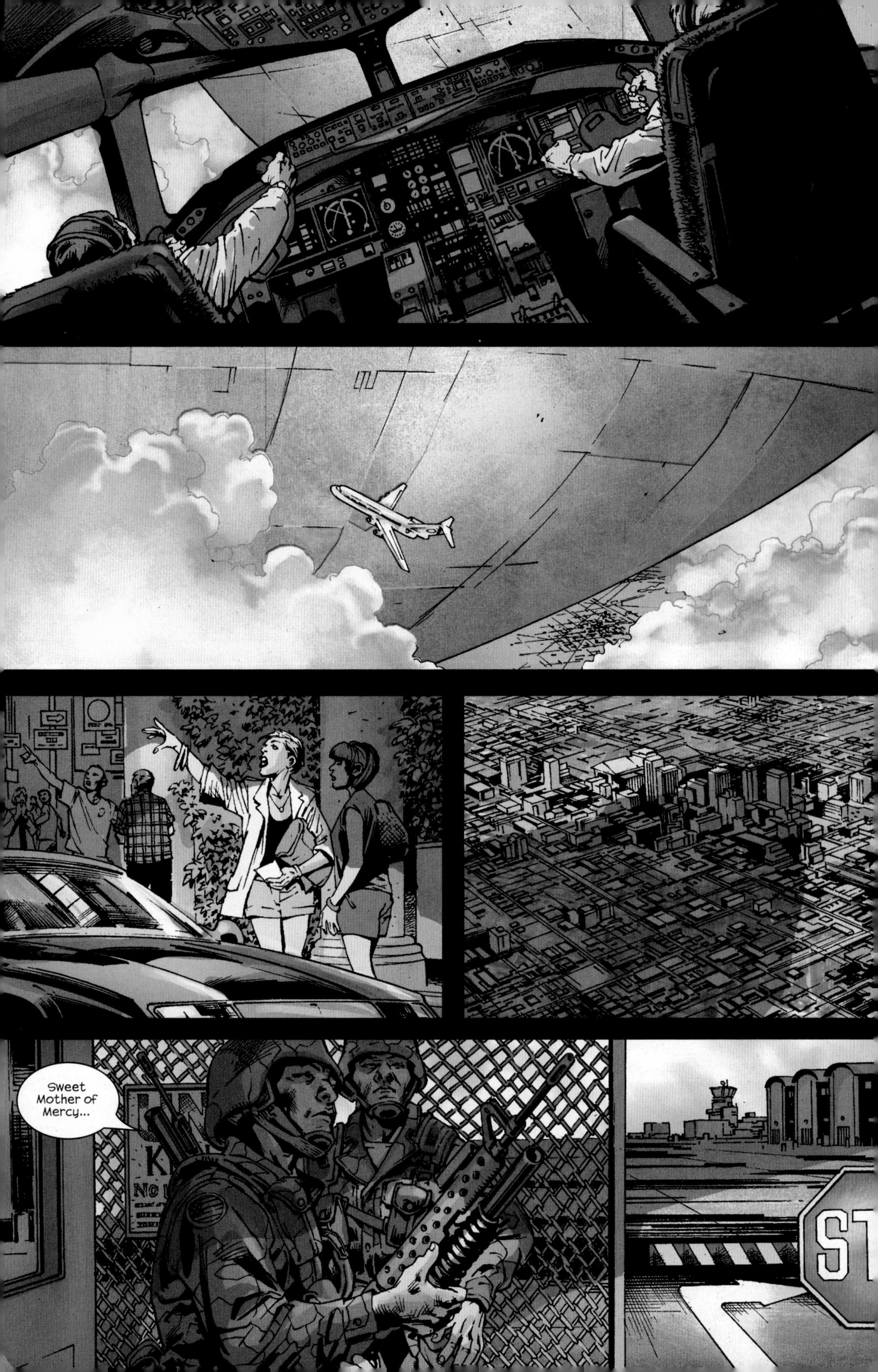
Sweet Mother of Mercy...

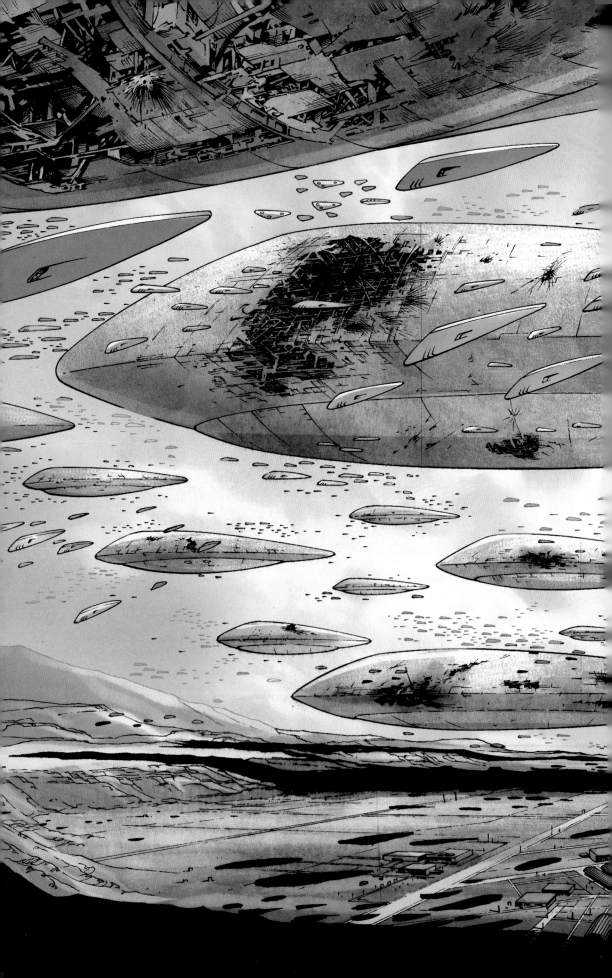

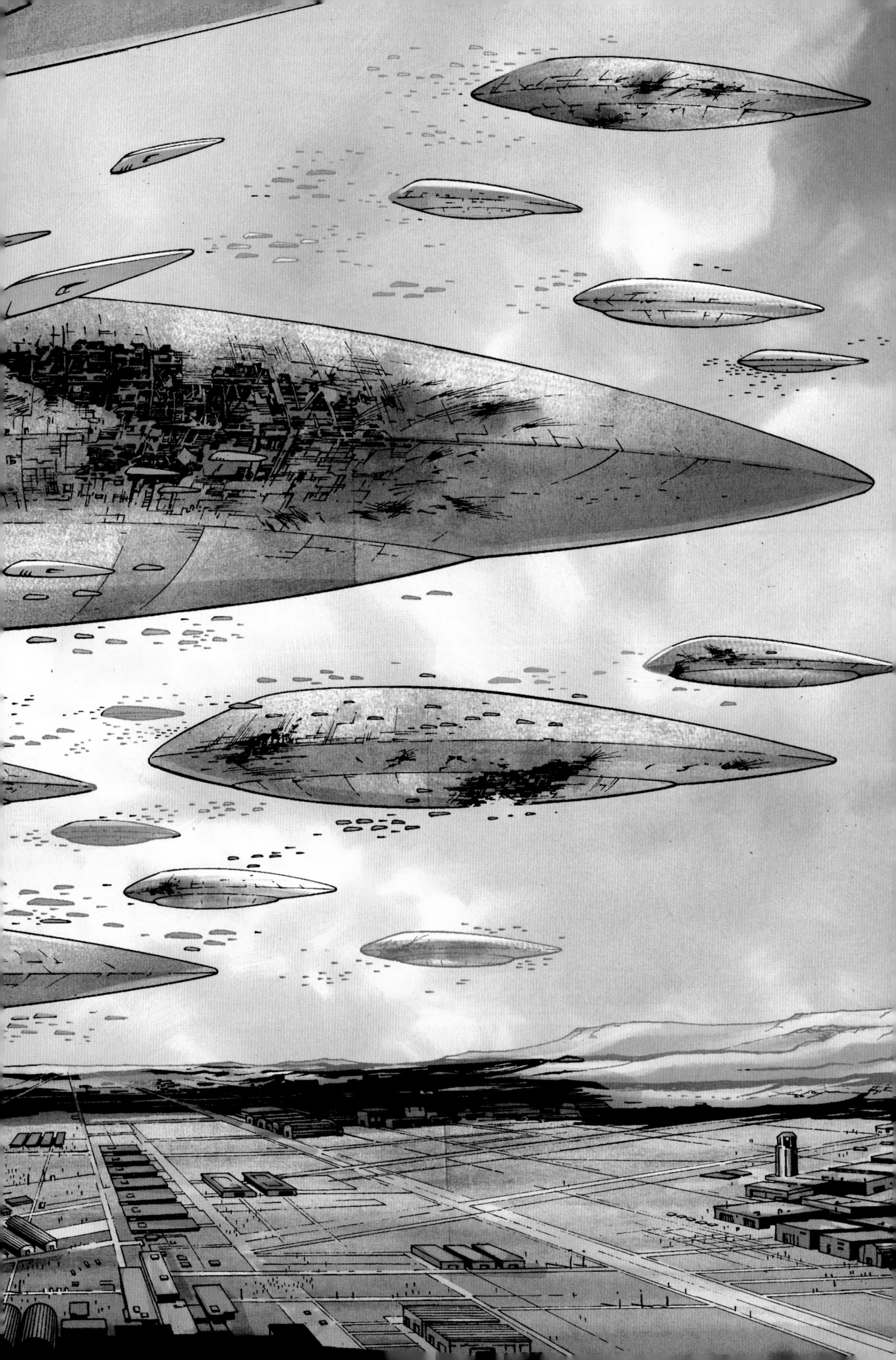

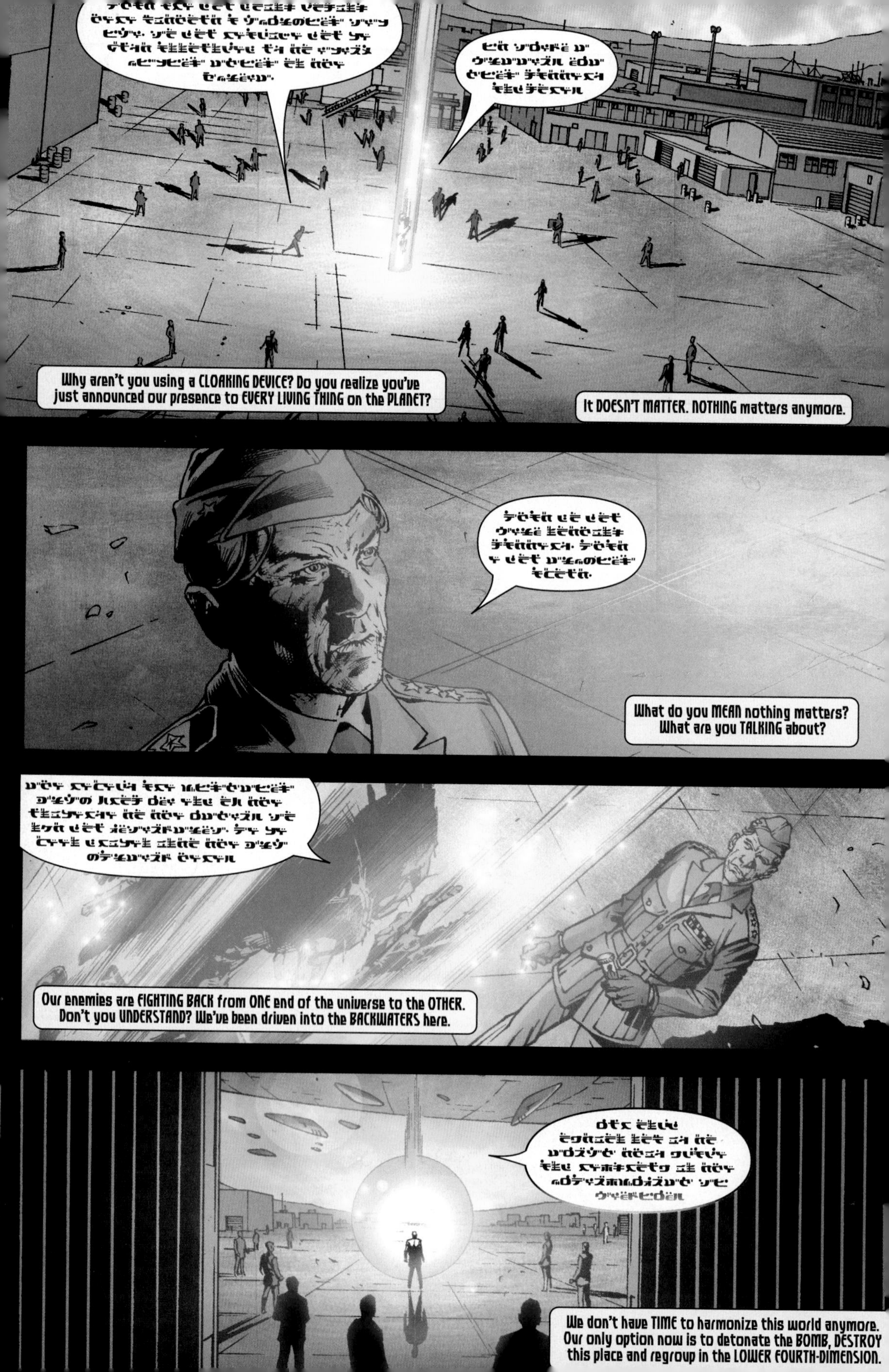
Why aren't you using a CLOAKING DEVICE? Do you realize you've just announced our presence to EVERY LIVING THING on the PLANET?
It DOESN'T MATTER. NOTHING matters anymore.
What do you MEAN nothing matters? What are you TALKING about?
Our enemies are FIGHTING BACK from ONE end of the universe to the OTHER. Don't you UNDERSTAND? We've been driven into the BACKWATERS here.
We don't have TIME to harmonize this world anymore. Our only option now is to detonate the BOMB, DESTROY this place and regroup in the LOWER FOURTH-DIMENSION.

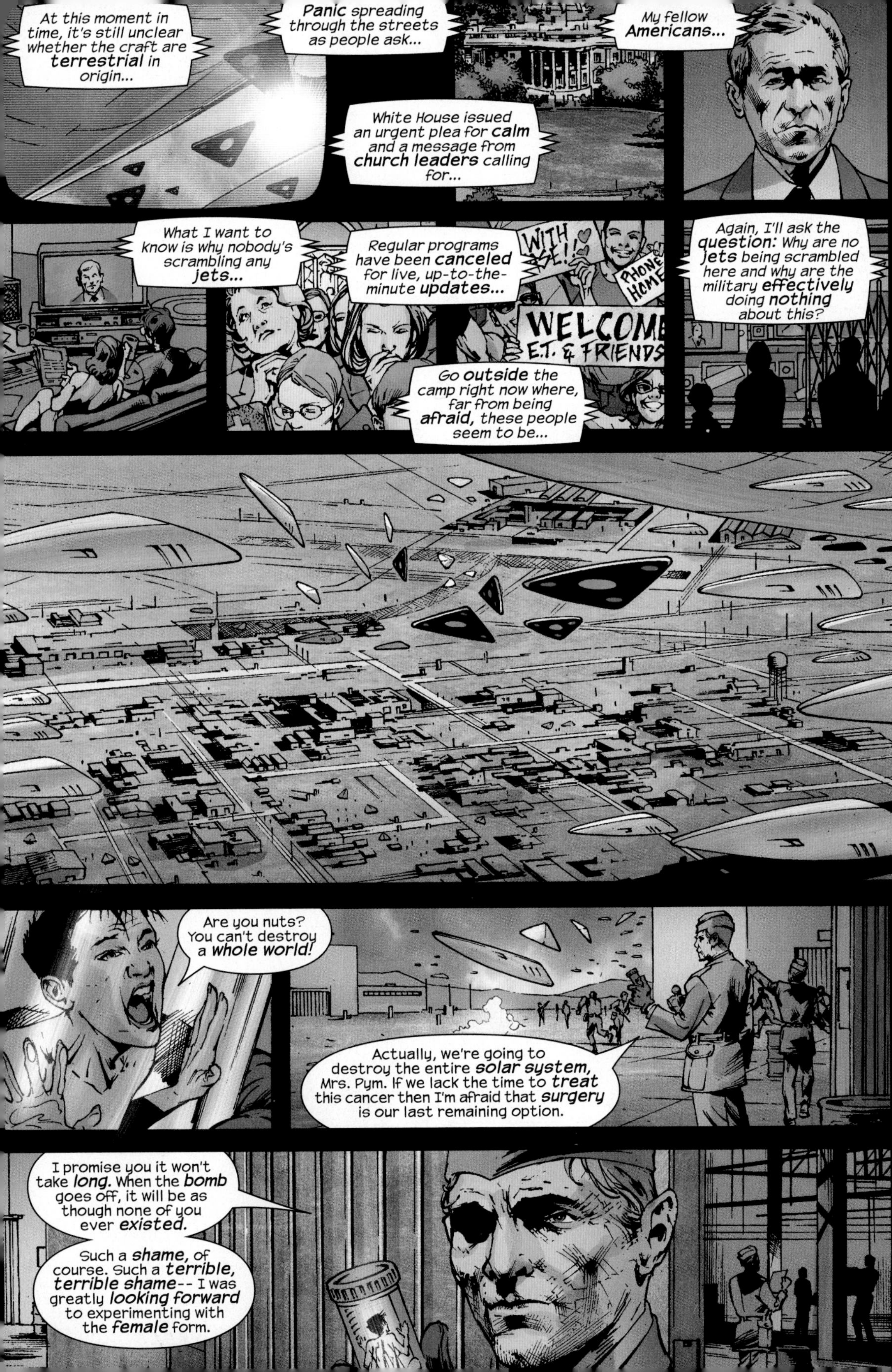

At this moment in time, it's still unclear whether the craft are terrestrial in origin...
Panic spreading through the streets as people ask...
White House issued an urgent plea for calm and a message from church leaders calling for...
My fellow Americans...
What I want to know is why nobody's scrambling any jets...
Regular programs have been canceled for live, up-to-the-minute updates...
PHONE HOME
WELCOME
E.T. & FRIENDS
Go outside the camp right now where, far from being afraid, these people seem to be...
Again, I'll ask the question: Why are no jets being scrambled here and why are the military effectively doing nothing about this?
Are you nuts? You can't destroy a whole world!
Actually, we're going to destroy the entire solar system, Mrs. Pym. If we lack the time to treat this cancer then I'm afraid that surgery is our last remaining option.
I promise you it won't take long. When the bomb goes off, it will be as though none of you ever existed.
Such a shame, of course. Such a terrible, terrible shame-- I was greatly looking forward to experimenting with the female form.

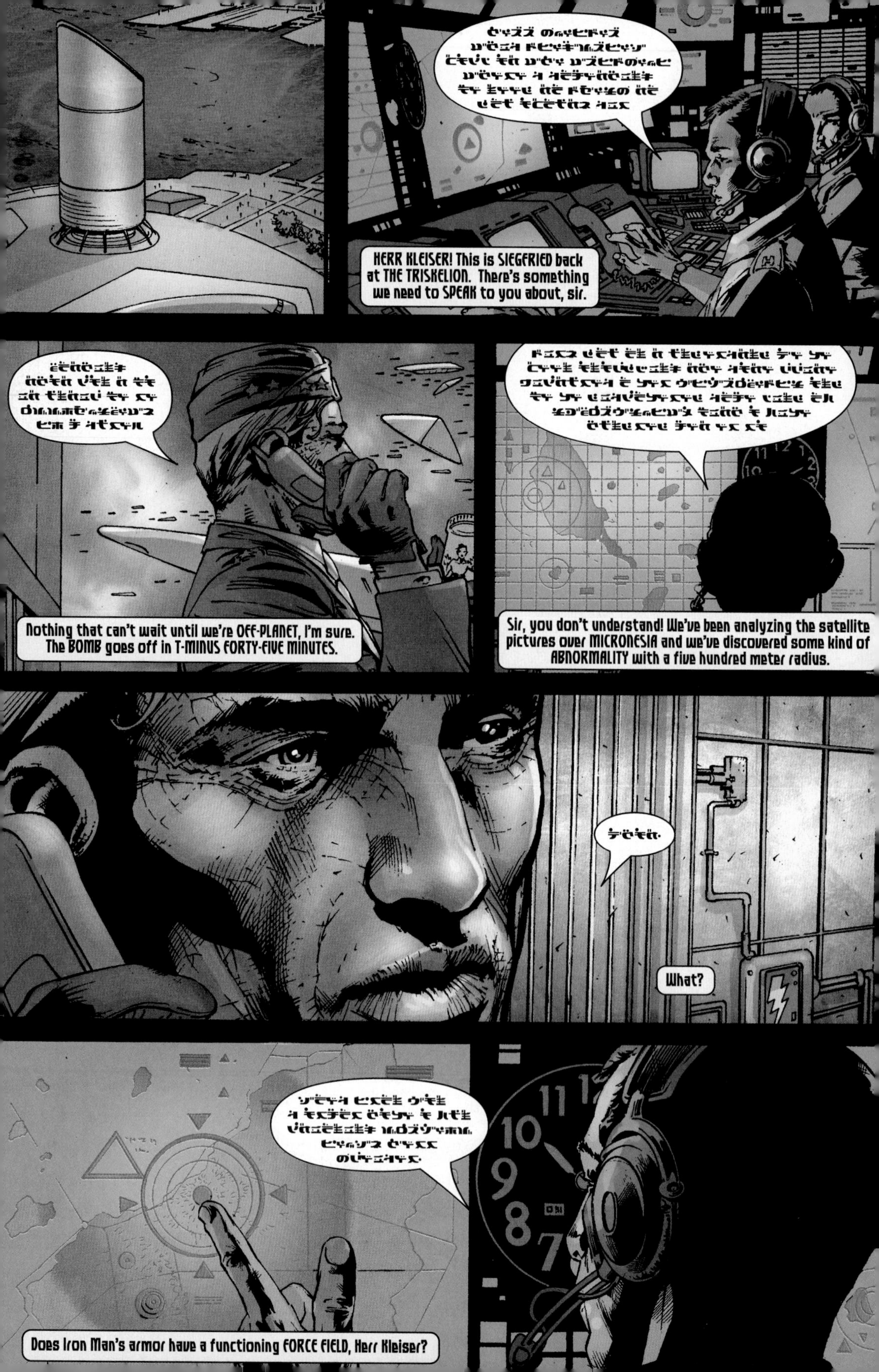
HERR KLEISER! This is SIEGFRIED back at THE TRISKELION. There's something we need to SPEAK to you about, sir.
Nothing that can't wait until we're OFF-PLANET, I'm sure. The BOMB goes off in T-MINUS FORTY-FIVE MINUTES.
Sir, you don't understand! We've been analyzing the satellite pictures over MICRONESIA and we've discovered some kind of ABNORMALITY with a five hundred meter radius.
What?
Does Iron Man's armor have a functioning FORCE FIELD, Herr Kleiser?

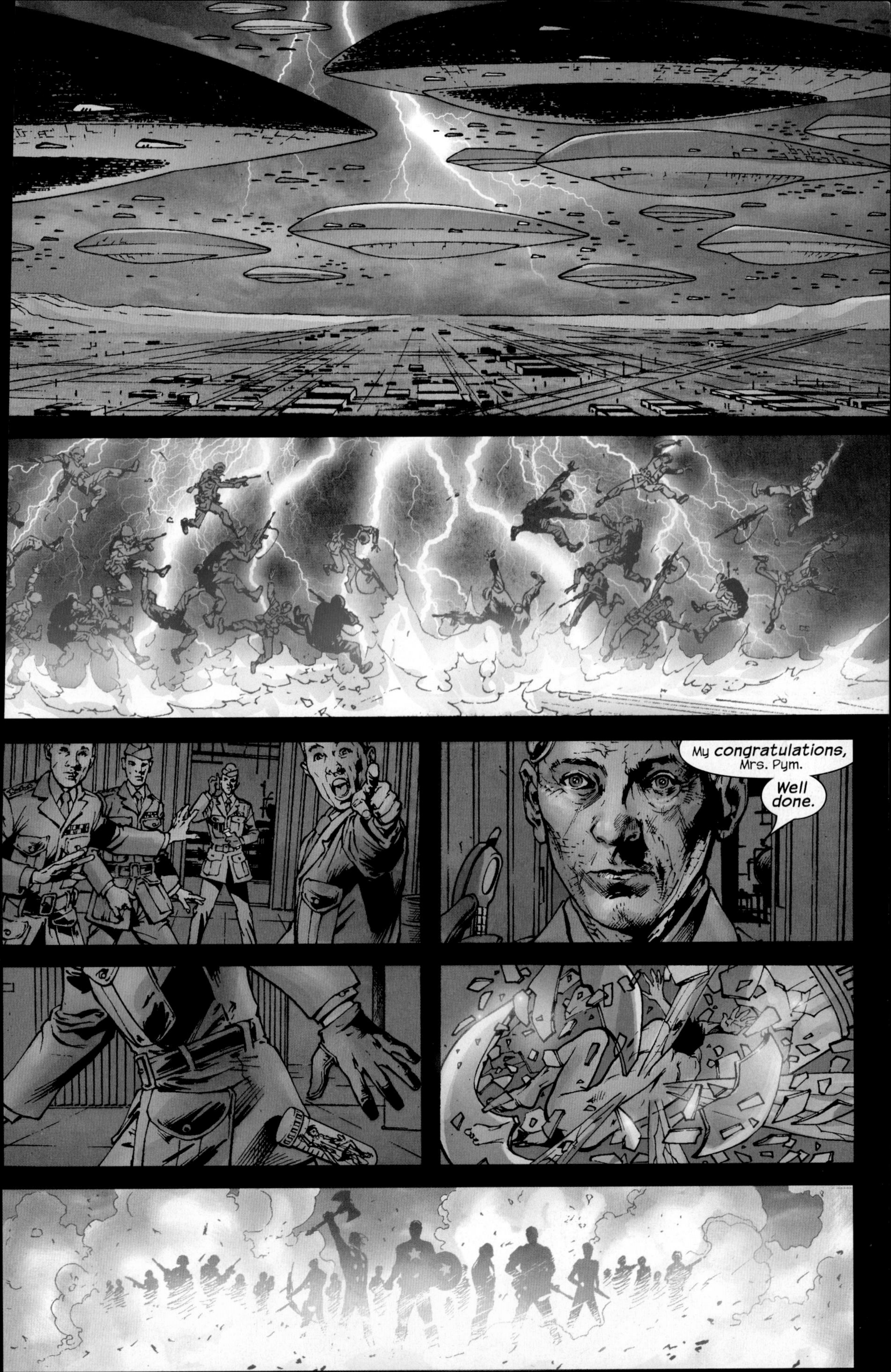
My congratulations, Mrs. Pym.
Well done.

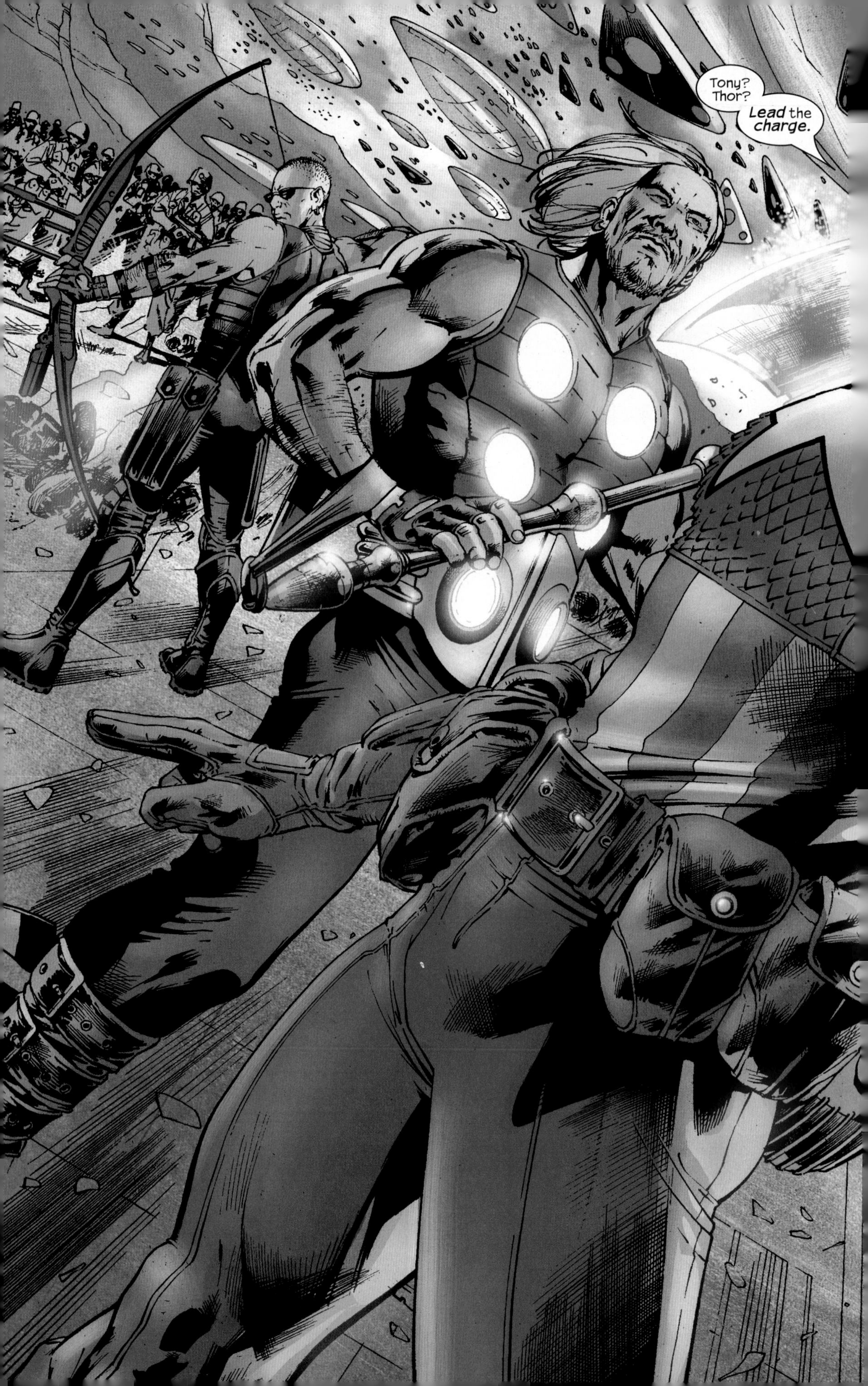
Tony? Thor? *Lead* the *charge.*

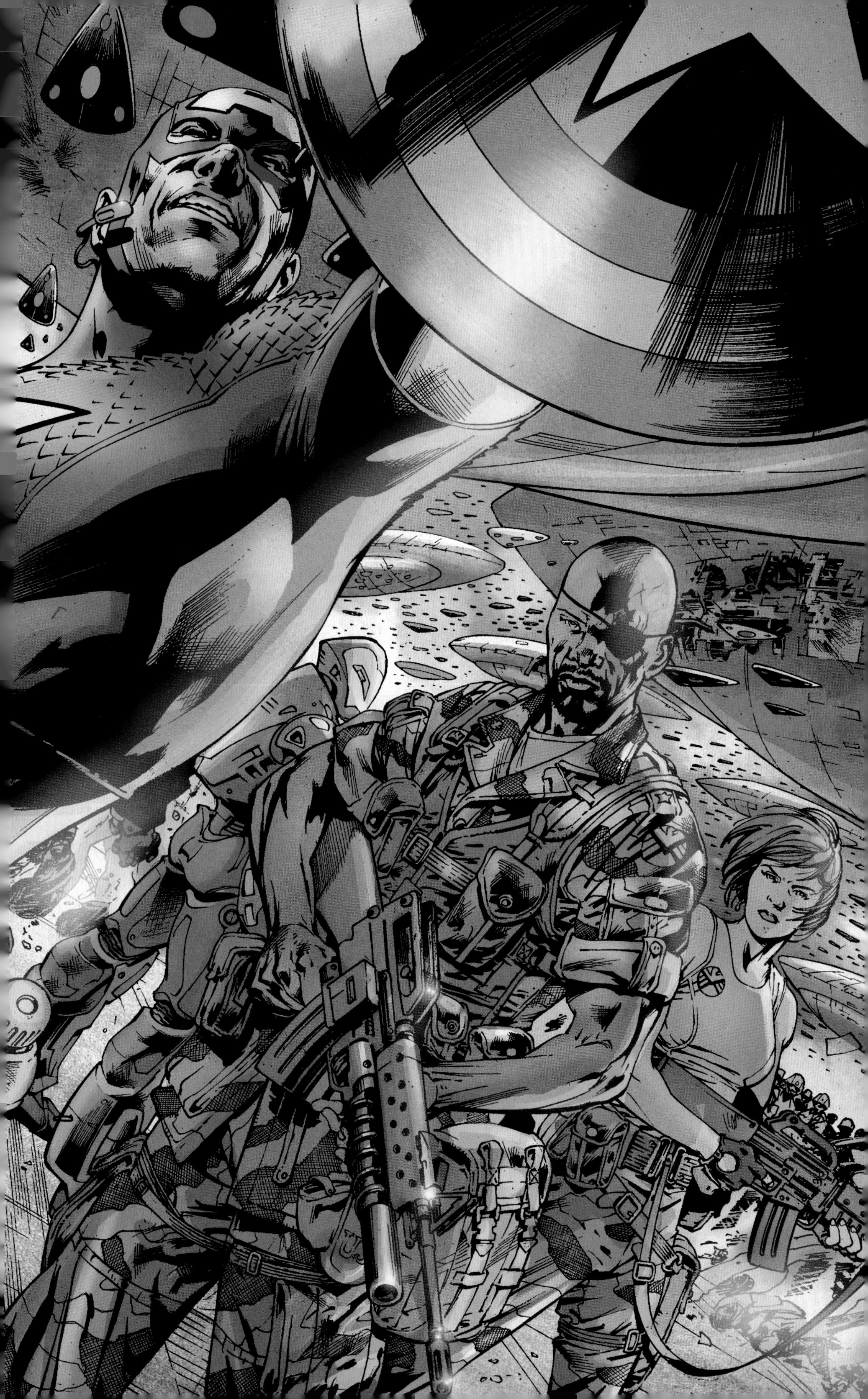

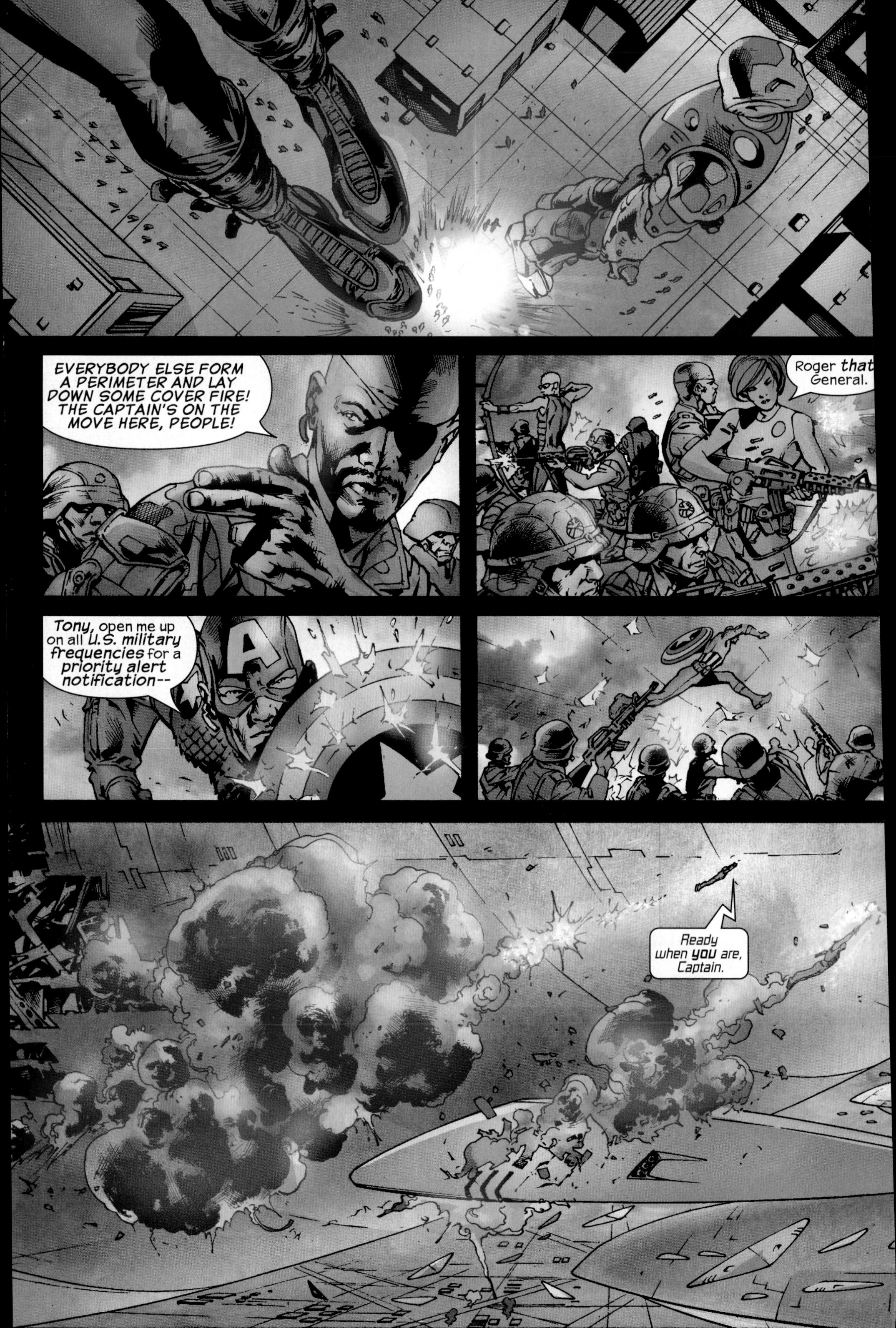
EVERYBODY ELSE FORM A PERIMETER AND LAY DOWN SOME COVER FIRE! THE CAPTAIN'S ON THE MOVE HERE, PEOPLE!
Roger that General.
Tony, open me up on all U.S. military frequencies for a priority alert notification--
Ready when you are, Captain.

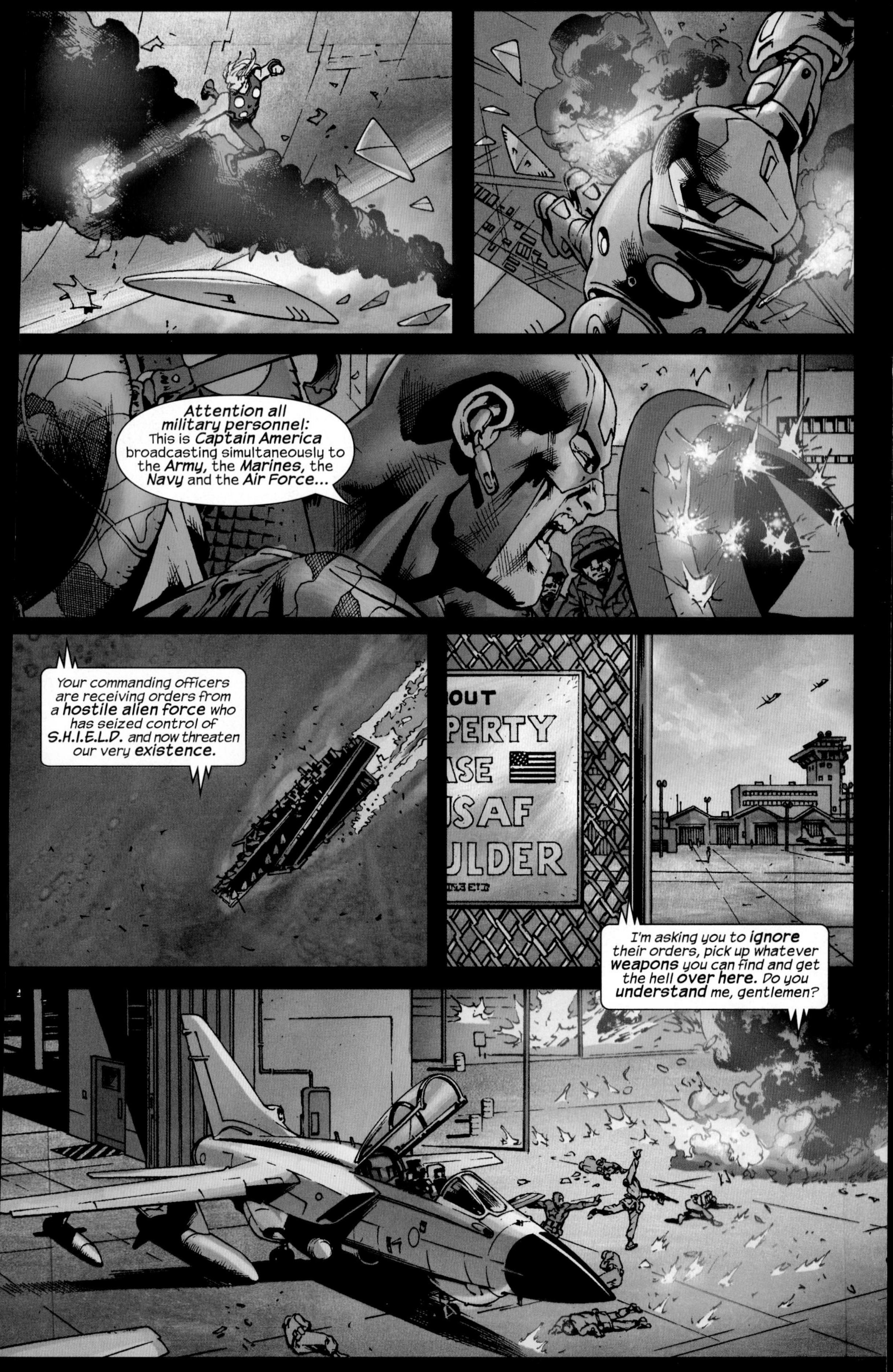
Attention all military personnel: This is Captain America broadcasting simultaneously to the Army, the Marines, the Navy and the Air Force...
Your commanding officers are receiving orders from a hostile alien force who has seized control of S.H.I.E.L.D. and now threaten our very existence.
OUT
PERTY
ASE
USAF
ULDER
I'm asking you to ignore their orders, pick up whatever weapons you can find and get the hell over here. Do you understand me, gentlemen?

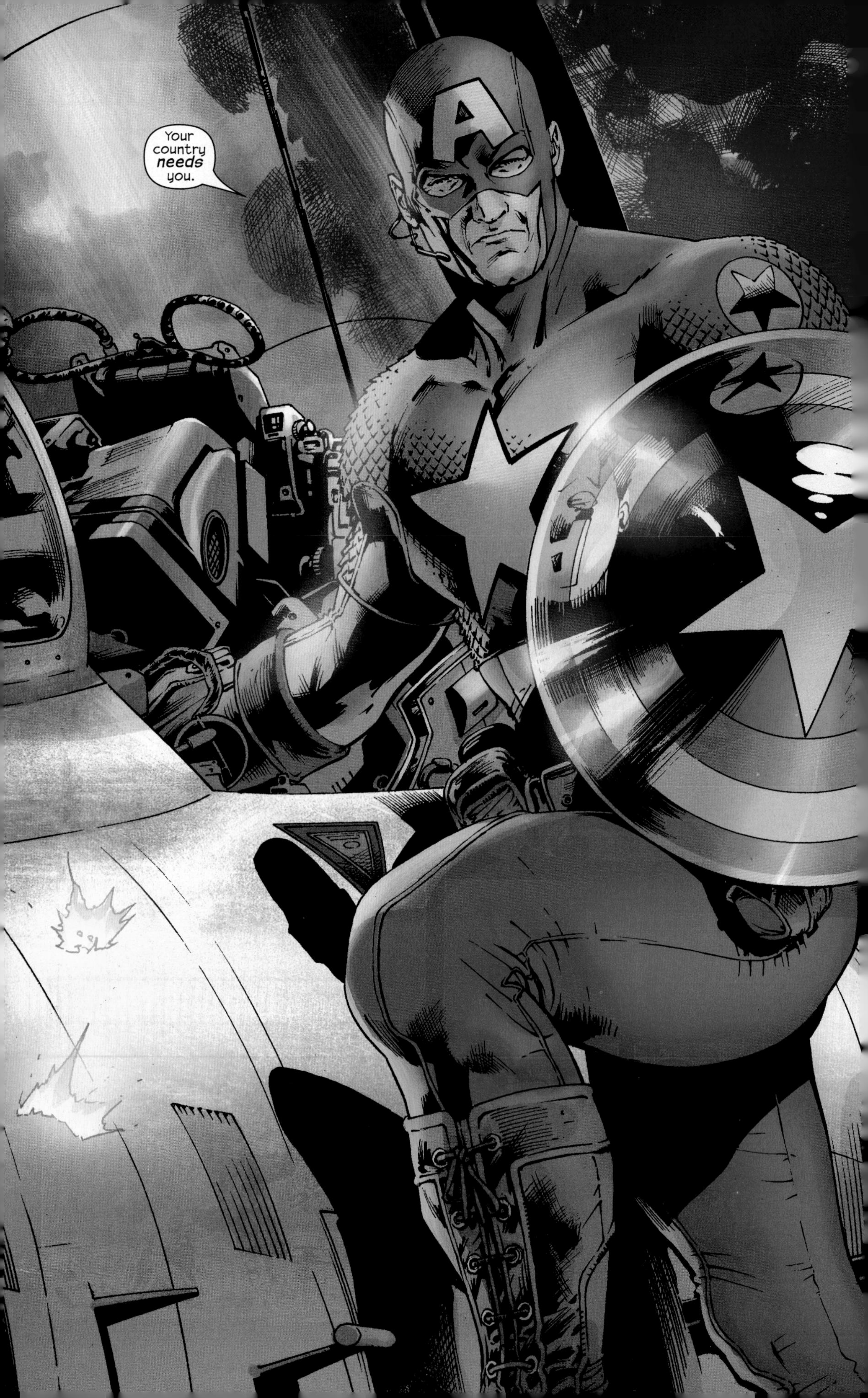
Your country **needs** you.

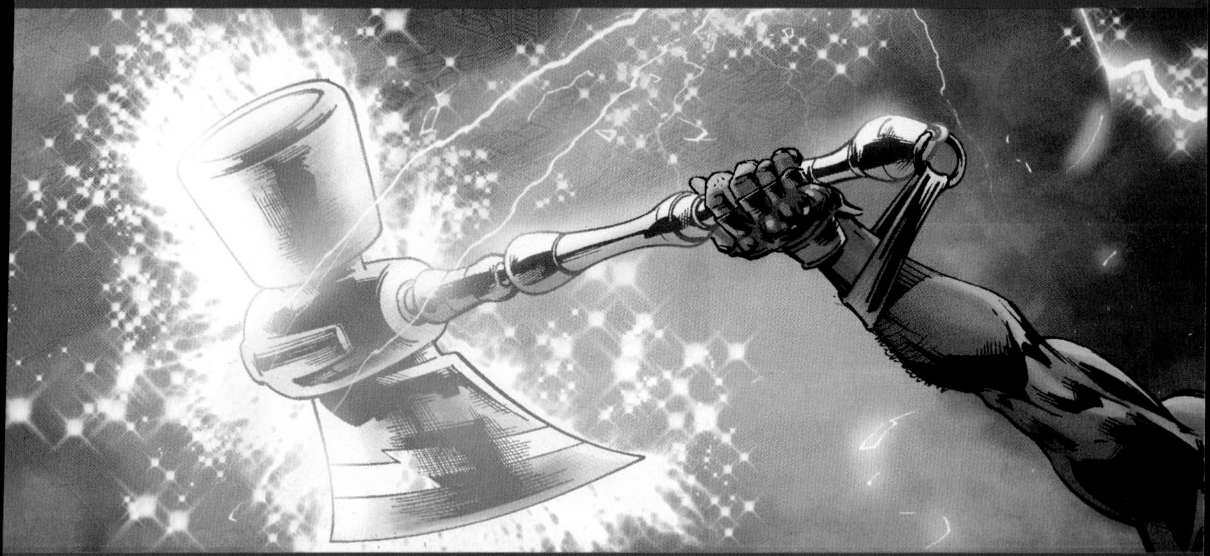

CHAPTER TWELVE

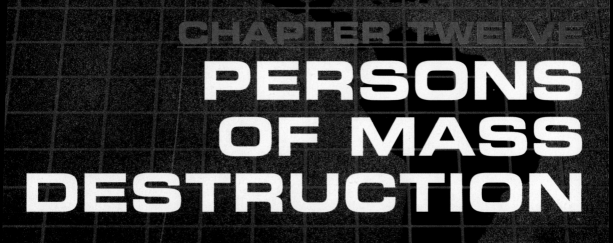

PERSONS OF MASS DESTRUCTION

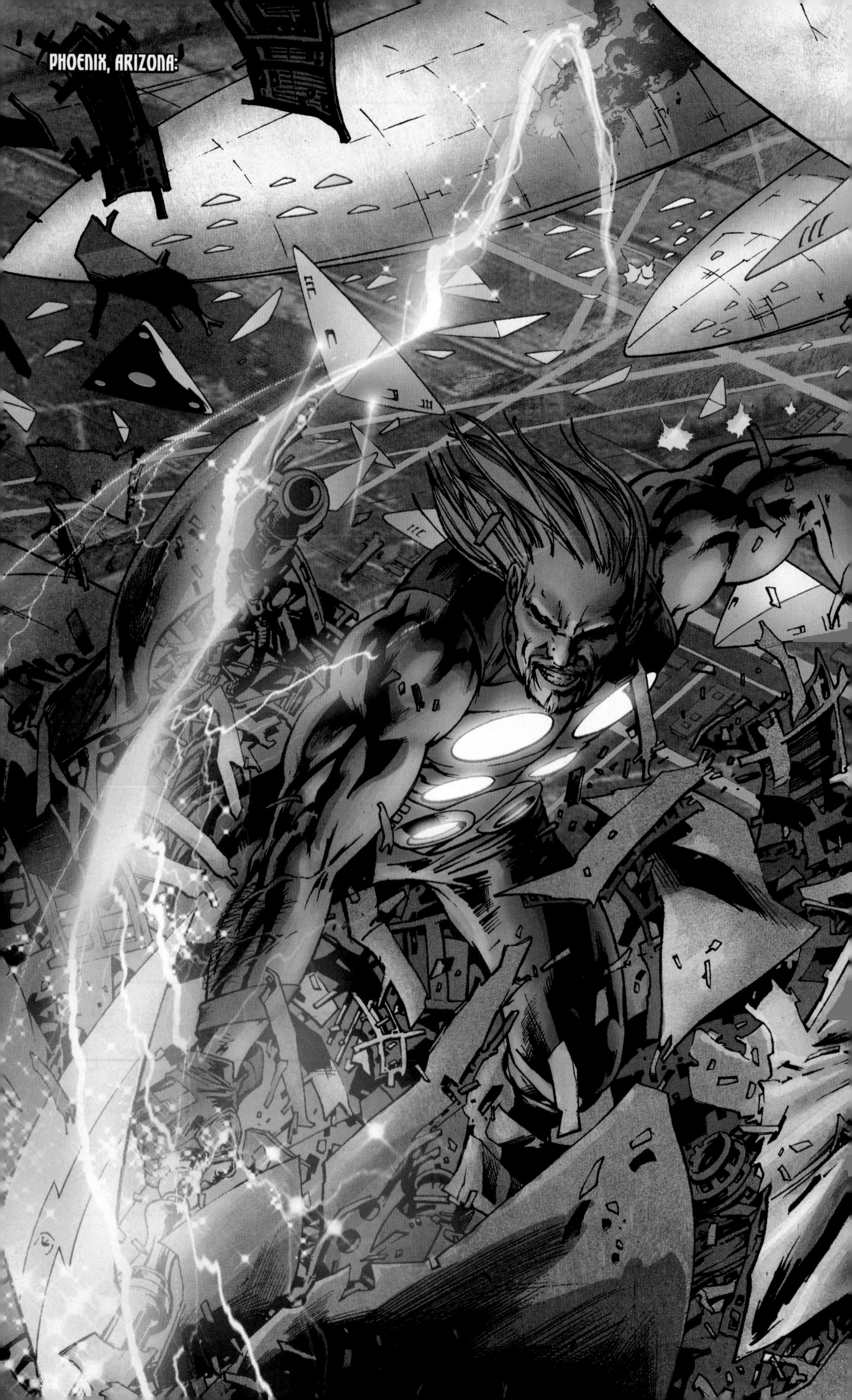
PHOENIX, ARIZONA:

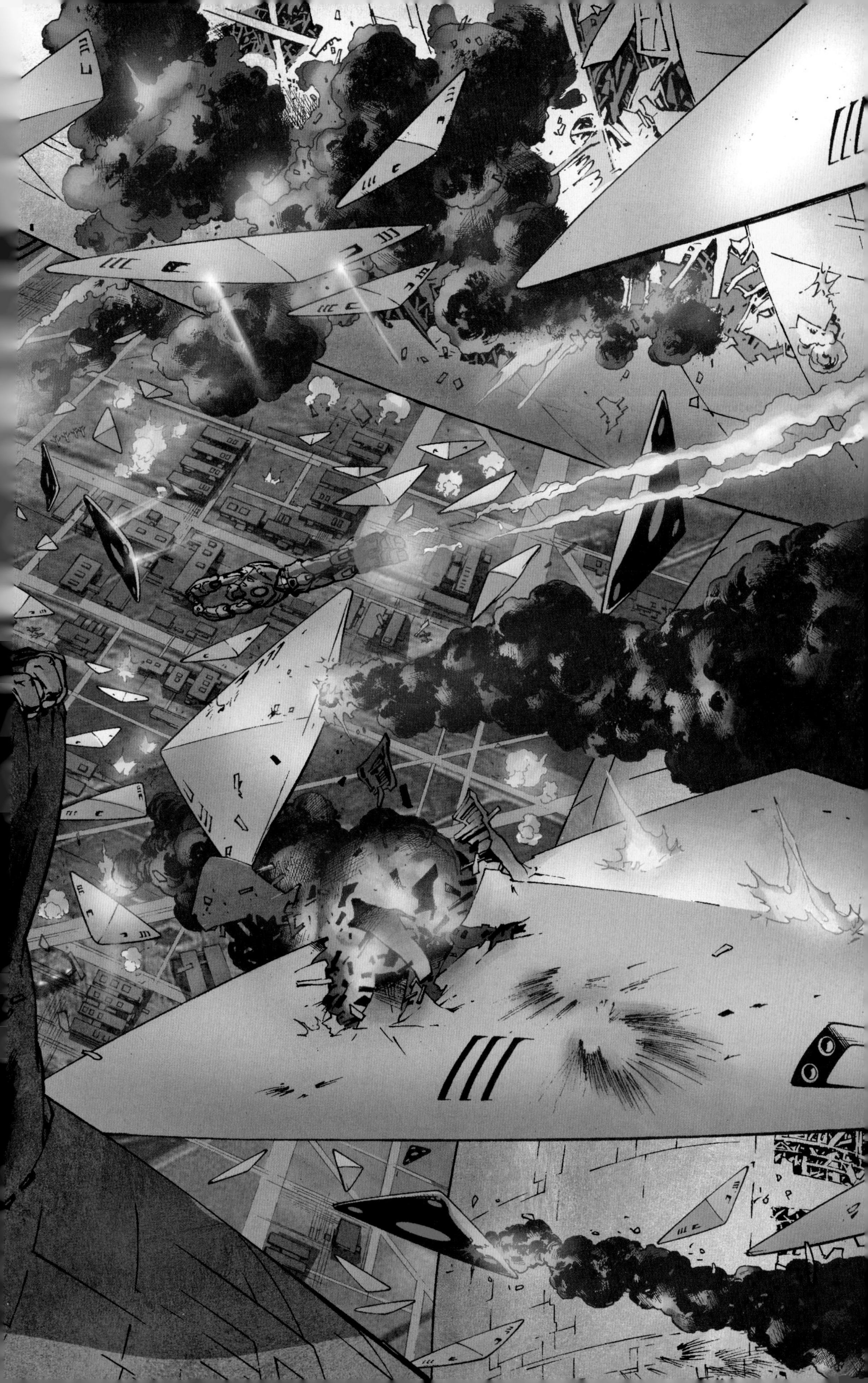

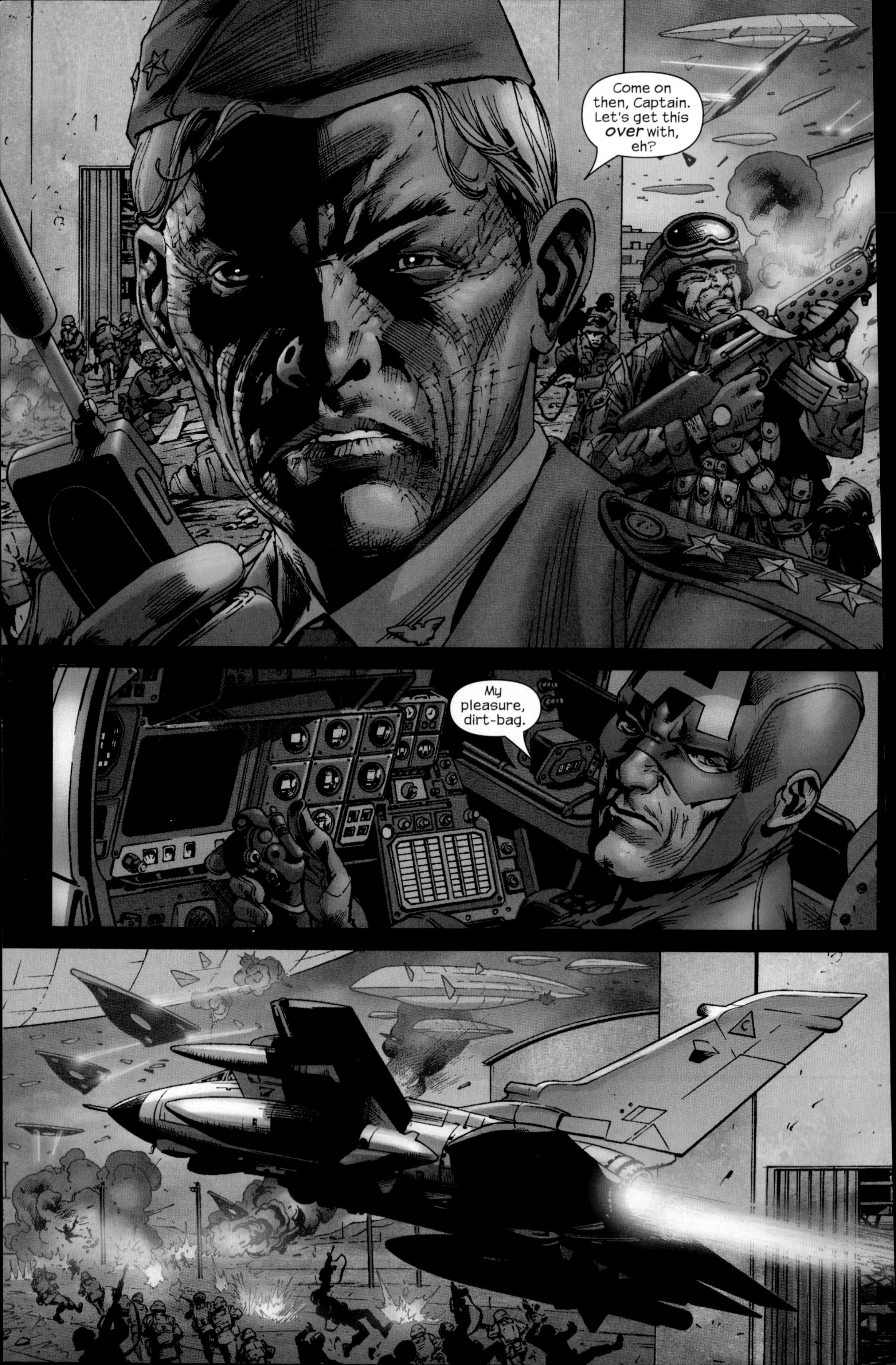
Come on then, Captain. Let's get this *over* with, eh?
My pleasure, dirt-bag.

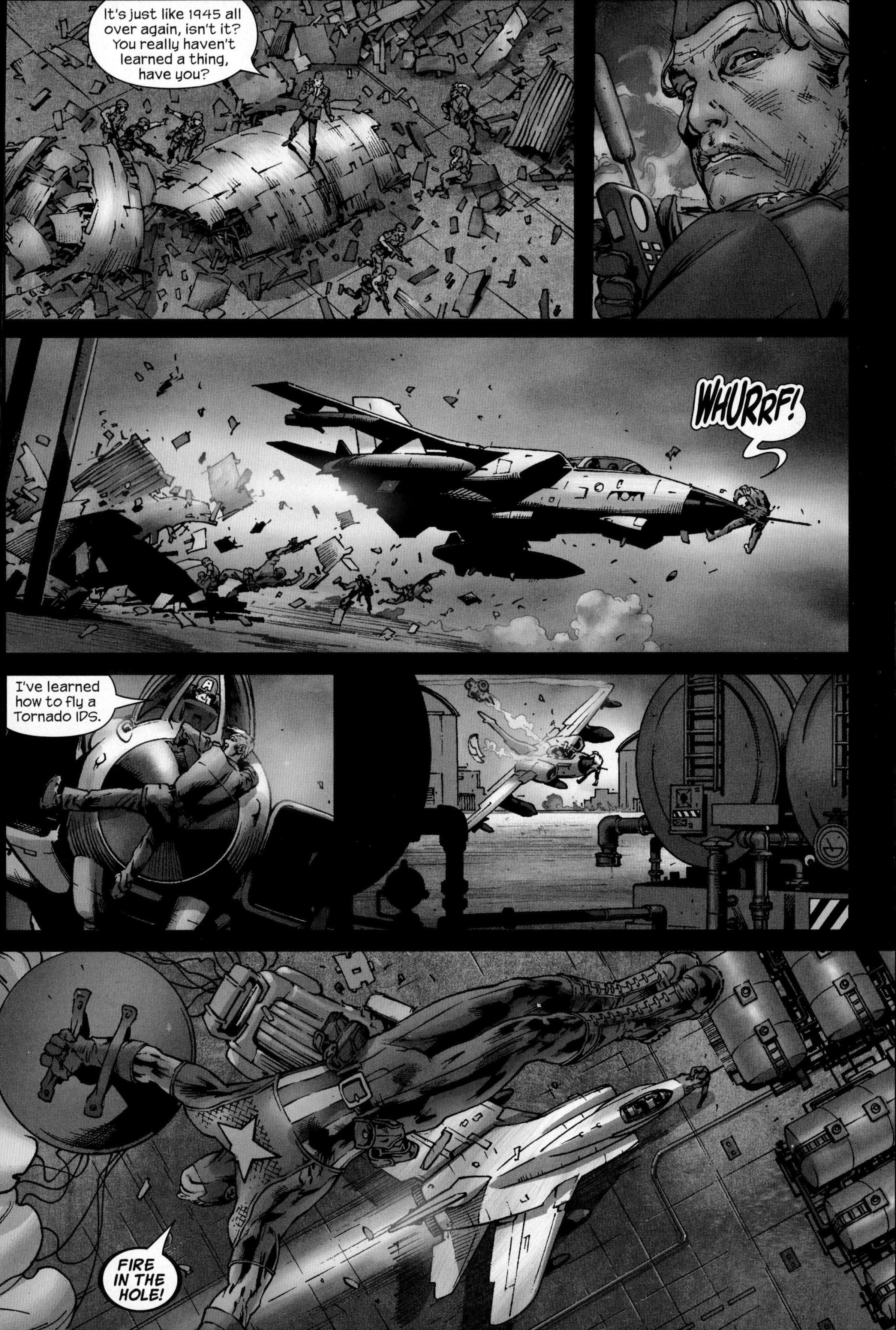
It's just like 1945 all over again, isn't it? You really haven't learned a thing, have you?
WHURRF!
I've learned how to fly a Tornado IDS.
FIRE IN THE HOLE!

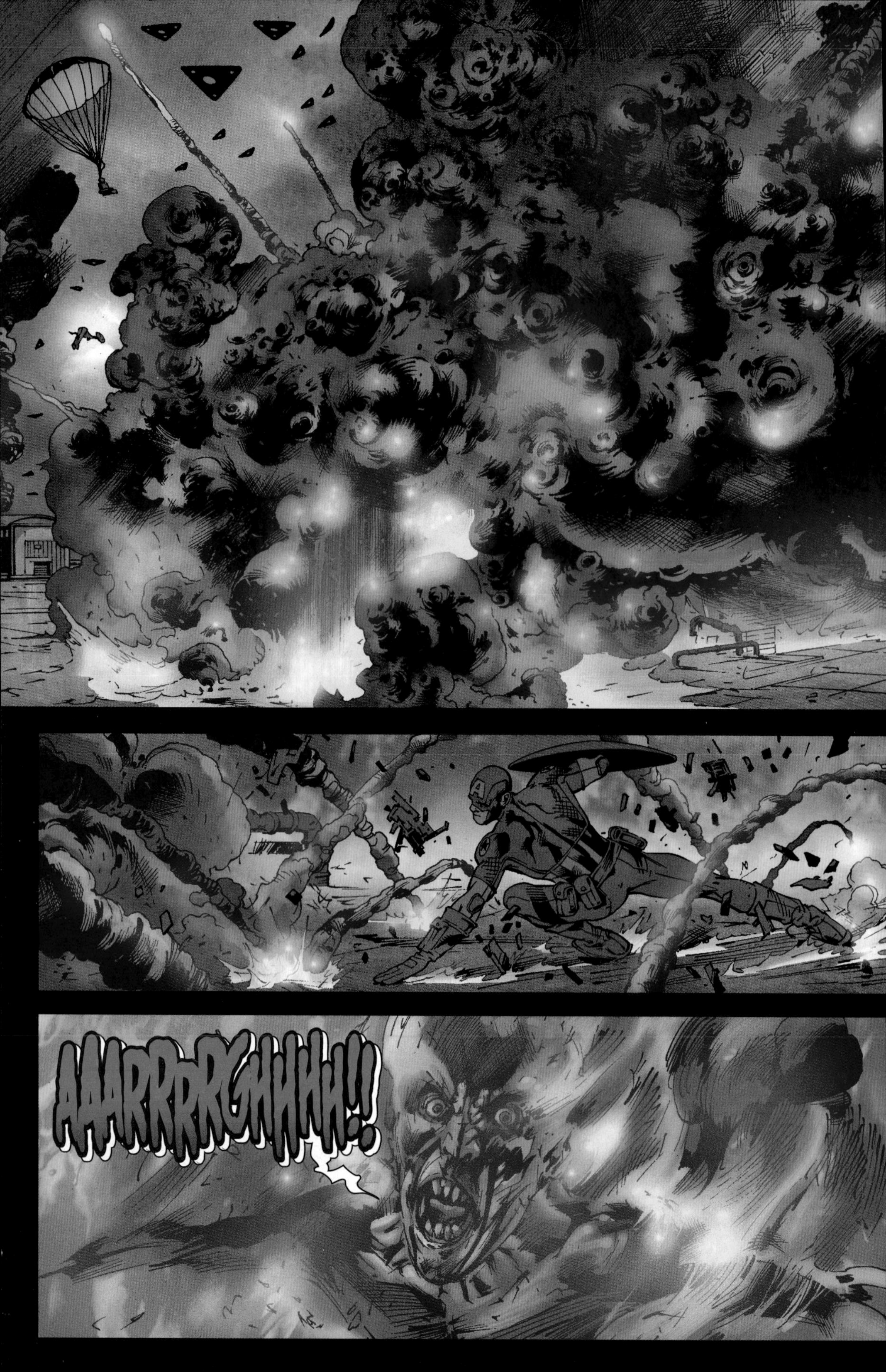
AAARRRRGHHHH!!

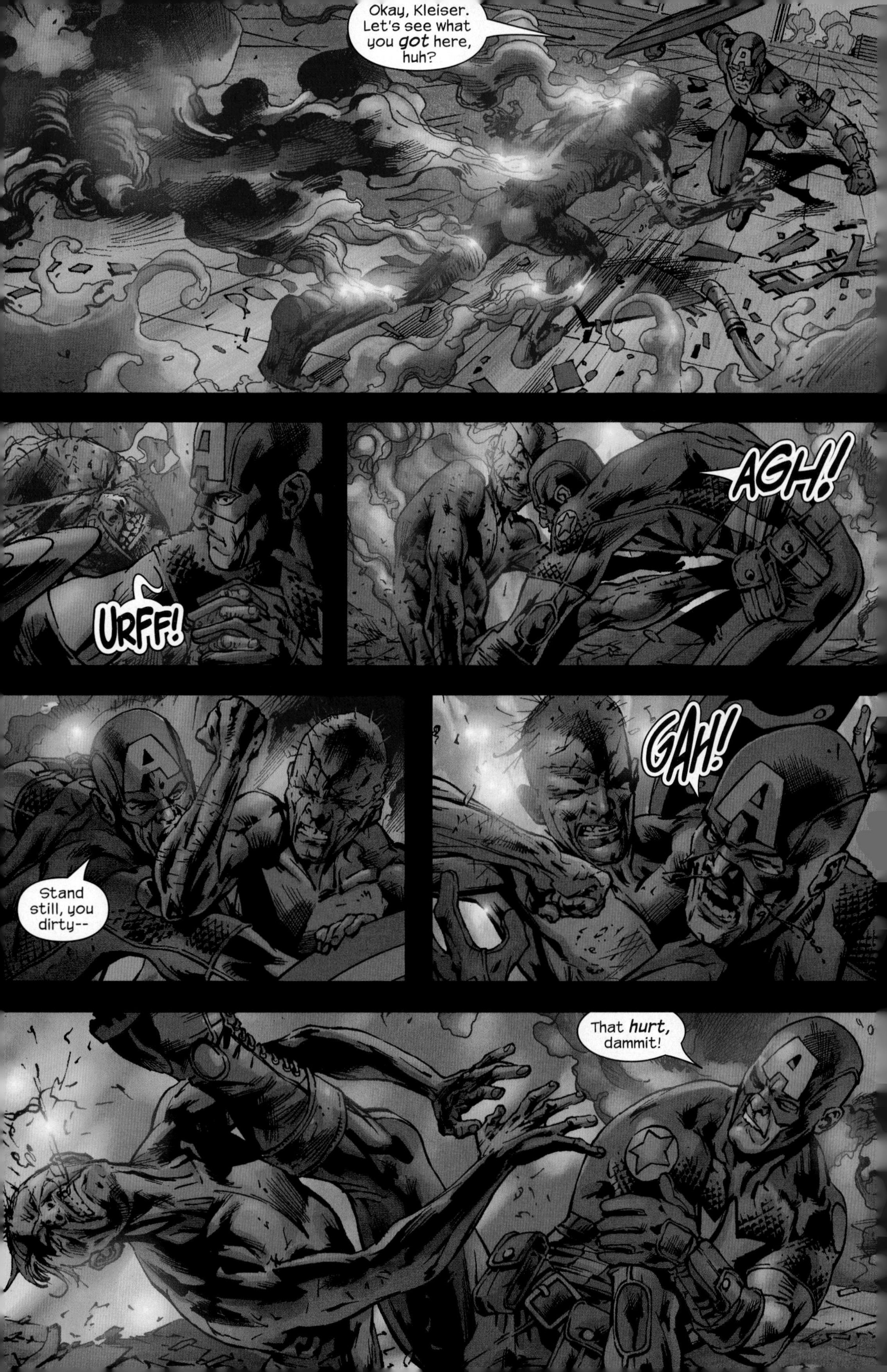

Okay, Kleiser. Let's see what you got here, huh?
URFF!
AGH!
Stand still, you dirty--
GAH!
That hurt, dammit!

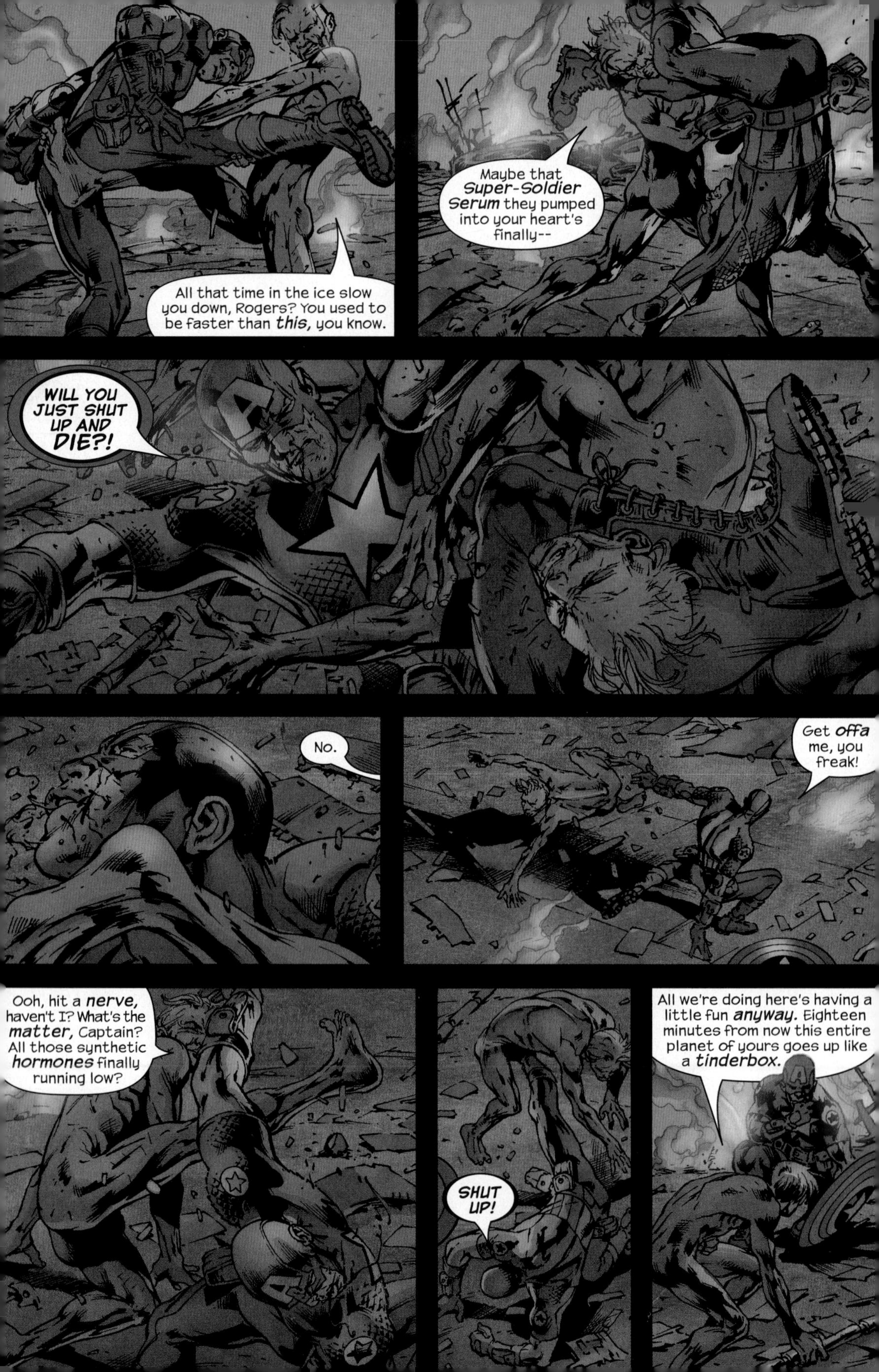
All that time in the ice slow you down, Rogers? You used to be faster than *this*, you know.
Maybe that *Super-Soldier Serum* they pumped into your heart's finally--
WILL YOU JUST SHUT UP AND DIE?!
No.
Get *offa* me, you freak!
Ooh, hit a *nerve*, haven't I? What's the *matter*, Captain? All those synthetic *hormones* finally running low?
SHUT UP!
All we're doing here's having a little fun *anyway*. Eighteen minutes from now this entire planet of yours goes up like a *tinderbox*.

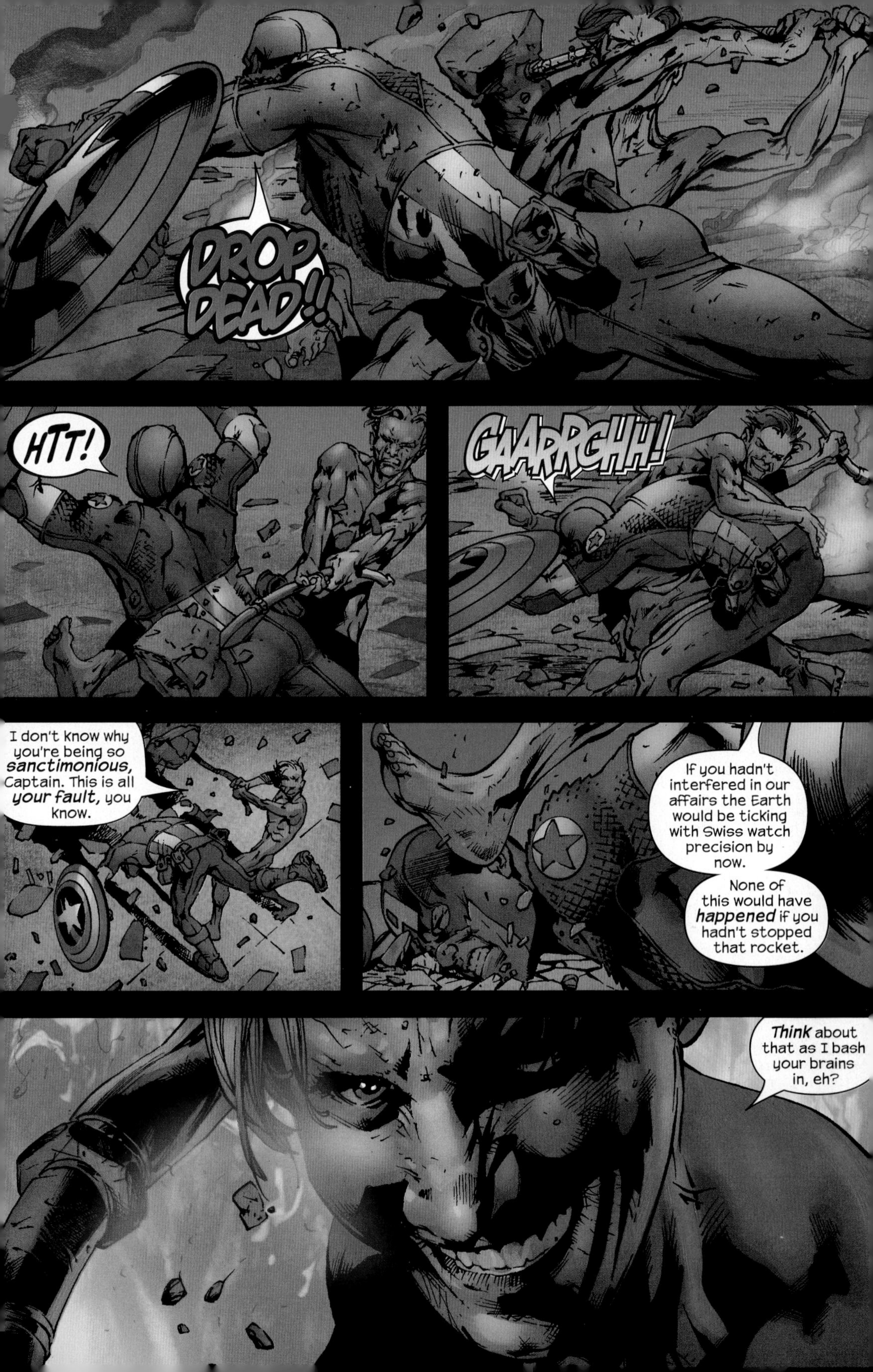
DROP DEAD!!
HTT!
GAARRGHH!
I don't know why you're being so *sanctimonious*, Captain. This is all *your fault*, you know.
If you hadn't interfered in our affairs the Earth would be ticking with Swiss watch precision by now.
None of this would have *happened* if you hadn't stopped that rocket.
Think about that as I bash your brains in, eh?

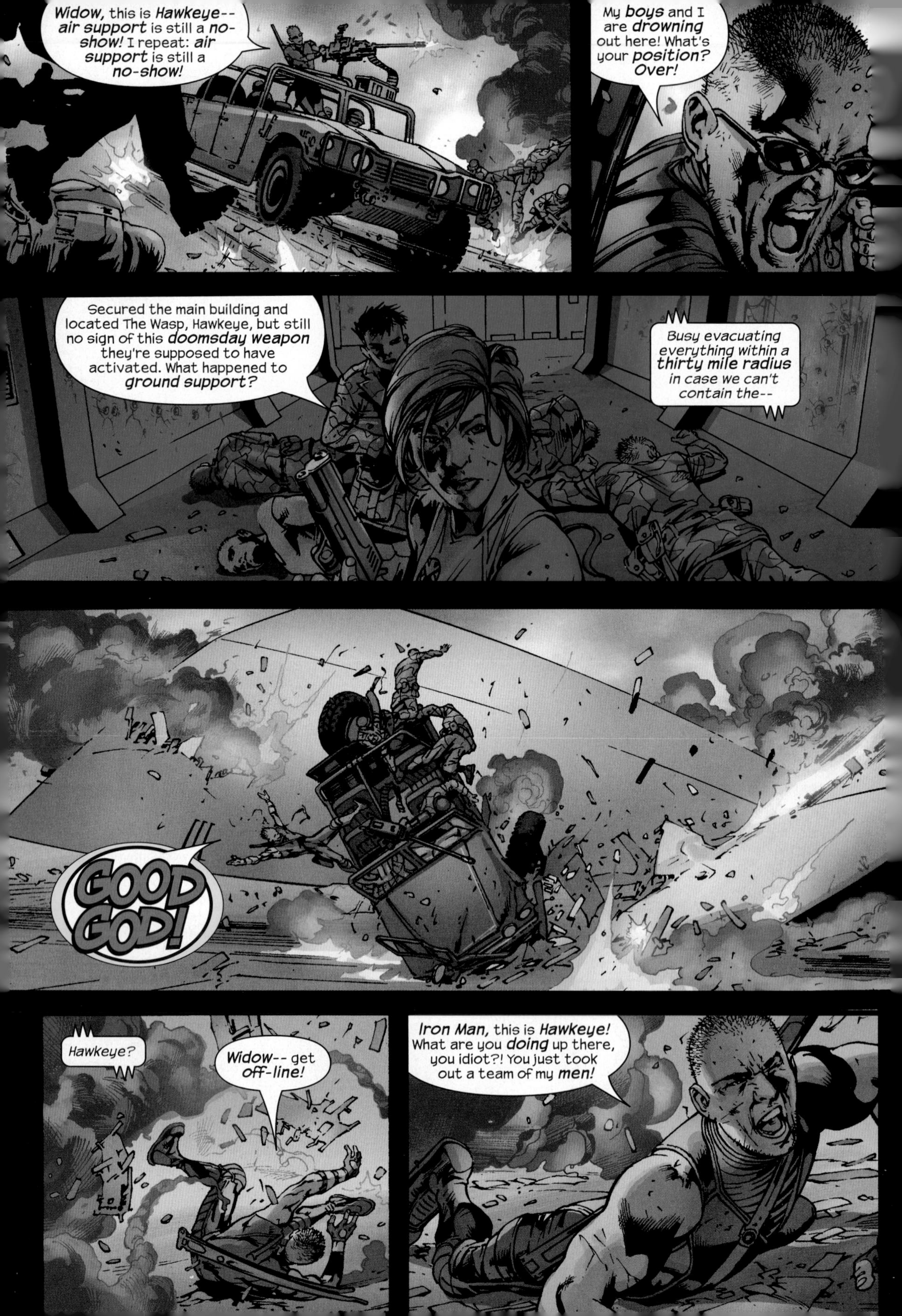
Widow, this is Hawkeye-- air support is still a no-show! I repeat: air support is still a no-show!
My boys and I are drowning out here! What's your position? Over!
Secured the main building and located The Wasp, Hawkeye, but still no sign of this doomsday weapon they're supposed to have activated. What happened to ground support?
Busy evacuating everything within a thirty mile radius in case we can't contain the--
GOOD GOD!
Hawkeye?
Widow-- get off-line!
Iron Man, this is Hawkeye! What are you doing up there, you idiot?! You just took out a team of my men!

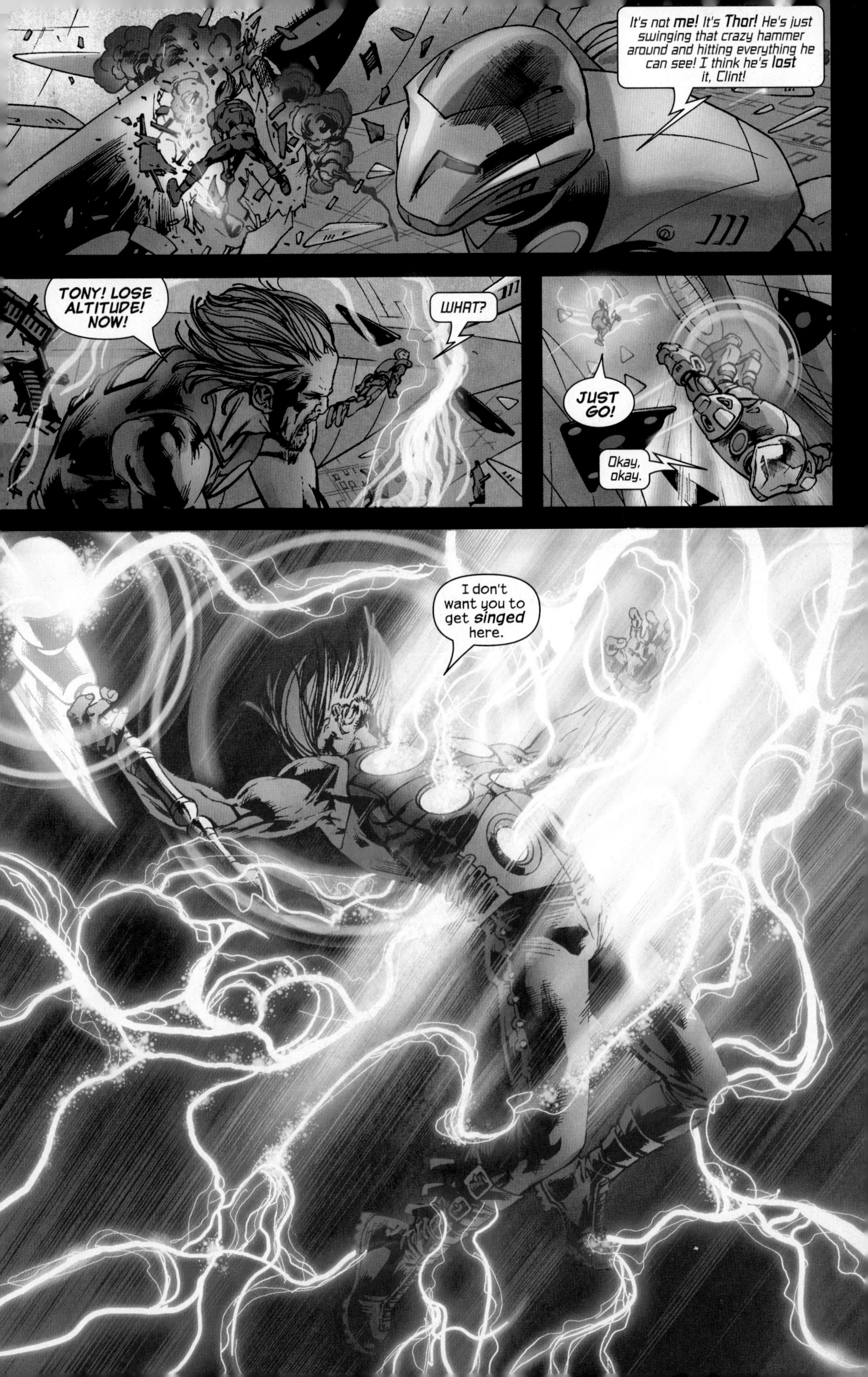
It's not **me!** It's **Thor!** He's just swinging that crazy hammer around and hitting everything he can see! I think he's **lost** it, Clint!
TONY! LOSE ALTITUDE! NOW!
WHAT?
JUST GO!
Okay, okay.
I don't want you to get ***singed*** here.

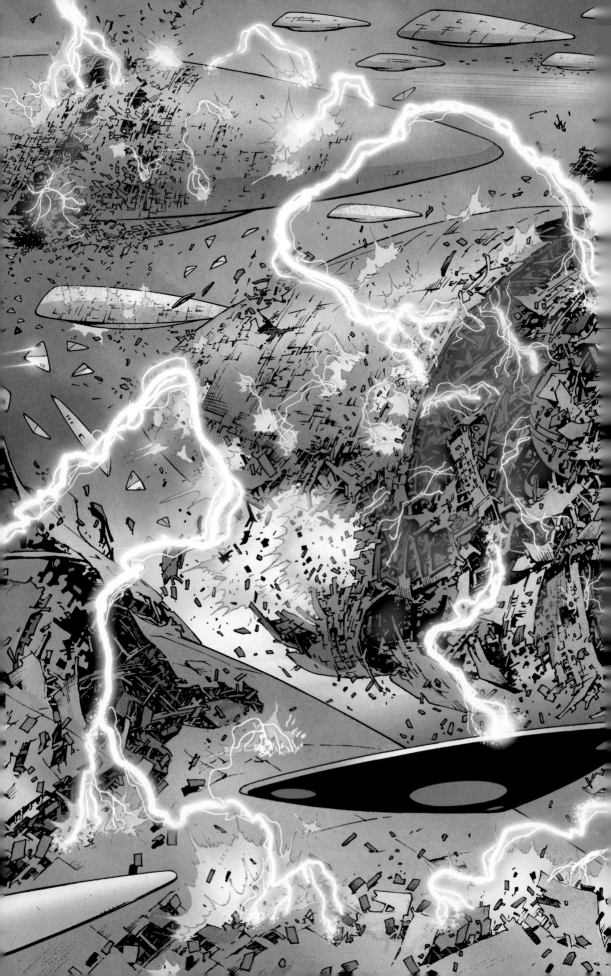

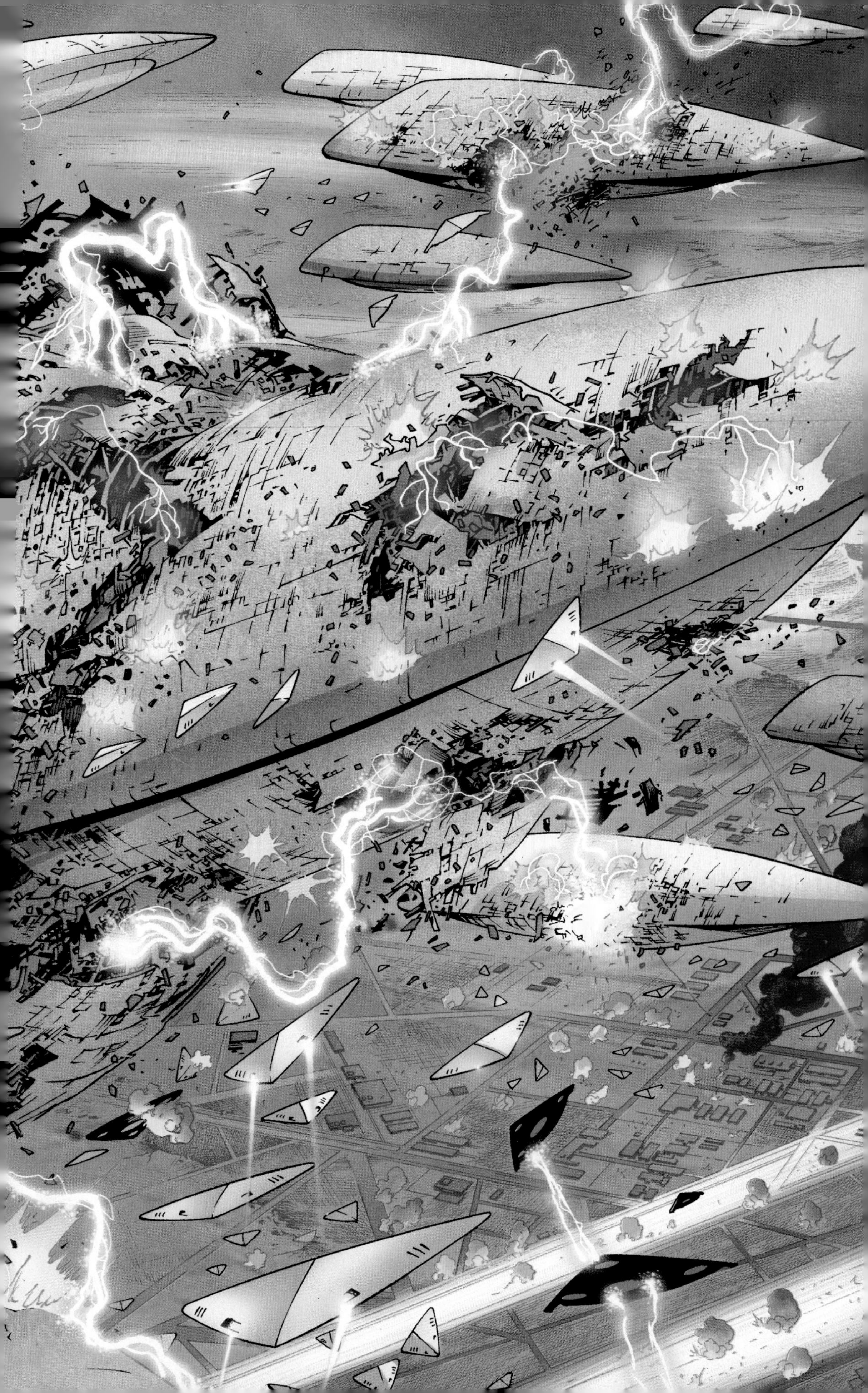

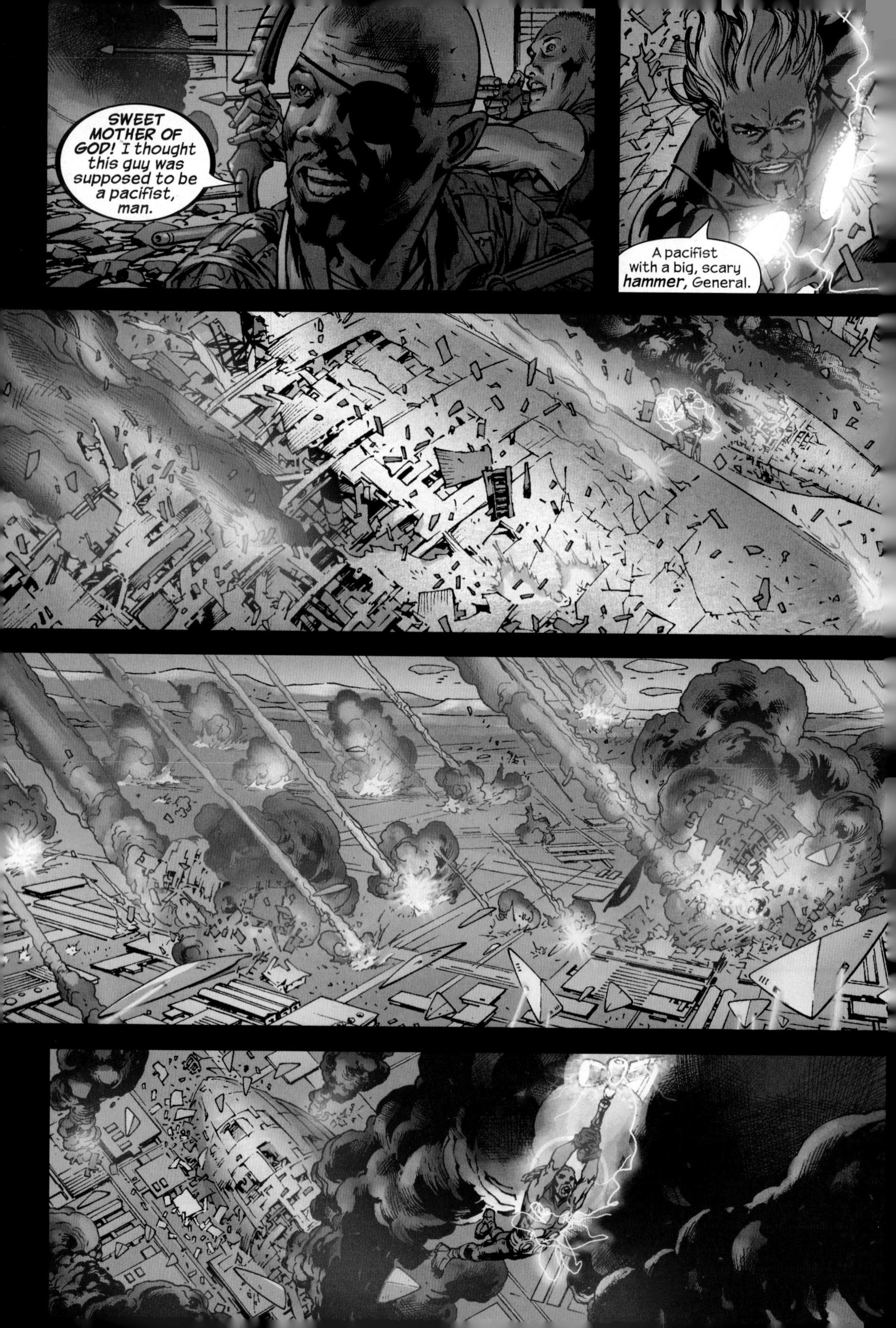
SWEET MOTHER OF GOD! I thought this guy was supposed to be a pacifist, man.
A pacifist with a big, scary hammer, General.

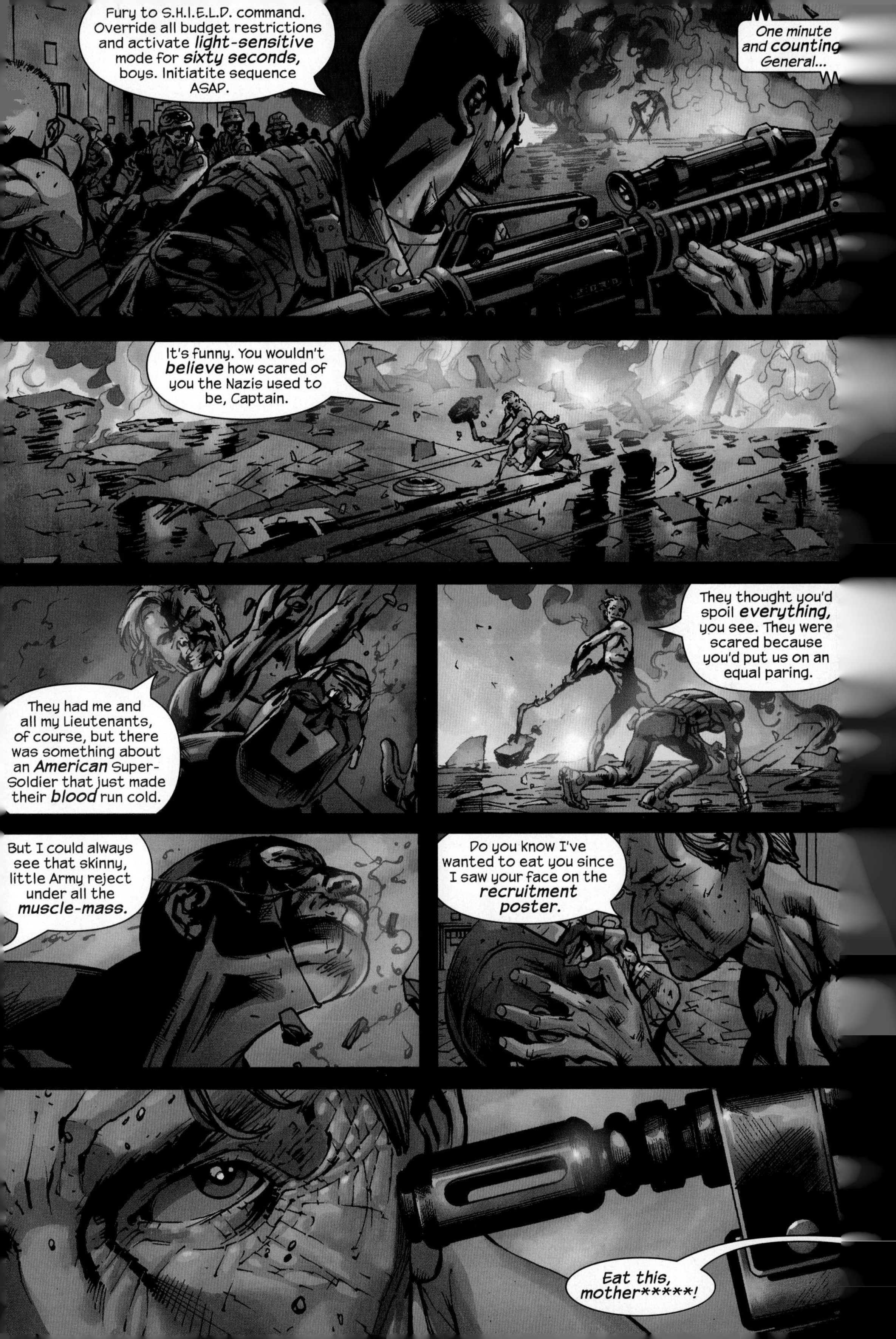
Fury to S.H.I.E.L.D. command. Override all budget restrictions and activate light-sensitive mode for sixty seconds, boys. Initiatite sequence ASAP.
One minute and counting General...
It's funny. You wouldn't believe how scared of you the Nazis used to be, Captain.
They had me and all my Lieutenants, of course, but there was something about an American Super-Soldier that just made their blood run cold.
They thought you'd spoil everything, you see. They were scared because you'd put us on an equal paring.
But I could always see that skinny, little Army reject under all the muscle-mass.
Do you know I've wanted to eat you since I saw your face on the recruitment poster.
Eat this, mother*****!

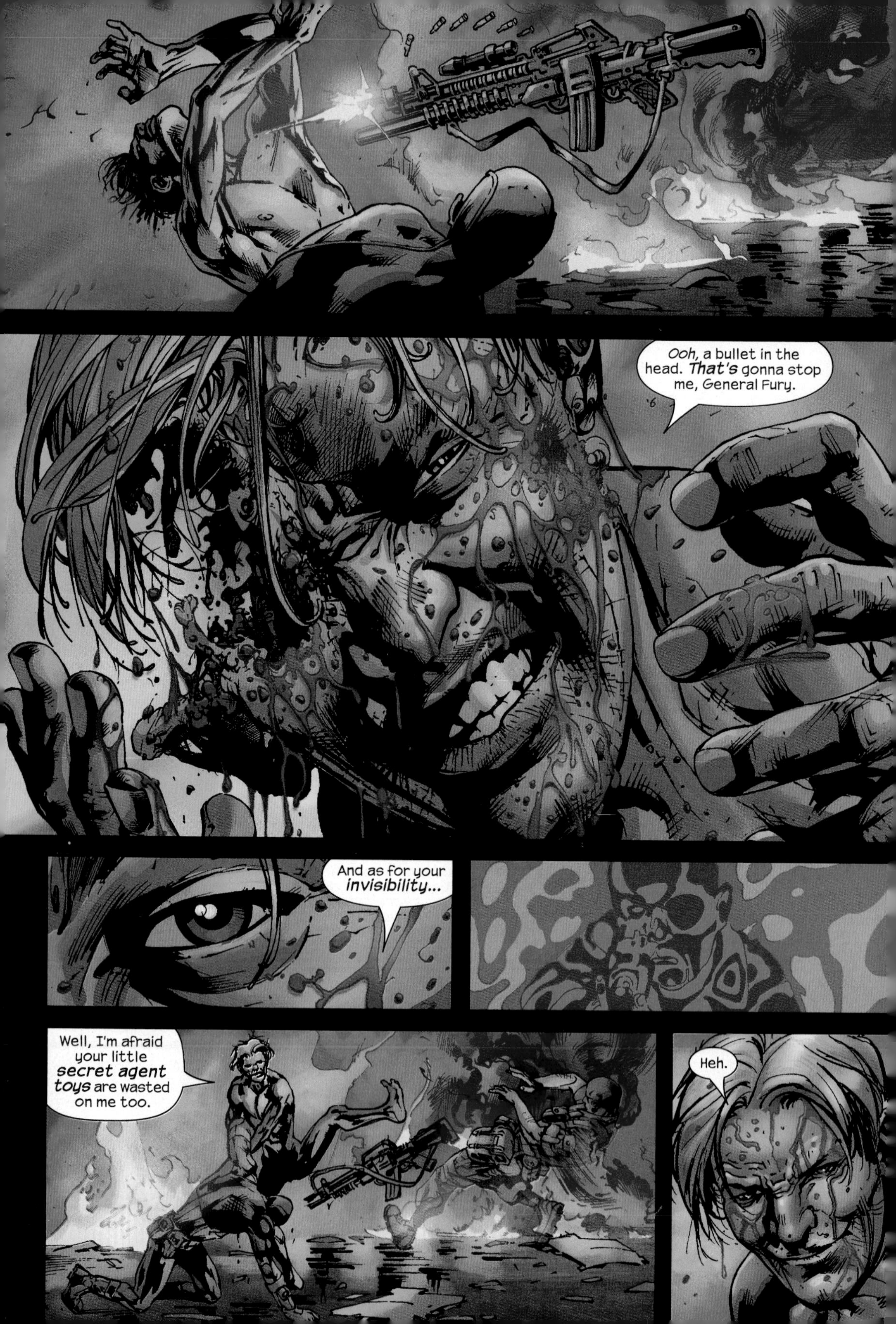
Ooh, a bullet in the head. That's gonna stop me, General Fury.
And as for your invisibility...
Well, I'm afraid your little secret agent toys are wasted on me too.
Heh.

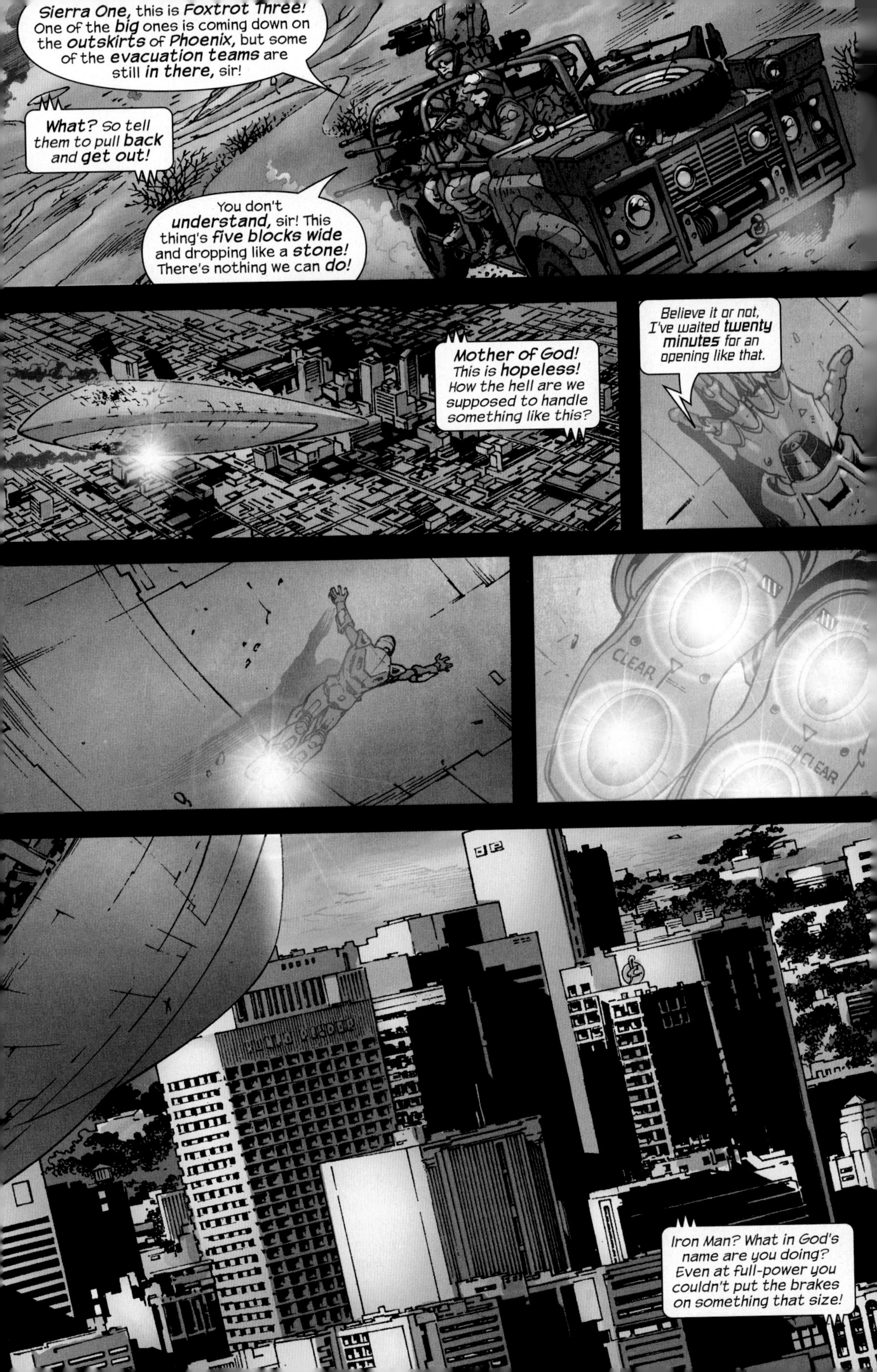
Sierra One, this is Foxtrot Three! One of the big ones is coming down on the outskirts of Phoenix, but some of the evacuation teams are still in there, sir!
What? So tell them to pull back and get out!
You don't understand, sir! This thing's five blocks wide and dropping like a stone! There's nothing we can do!
Mother of God! This is hopeless! How the hell are we supposed to handle something like this?
Believe it or not, I've waited twenty minutes for an opening like that.
CLEAR
CLEAR
Iron Man? What in God's name are you doing? Even at full-power you couldn't put the brakes on something that size!

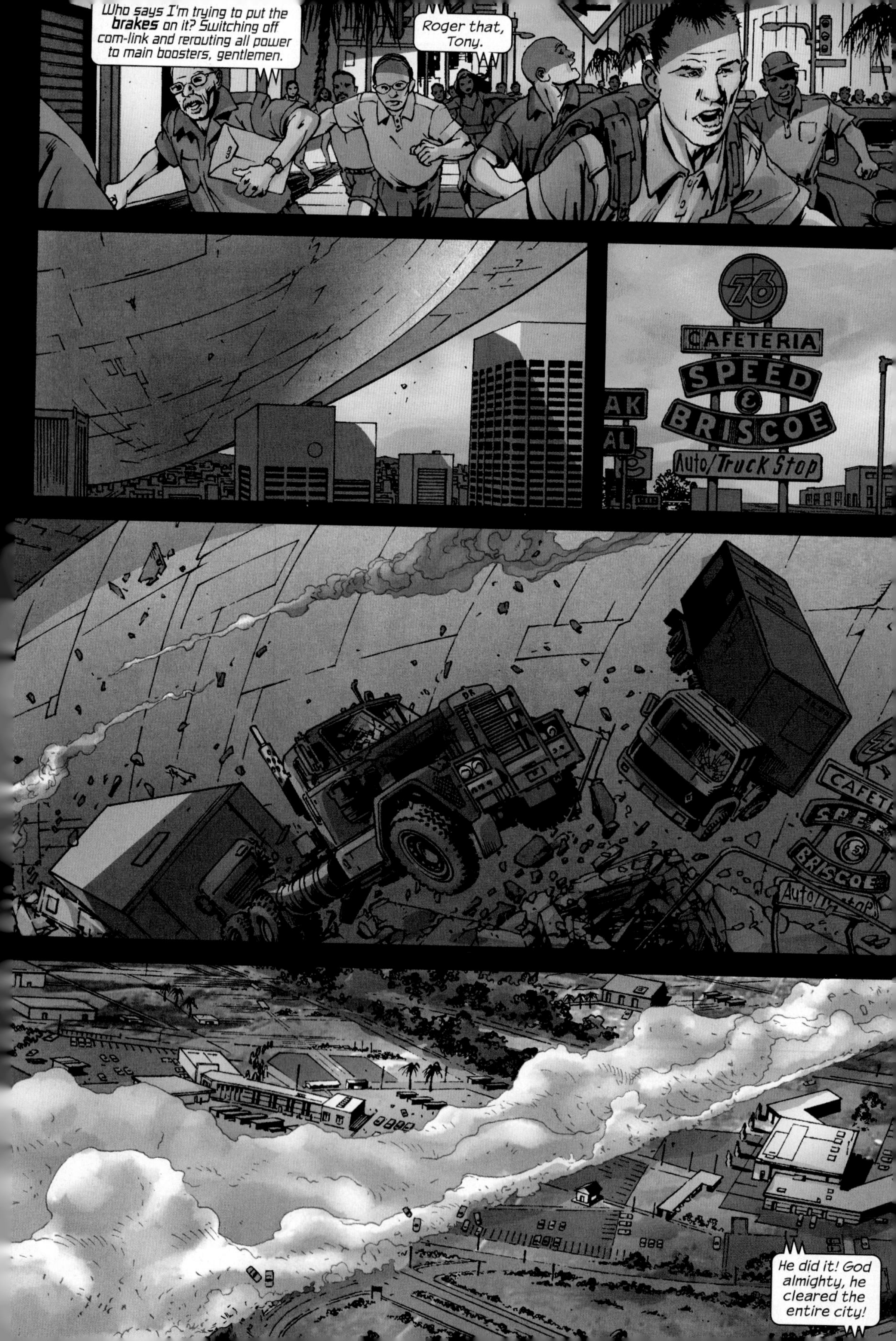
Who says I'm trying to put the brakes on it? Switching off com-link and rerouting all power to main boosters, gentlemen.
Roger that, Tony.
76
CAFETERIA
SPEED
&
BRISCOE
Auto/Truck Stop
CAFETE
SPE
BRISCOE
He did it! God almighty, he cleared the entire city!

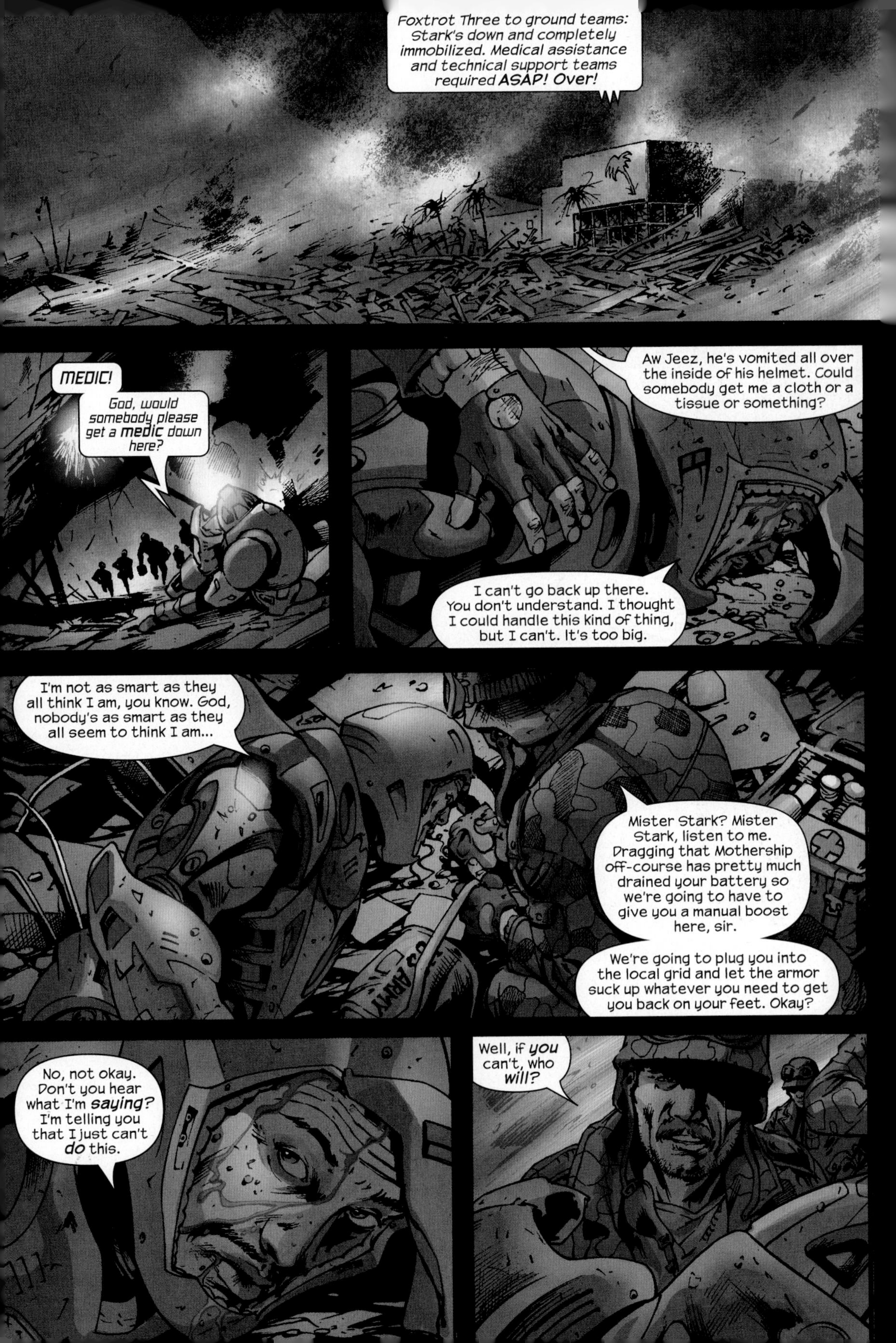
Foxtrot Three to ground teams: Stark's down and completely immobilized. Medical assistance and technical support teams required ASAP! Over!
MEDIC!
God, would somebody please get a medic down here?
Aw Jeez, he's vomited all over the inside of his helmet. Could somebody get me a cloth or a tissue or something?
I can't go back up there. You don't understand. I thought I could handle this kind of thing, but I can't. It's too big.
I'm not as smart as they all think I am, you know. God, nobody's as smart as they all seem to think I am...
Mister Stark? Mister Stark, listen to me. Dragging that Mothership off-course has pretty much drained your battery so we're going to have to give you a manual boost here, sir.
We're going to plug you into the local grid and let the armor suck up whatever you need to get you back on your feet. Okay?
No, not okay. Don't you hear what I'm saying? I'm telling you that I just can't do this.
Well, if you can't, who will?

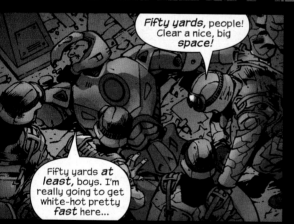

Okay, get me over by that streetlight, but if anything happens to me up there you've got a hundred and fifty thousand jobless Stark employees on your conscience.

Fifty yards, people! Clear a nice, big space!

Fifty yards at least, boys. I'm really going to get white-hot pretty fast here...

What the hell's going on here?

We're losing power from Flagstaff all the way down to Tucson, sir. Grid control says the whole network's been redirected to Phoenix, Arizona.

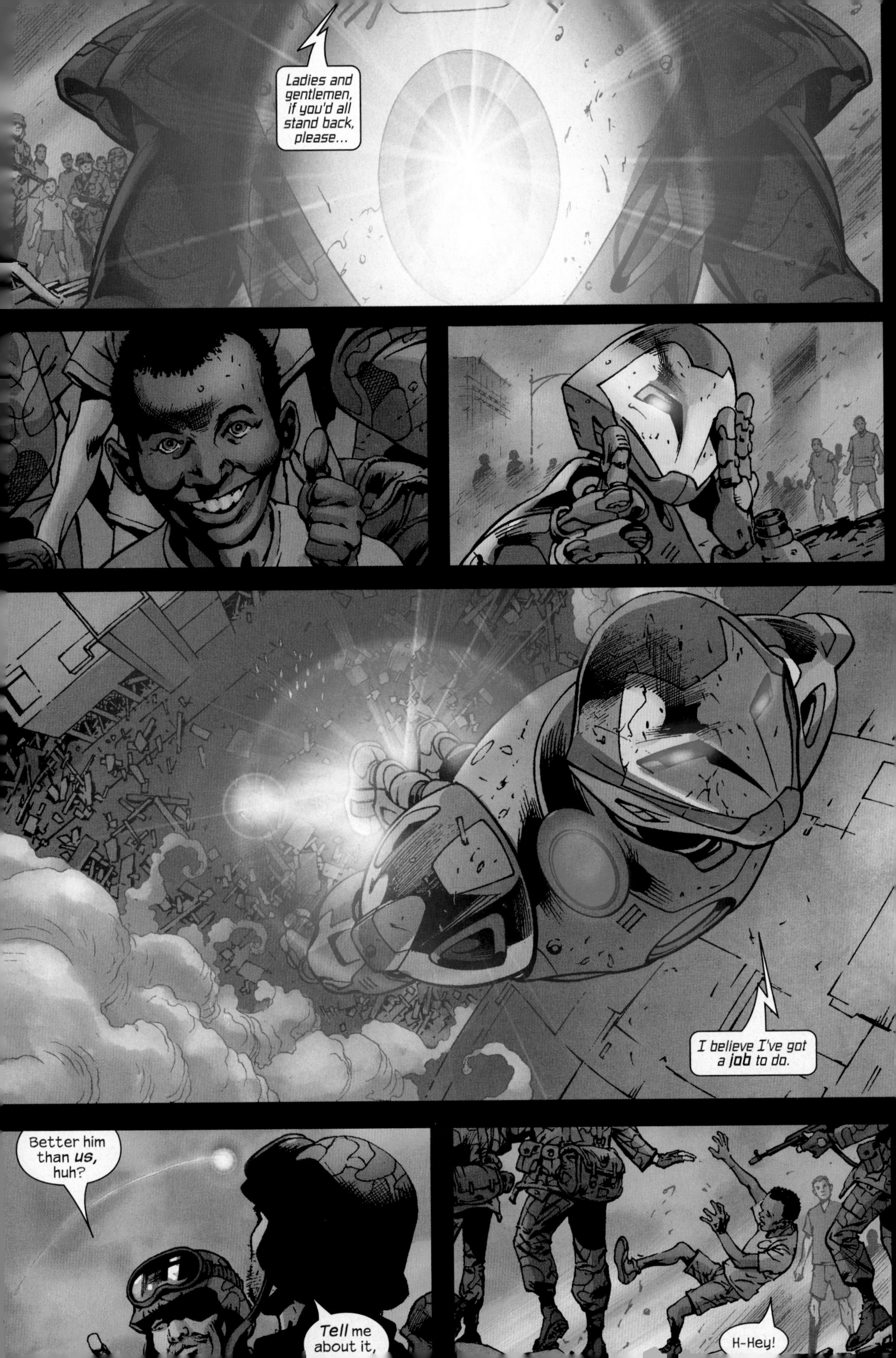

Ladies and gentlemen, if you'd all stand back, please...
I believe I've got a *job* to do.
Better him than *us*, huh?
Tell me about it,
H-Hey!

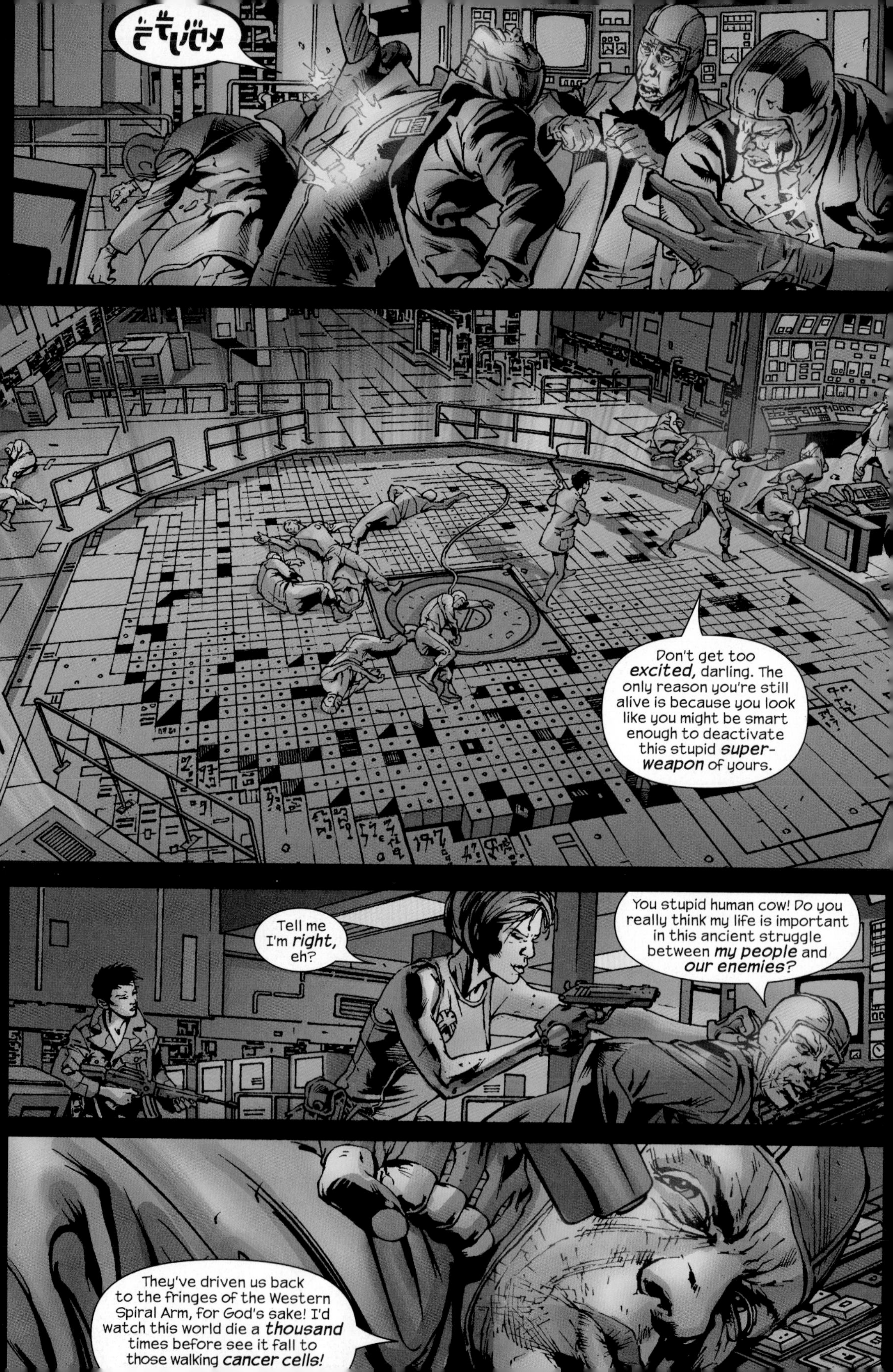
Don't get too excited, darling. The only reason you're still alive is because you look like you might be smart enough to deactivate this stupid super-weapon of yours.
Tell me I'm right, eh?
You stupid human cow! Do you really think my life is important in this ancient struggle between my people and our enemies?
They've driven us back to the fringes of the Western Spiral Arm, for God's sake! I'd watch this world die a thousand times before see it fall to those walking cancer cells!

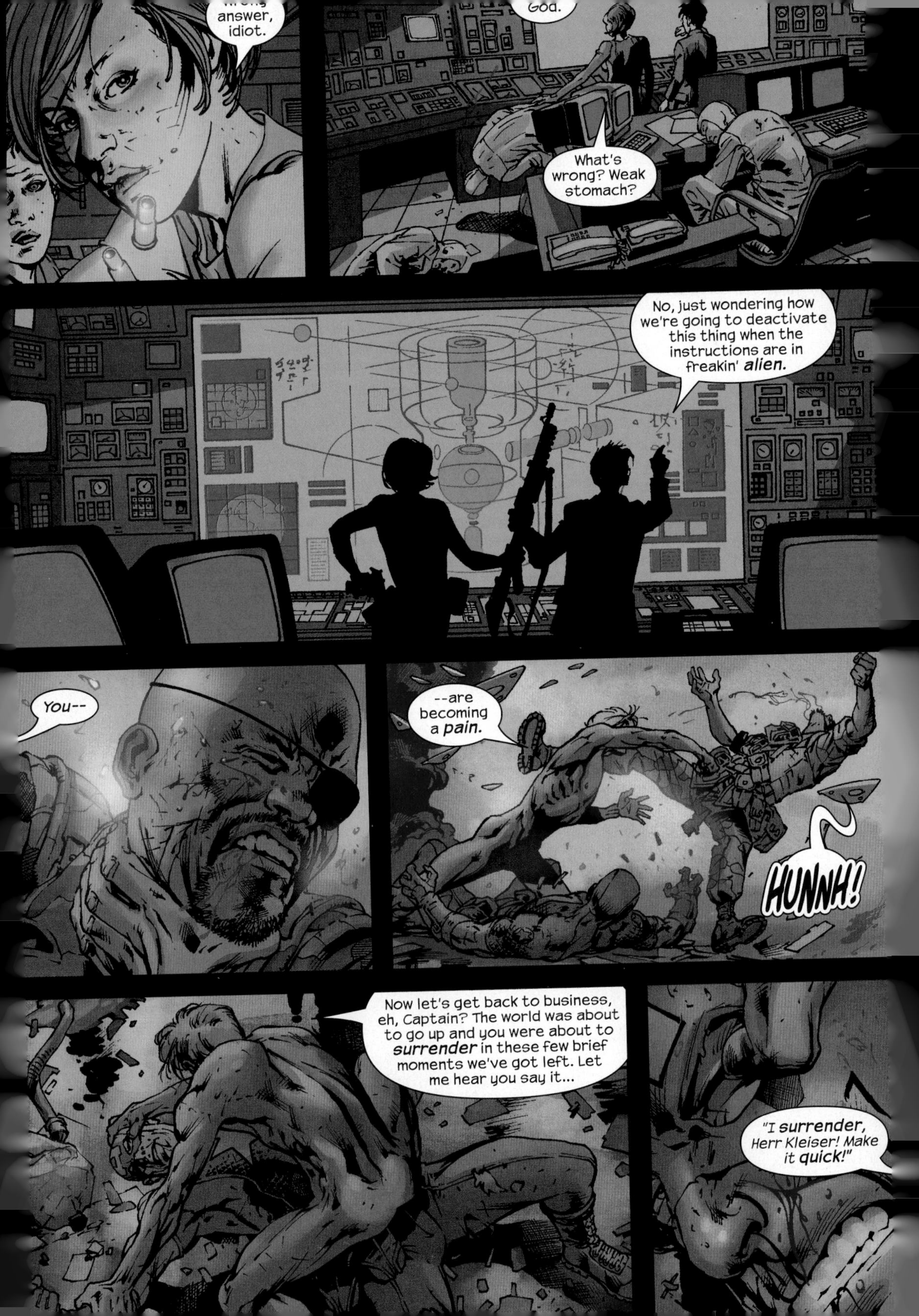

answer,
idiot.
God.
What's wrong? Weak stomach?
No, just wondering how we're going to deactivate this thing when the instructions are in freakin' *alien.*
You--
--are becoming a *pain.*
HUNNH!
Now let's get back to business, eh, Captain? The world was about to go up and you were about to *surrender* in these few brief moments we've got left. Let me hear you say it...
"I *surrender,* Herr Kleiser! Make it *quick!*"

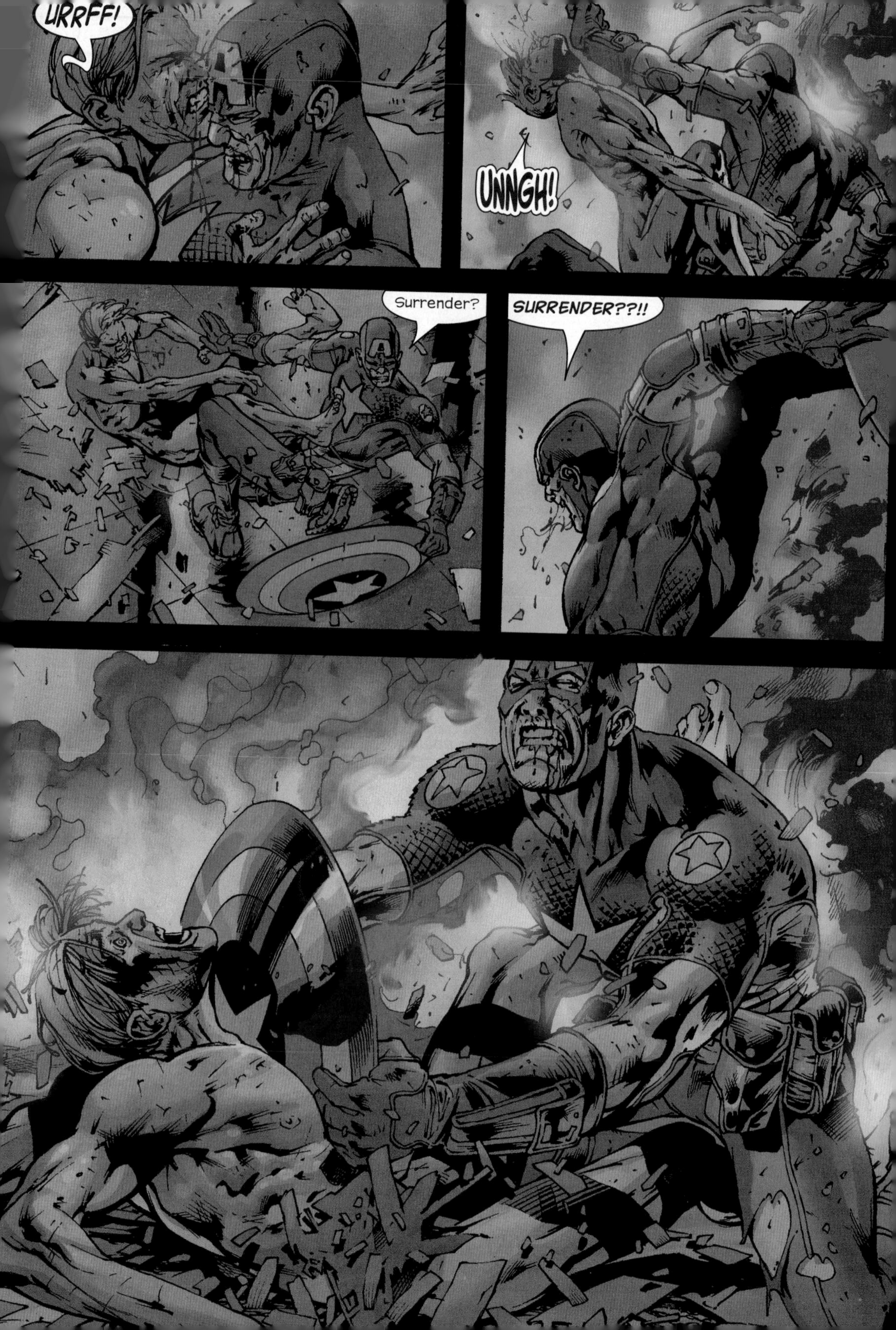
URRFF!
UNNGH!
Surrender?
SURRENDER??!!

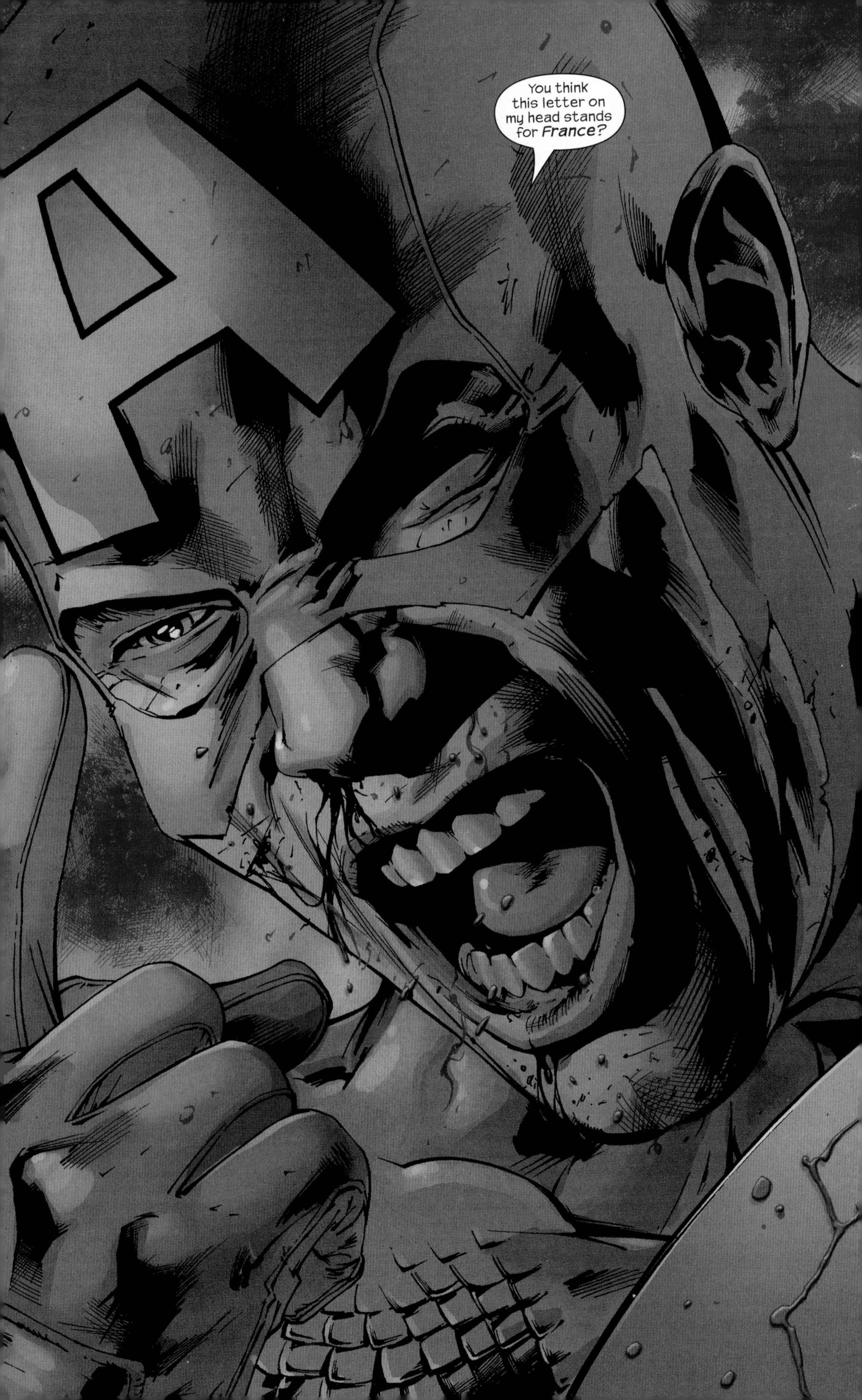
You think this letter on my head stands for *France*?

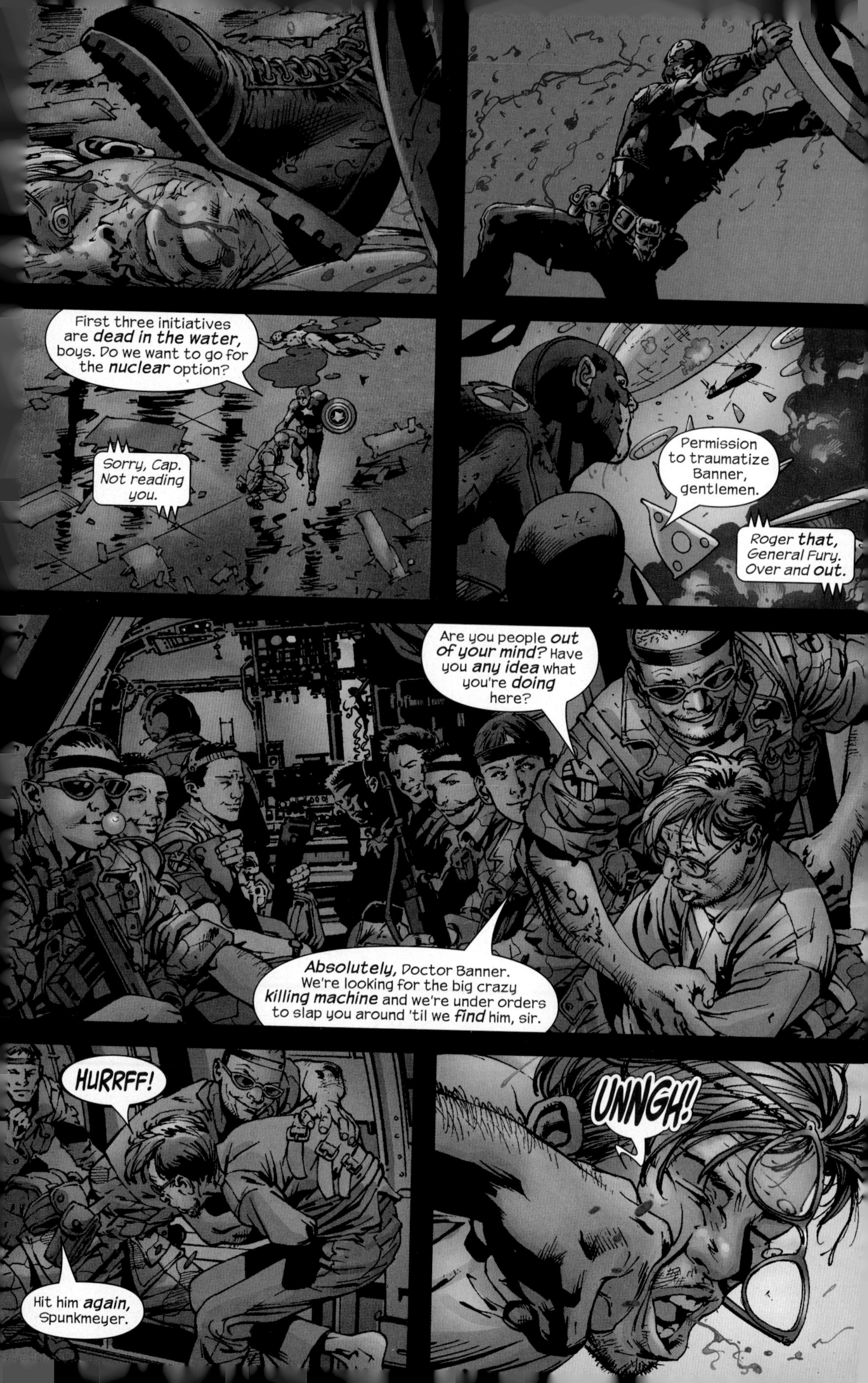
First three initiatives are dead in the water, boys. Do we want to go for the nuclear option?
Sorry, Cap. Not reading you.
Permission to traumatize Banner, gentlemen.
Roger that, General Fury. Over and out.
Are you people out of your mind? Have you any idea what you're doing here?
Absolutely, Doctor Banner. We're looking for the big crazy killing machine and we're under orders to slap you around 'til we find him, sir.
HURRFF!
Hit him again, Spunkmeyer.
UNNGH!

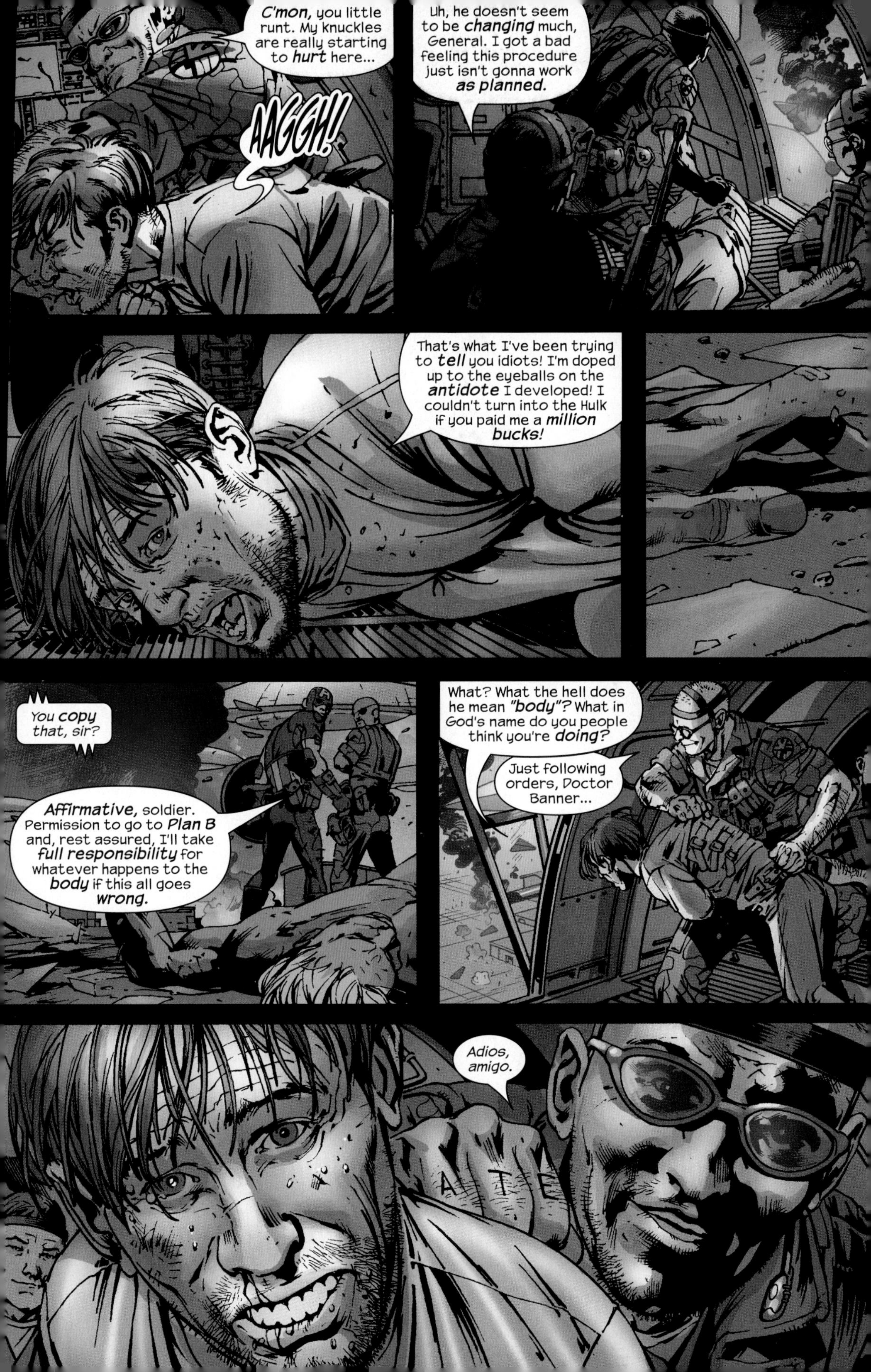
C'mon, you little runt. My knuckles are really starting to hurt here...
AAGGH!!
Uh, he doesn't seem to be changing much, General. I got a bad feeling this procedure just isn't gonna work as planned.
That's what I've been trying to tell you idiots! I'm doped up to the eyeballs on the antidote I developed! I couldn't turn into the Hulk if you paid me a million bucks!
You copy that, sir?
Affirmative, soldier. Permission to go to Plan B and, rest assured, I'll take full responsibility for whatever happens to the body if this all goes wrong.
What? What the hell does he mean "body"? What in God's name do you people think you're doing?
Just following orders, Doctor Banner...
Adios, amigo.

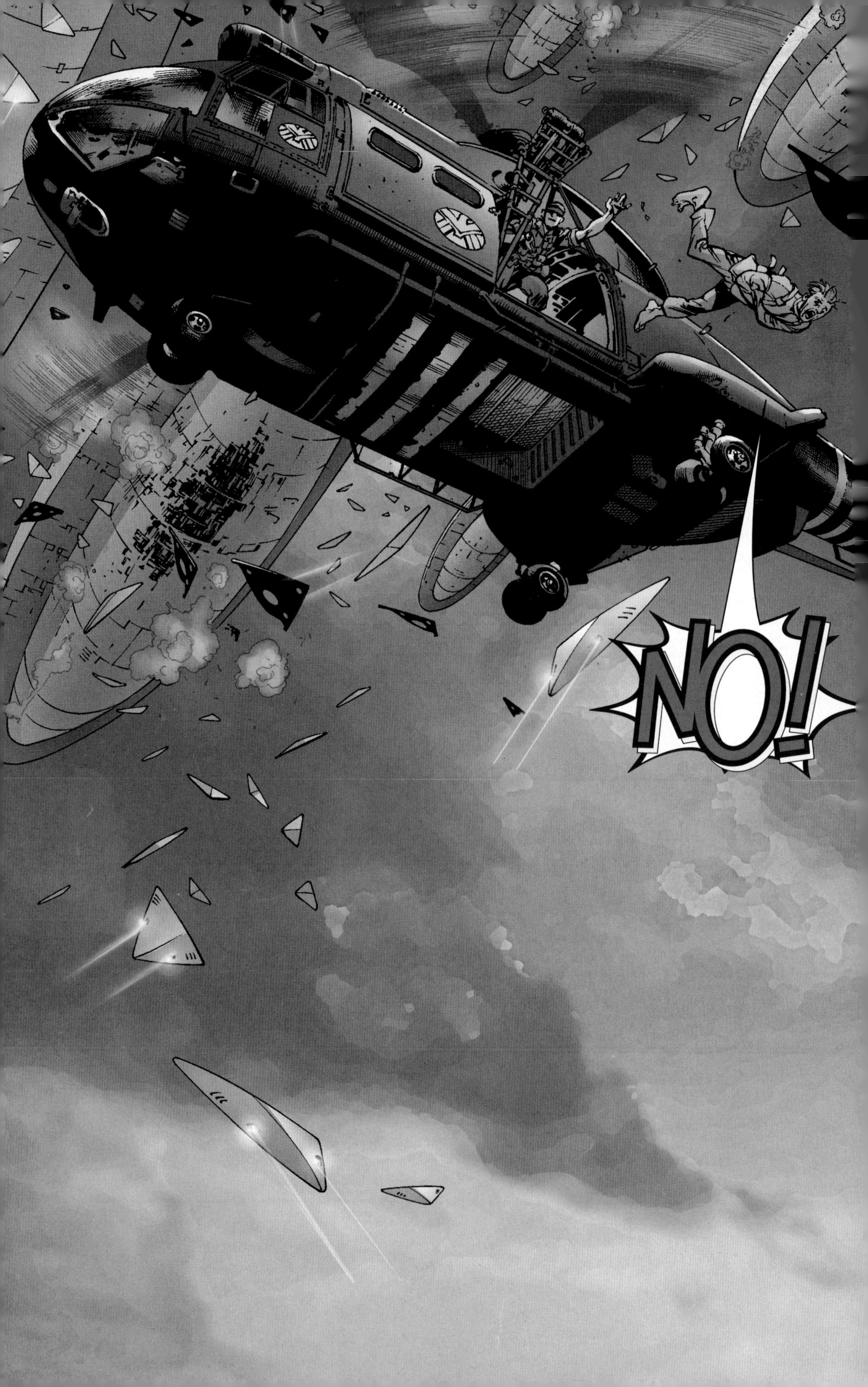
NO!

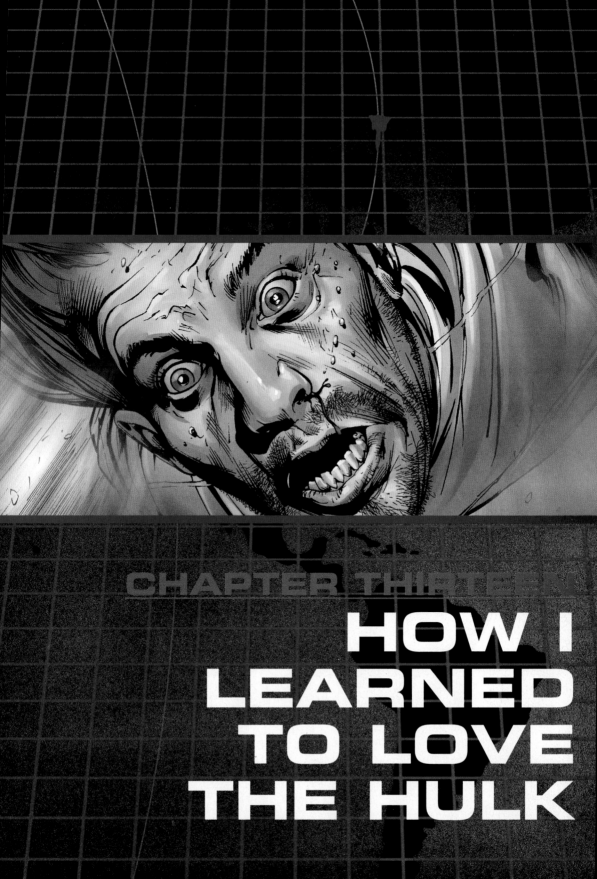

CHAPTER THIRTEEN

HOW I LEARNED TO LOVE THE HULK

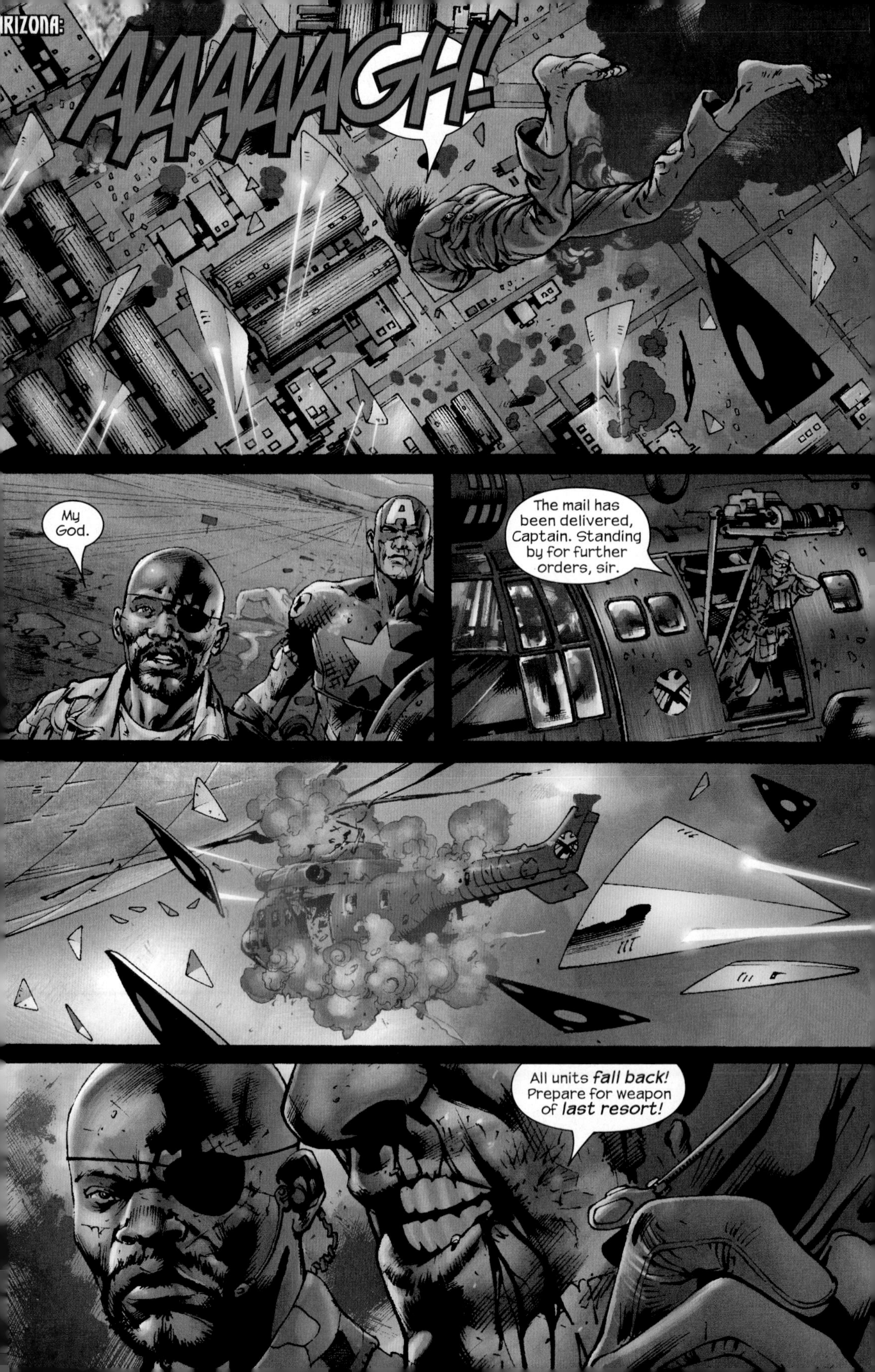
RIZONA:
AAAAAAGH!
My God.
The mail has been delivered, Captain. Standing by for further orders, sir.
All units *fall back!* Prepare for weapon of *last resort!*

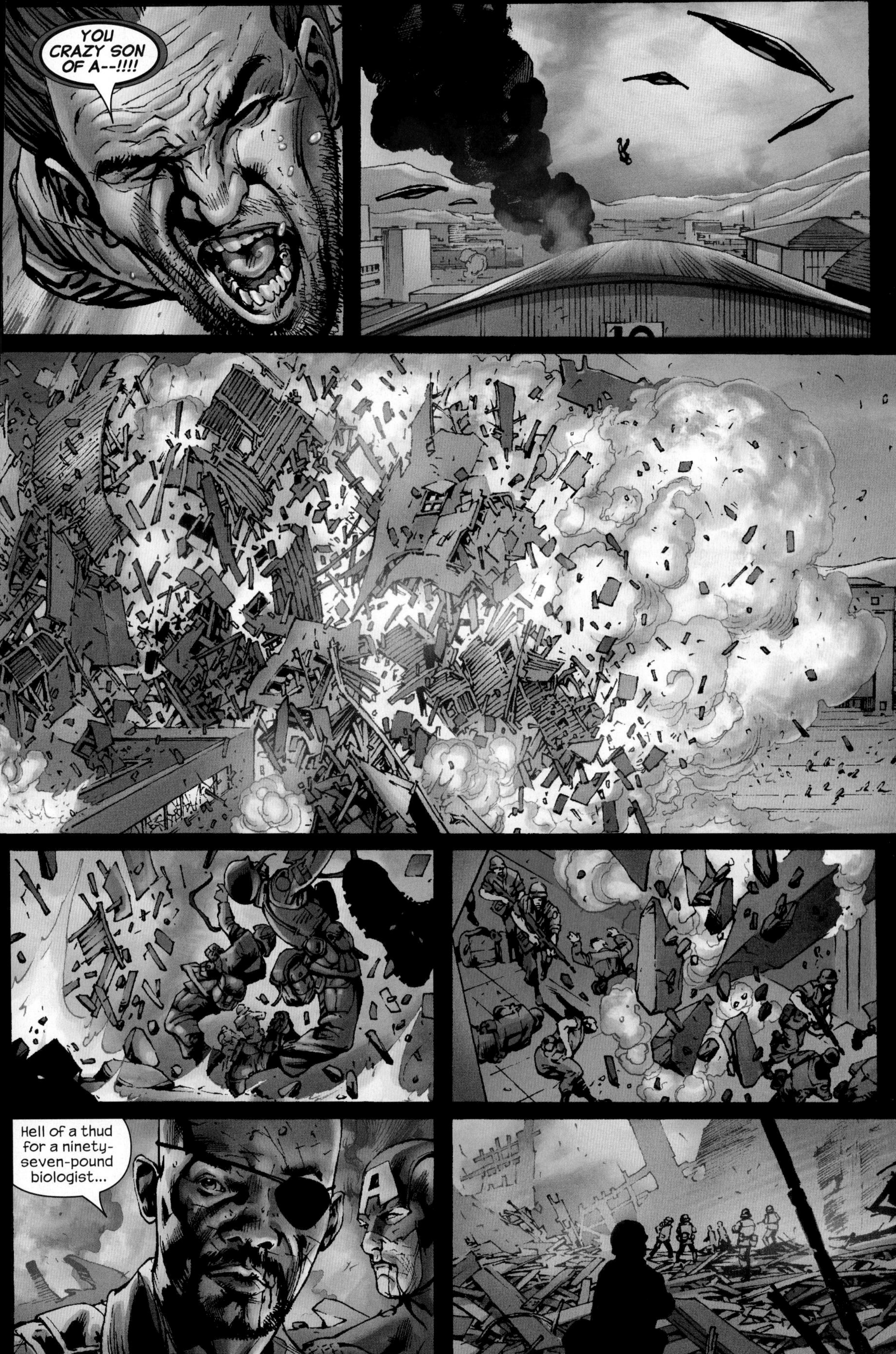
YOU CRAZY SON OF A--!!!!
Hell of a thud for a ninety-seven-pound biologist...

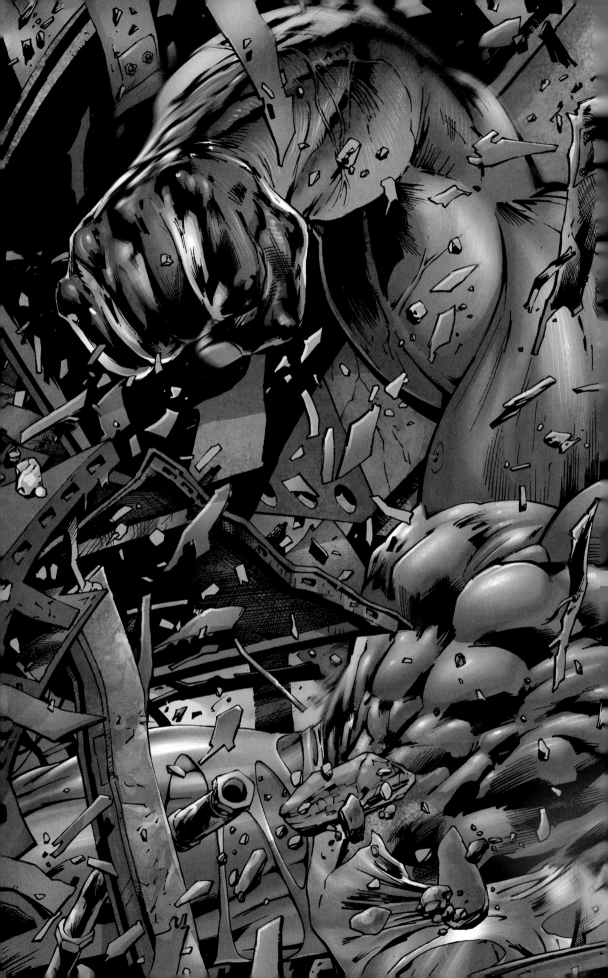

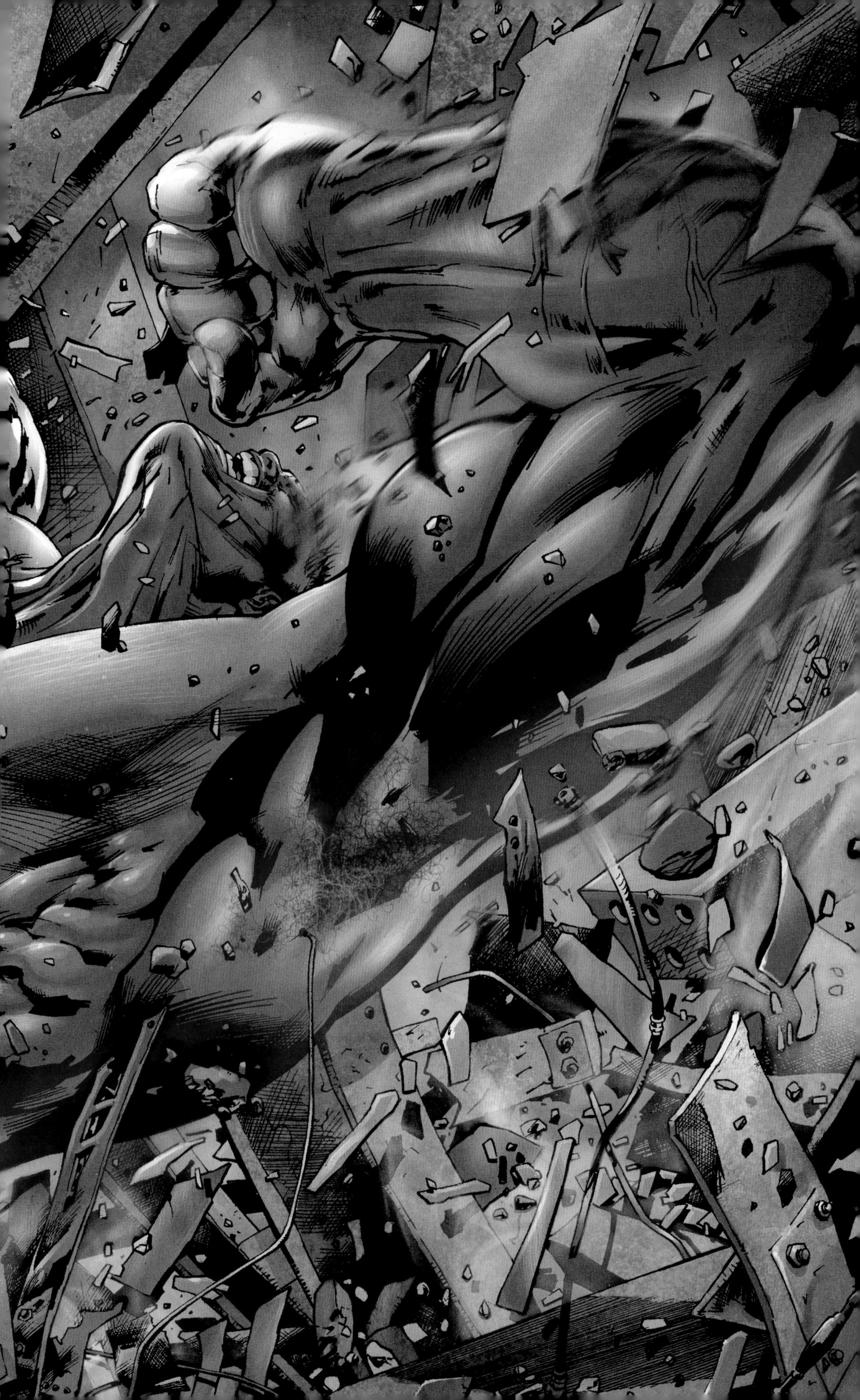

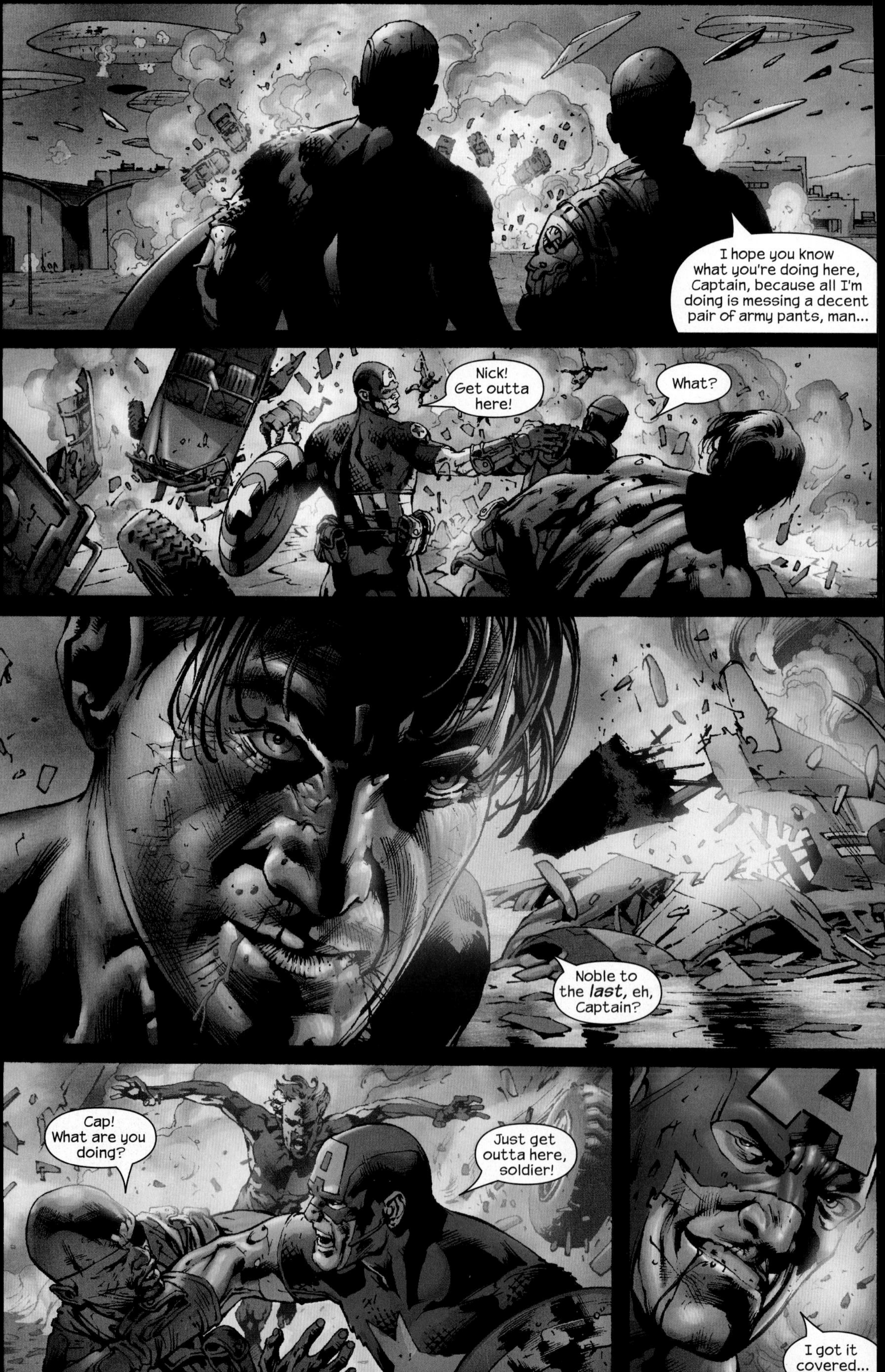
I hope you know what you're doing here, Captain, because all I'm doing is messing a decent pair of army pants, man...
Nick! Get outta here!
What?
Noble to the *last,* eh, Captain?
Cap! What are you doing?
Just get outta here, soldier!
I got it covered...

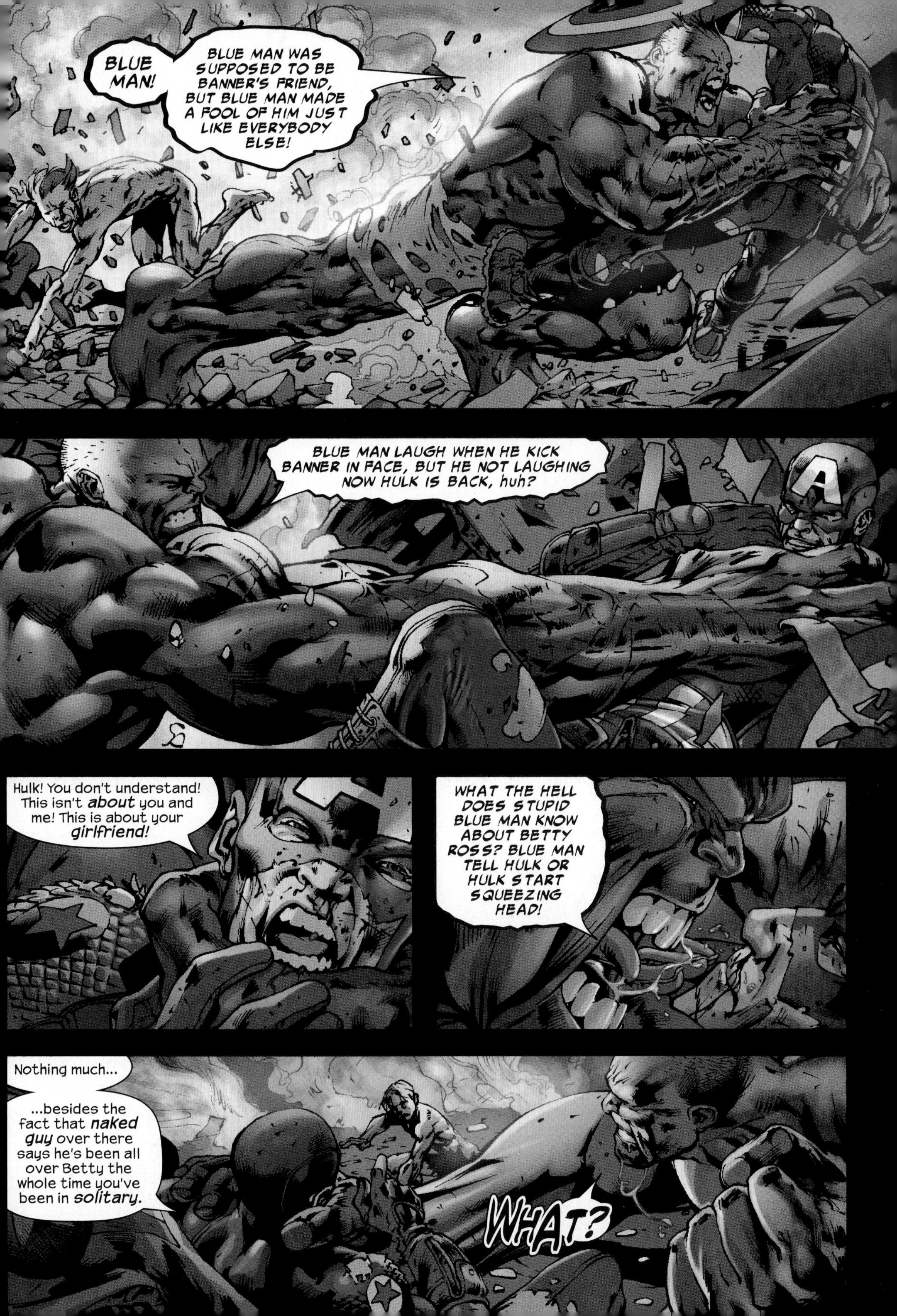
BLUE MAN!
BLUE MAN WAS SUPPOSED TO BE BANNER'S FRIEND, BUT BLUE MAN MADE A FOOL OF HIM JUST LIKE EVERYBODY ELSE!
BLUE MAN LAUGH WHEN HE KICK BANNER IN FACE, BUT HE NOT LAUGHING NOW HULK IS BACK, huh?
Hulk! You don't understand! This isn't about you and me! This is about your girlfriend!
WHAT THE HELL DOES STUPID BLUE MAN KNOW ABOUT BETTY ROSS? BLUE MAN TELL HULK OR HULK START SQUEEZING HEAD!
Nothing much...
...besides the fact that naked guy over there says he's been all over Betty the whole time you've been in solitary.
WHAT?

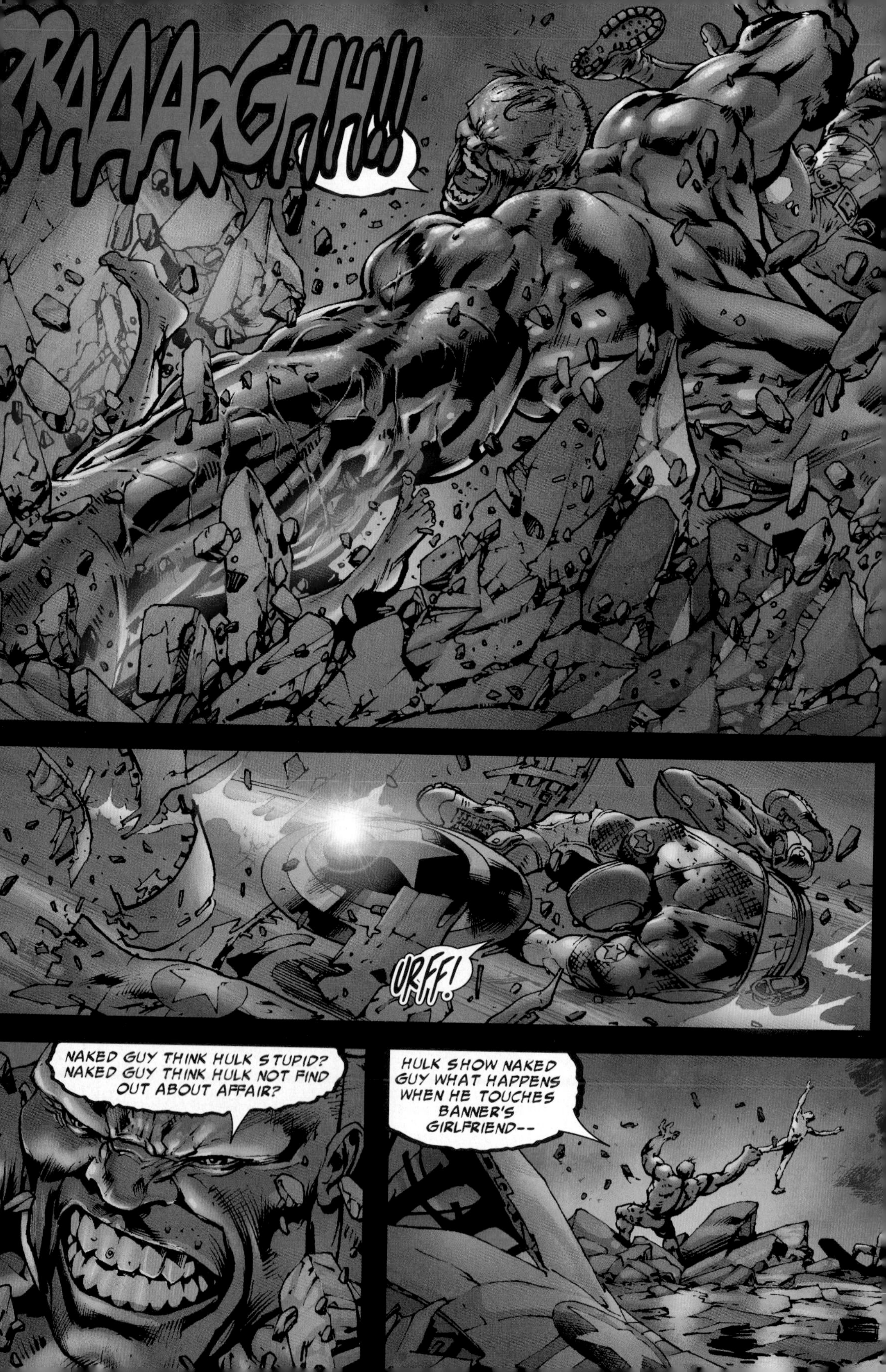
RAAARGHH!!
URFF!
NAKED GUY THINK HULK STUPID? NAKED GUY THINK HULK NOT FIND OUT ABOUT AFFAIR?
HULK SHOW NAKED GUY WHAT HAPPENS WHEN HE TOUCHES BANNER'S GIRLFRIEND--

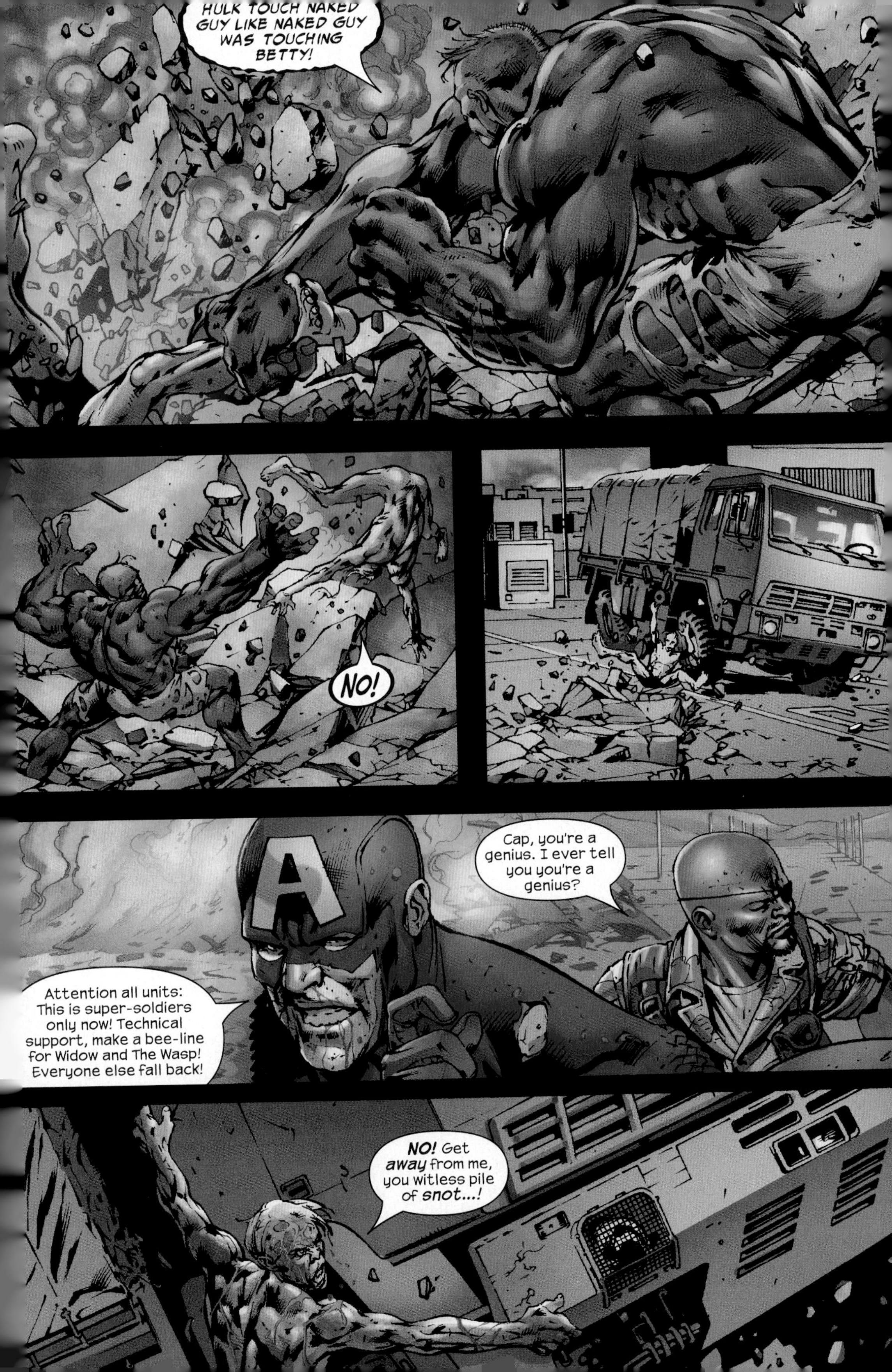
HULK TOUCH NAKED GUY LIKE NAKED GUY WAS TOUCHING BETTY!
NO!
Cap, you're a genius. I ever tell you you're a genius?
Attention all units: This is super-soldiers only now! Technical support, make a bee-line for Widow and The Wasp! Everyone else fall back!
NO! Get away from me, you witless pile of snot...!

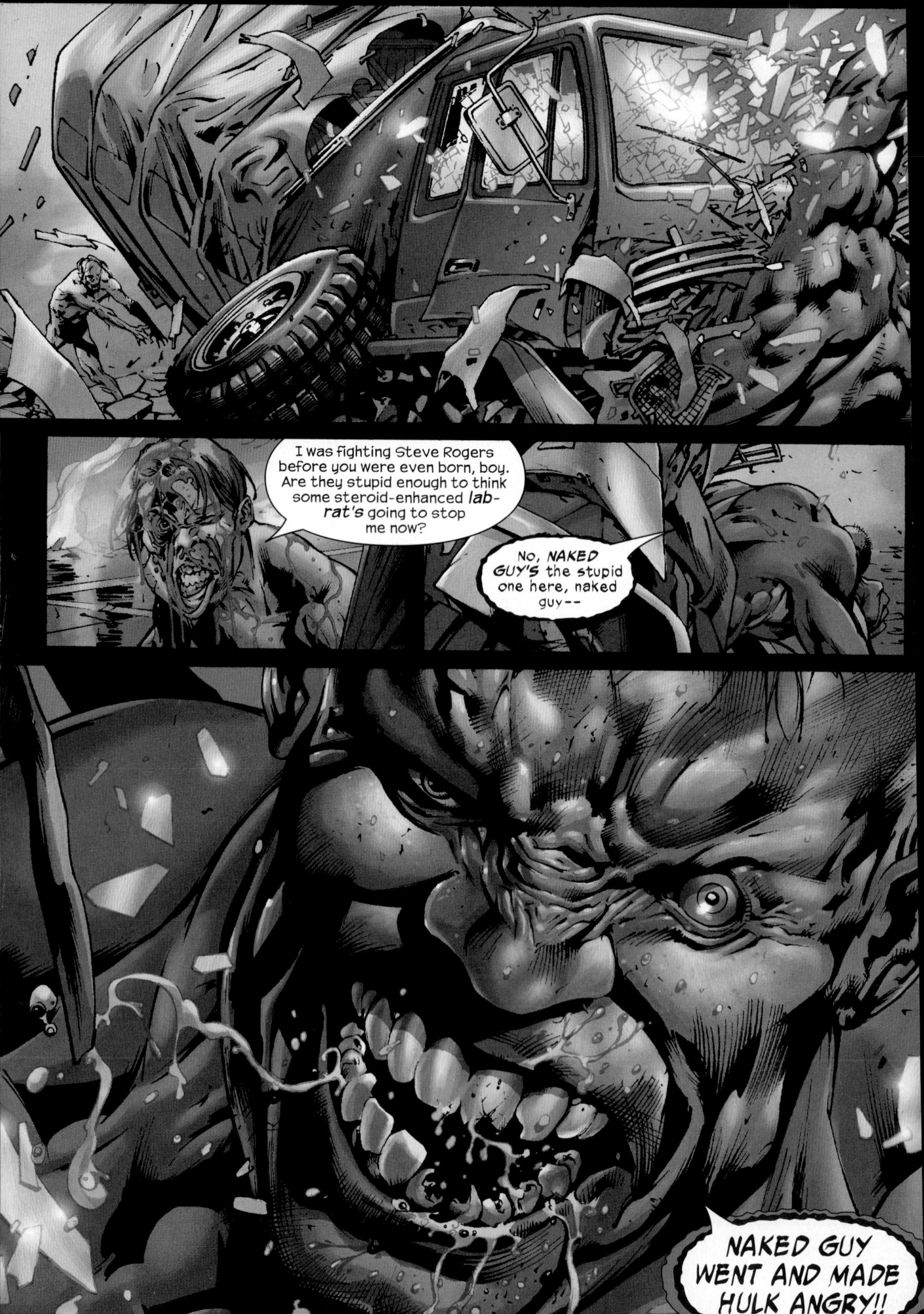
I was fighting Steve Rogers before you were even born, boy. Are they stupid enough to think some steroid-enhanced lab-rat's going to stop me now?
No, NAKED GUY'S the stupid one here, naked guy--
NAKED GUY WENT AND MADE HULK ANGRY!!

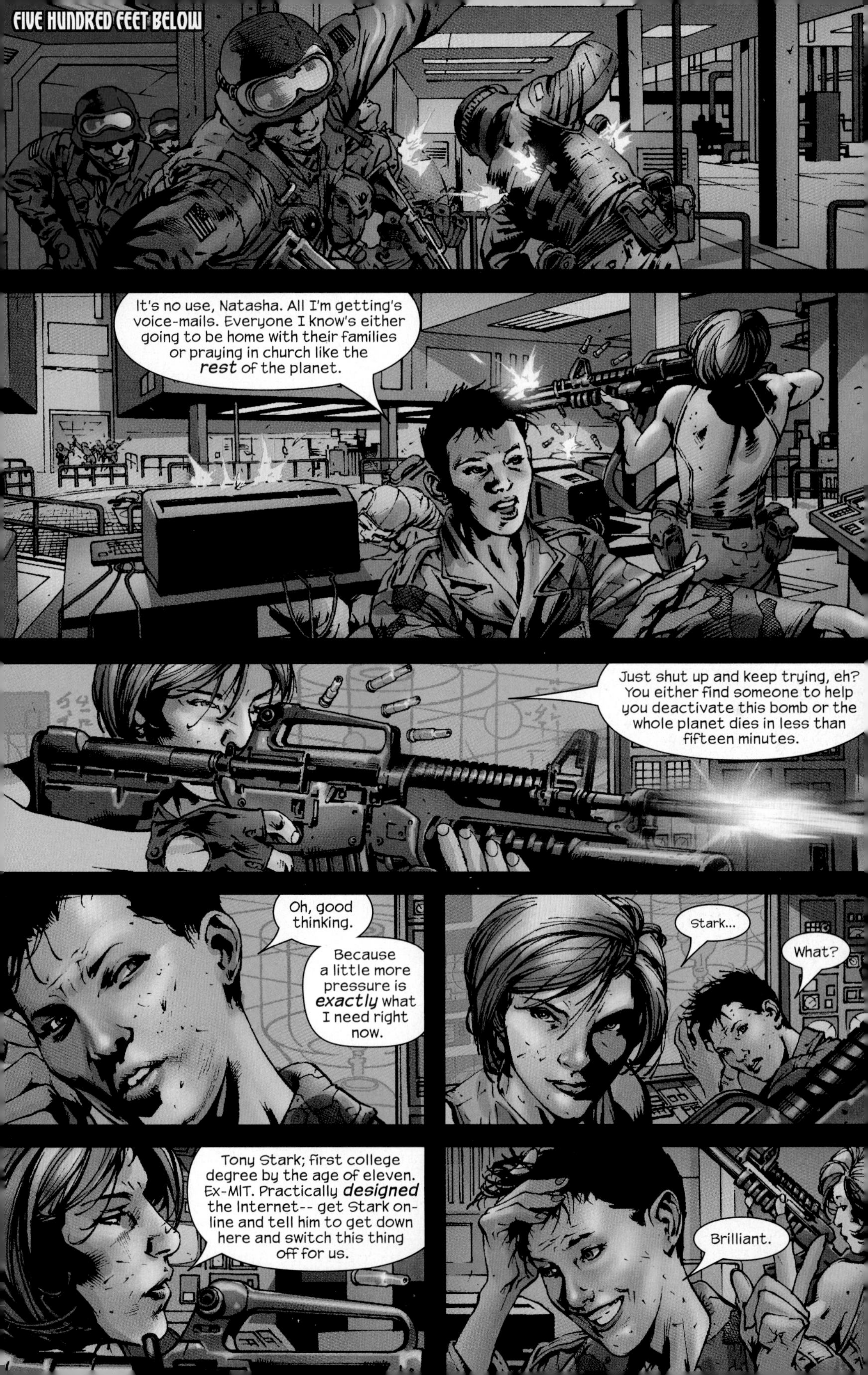
FIVE HUNDRED FEET BELOW
It's no use, Natasha. All I'm getting's voice-mails. Everyone I know's either going to be home with their families or praying in church like the *rest* of the planet.
Just shut up and keep trying, eh? You either find someone to help you deactivate this bomb or the whole planet dies in less than fifteen minutes.
Oh, good thinking.
Because a little more pressure is *exactly* what I need right now.
Stark...
What?
Tony Stark; first college degree by the age of eleven. Ex-MIT. Practically *designed* the Internet-- get Stark on-line and tell him to get down here and switch this thing off for us.
Brilliant.

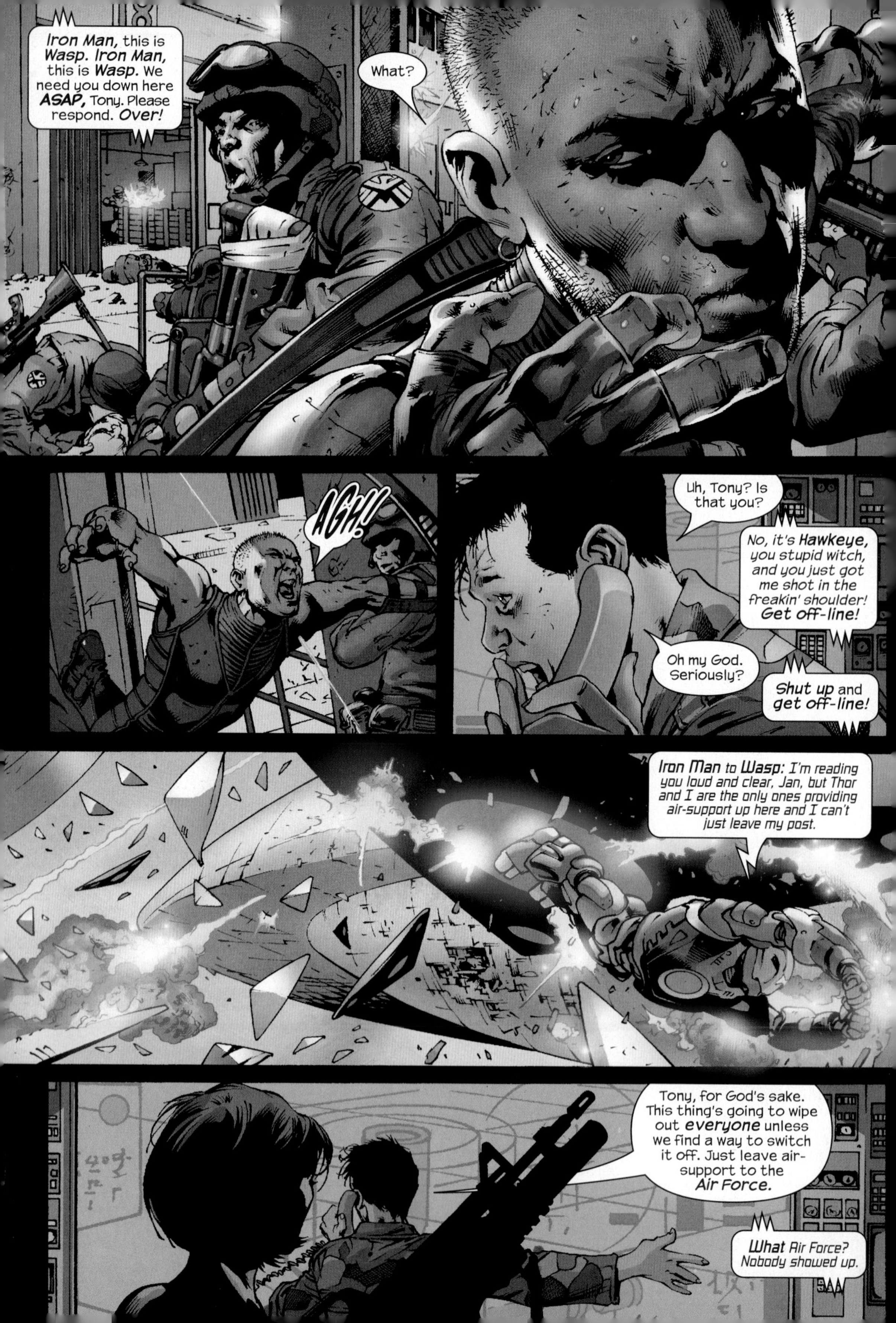
Iron Man, this is Wasp. Iron Man, this is Wasp. We need you down here ASAP, Tony. Please respond. Over!
What?
AGH!!
Uh, Tony? Is that you?
No, it's Hawkeye, you stupid witch, and you just got me shot in the freakin' shoulder! Get off-line!
Oh my God. Seriously?
Shut up and get off-line!
Iron Man to Wasp: I'm reading you loud and clear, Jan, but Thor and I are the only ones providing air-support up here and I can't just leave my post.
Tony, for God's sake. This thing's going to wipe out everyone unless we find a way to switch it off. Just leave air-support to the Air Force.
What Air Force? Nobody showed up.

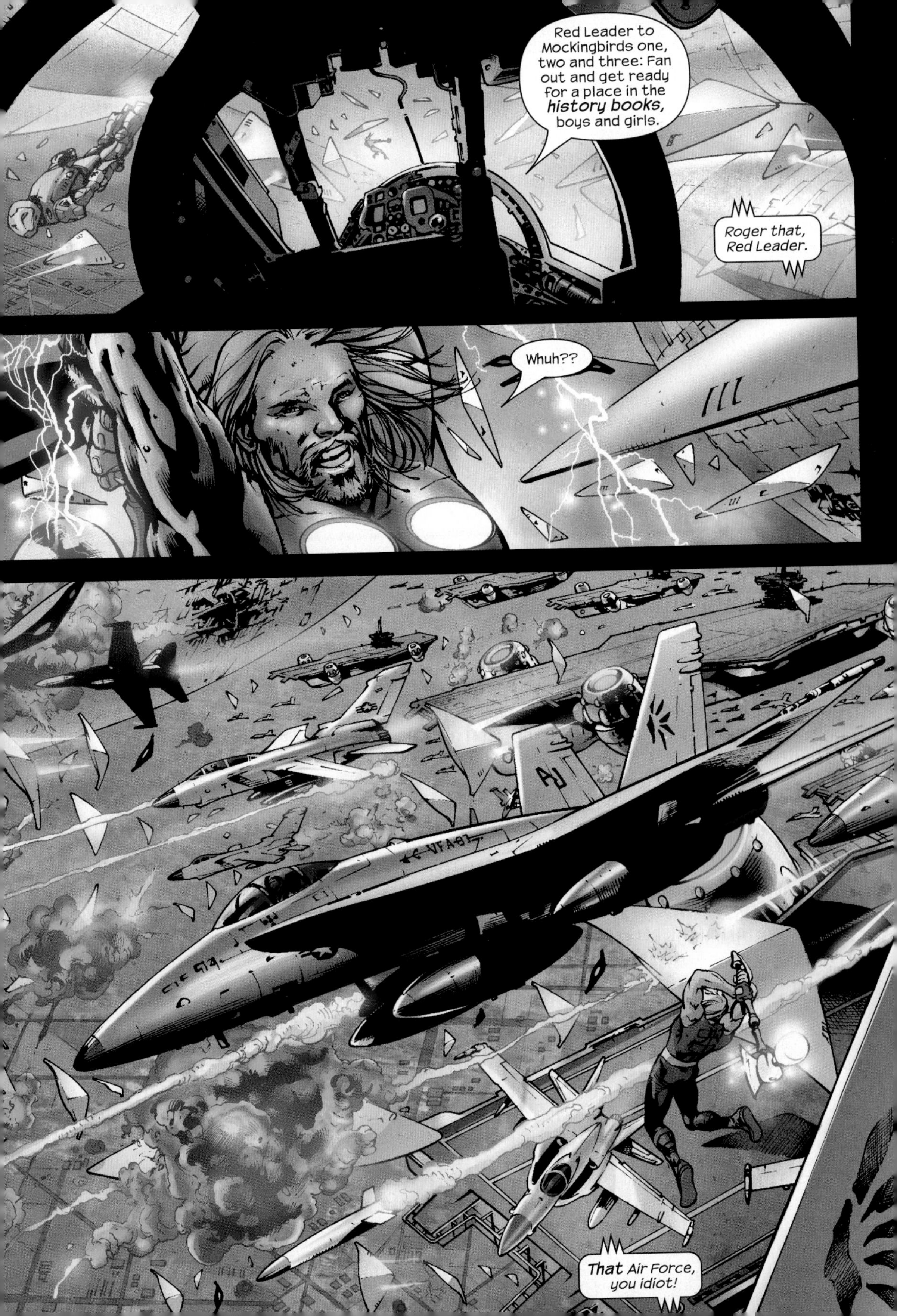
Red Leader to Mockingbirds one, two and three: Fan out and get ready for a place in the ***history books,*** boys and girls.
Roger that, Red Leader.
Whuh??
That *Air Force, you idiot!*

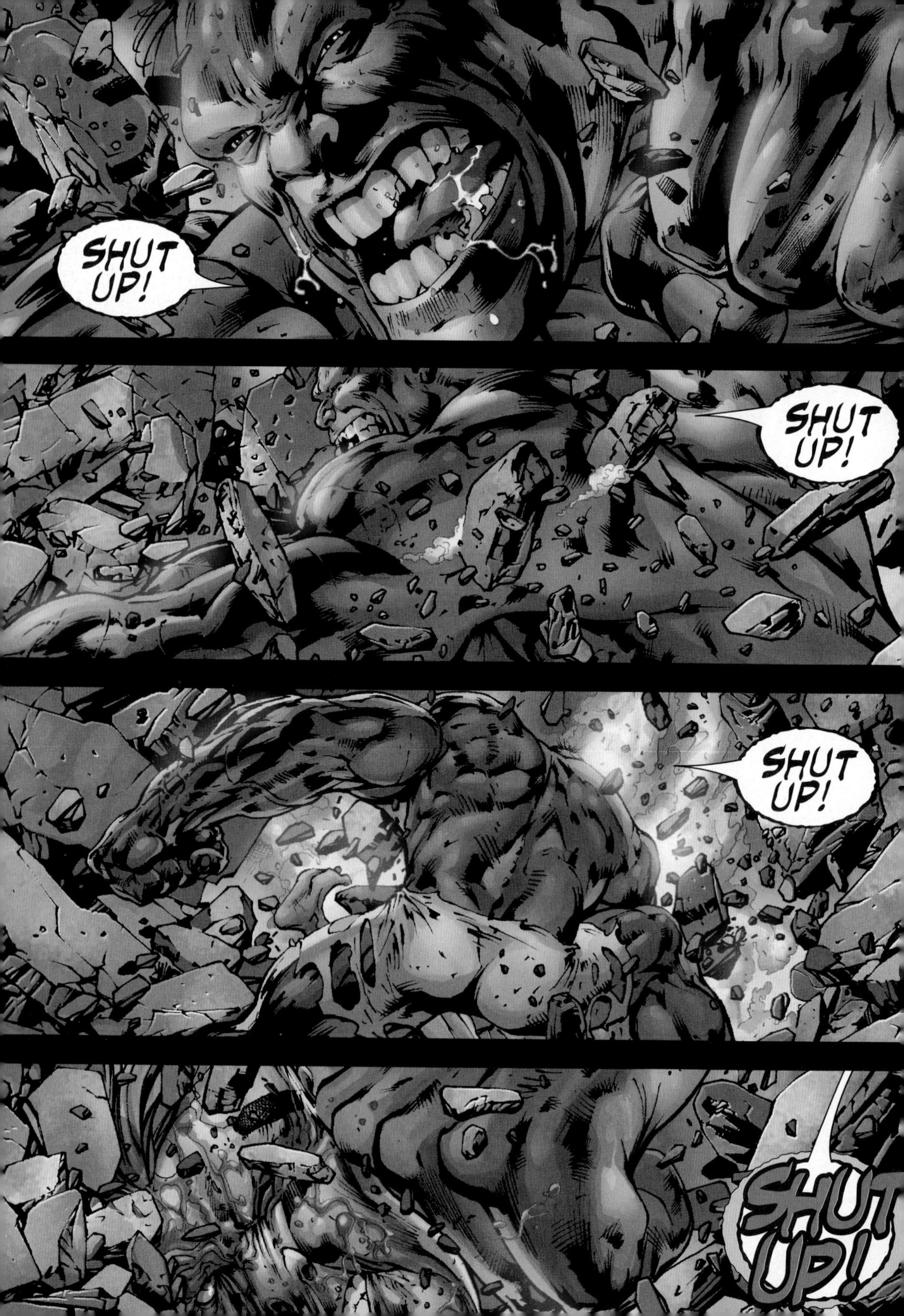
SHUT UP!
SHUT UP!
SHUT UP!
SHUT UP!

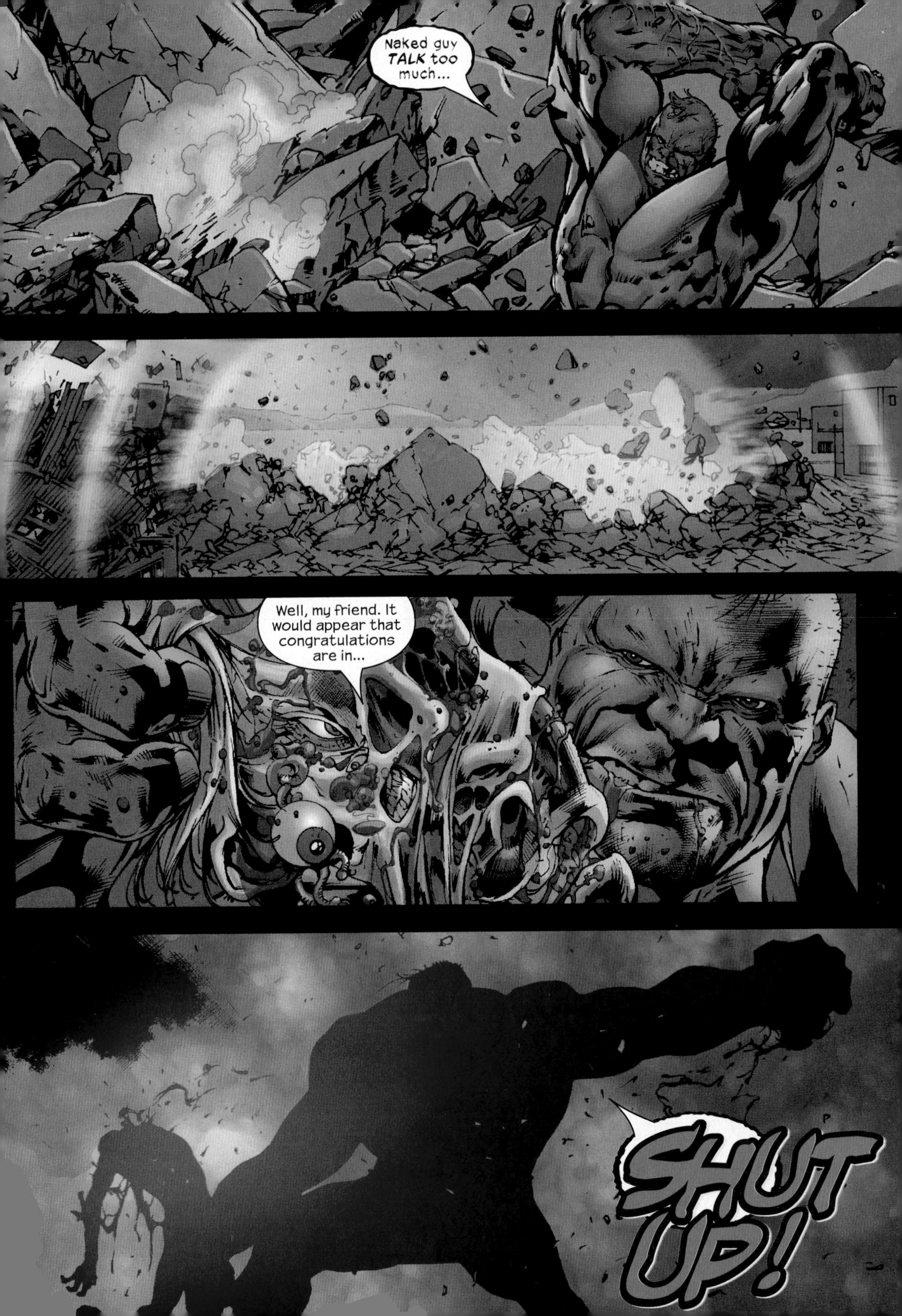
Naked guy TALK too much...
Well, my friend. It would appear that congratulations are in...
SHUT UP!

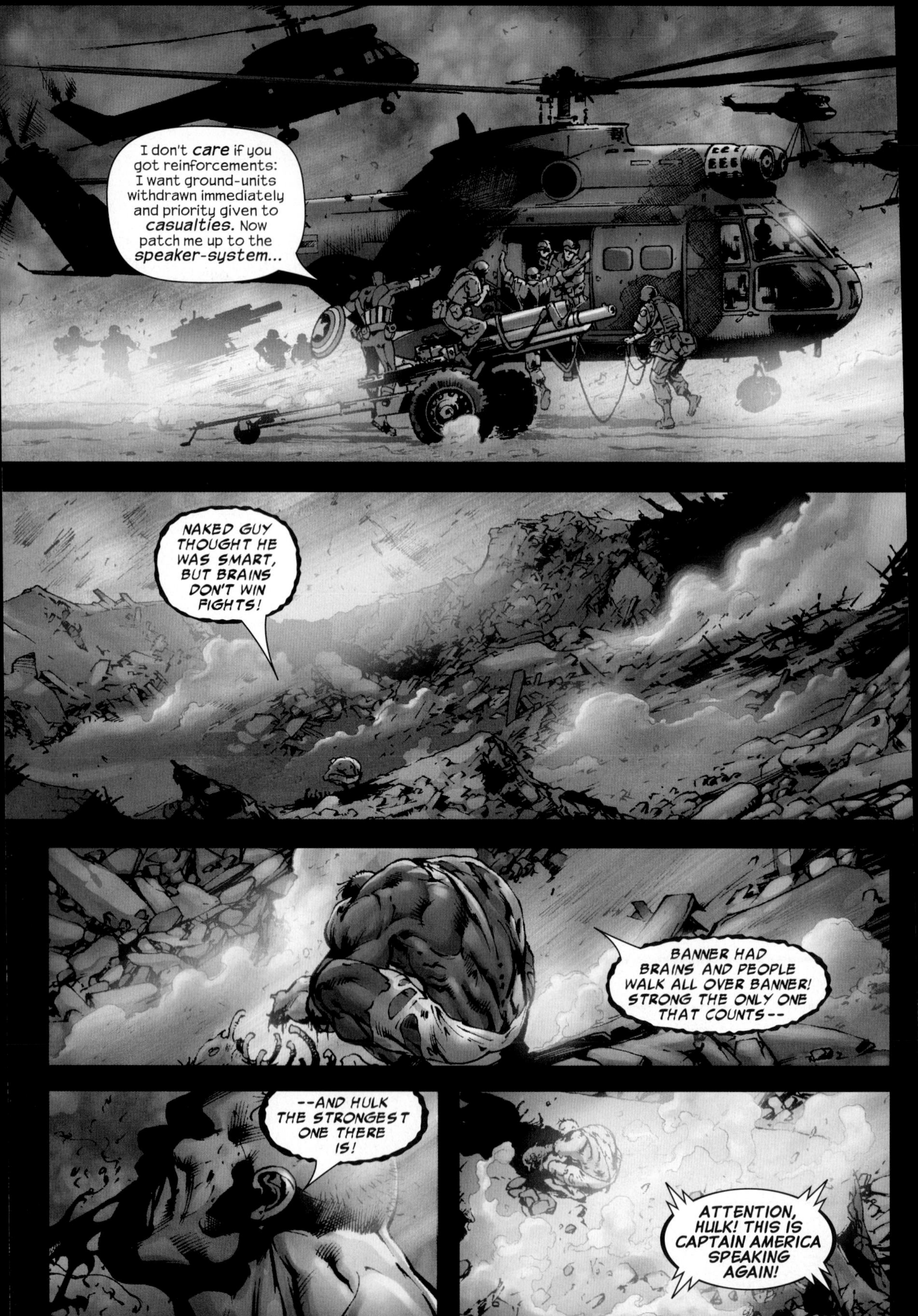
I don't care if you got reinforcements: I want ground-units withdrawn immediately and priority given to casualties. Now patch me up to the speaker-system...
NAKED GUY THOUGHT HE WAS SMART, BUT BRAINS DON'T WIN FIGHTS!
BANNER HAD BRAINS AND PEOPLE WALK ALL OVER BANNER! STRONG THE ONLY ONE THAT COUNTS--
--AND HULK THE STRONGEST ONE THERE IS!
ATTENTION, HULK! THIS IS CAPTAIN AMERICA SPEAKING AGAIN!

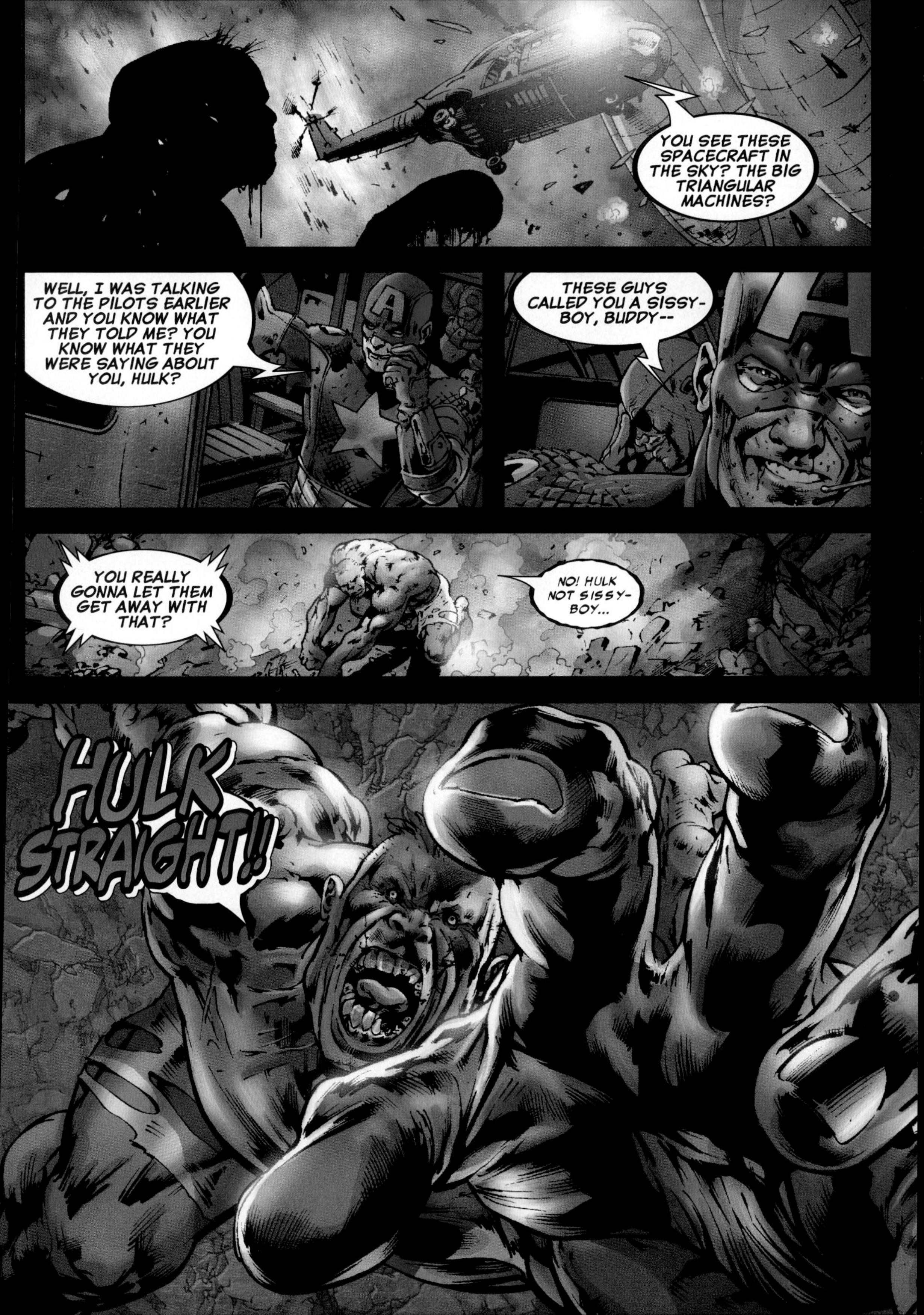

YOU SEE THESE SPACECRAFT IN THE SKY? THE BIG TRIANGULAR MACHINES?
WELL, I WAS TALKING TO THE PILOTS EARLIER AND YOU KNOW WHAT THEY TOLD ME? YOU KNOW WHAT THEY WERE SAYING ABOUT YOU, HULK?
THESE GUYS CALLED YOU A SISSY-BOY, BUDDY--
YOU REALLY GONNA LET THEM GET AWAY WITH THAT?
NO! HULK NOT SISSY-BOY...
HULK STRAIGHT!!

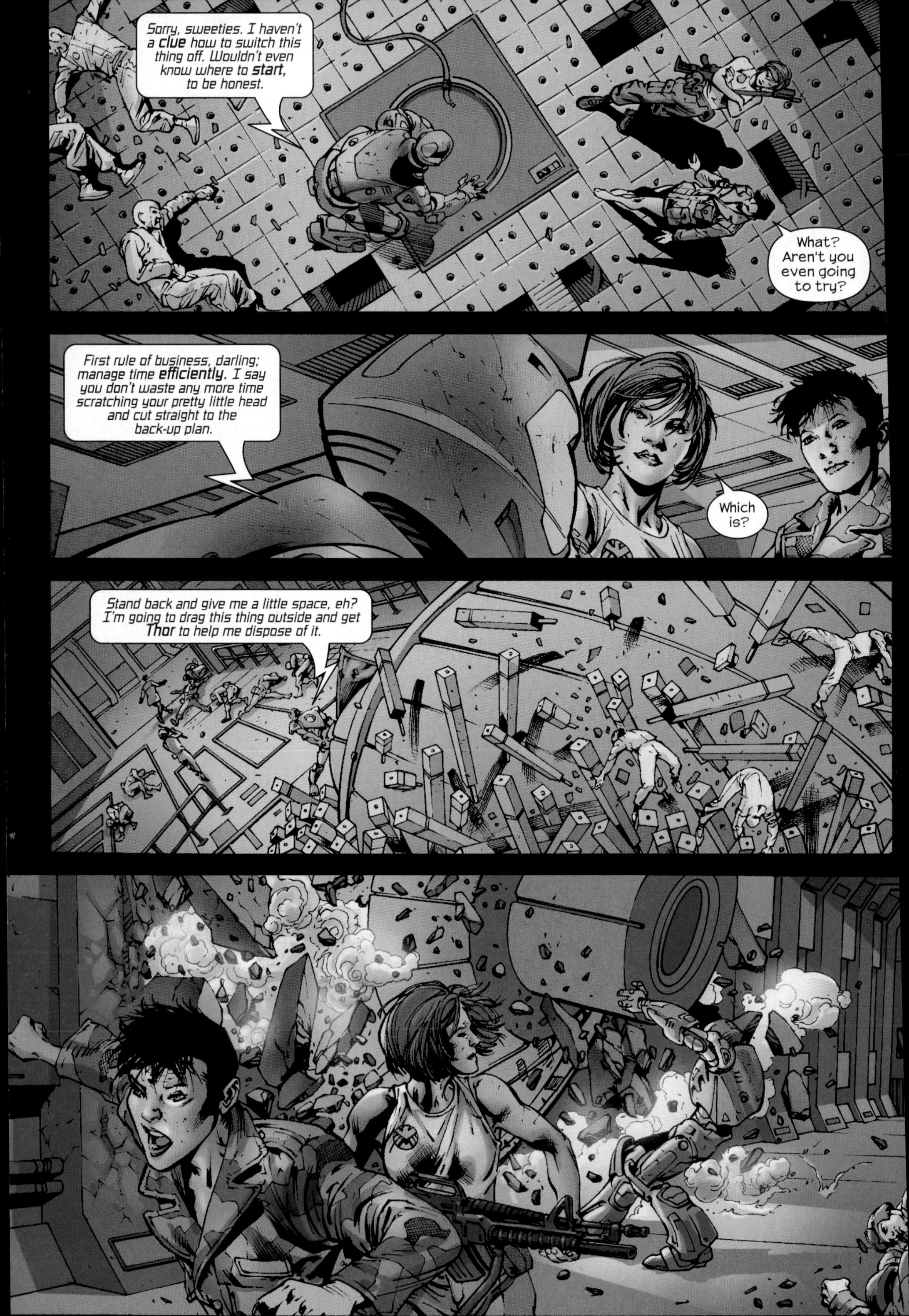
Sorry, sweeties. I haven't a clue how to switch this thing off. Wouldn't even know where to start, to be honest.
What? Aren't you even going to try?
First rule of business, darling; manage time efficiently. I say you don't waste any more time scratching your pretty little head and cut straight to the back-up plan.
Which is?
Stand back and give me a little space, eh? I'm going to drag this thing outside and get Thor to help me dispose of it.

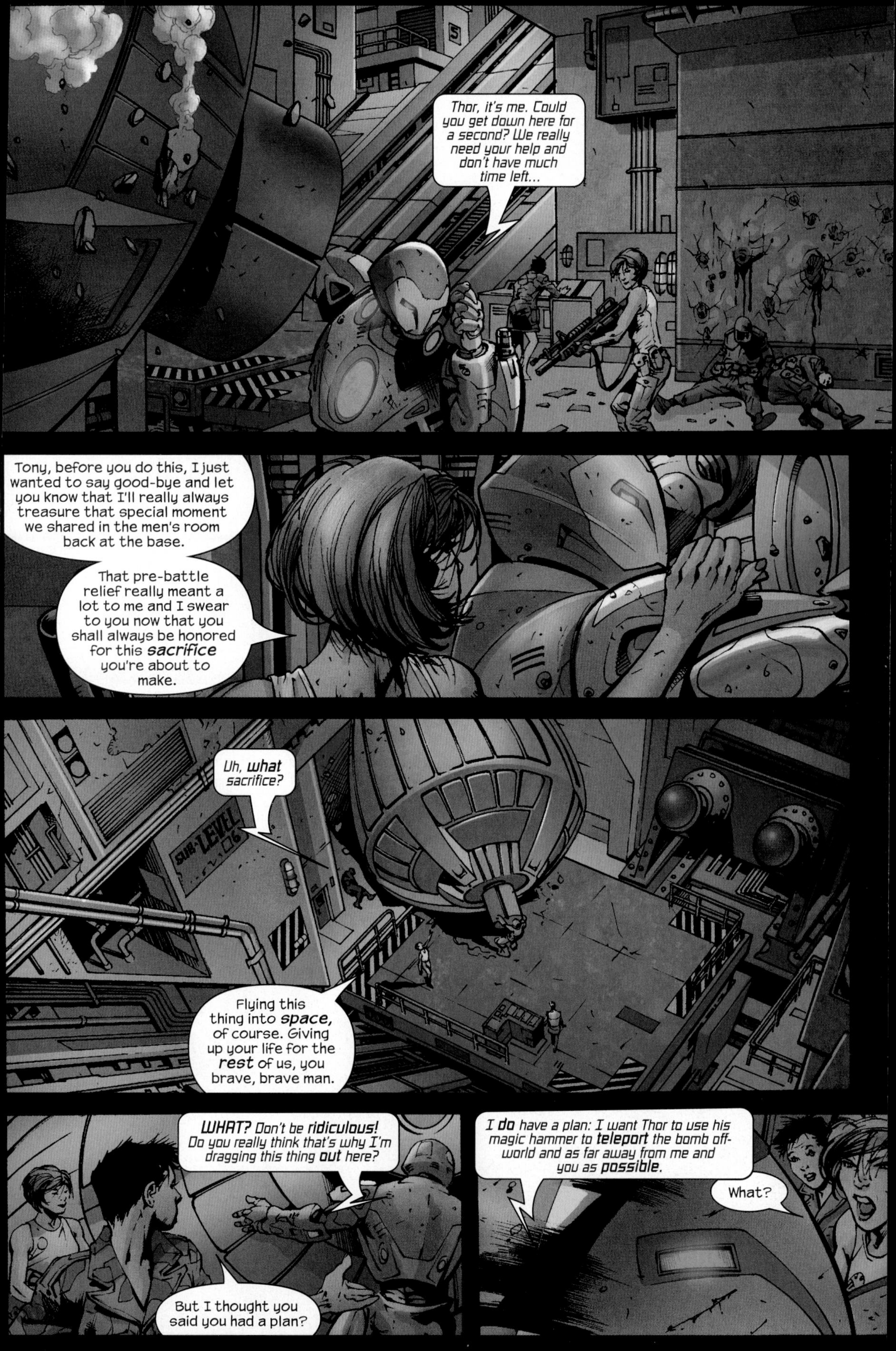
Thor, it's me. Could you get down here for a second? We really need your help and don't have much time left...
Tony, before you do this, I just wanted to say good-bye and let you know that I'll really always treasure that special moment we shared in the men's room back at the base.
That pre-battle relief really meant a lot to me and I swear to you now that you shall always be honored for this sacrifice you're about to make.
SUB-LEVEL 06
Uh, what sacrifice?
Flying this thing into space, of course. Giving up your life for the rest of us, you brave, brave man.
WHAT? Don't be ridiculous! Do you really think that's why I'm dragging this thing out here?
But I thought you said you had a plan?
I do have a plan: I want Thor to use his magic hammer to teleport the bomb off-world and as far away from me and you as possible.
What?

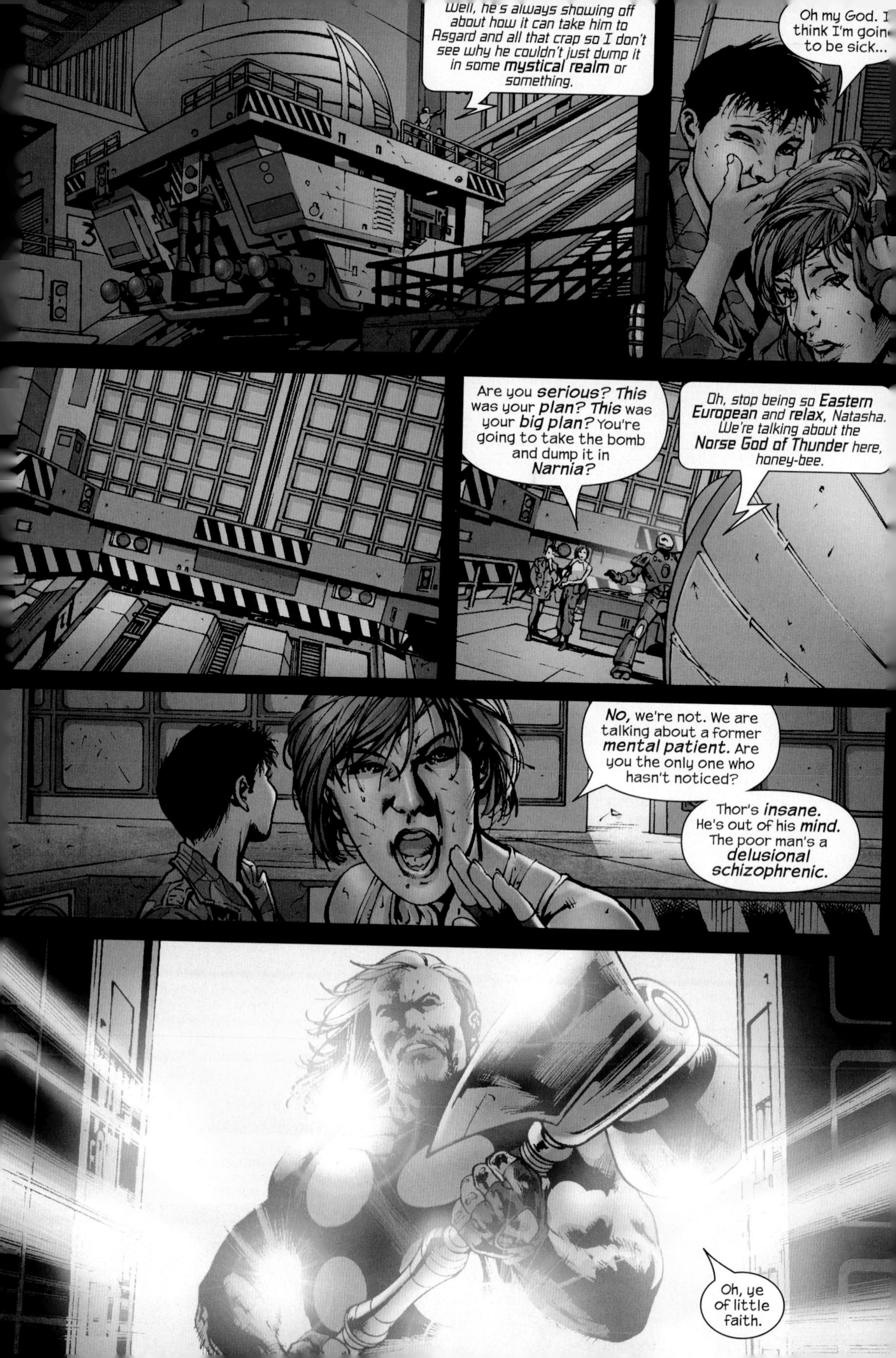

Well, he's always showing off about how it can take him to Asgard and all that crap so I don't see why he couldn't just dump it in some mystical realm or something.
Oh my God. I think I'm goin to be sick...
Are you serious? This was your plan? This was your big plan? You're going to take the bomb and dump it in Narnia?
Oh, stop being so Eastern European and relax, Natasha. We're talking about the Norse God of Thunder here, honey-bee.
No, we're not. We are talking about a former mental patient. Are you the only one who hasn't noticed?
Thor's insane. He's out of his mind. The poor man's a delusional schizophrenic.
Oh, ye of little faith.

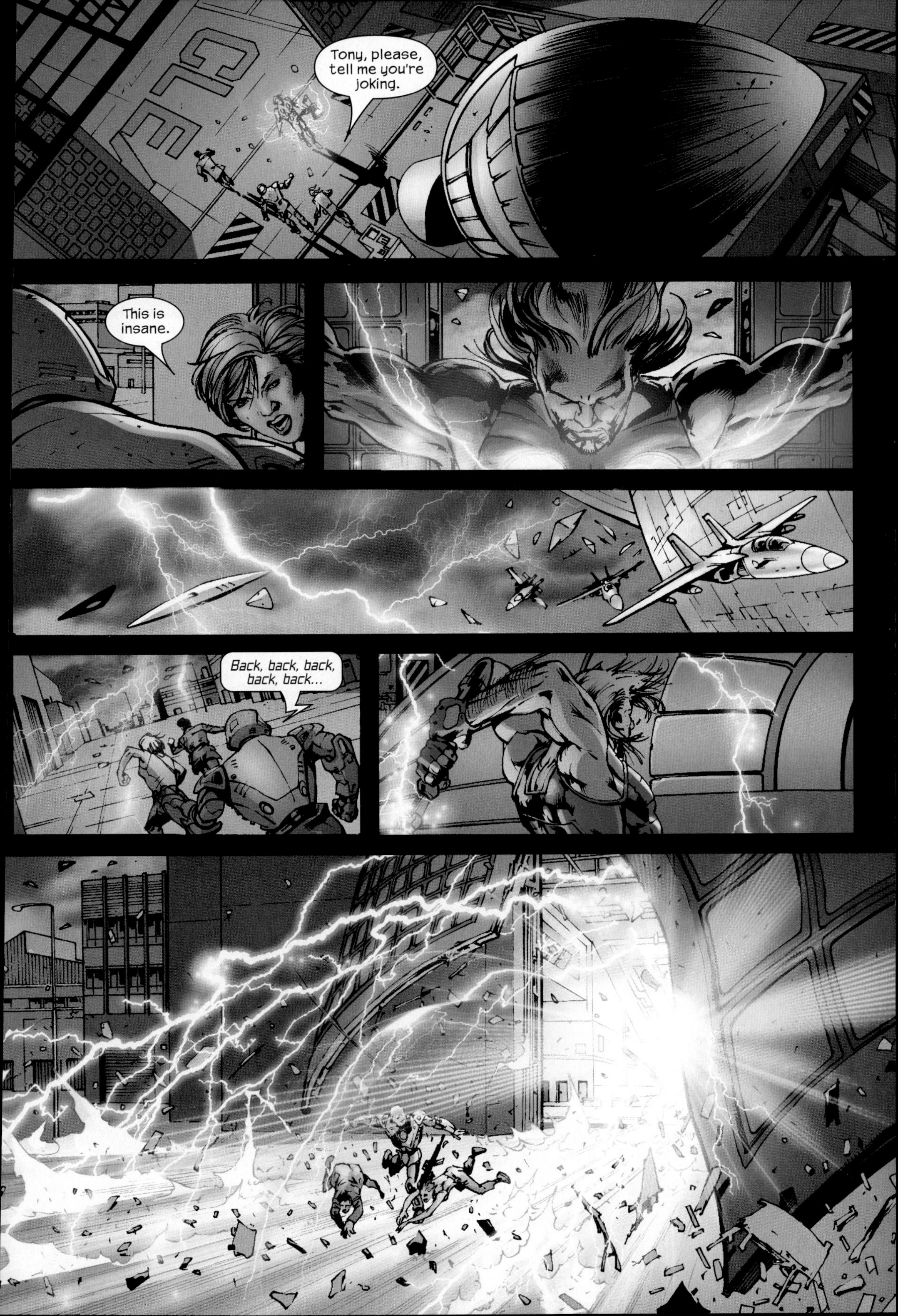
Tony, please, tell me you're joking.
This is insane.
Back, back, back, back, back...

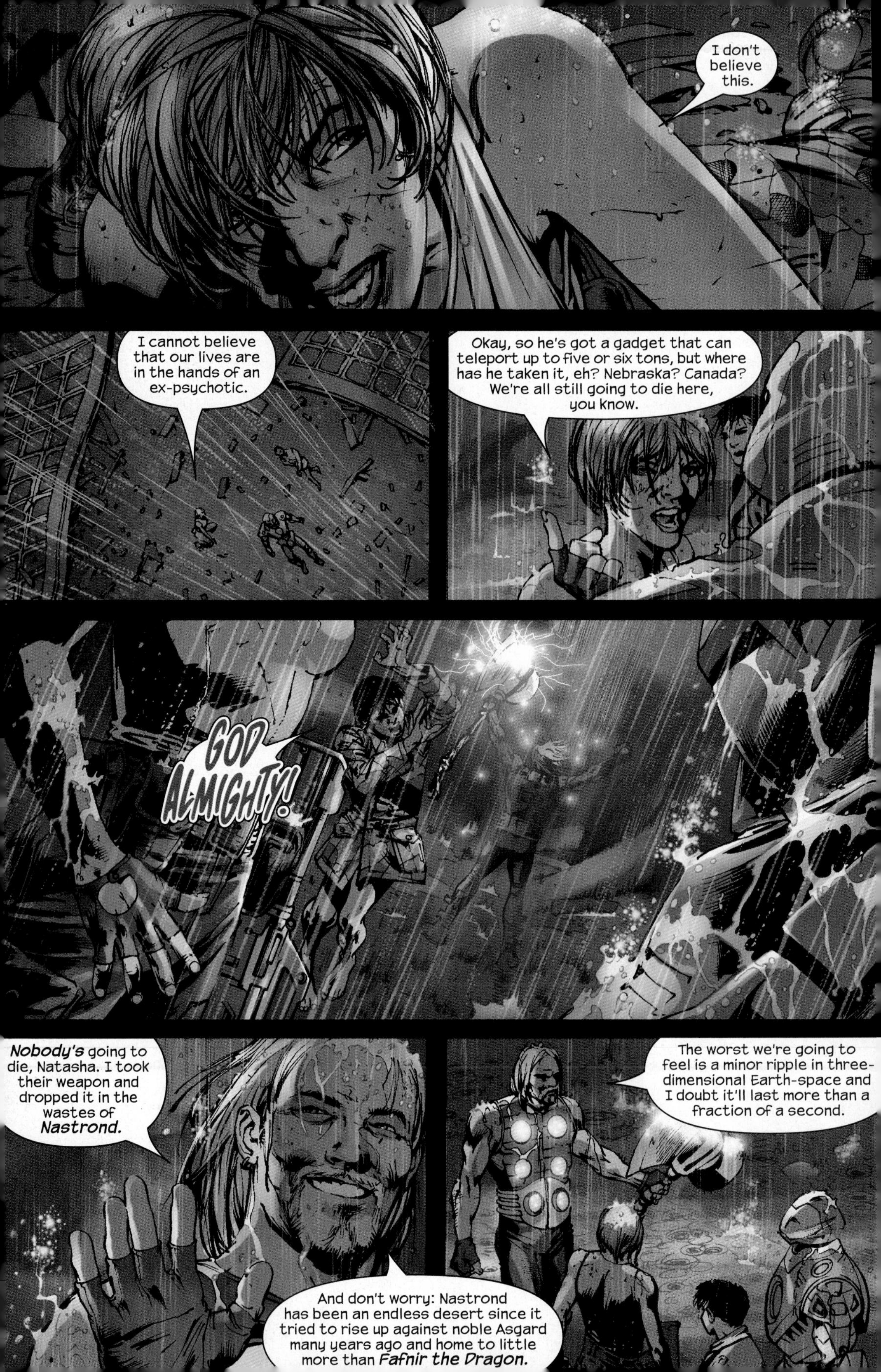
I don't believe this.
I cannot believe that our lives are in the hands of an ex-psychotic.
Okay, so he's got a gadget that can teleport up to five or six tons, but where has he taken it, eh? Nebraska? Canada? We're all still going to die here, you know.
GOD ALMIGHTY!
Nobody's going to die, Natasha. I took their weapon and dropped it in the wastes of ***Nastrond.***
The worst we're going to feel is a minor ripple in three-dimensional Earth-space and I doubt it'll last more than a fraction of a second.
And don't worry: Nastrond has been an endless desert since it tried to rise up against noble Asgard many years ago and home to little more than ***Fafnir the Dragon.***

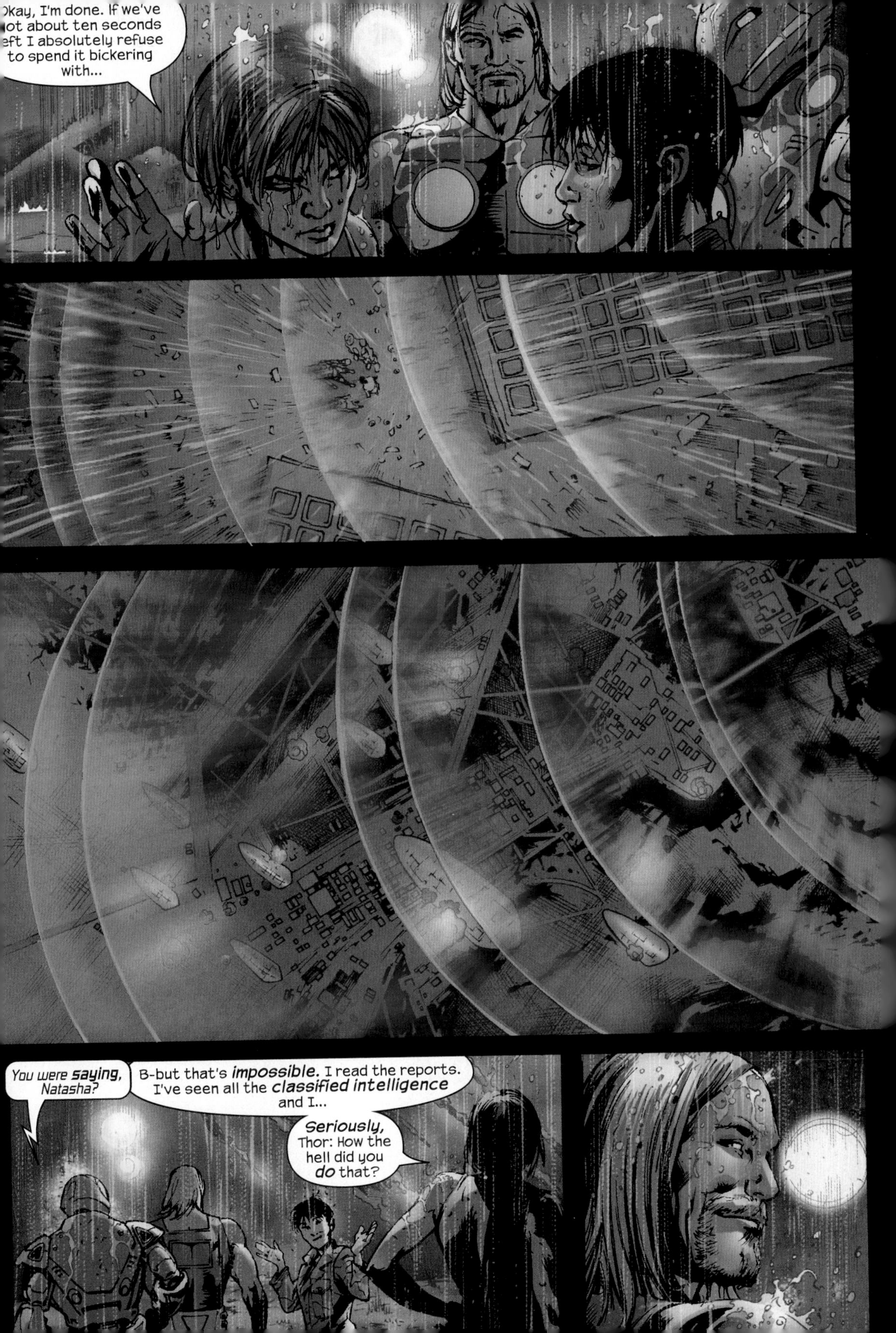
Okay, I'm done. If we've got about ten seconds left I absolutely refuse to spend it bickering with...
You were saying, Natasha?
B-but that's impossible. I read the reports. I've seen all the classified intelligence and I...
Seriously, Thor: How the hell did you do that?

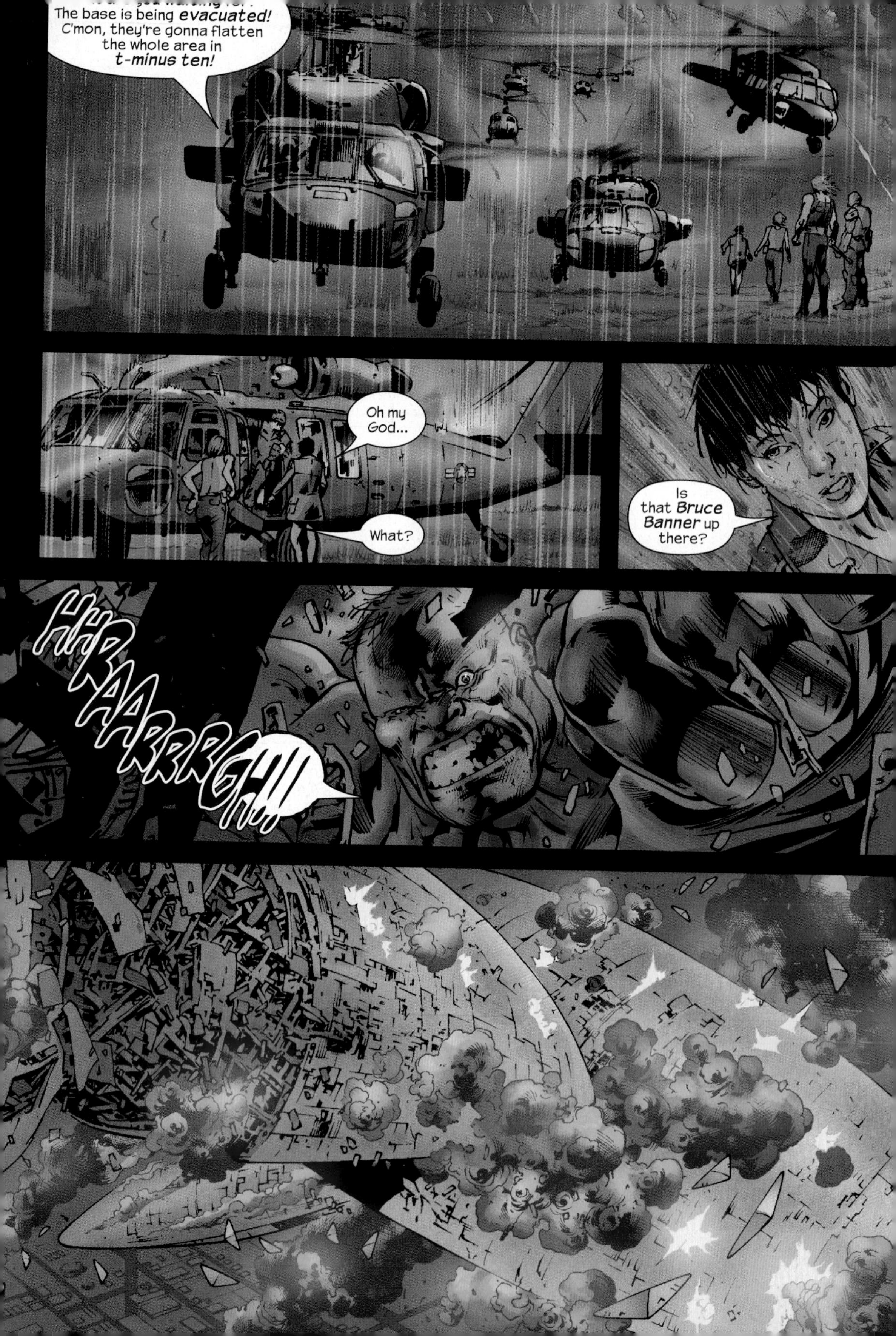

The base is being evacuated! C'mon, they're gonna flatten the whole area in t-minus ten!
Oh my God...
What?
Is that Bruce Banner up there?
HHRAARRRGH!!

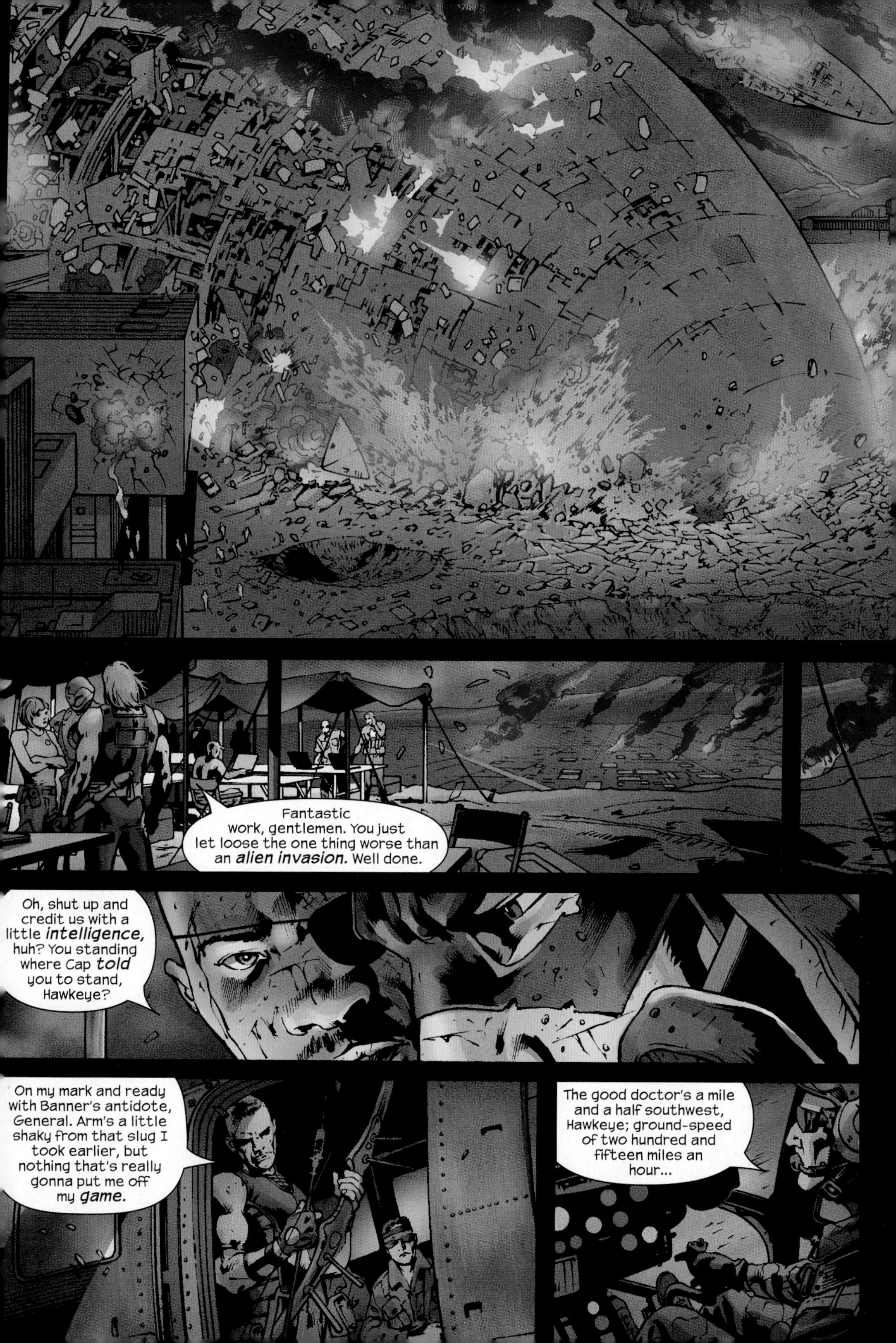

Fantastic work, gentlemen. You just let loose the one thing worse than an *alien invasion.* Well done.
Oh, shut up and credit us with a little *intelligence,* huh? You standing where Cap *told* you to stand, Hawkeye?
On my mark and ready with Banner's antidote, General. Arm's a little shaky from that slug I took earlier, but nothing that's really gonna put me off my *game.*
The good doctor's a mile and a half southwest, Hawkeye; ground-speed of two hundred and fifteen miles an hour...

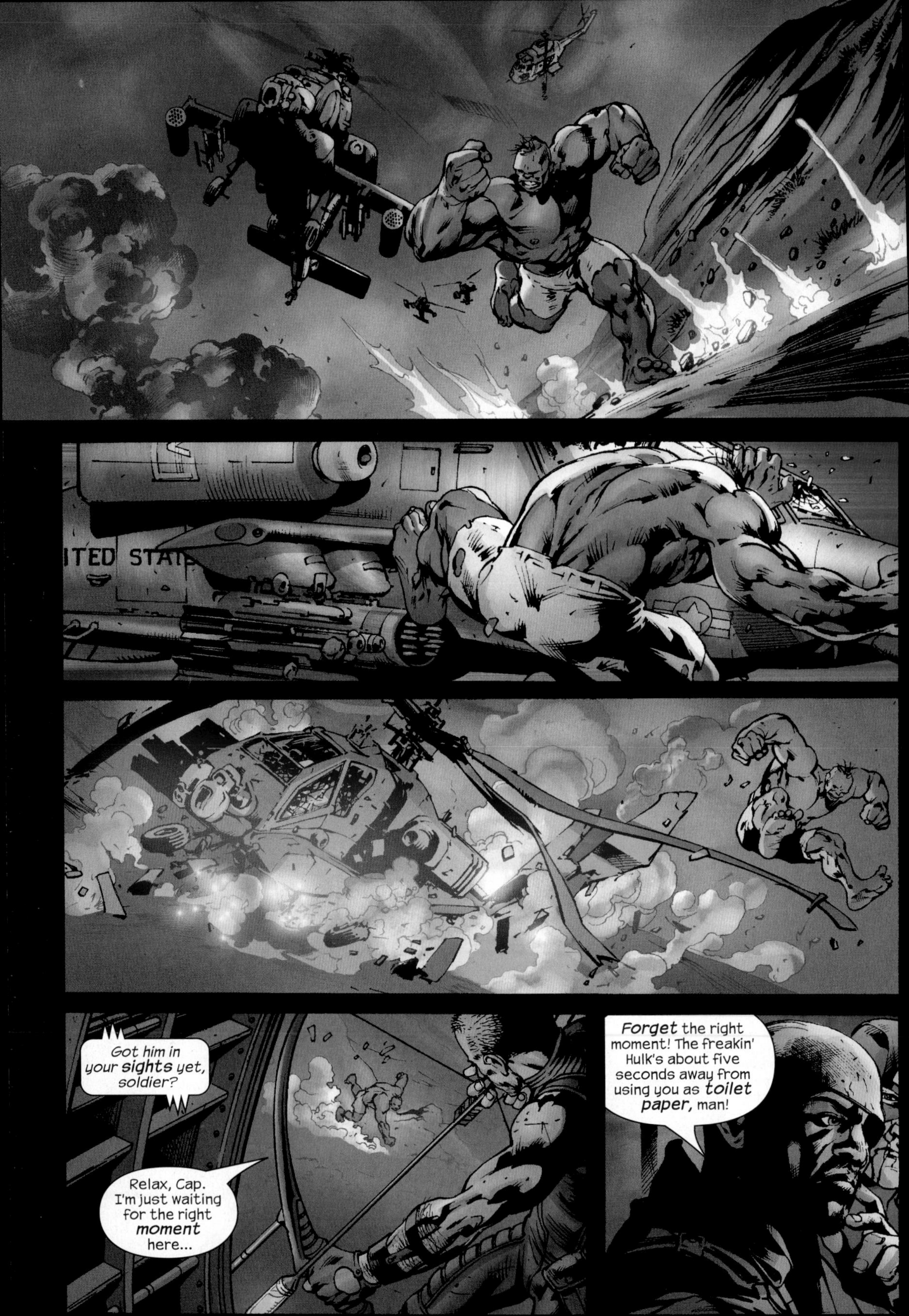
ITED STAT
Got him in your sights yet, soldier?
Relax, Cap. I'm just waiting for the right moment here...
Forget the right moment! The freakin' Hulk's about five seconds away from using you as toilet paper, man!

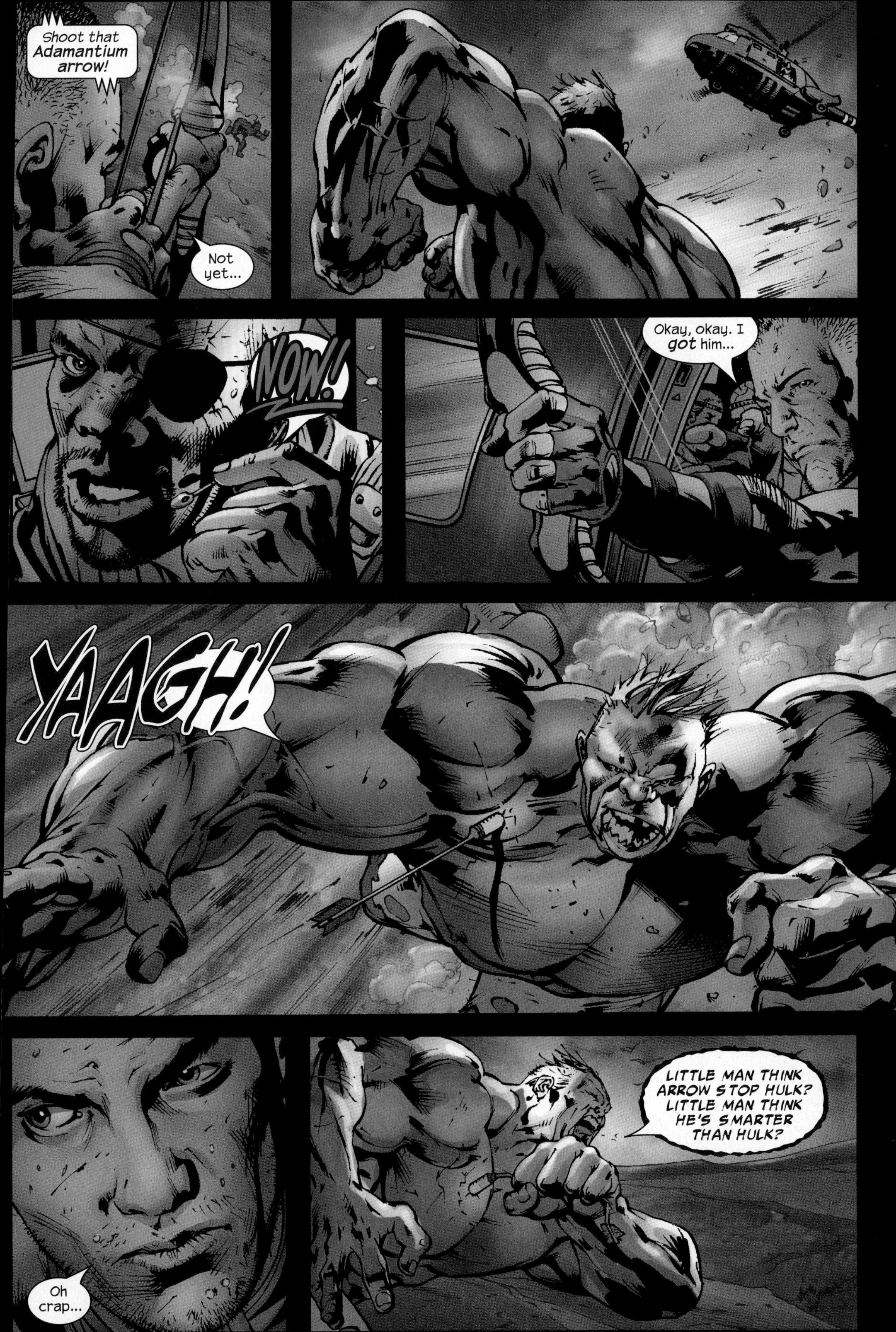
Shoot that Adamantium arrow!
Not yet...
NOW!
Okay, okay. I got him...
YAAGH!
Oh crap...
LITTLE MAN THINK ARROW STOP HULK? LITTLE MAN THINK HE'S SMARTER THAN HULK?

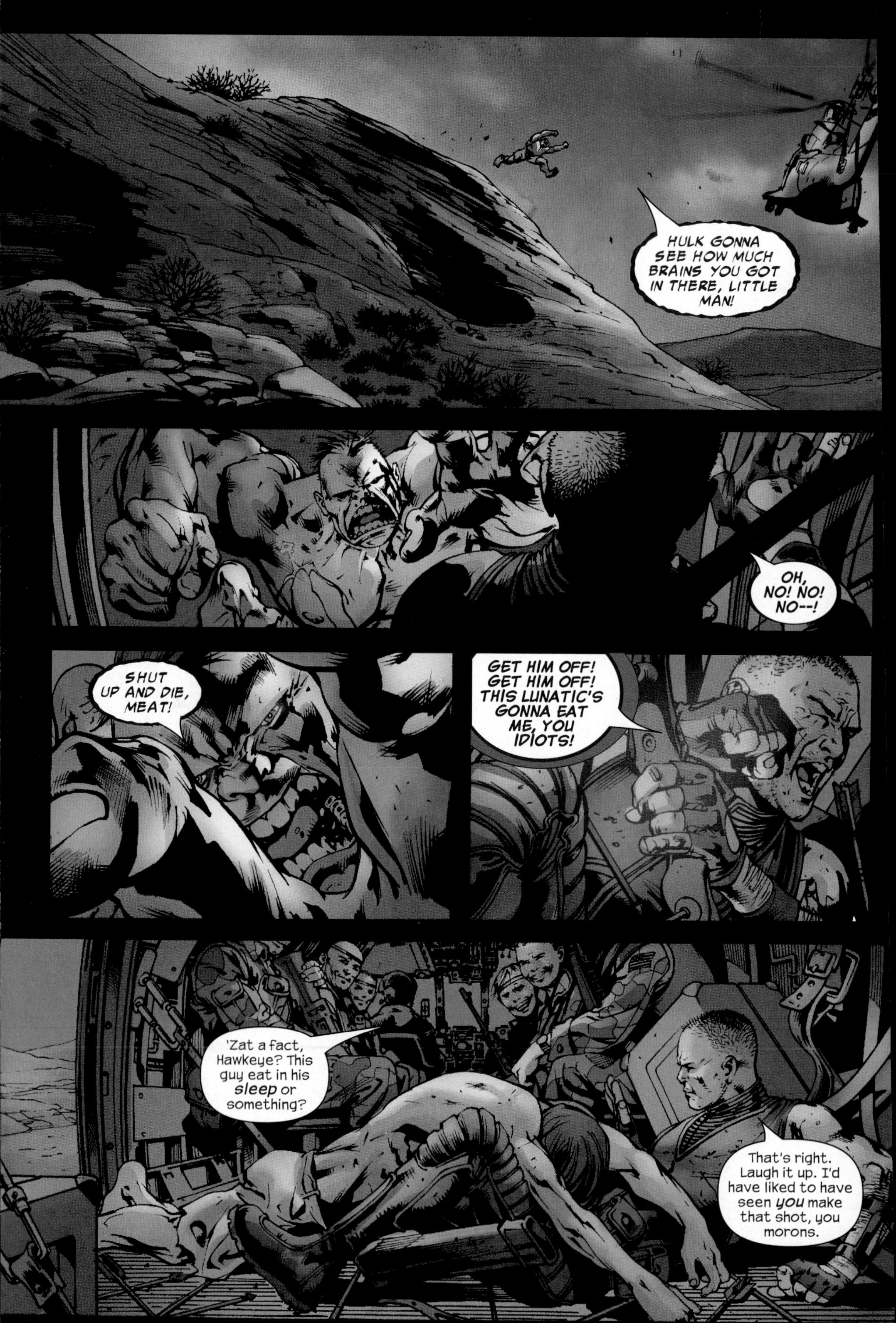
HULK GONNA SEE HOW MUCH BRAINS YOU GOT IN THERE, LITTLE MAN!
OH, NO! NO! NO--!
SHUT UP AND DIE, MEAT!
GET HIM OFF! GET HIM OFF! THIS LUNATIC'S GONNA EAT ME, YOU IDIOTS!
'Zat a fact, Hawkeye? This guy eat in his *sleep* or something?
That's right. Laugh it up. I'd have liked to have seen *you* make that shot, you morons.

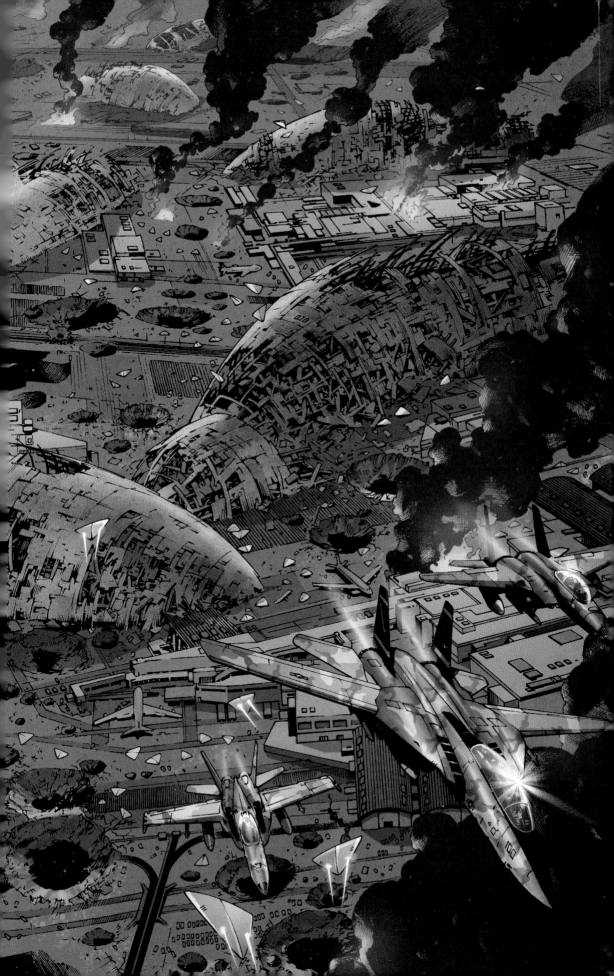

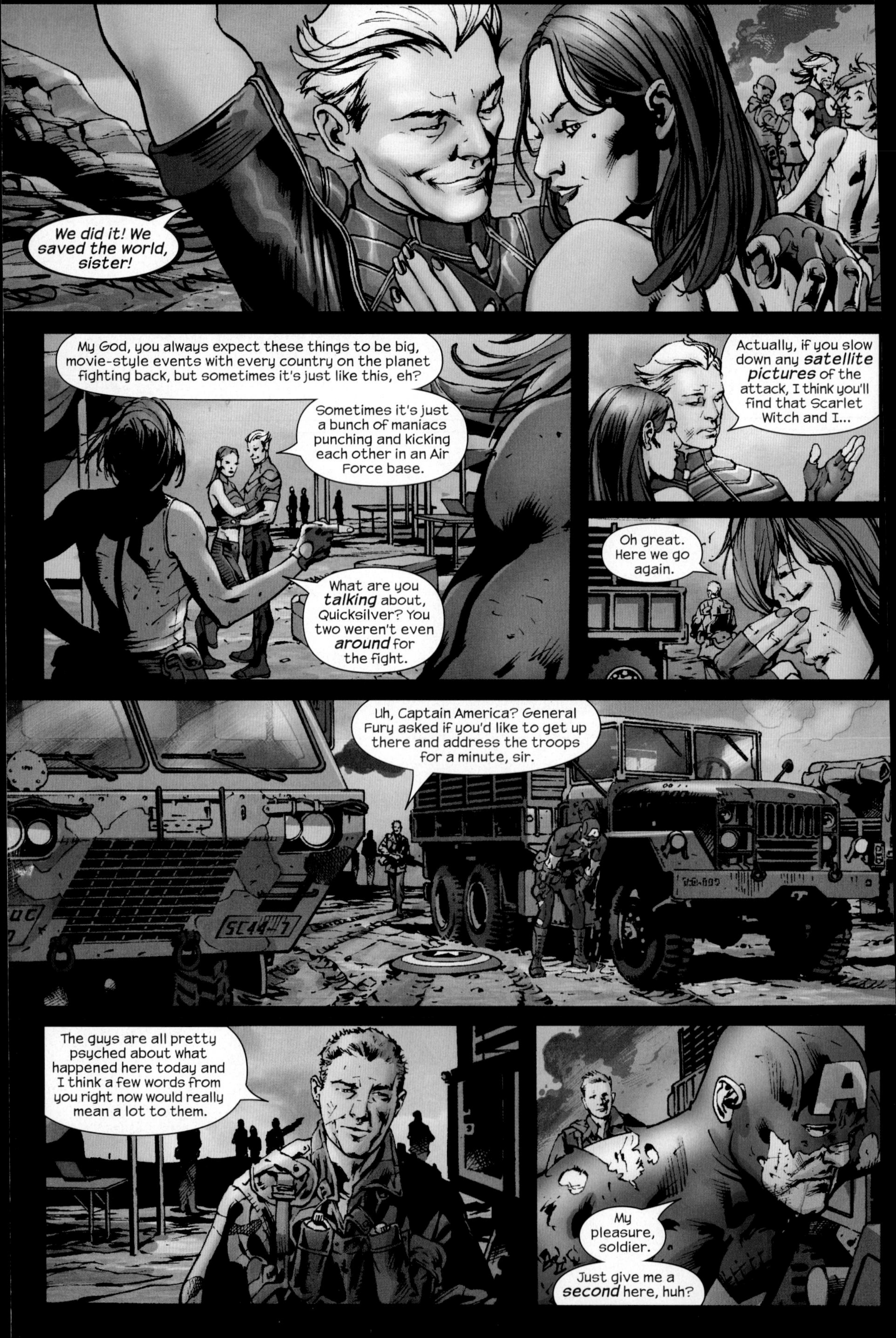
We did it! We saved the world, sister!
My God, you always expect these things to be big, movie-style events with every country on the planet fighting back, but sometimes it's just like this, eh?
Sometimes it's just a bunch of maniacs punching and kicking each other in an Air Force base.
What are you talking about, Quicksilver? You two weren't even around for the fight.
Actually, if you slow down any satellite pictures of the attack, I think you'll find that Scarlet Witch and I...
Oh great. Here we go again.
Uh, Captain America? General Fury asked if you'd like to get up there and address the troops for a minute, sir.
The guys are all pretty psyched about what happened here today and I think a few words from you right now would really mean a lot to them.
My pleasure, soldier.
Just give me a second here, huh?

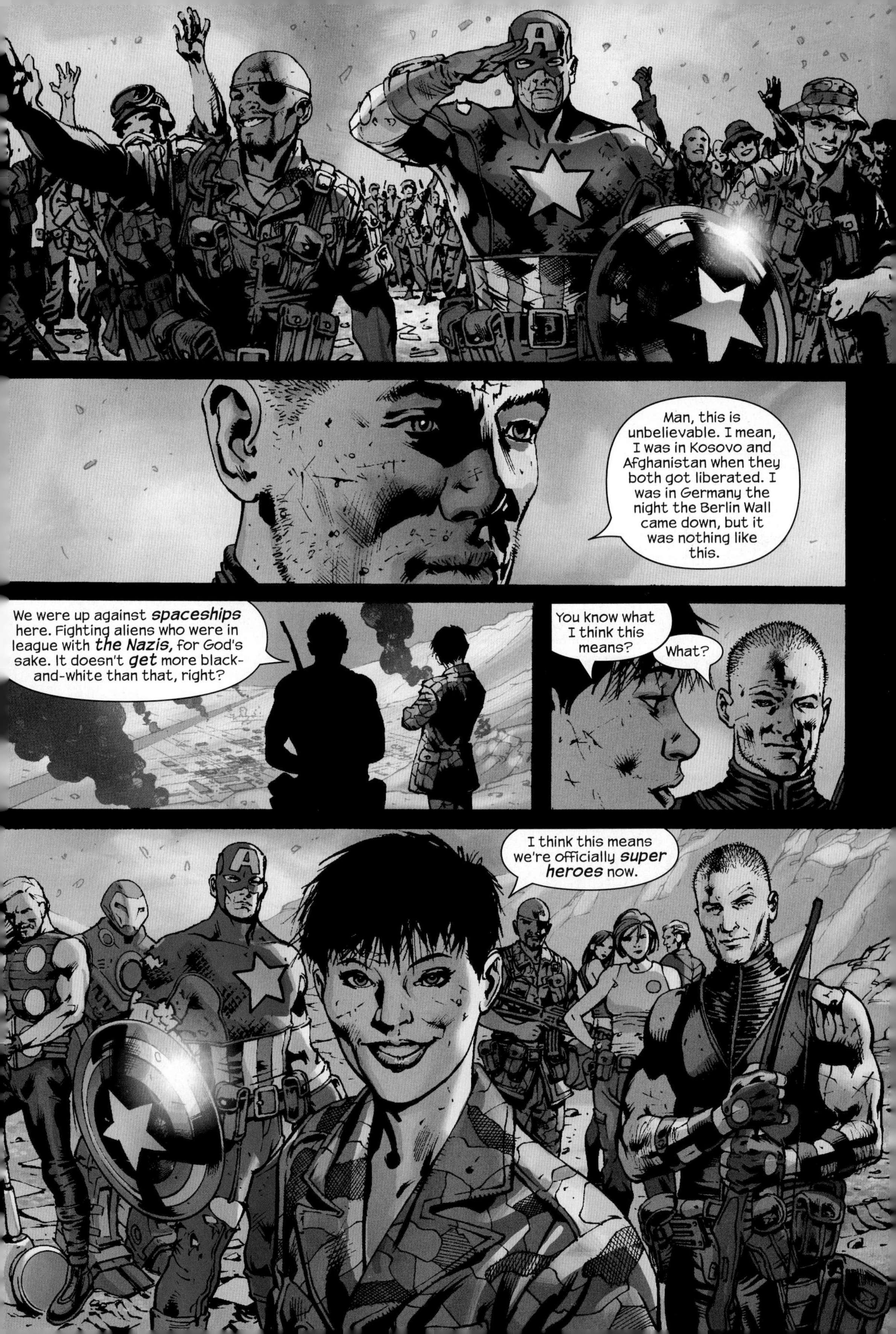
Man, this is unbelievable. I mean, I was in Kosovo and Afghanistan when they both got liberated. I was in Germany the night the Berlin Wall came down, but it was nothing like this.
We were up against *spaceships* here. Fighting aliens who were in league with ***the Nazis,*** for God's sake. It doesn't ***get*** more black-and-white than that, right?
You know what I think this means?
What?
I think this means we're officially ***super heroes*** now.

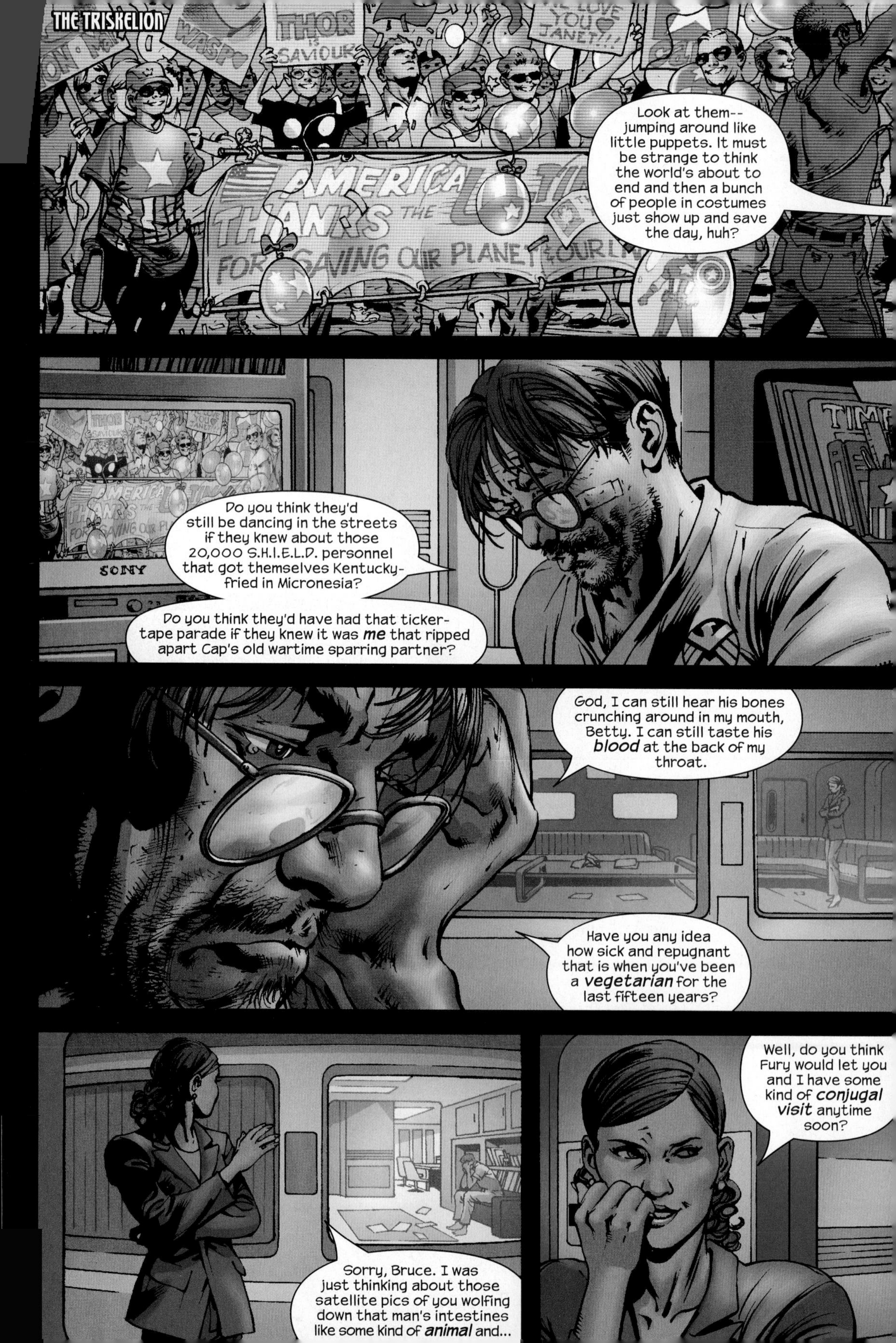
THE TRISKELION
THOR IS SAVIOUR
WASP
WE LOVE YOU JANET!!!
AMERICA THANKS THE ULTIMATES FOR SAVING OUR PLANET & OUR LIVES
Look at them--jumping around like little puppets. It must be strange to think the world's about to end and then a bunch of people in costumes just show up and save the day, huh?
SONY
Do you think they'd still be dancing in the streets if they knew about those 20,000 S.H.I.E.L.D. personnel that got themselves Kentucky-fried in Micronesia?
Do you think they'd have had that ticker-tape parade if they knew it was *me* that ripped apart Cap's old wartime sparring partner?
God, I can still hear his bones crunching around in my mouth, Betty. I can still taste his *blood* at the back of my throat.
Have you any idea how sick and repugnant that is when you've been a *vegetarian* for the last fifteen years?
Sorry, Bruce. I was just thinking about those satellite pics of you wolfing down that man's intestines like some kind of *animal* and...
Well, do you think Fury would let you and I have some kind of *conjugal visit* anytime soon?

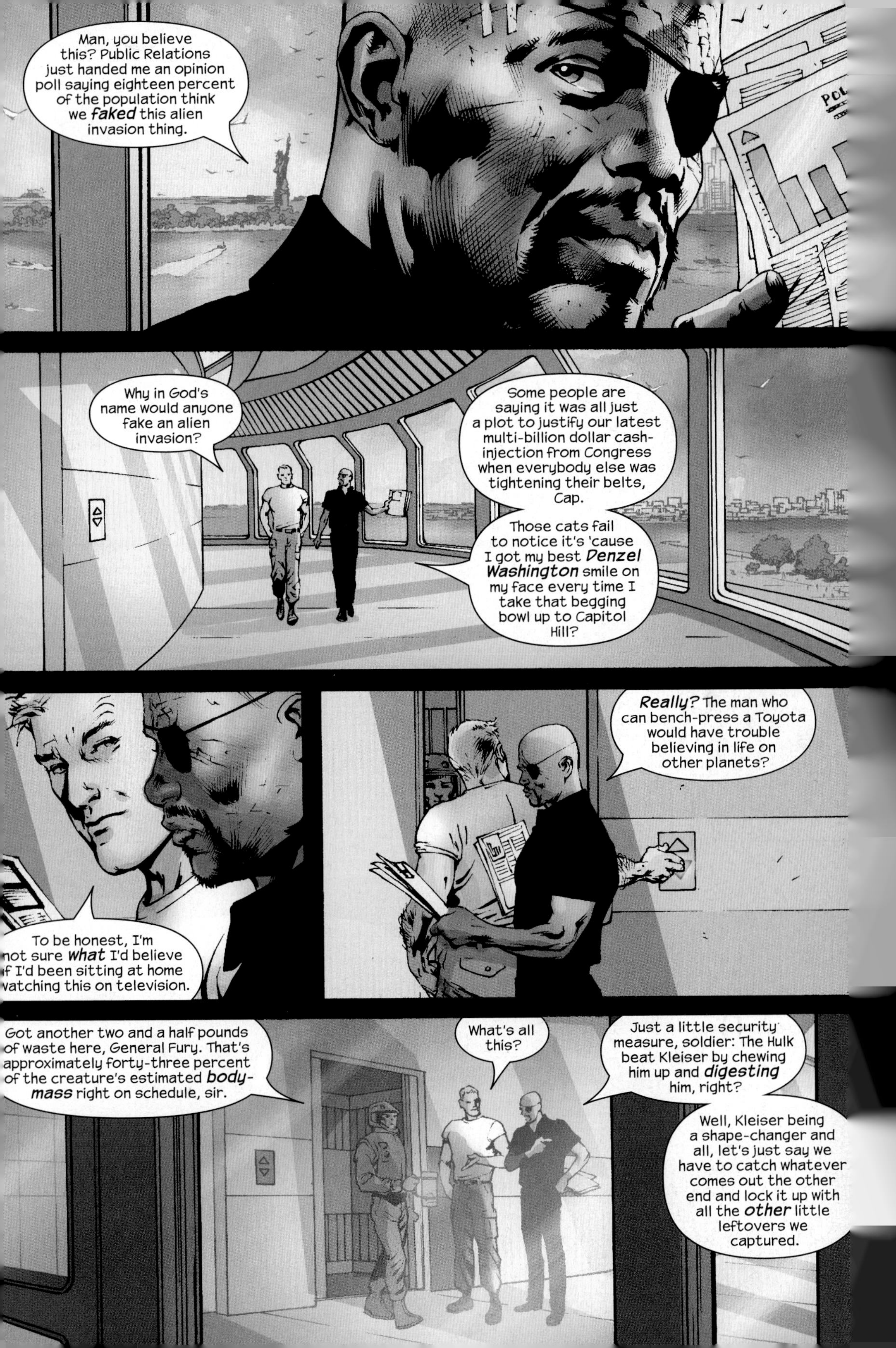
Man, you believe this? Public Relations just handed me an opinion poll saying eighteen percent of the population think we *faked* this alien invasion thing.
Why in God's name would anyone fake an alien invasion?
Some people are saying it was all just a plot to justify our latest multi-billion dollar cash-injection from Congress when everybody else was tightening their belts, Cap.
Those cats fail to notice it's 'cause I got my best *Denzel Washington* smile on my face every time I take that begging bowl up to Capitol Hill?
To be honest, I'm not sure *what* I'd believe if I'd been sitting at home watching this on television.
Really? The man who can bench-press a Toyota would have trouble believing in life on other planets?
Got another two and a half pounds of waste here, General Fury. That's approximately forty-three percent of the creature's estimated *body-mass* right on schedule, sir.
What's all this?
Just a little security measure, soldier: The Hulk beat Kleiser by chewing him up and *digesting* him, right?
Well, Kleiser being a shape-changer and all, let's just say we have to catch whatever comes out the other end and lock it up with all the *other* little leftovers we captured.

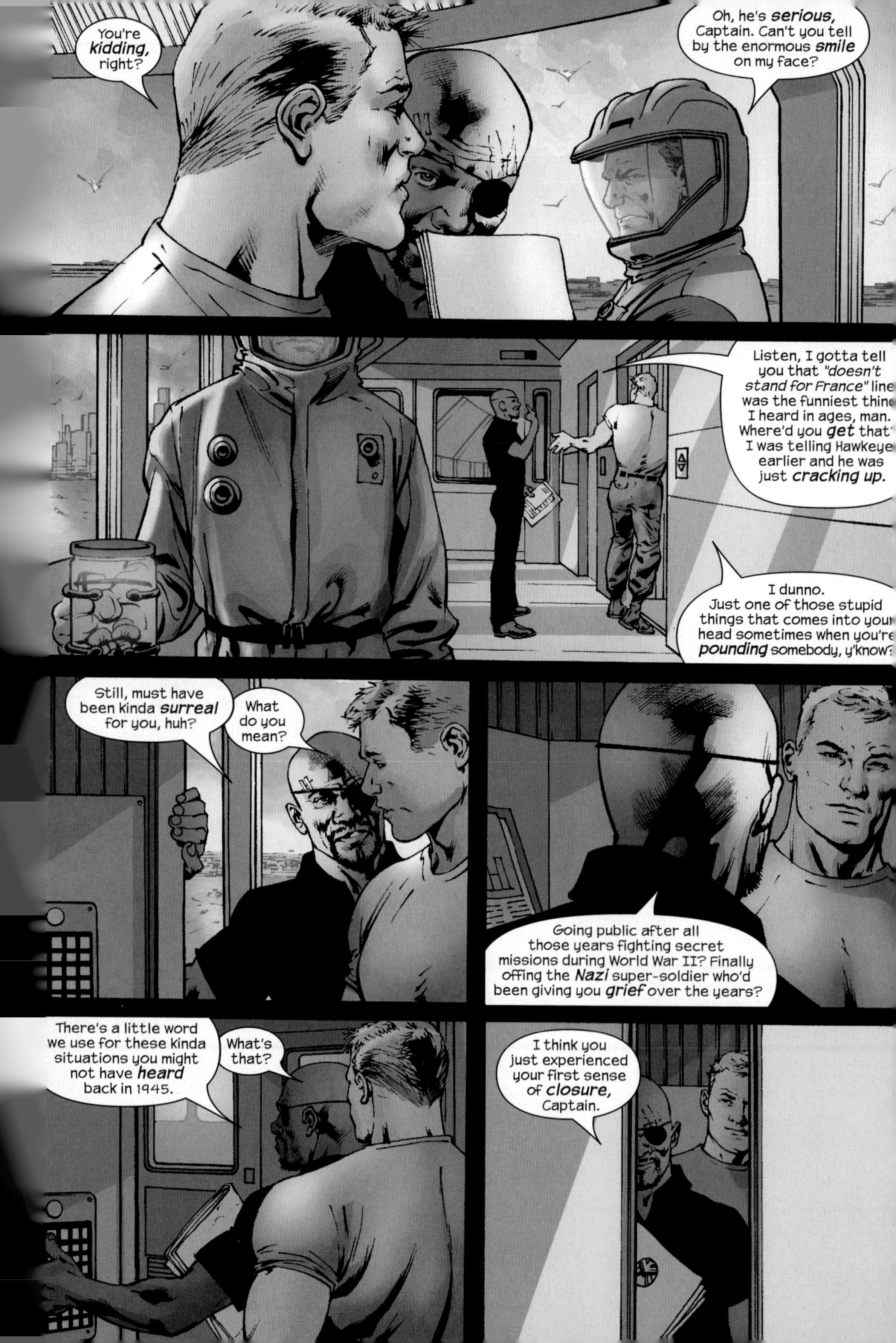
You're kidding, right?
Oh, he's serious, Captain. Can't you tell by the enormous smile on my face?
Listen, I gotta tell you that "doesn't stand for France" line was the funniest thing I heard in ages, man. Where'd you get that? I was telling Hawkeye earlier and he was just cracking up.
I dunno. Just one of those stupid things that comes into your head sometimes when you're pounding somebody, y'know?
Still, must have been kinda surreal for you, huh?
What do you mean?
Going public after all those years fighting secret missions during World War II? Finally offing the Nazi super-soldier who'd been giving you grief over the years?
There's a little word we use for these kinda situations you might not have heard back in 1945.
What's that?
I think you just experienced your first sense of closure, Captain.

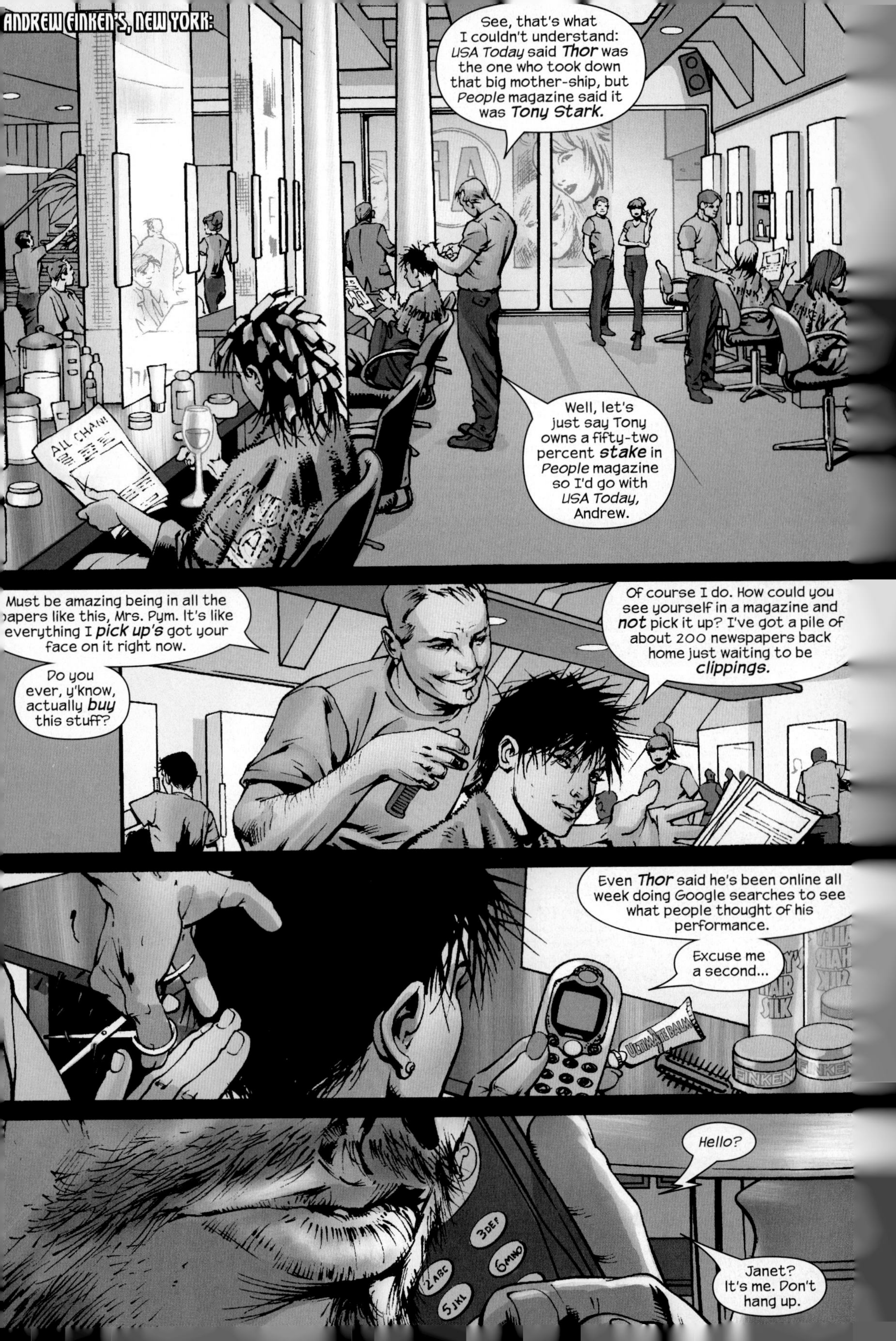
ANDREW FINKEN'S, NEW YORK:
See, that's what I couldn't understand: USA Today said Thor was the one who took down that big mother-ship, but People magazine said it was Tony Stark.
Well, let's just say Tony owns a fifty-two percent stake in People magazine so I'd go with USA Today, Andrew.
Must be amazing being in all the papers like this, Mrs. Pym. It's like everything I pick up's got your face on it right now.
Do you ever, y'know, actually buy this stuff?
Of course I do. How could you see yourself in a magazine and not pick it up? I've got a pile of about 200 newspapers back home just waiting to be clippings.
Even Thor said he's been online all week doing Google searches to see what people thought of his performance.
Excuse me a second...
ULTIMATE BALM
FINKEN
Hello?
Janet? It's me. Don't hang up.

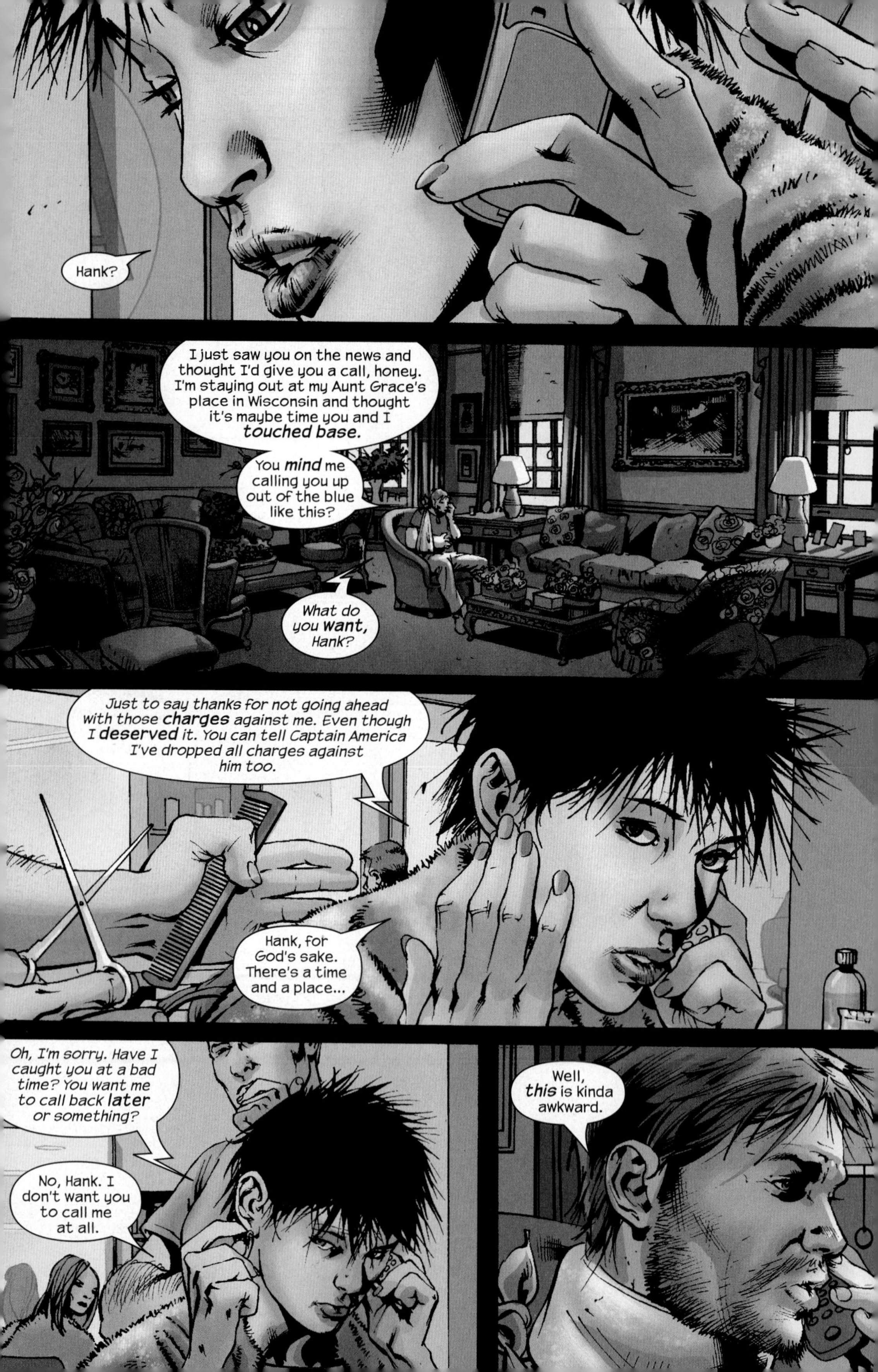
Hank?
I just saw you on the news and thought I'd give you a call, honey. I'm staying out at my Aunt Grace's place in Wisconsin and thought it's maybe time you and I touched base.
You mind me calling you up out of the blue like this?
What do you want, Hank?
Just to say thanks for not going ahead with those charges against me. Even though I deserved it. You can tell Captain America I've dropped all charges against him too.
Hank, for God's sake. There's a time and a place...
Oh, I'm sorry. Have I caught you at a bad time? You want me to call back later or something?
No, Hank. I don't want you to call me at all.
Well, this is kinda awkward.

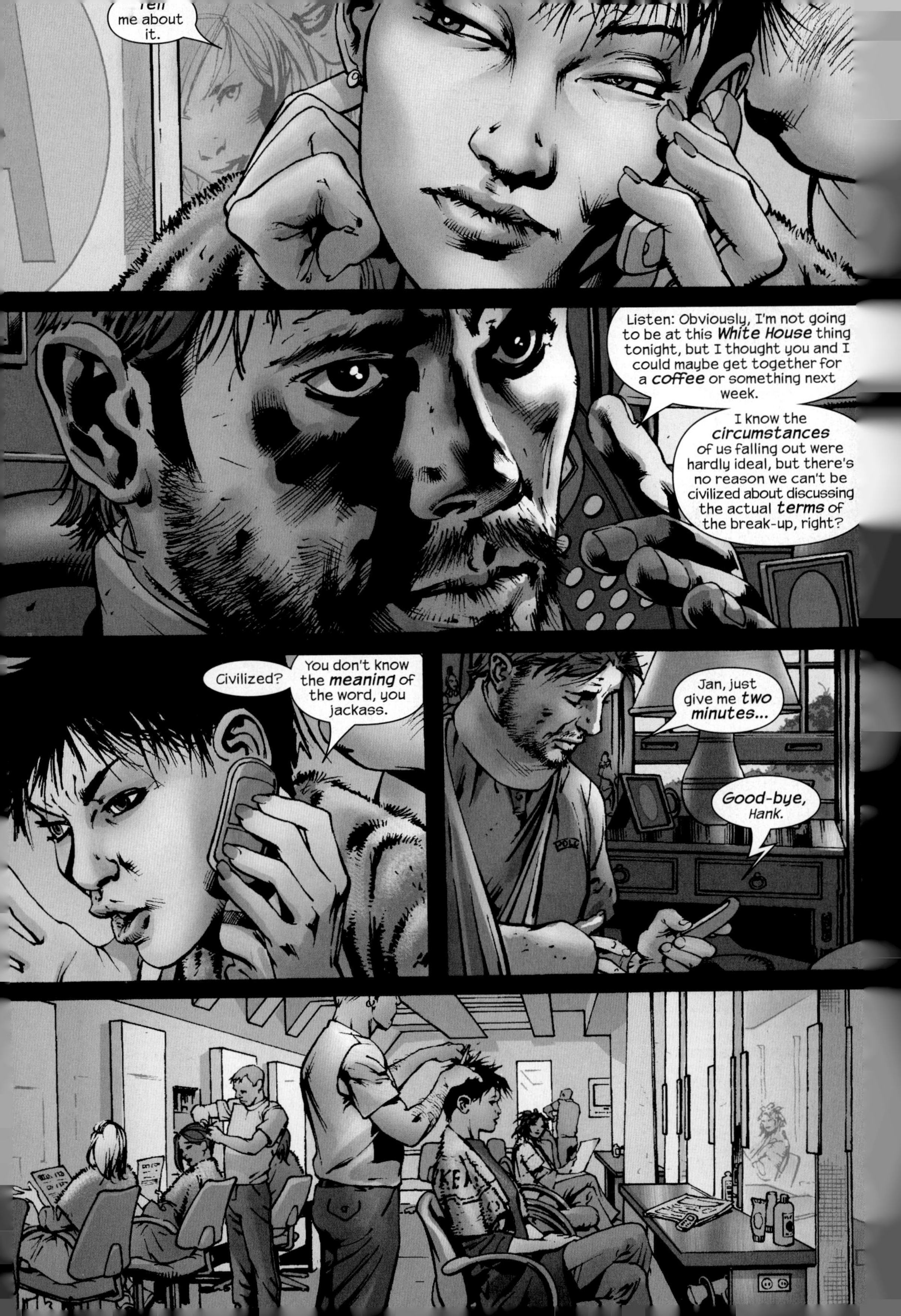
Tell me about it.
Listen: Obviously, I'm not going to be at this White House thing tonight, but I thought you and I could maybe get together for a coffee or something next week.
I know the circumstances of us falling out were hardly ideal, but there's no reason we can't be civilized about discussing the actual terms of the break-up, right?
Civilized?
You don't know the meaning of the word, you jackass.
Jan, just give me two minutes...
Good-bye, Hank.

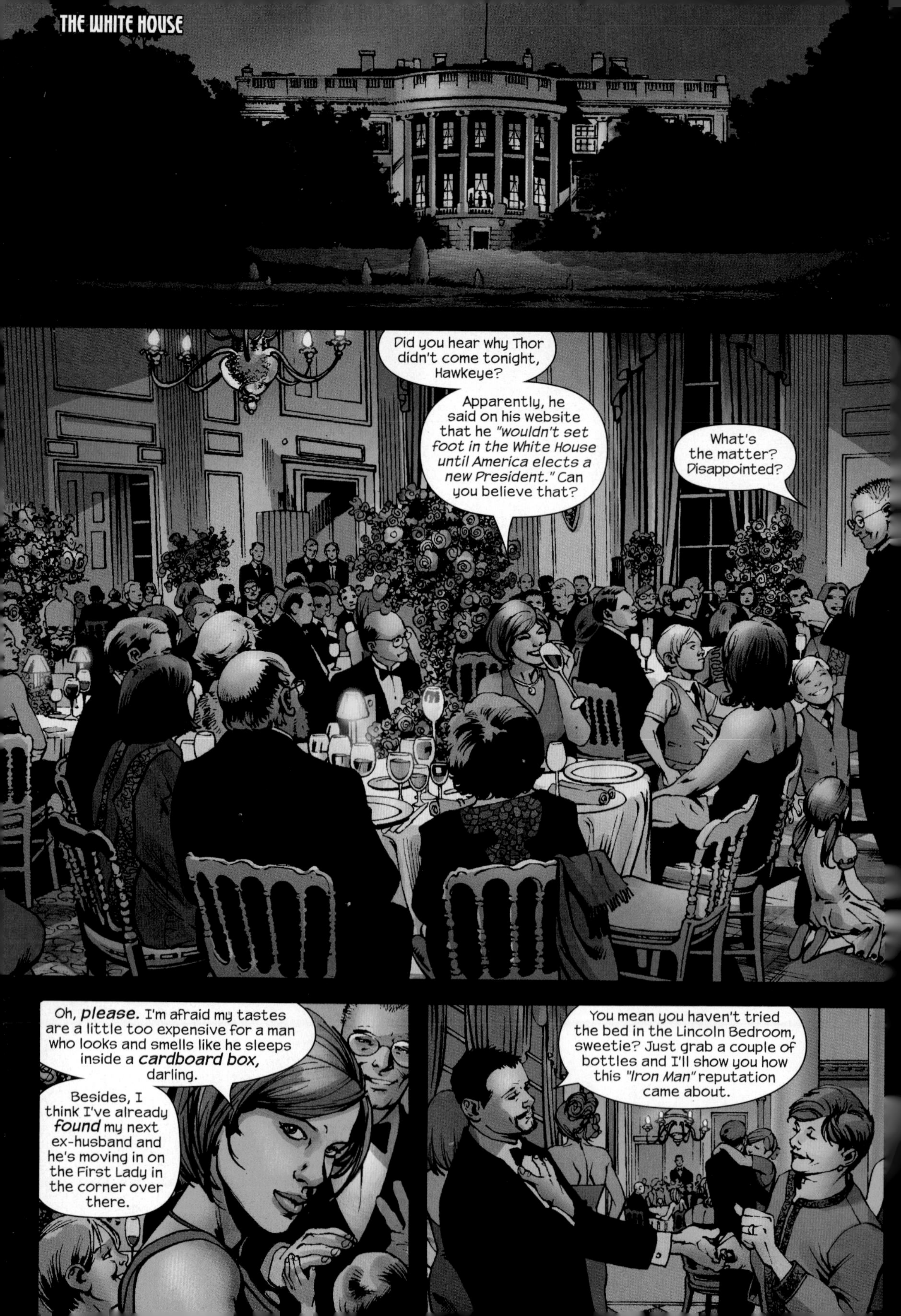

THE WHITE HOUSE
Did you hear why Thor didn't come tonight, Hawkeye?
Apparently, he said on his website that he *"wouldn't set foot in the White House until America elects a new President."* Can you believe that?
What's the matter? Disappointed?
Oh, **please.** I'm afraid my tastes are a little too expensive for a man who looks and smells like he sleeps inside a ***cardboard box,*** darling.
Besides, I think I've already ***found*** my next ex-husband and he's moving in on the First Lady in the corner over there.
You mean you haven't tried the bed in the Lincoln Bedroom, sweetie? Just grab a couple of bottles and I'll show you how this *"Iron Man"* reputation came about.

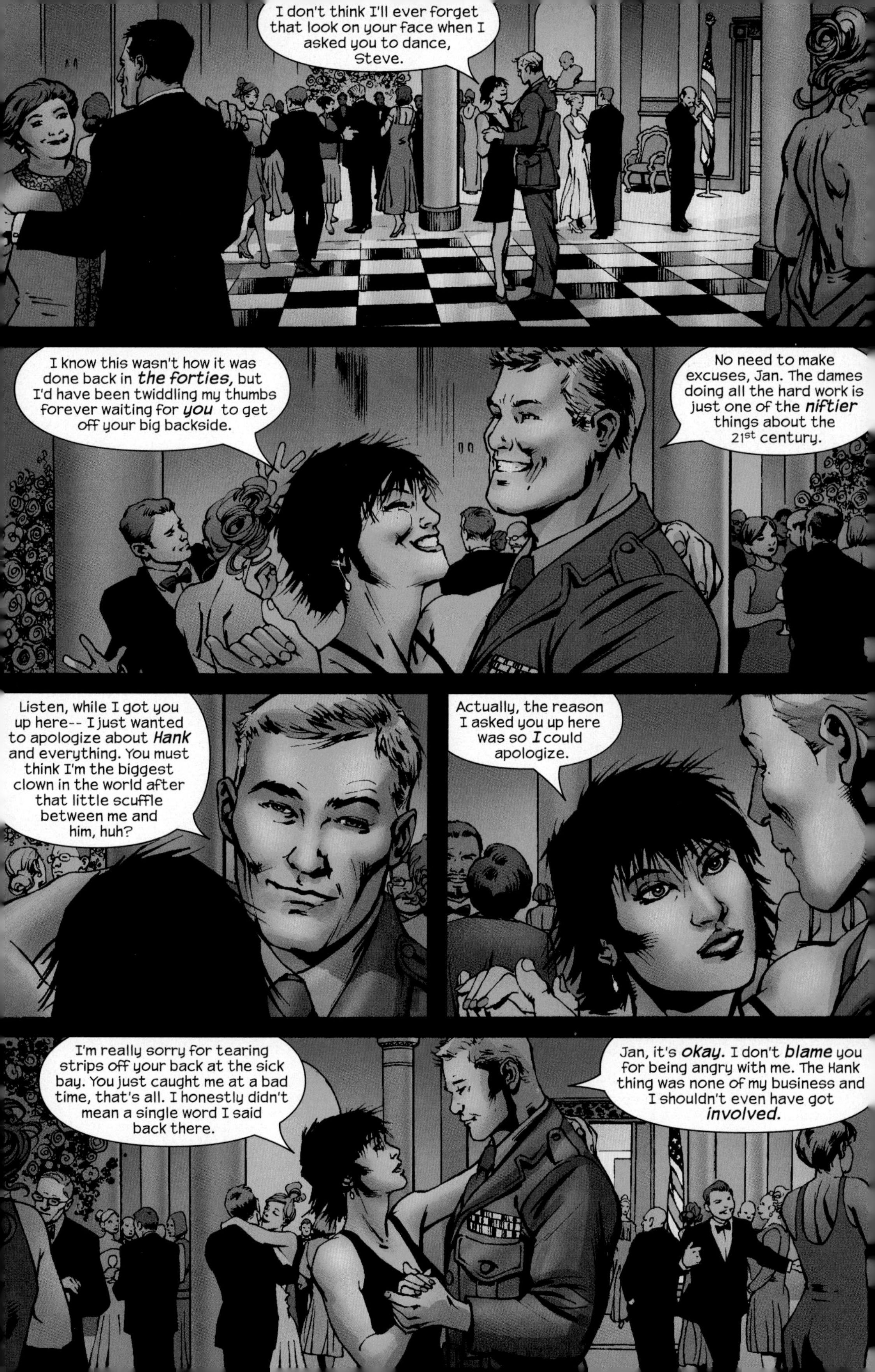

I don't think I'll ever forget that look on your face when I asked you to dance, Steve.
I know this wasn't how it was done back in *the forties*, but I'd have been twiddling my thumbs forever waiting for *you* to get off your big backside.
No need to make excuses, Jan. The dames doing all the hard work is just one of the *niftier* things about the 21st century.
Listen, while I got you up here-- I just wanted to apologize about *Hank* and everything. You must think I'm the biggest clown in the world after that little scuffle between me and him, huh?
Actually, the reason I asked you up here was so *I* could apologize.
I'm really sorry for tearing strips off your back at the sick bay. You just caught me at a bad time, that's all. I honestly didn't mean a single word I said back there.
Jan, it's *okay.* I don't *blame* you for being angry with me. The Hank thing was none of my business and I shouldn't even have got *involved.*

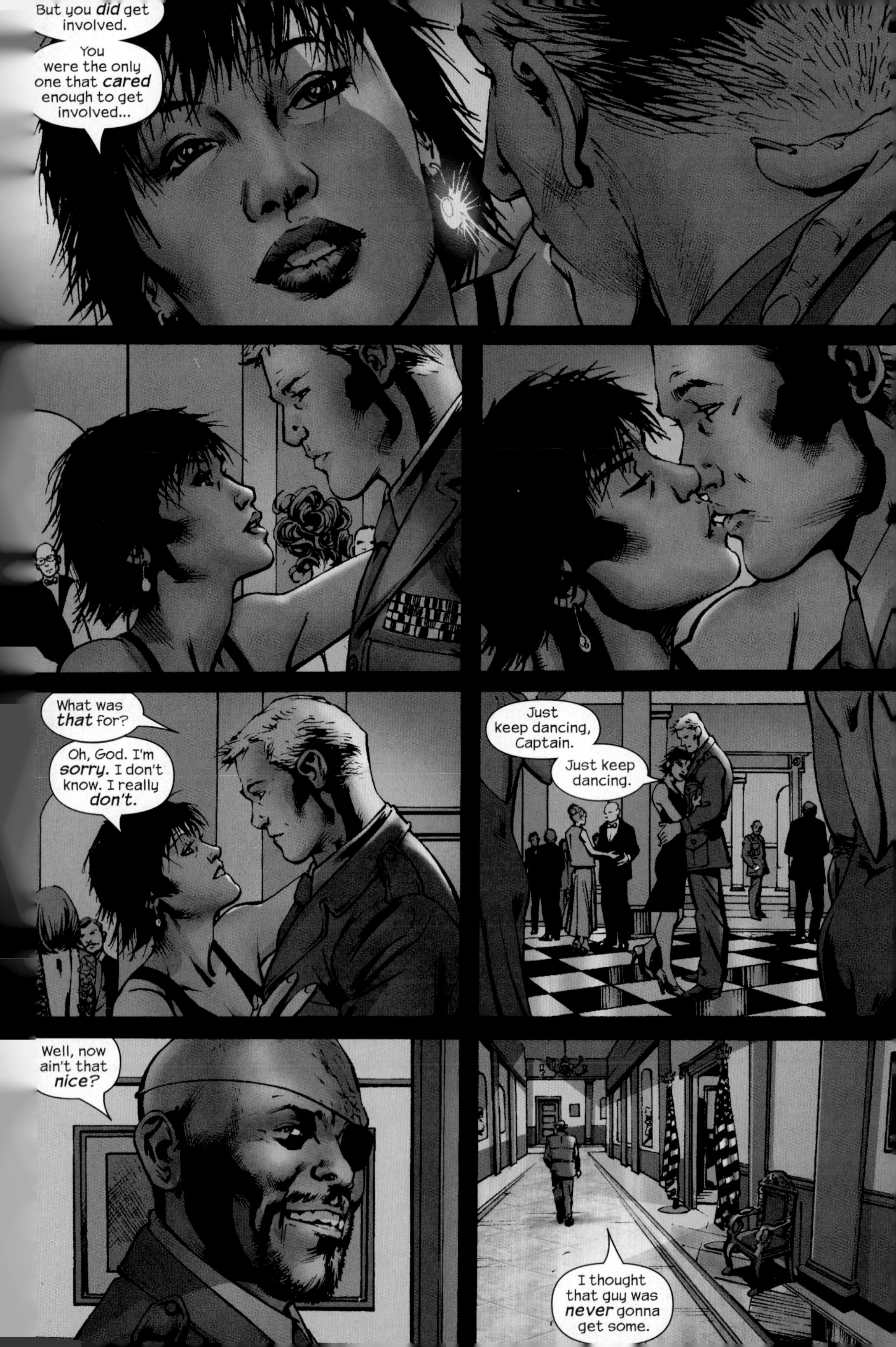
But you did get involved.
You were the only one that cared enough to get involved...
What was that for?
Oh, God. I'm sorry. I don't know. I really don't.
Just keep dancing, Captain.
Just keep dancing.
Well, now ain't that nice?
I thought that guy was never gonna get some.

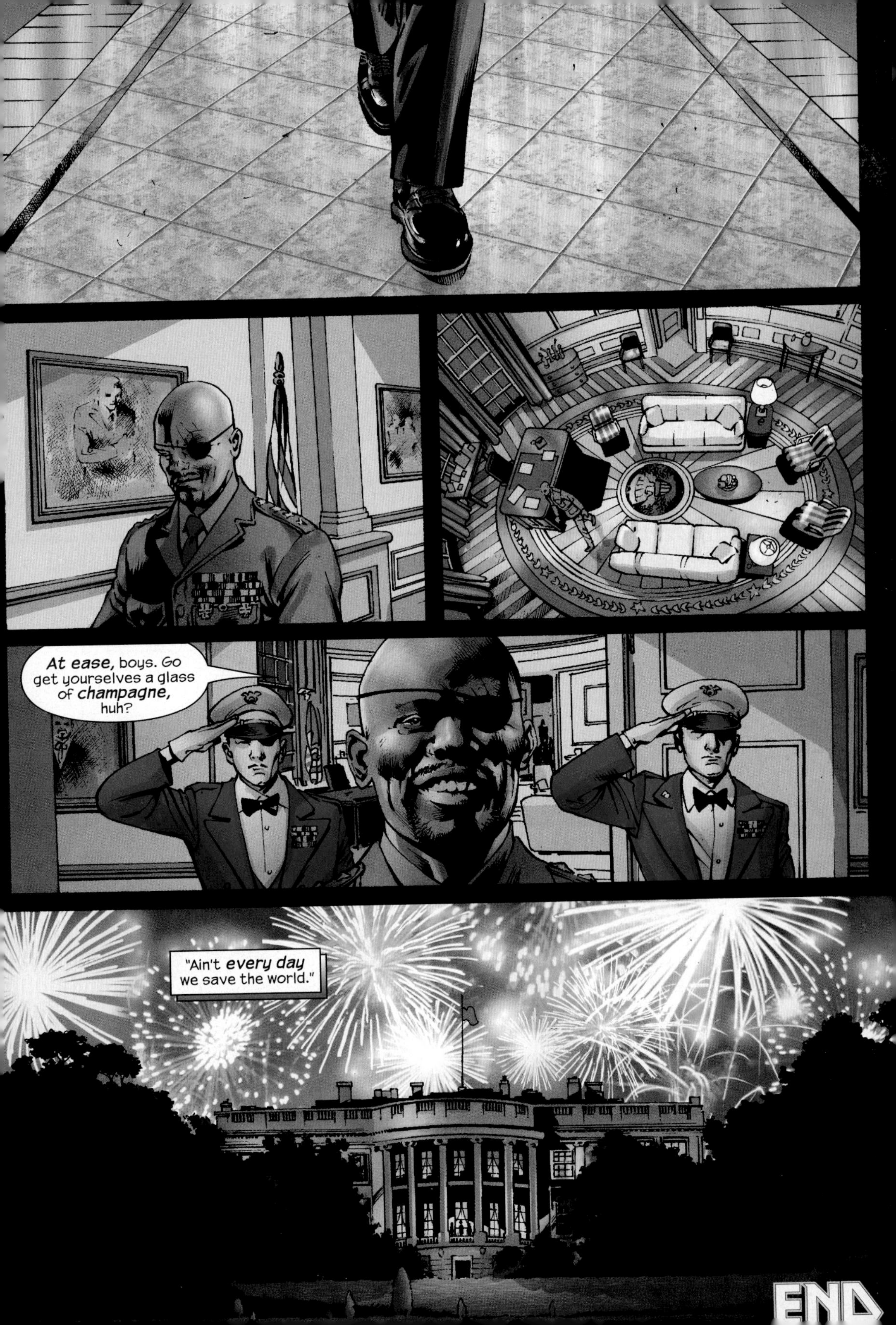
At ease, boys. Go get yourselves a glass of *champagne*, huh?
"Ain't *every day* we save the world."
END

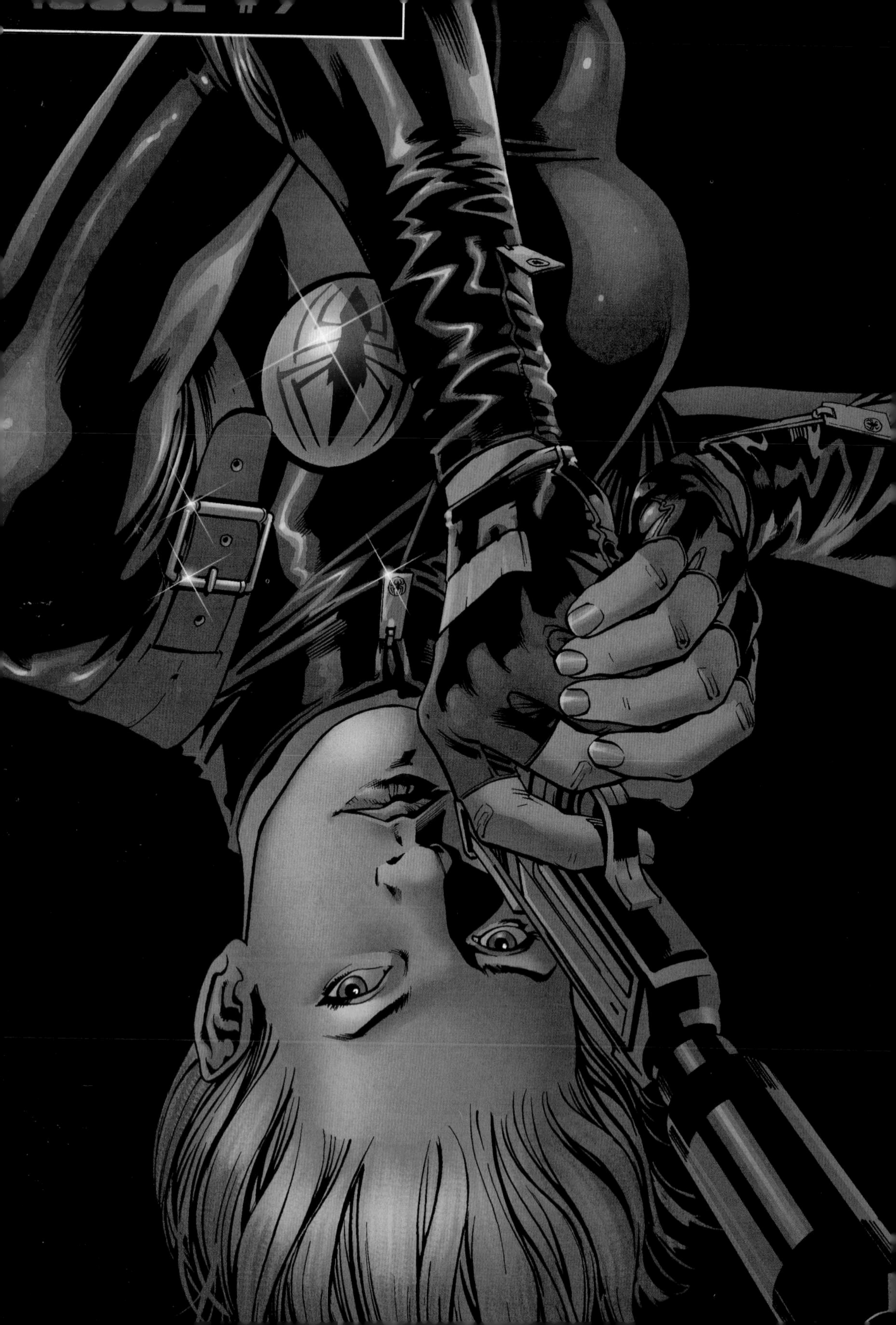

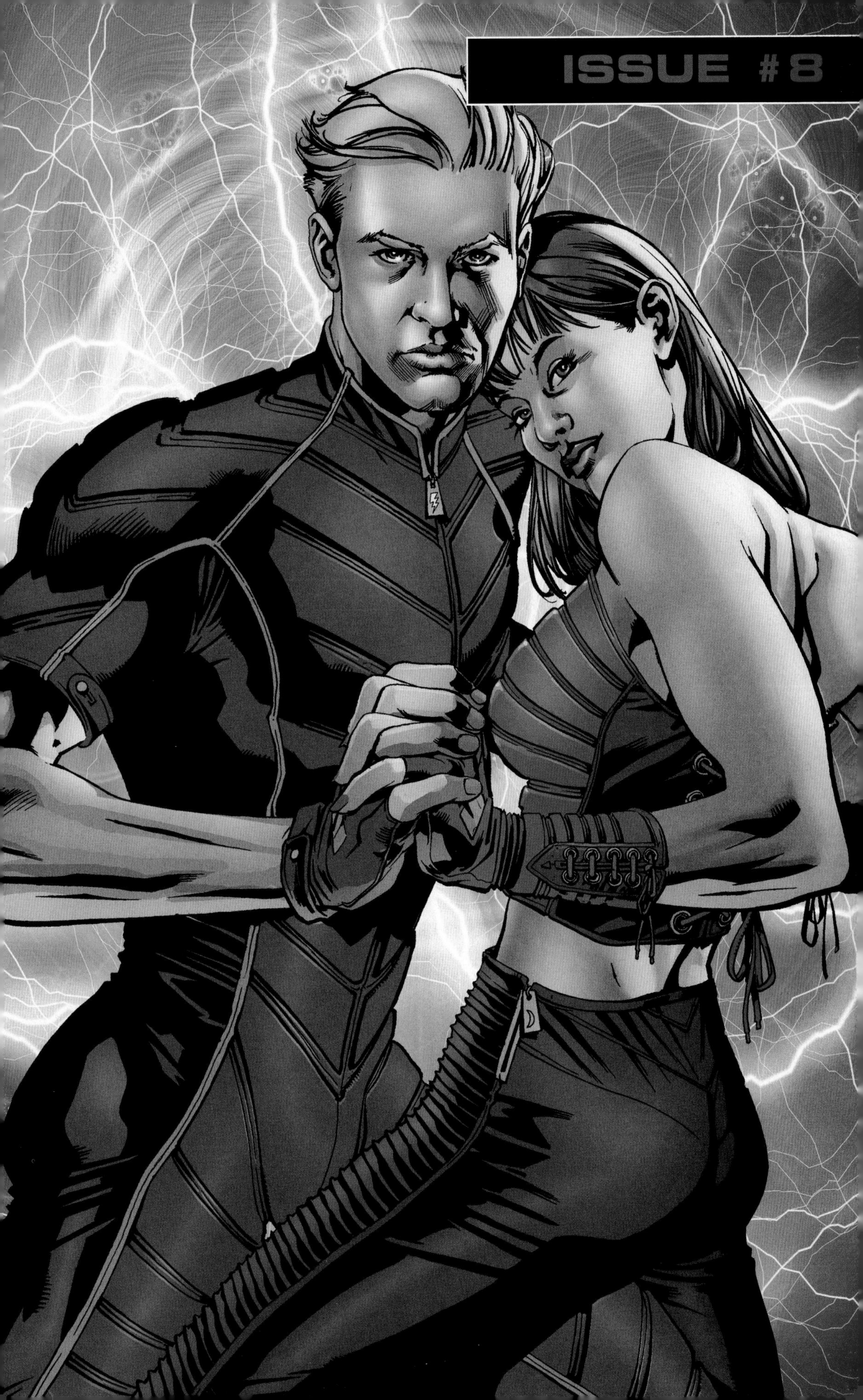
ISSUE #8

ISSUE #9

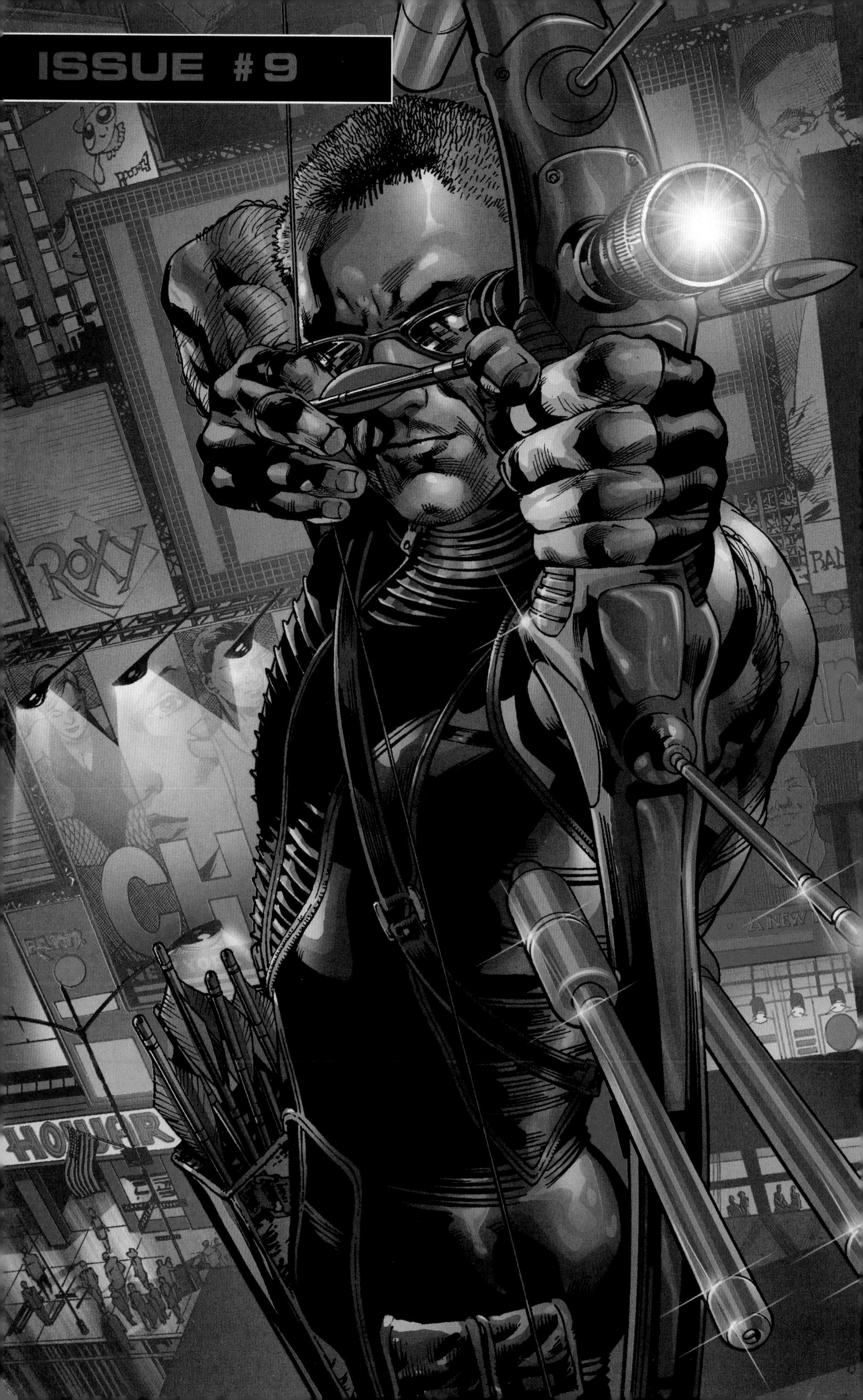
ROXY

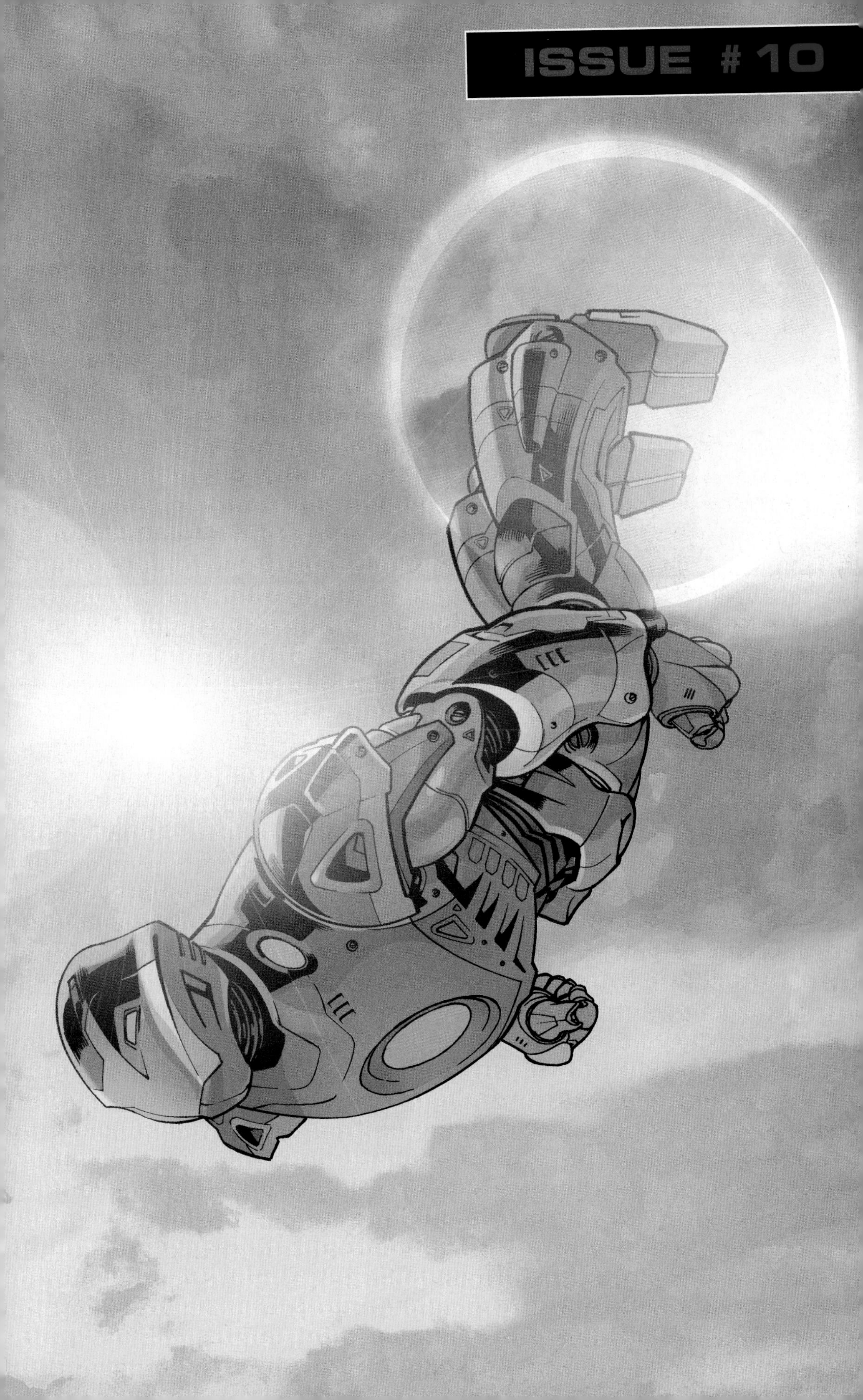
ISSUE #10

ISSUE #11

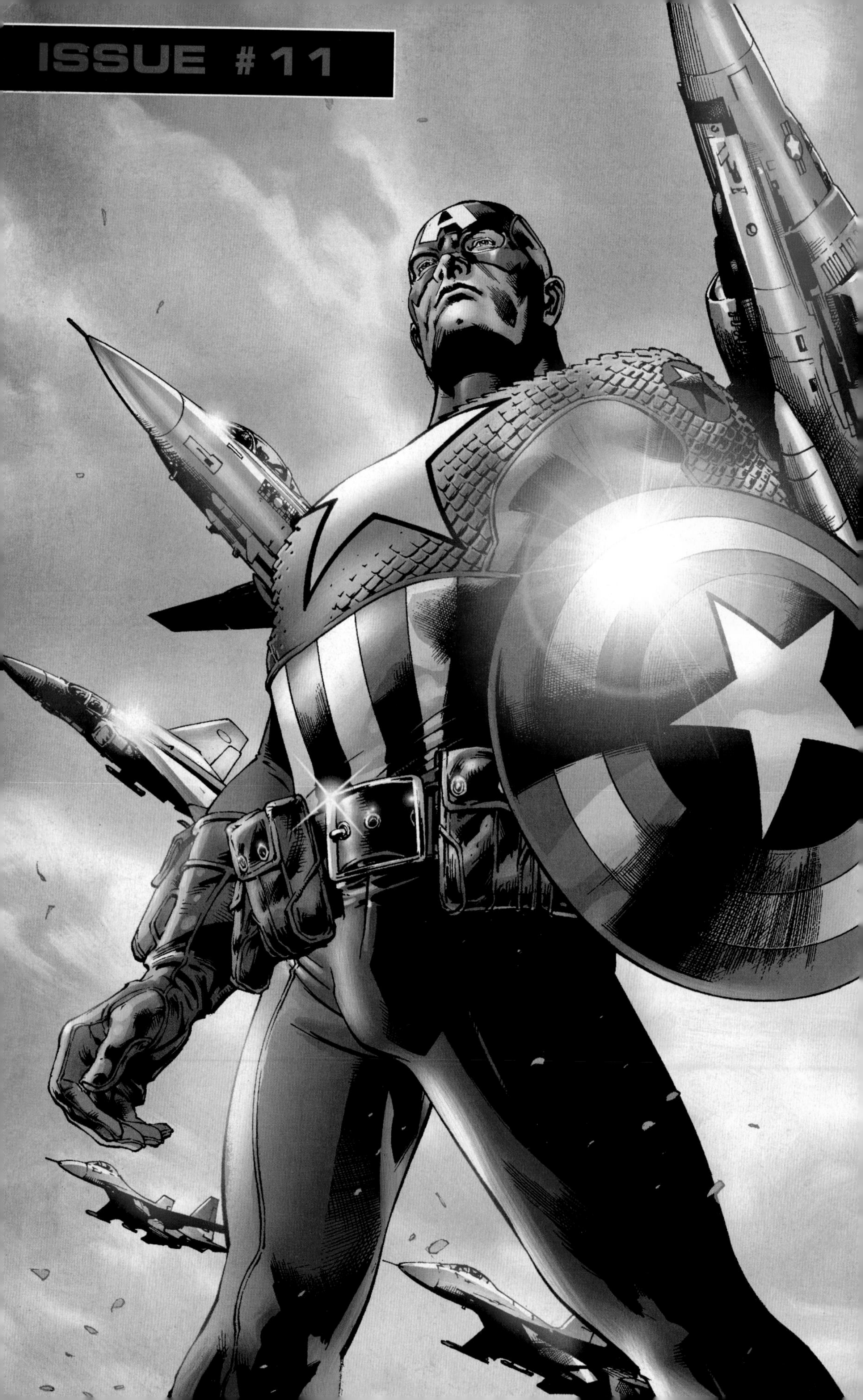

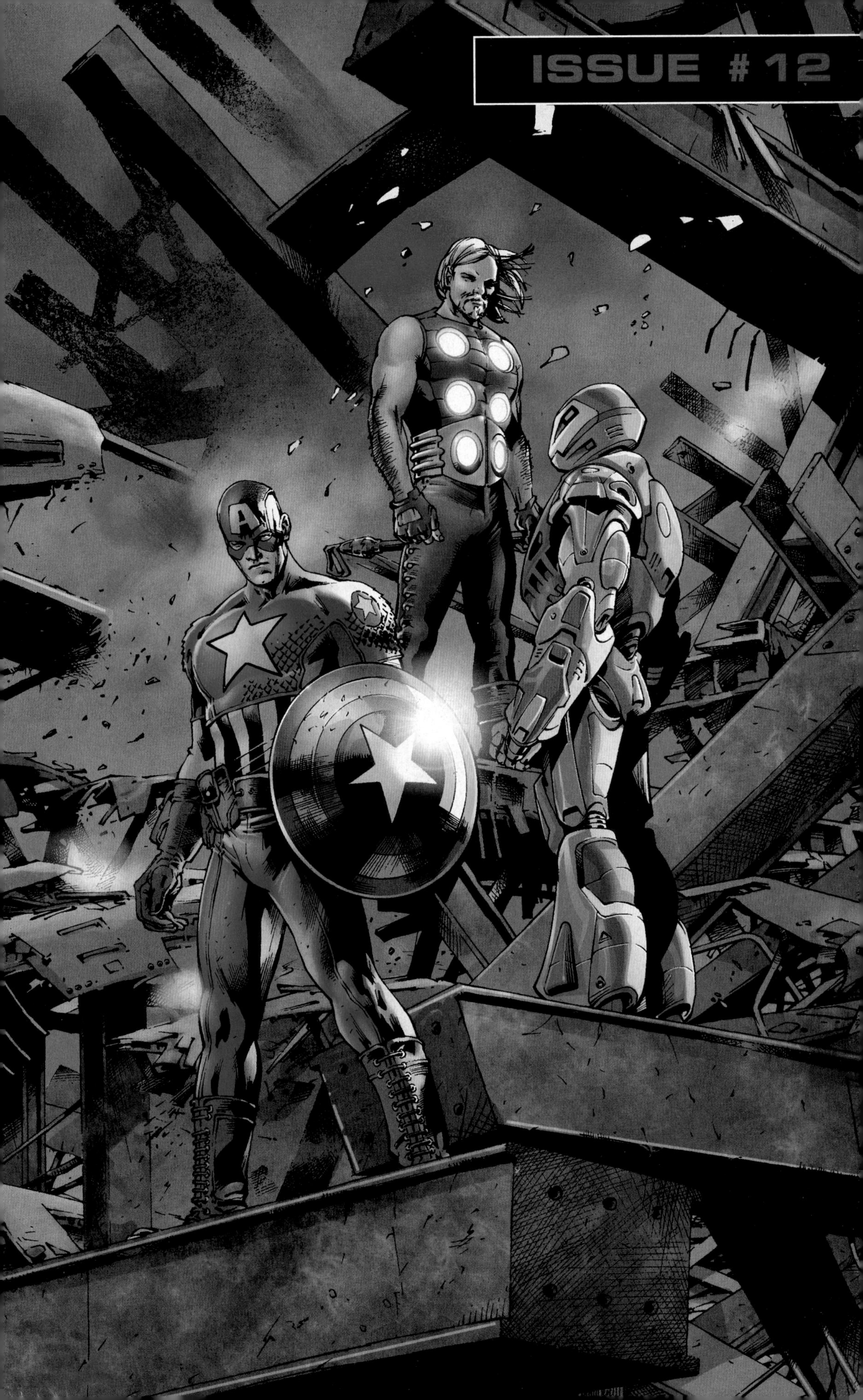
ISSUE # 12

ISSUE #13

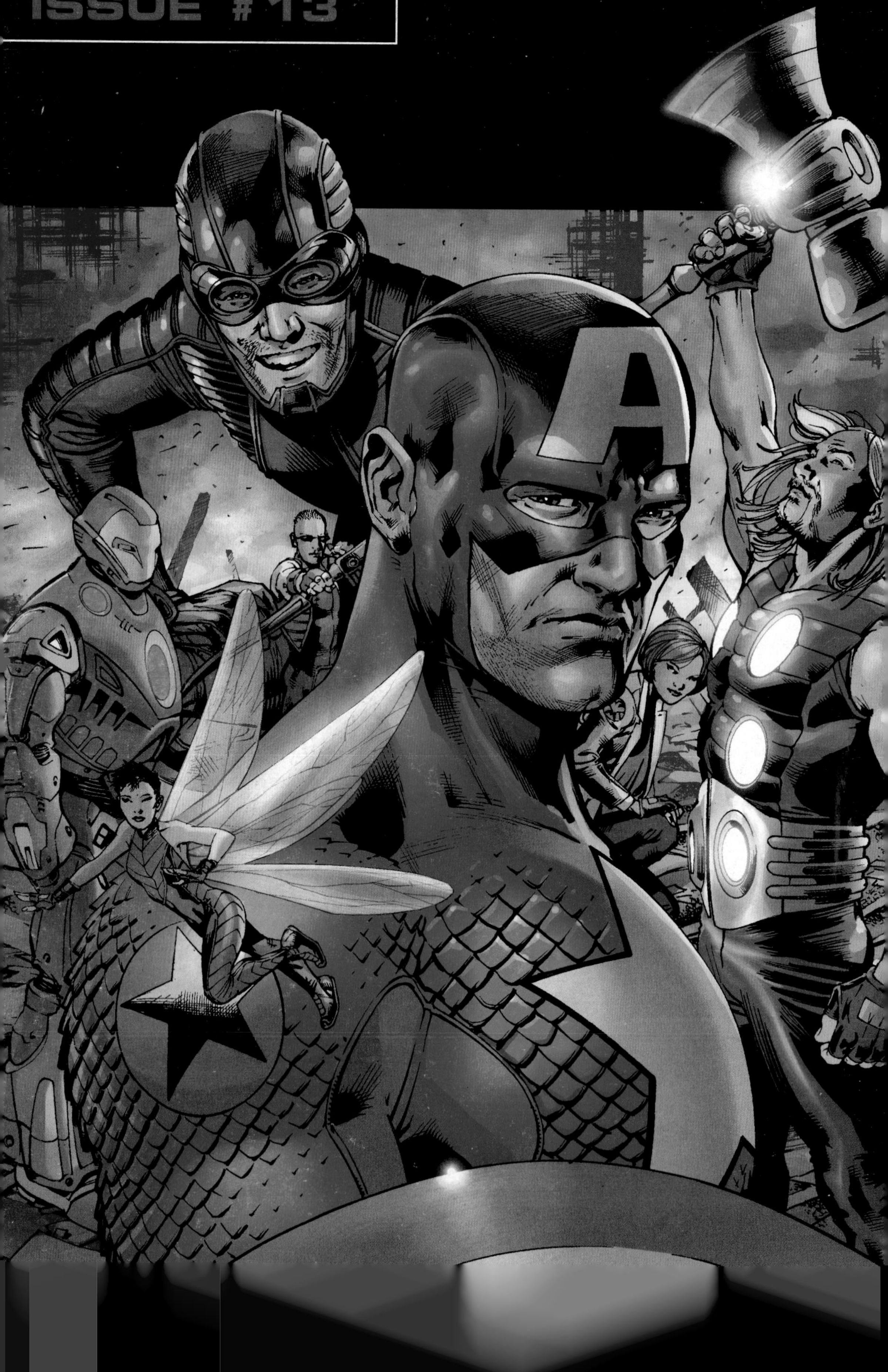